CONSUMER BEHAVIOR
IN LATIN AMERICA

PHILIP MUSGROVE

CONSUMER BEHAVIOR IN LATIN AMERICA

Income and Spending of Families in Ten Andean Cities

AN ECIEL STUDY

THE BROOKINGS INSTITUTION

Washington, D.C.

Library of Congress Cataloging in Publication Data:

Musgrove, Philip.
    Consumer behavior in Latin America.
    "An ECIEL study."
    Includes bibliographical references and index.
    1. Income—South America. 2. Consumption
(Economics)—South America. 3. Consumers—South
America. 4. Cost and standard of living—South
America. I. Title.
HC170.15M87   339.4′1′098   77-1108
ISBN 0-8157-5914-2

THE BROOKINGS INSTITUTION is an independent organization devoted to nonpartisan research, education, and publication in economics, government, foreign policy, and the social sciences generally. Its principal purposes are to aid in the development of sound public policies and to promote public understanding of issues of national importance.

The Institution was founded on December 8, 1927, to merge the activities of the Institute for Government Research, founded in 1916, the Institute of Economics, founded in 1922, and the Robert Brookings Graduate School of Economics and Government, founded in 1924.

The Board of Trustees is responsible for the general administration of the Institution, while the immediate direction of the policies, program, and staff is vested in the President, assisted by an advisory committee of the officers and staff. The by-laws of the Institution state: "It is the function of the Trustees to make possible the conduct of scientific research, and publication, under the most favorable conditions, and to safeguard the independence of the research staff in the pursuit of their studies and in the publication of the results of such studies. It is not a part of their function to determine, control, or influence the conduct of particular investigations or the conclusions reached."

The President bears final responsibility for the decision to publish a manuscript as a Brookings book. In reaching his judgment on the competence, accuracy, and objectivity of each study, the President is advised by the director of the appropriate research program and weighs the views of a panel of expert outside readers who report to him in confidence on the quality of the work. Publication of a work signifies that it is deemed a competent treatment worthy of public consideration but does not imply endorsement of conclusions or recommendations.

The Institution maintains its position of neutrality on issues of public policy in order to safeguard the intellectual freedom of the staff. Hence interpretations or conclusions in Brookings publications should be understood to be solely those of the authors and should not be attributed to the Institution, to its trustees, officers, or other staff members, or to the organizations that support its research.

Foreword

PRIVATE CONSUMPTION by households and individuals absorbs about three-fourths of all the income generated in Latin America, as it does in many other economies. The way income is distributed, spent, and saved strongly influences the welfare of the population, the level and composition of output, and the prospects for economic growth and development. Very little was known until recently about the structure of private spending in Latin America and its relation to economic, demographic, and cultural factors. The information that did exist was incomplete, difficult to compare among countries, and of doubtful reliability, even for the major cities of the region. And not all of it was analyzed thoroughly.

In this book Philip Musgrove presents a comparative analysis of household income and spending, based on new and relatively uniform survey data, for ten cities in five South American countries. The study is the result of a joint project in which several Latin American research institutions participated. That project was undertaken as part of the Program of Joint Studies on Latin American Economic Integration, known by the acronym ECIEL and briefly described in the prefatory note.

Beginning with the distribution and structure of family income, Musgrove examines the allocation of income between spending and saving; he then analyzes the composition of expenditures and its relation to the characteristics of individual families and of the different national economies. The study's emphasis on international comparisons and on a common set of explanatory factors makes it possible to discern patterns of consumer behavior in different economic and cultural settings, and to illuminate the features that give rise to differences in those patterns. The

vii

information brought together is fundamental for understanding how the economies of the region operate and for evaluating alternatives for their further development.

This study results from parallel work by various private and public research institutions in six countries. It was the largest ECIEL project undertaken from 1966 to 1974, and it constituted the first wide-coverage general-purpose survey of household economic behavior anywhere in Latin America. The individuals and institutions in Latin America principally responsible for the study are listed in the prefatory note.

Four persons were responsible for coordinating the collection and analysis of data at Brookings. During the first year Joseph Grunwald, the founder and first General Coordinator of ECIEL and a senior fellow in the Brookings Foreign Policy Studies program, was in charge and organized the study. Philip Musgrove's responsibility, assumed in 1967, was interrupted between July 1968 and July 1971, during which time Howard Howe (1968–70) and Arturo Meyer (1970–71) coordinated the project. During their involvement with the project, Musgrove, Howe, and Meyer were research associates in the Brookings Foreign Policy Studies program. Howe and Meyer also served as consultants to the project after their terms as technical coordinators. Howe was largely responsible for the original organization of the data and for the first empirical results to be completed, those for Colombia. In the early stages of the work, he also made many of the methodological decisions and was in charge of analysis and the verification of data. Meyer revised certain of the Colombian calculations, began the work for Peru, and developed the basic econometric specification. Musgrove was in charge of the harmonization of the data from different countries and the processing for Peru, Chile, Ecuador, and Venezuela. He was solely responsible for writing this volume.

Robert Ferber, director of the Survey Research Center at the University of Illinois, was a consultant and of great help to the project from its beginning. He contributed to every stage of the study, being particularly responsible for the design of the samples and questionnaires and the choice of statistical results. His careful reading greatly improved the manuscript.

Five research assistants were responsible for handling the data and preparing statistical results: Ximena Cheetham, Joy Dunkerley, Jorge Lamas, Marily Luders, and Danuta Nowicki. Cheetham was largely responsible for the work on Colombia and Chile, Nowicki for Peru and Venezuela, and Luders for Ecuador. Dunkerley and Lamas contributed to work on several of these countries.

The project required the creation of a series of computer programs for eliminating spurious data as well as for statistical analysis. The chief programmer was Marcia Mason of the Brookings Social Science Computation Center; she was also in charge of creating and maintaining the files. The study also used programs written wholly or in part by Leo Bourne, Christine de Fontenay, Alicia DeNood, and Jorge Spencer of Brookings, and by Roberto Villaveces of the Centro de Estudios sobre Desarrollo Económico of Colombia, who worked for several months at Brookings and helped install ECIEL programs in several of the Latin American institutes.

Felipe Herrera, who succeeded Joseph Grunwald as general coordinator, provided important support after ECIEL coordination was transferred to Brazil in 1974.

The project was financed primarily by the Ford Foundation and the Inter-American Development Bank, with assistance from the World Bank and the Tinker Foundation. Funds from the Banco Central de Venezuela, the Junta del Acuerdo de Cartagena, and the U.S. Bureau of Labor Statistics helped defray the costs of some parts of the work. The participating ECIEL institutions in Chile, Ecuador, and Venezuela also contributed resources. The Colombian study was partially financed by the Departamento Nacional de Planeación, the Banco de la República, the Instituto Colombiano de la Reforma Agraria, and the Fondo Colombiano de Investigación; the Peruvian study was partially supported by the Ministerio de Economía y Finanzas.

Although the author drew on the knowledge and advice of the people and institutions previously mentioned, none of them is responsible for his interpretation of the results or for any errors of fact. The use of the first person singular throughout the book is a recognition of his sole responsibility and is not meant to detract from the contributions of the collaborators in the study on which the book is based. The author thanks Roger Betancourt, William R. Cline, Philip Friedman, Jorge Salazar-Carrillo, Eleanor B. Steinberg, Lester D. Taylor, and an anonymous reader for helpful comments.

The burden of typing the manuscript was ably borne by Cristina Gobin, Florence Seldes, and Rosa Smith. The manuscript was checked for factual errors by Penelope S. Harpold and Judy Conmy and edited by Vivienne Killingsworth; the index was prepared by Florence Robinson.

The views expressed here should not be ascribed to any of the organizations that supported the research, or to the officers, trustees, or other staff members of the Brookings Institution.

BRUCE K. MAC LAURY
President

May 1978
Washington, D.C.

The ECIEL Program:
A Prefatory Note

WHEN the Latin American integration movement began during the early 1960s, research institutions from several countries in the region joined forces to collaborate in comparative studies of important aspects of Latin American economic development. The program of joint studies on Latin American economic integration on which they embarked became known as ECIEL (in Spanish, "Estudios Conjuntos sobre Integración Económica Latinoamericana"; in Portuguese, "Estudos Conjuntos de Integração Econômica da América Latina"). Beginning with the participation of three Latin American institutions and a coordinating staff at the Brookings Institution, ECIEL grew to encompass more than thirty collaborating public and private research centers in every nation of Latin America except the Caribbean islands and some of the Central American countries. In 1974 the coordinating responsibility was transferred from Brookings to a specially created, autonomous coordination center in Rio de Janeiro.

The first ECIEL study, *Industrialization in a Latin American Common Market,* prepared by Martin Carnoy, was published by Brookings in 1972. The Instituto Torcuato Di Tella of Buenos Aires published a Spanish edition of it in 1975. The present volume is the second ECIEL book published by Brookings. Other ECIEL projects have dealt with the structure of wages, price comparisons, labor force absorption, and the role of education in development.

ECIEL studies have been coordinated primarily through semiannual seminars held at the participating institutes. Between seminars, the coordinating staff has communicated with the institutes by letter and personal visit. In each project the coordinating staff sought agreement on a common methodology that would be followed by all participating institutes to facilitate international comparisons. In preparing the international studies, the institutes added items of particular relevance to their countries to the common methodology and objectives. Thus collaboration in ECIEL has yielded national studies of direct interest to the participating institutions and their countries, as well as international comparisons with other Latin American nations providing perspective for national and regional economic policies.

While the focus of ECIEL is on increasing knowledge about the economic development of Latin America, an important by-product has been a higher level of empirical economic research in the region. By bringing together researchers with different training from several countries with different development experience, it has been possible for the participants to learn from one another as well as to undertake advanced research.

The Present Study

In undertaking the income and consumption study, ECIEL pursued two objectives. The first was to extend knowledge of a vital but little-known sector of Latin American economies so as to promote understanding of that region and of household economic behavior in general. The second, more difficult to attain but ultimately more important, was to contribute to economic development and to improving the welfare of the people studied and of others like them.

The project was first discussed by the participating institutes and its objectives were agreed upon at the fifth seminar in São Paulo in November 1965. At the next seminar in Lima in July 1966, the information to be collected was outlined and the general survey design was approved.

Rather than insist on a uniform survey questionnaire for all countries studied, the coordinating staff decided to give the institutes maximum leeway in designing the interview forms, within the agreed-upon framework. Therefore, much effort, time, and resources had to be expended in preparing a uniform code to combine all the information obtained in the various national surveys and permit international comparisons of the results. Intensive effort was also devoted to highly rigorous testing and "cleaning" procedures to ensure the reliability and comparability of the data.

The choice of information to collect in a household survey, and of the best way to obtain it, is obviously guided by some hypotheses about how consumers behave. Once the data are collected, however, there is a choice between analyzing them according to specific models or hypotheses and presenting descriptive statistics that can be derived without any such restrictions. It was decided to concentrate on the latter in the ECIEL study, largely because of the scarcity of comparable data and the desire to get a general view of income and consumption as quickly as possible. Also, it was not clear, before seeing any results of the investigation, which specific hypotheses would be most important to test.

Initially the study was to cover all eleven member countries of the Latin American Free Trade Association (LAFTA). Surveys were conducted in the ten South American countries, including eighteen cities; Mexico was not included because a comparable survey was undertaken at the same time by the Banco de Mexico.

This book covers five of the then six member countries of the Andean Pact: Chile, Colombia, Ecuador, Peru, and Venezuela—only Bolivia is omitted. The five countries and ten cities analyzed here are the first for which the data processing was completed. In the future ECIEL hopes to publish the results for Argentina, Bolivia, Brazil, and Paraguay, including international comparisons among them and with the countries presented here.

The original intent was to present a series of country chapters, prepared by the participating institutes, and an introduction and an international comparison of results prepared by the ECIEL coordinating staff. Much of the material for the national chapters, however, had already been published as monographs by several institutes for their respective countries. Furthermore, the wealth of data allowed many important comparisons among countries that could not be accommodated in the original design. In addition to the country studies, the participating institutes and coordinating staff have published papers and articles on specific questions based on information derived from the ECIEL surveys. This volume is therefore designed to offer the first fairly complete look at the results. The detailed comparisons of countries and across different modes of analysis make up the bulk of the book.

The Collaborators

The participating Latin American institutions contributed the survey data and much of the analysis that form the basis of this book. In several instances the Latin American institution responsible for part of the research relied on other organizations in the same country for help with particular phases of the work, such as interviewing or data processing. Detailed acknowledgments appear in the publications listed in the bibliographic note at the end of the first chapter; the following acknowledgments refer to the institutions and individuals principally responsible for the study.

In Chile, the research was conducted by the Instituto de Economía of the Universidad de Chile in Santiago, in collaboration with the Dirección Nacional de Estadística, which carried out the survey. Gastón Ormeño and César Tapia were chiefly responsible for the survey work. The principal researcher at the University of Chile was Sergio Chaigneau. Luis Federici, Juan Braun, Carlos Clavel, Gunther Held, Gustavo Sanfeliú, and Aquiles Arellano participated in the early stages of the project; Raquel Szalachman collaborated in its completion; and Guillermo Arriagada was in charge of computation.

In Colombia, the research was carried out by the Centro de Estudios sobre Desarrollo Económico of the economics faculty of the Universidad de los Andes in Bogotá. Regional universities undertook the surveys in three other cities and collaborated in the initial stages of data preparation. The project was organized and initially directed by Francisco J. Ortega. Rafael Prieto D. participated in the study from its inception and was the principal researcher until its completion. Roberto Villaveces was in charge of data processing, including all the computing undertaken in Colombia and also a portion of that done at Brookings. Rafael Isaza B. and Eduardo Wiesner also collaborated in the study.

In Ecuador, the research was conducted by the Instituto Nacional de Estadística in Quito, following the participation in the planning stage of the Centro de Estudios sobre Desarrollo, also in Quito. Jorge Yépez of the Instituto Nacional was chiefly responsible for the work throughout the project.

The Peruvian study began with a pilot survey undertaken by the Universidad de San Marcos, but the full project was carried out by the Centro de Investigaciones Sociales, Económicas, Políticas y Antropológicas of the Pontificia Universidad Católica del Perú, in Lima. The field work and the initial stages of data preparation were directed by Marinus Boenders of the University of Nijmegen in the Netherlands, who was on the faculty of the Catholic University of Peru for the first four years of the project. His place as principal investigator was taken by Adolfo Figueroa A. until the study was completed. Jan Kess Ver-Kooyen, Jorge Málaga, Gustavo Ríofrío, Ana Zegarra, and Leonardo Matos collaborated in the early stages; and Octavio Chirinos, Cecilia Arévalo, Tereza Ortiz de Zavallos, and Oscar Millones helped finish the research. Assistance in computing was provided by Fred Zappert of the Ministerio de Economía y Finanzas.

The Venezuelan portion of the study was carried out in Caracas by the Departmento de Estadística of the Banco Central de Venezuela, and in Maracaibo by the Universidad del Zulia and by the Consejo Zuliano de Planificación. The principal researchers throughout the project were Antonio José Fernández of the Banco Central and Beatriz A. de Khan of the University of Zulia and the Consejo Zuliano. The Universidad Central de Venezuela in Caracas was instrumental in bringing these institutions into the ECIEL program through its Centro de Estudios del Desarrollo. Later, the university participated through the Centro de Computación of the physics and mathematics faculty in the initial processing of the data; Margarita Blei was in charge of this stage of the work.

JOSEPH GRUNWALD
General Coordinator, ECIEL Program, 1963–74

FELIPE HERRERA
General Coordinator, ECIEL Program, 1974–

Contents

Appendix Tables

Text Figures

CHAPTER ONE

Introduction

OF THE TOTAL INCOME generated in Latin America, approximately three-quarters accrues to households or individual consumers as disposable income, to be spent for consumption or saved. The share varies according to the size of the public sector, much of whose output also goes to meet consumers' demands, and according to the pace of public and private investment, but private consumption is always much the largest component of total national income or product.[1] However, we know little about the incomes and spending of consumers. In fact, consumption is usually estimated residually in national accounts as the difference between estimated total product and the sum of government spending and investment (the latter being equal to total saving by consumers, business firms, and the public sector). Even if such estimates are reasonably accurate, they contain no information about the composition or the sources of final demand: that is, they permit no disaggregation either among the goods and services consumed or among the different groups in the population who buy those goods and services. Neither do they give any indication of how families acquire their incomes or of what portion of that income is saved.

Of course, such disaggregation is difficult, given the great variety of expenditure categories and the large number and variety of decisionmaking

---

1. In 1968, the year corresponding most closely to this study, private consumption accounted for 73.1 percent of total income in the eleven major countries of Latin America. For the five countries studied here, the share was 57.5 percent in Venezuela (because of a very high rate of investment of government oil revenues) and ranged from 71.2 percent (Chile) to 78.0 percent (Ecuador) in the other four countries.

1

units. Furthermore, disaggregation may be unnecessary for many analytical and policy purposes. However, a number of vital questions cannot be answered or even addressed on the basis of highly aggregated information. In general, disaggregation is necessary to take account of incidence or distributional consequences. Still more generally, disaggregation always permits—in principle—a finer understanding of economic relations; and microeconomic information can always—again in principle—be combined to the macroeconomic level where this is desirable.

Considerations such as these, balanced against the costs and difficulties of the required survey research, have led to the establishment of periodic consumer expenditure surveys in all industrialized countries and in a number of less developed countries. The results of these surveys form the basis for a steadily growing body of microeconomic analysis and are of obvious interest and importance for framing social policy measures. (Two obvious examples are their use in making indexes of consumer prices and in setting eligibility standards, based on income, for public assistance programs.)

The ECIEL Surveys

In the last decade, a substantial number of consumer expenditure surveys have been undertaken in several Latin American countries, and it is increasingly recognized that such information should be gathered periodically, with as wide and consistent a coverage as possible. This volume describes and analyzes the findings of the first such wide coverage, general purpose surveys to be conducted in Latin America. The series of surveys was conducted between late 1966 and late 1969 by Estudios Conjuntos sobre Integración Económica Latinoamericana (ECIEL), and investigated income and consumption patterns in ten Latin American countries. This book presents the principal results of the study for ten cities in five of the countries surveyed: Colombia, Chile, Ecuador, Peru, and Venezuela.[2]

The ECIEL study was undertaken in order to answer a number of questions about how income is distributed and how it is saved or spent. First,

2. A number of studies of individual countries or of particular questions, based on the data gathered in this survey, have already been published, and more are under way. For a list of these studies, see the bibliographic note at the end of this chapter.

the participants in the project wanted to know how income levels compare among cities and countries; how important and how concentrated the different sources of income are; and how income is related to a variety of sociodemographic features of individuals, households, and national economies. These questions are treated in chapter 2. Second, the researchers were interested in how households allocate income between consumption and saving, and among the different forms of saving; and in how certain sociodemographic characteristics affect the level and composition of saving. This is the material of chapter 3. The third main purpose was to analyze spending patterns as functions of income, the variables that determine income, and the size and composition of the household. These questions are treated in chapters 4, 5, and 6.

In addition to analyzing the importance of particular household characteristics, the study was intended to facilitate international comparisons and to reveal the importance of national economic conditions and preferences in explaining differences in behavior. This question is considered in chapter 7, together with a summary of the detailed results presented in chapters 2 through 6.

These questions and results do not, of course, exhaust the information contained in the data; every finding may stimulate new questions. Rather, the results presented here are designed to provide a good summary description of household economic behavior and to permit an initial examination of relations that are known or expected to be important.

Concentration on Urban Families

Beacuse of the considerable difficulties of carrying out field work in rural areas, it was decided to limit the study to between one and four important cities in each country, chosen according to their size (300,000 persons or more) and the representativeness of the entire urban sector. This concentration on the urban sector was justified by three further reasons. First, the countries of Latin America are rather highly urbanized, with much of the population in the one or two largest cities. In the five countries studied here, the capital cities alone account for 18.1 percent of the total population, the share ranging from 8.9 percent in Ecuador to 32.8 percent in Chile. When all ten cities are considered, the share in population is 24.5 percent, with at least 22 percent of the population included in each country.

Second, incomes are much higher in the large cities than in small towns and rural areas, so the former account for an even larger share of total income and consumption than they do of population. The families living in the five capital cities alone appear to account for 33.6 percent of total private consumption in the five countries in 1968. The share is 17.7 percent for Quito, Ecuador, and 17.8 percent for Bogotá, Colombia: these relatively low shares justify the inclusion of other cities in those countries (three in Colombia and one in Ecuador). Caracas accounts for 36.8 percent of consumption in Venezuela (one other city was also included here), and the share rises to 47.9 percent in Lima, Peru, and 51.4 percent in Santiago, Chile.[3] Inclusion of the five non-capital cities raises the share in total private consumption to 42.5 percent for the five countries together: 32.6 percent in Colombia, 42.4 percent in Ecuador, and 44.4 percent in Venezuela. Except in Colombia, where the population is distributed in many cities rather than being concentrated in one or two, close to half of total private consumption in the country is accounted for by the population of the cities studied.

Third, a substantial part of rural income and consumption does not pass through the market but is consumed directly by farm families, whereas urban households have relatively little nonmarket consumption. The latter therefore constitute a very large share of total demand for those categories of goods and services provided only by the market economy, and particularly for manufactured goods.[4]

---

3. Total household income in each city is estimated as mean household income, divided by mean household size, multiplied by the city's total population. This estimate is then compared to a national accounts estimate of total private consumption, although survey and national accounts data are not perfectly comparable (International Monetary Fund, *International Financial Statistics,* March 1971). For summing across countries, all amounts are converted to Venezuelan bolívars by the parity exchange rates developed in chapter 2.

4. Within cities, demand is, of course, still further concentrated among the wealthiest households. The share that the subsistence sector (or nonmonetary activities in general) contributes to gross domestic product is estimated to be 5 percent in Venezuela and 8 percent in Ecuador. Estimates derived from the share of agriculture in gross domestic product (GDP) suggest that the subsistence sector accounts for 6 or 7 percent of product in Peru and Chile, and somewhat more in Colombia. See Derek W. Blades, "Subsistence Activities in the National Accounts of Developing Countries, with Special Reference to Latin America," *Review of Income and Wealth,* vol. 21 (December 1975), pp. 391–410.

Selection of Countries Studied

The study was initially intended to cover all eleven member countries of the Latin American Free Trade Area (LAFTA). Surveys were undertaken in the ten South American countries, including eighteen cities; Mexico was not included because a comparable survey was undertaken at the same time by the Banco de México.[5]

The present volume covers five of the then six member countries of the Andean Pact: Colombia, Chile, Ecuador, Peru, and Venezuela. Of the Pact countries, only Bolivia is omitted, partly because of delays in availability of the data (interviewing was not completed until 1972, and the data were not received until 1974) and partly because of some difficult problems in the analysis of samples collected in two cities at different times and with different procedures. The five countries and ten cities analyzed here were chosen for comparative study according to four criteria. First, they are among the first six countries (Paraguay is the sixth) for which the data processing was completed. Second, they are or were members of an active regional integration agreement—the Andean Pact or Cartagena Agreement—which involves not only reduction of trade barriers but joint planning of investment and harmonization of economic policies. Third, the data appear to be of comparable quality, with a few exceptions which can be readily taken into account, so that international comparison is relatively safe. Finally, the data for each country have been used for one or more specialized national or international investigations whose results complement the analyses common to all countries.

According to the first and fourth of these criteria, Paraguay might also have been included. It is not, however, a member of the Andean Pact, and its economy is connected much more closely—by trade, migration, and capital flows—to Argentina and Brazil than to any of the Pact countries. The latter two countries are omitted from this study because the re-

<hr>

5. The survey, in March 1968, covered both urban and rural areas of Mexico. The data were not made available to ECIEL for comparative analysis, but a full description of the study, together with large amounts of statistical material, has been published by the Dirección General Coordinadora de la Programación Económica y Social, Secretaría de la Presidencia, *Estados Unidos Mexicanos: Estudio de Ingresos y Gastos de las Familias,* 6 vols. (Mexico, July 1974).

Table 1-1. *Time Periods during Which ECIEL Survey Interviews Were Conducted, Ten Latin American Cities*

	Time periods of interviews			
City	*First*	*Second*	*Third*	*Fourth*
Colombia				
Bogotá	2/1/67–2/28/67	8/1/67–8/31/67	11/1/67–11/30/67	5/1/68–5/31/68
Barranquilla	2/1/67–2/28/67	8/1/67–8/31/67	11/1/67–11/30/67	5/1/68–5/31/68
Cali	2/1/67–2/28/67	8/1/67–8/31/67	11/1/67–11/30/67	5/1/68–5/31/68
Medellin	2/1/67–2/28/67	8/1/67–8/31/67	11/1/67–11/30/67	5/1/68–5/31/68
Chile				
Santiago	9/15/68–12/15/68	12/16/68–3/30/69	3/17/69–6/30/69	6/15/69–11/14/69
Ecuador				
Quito	5/26/67–11/30/67	12/1/67–4/29/68	4/1/68–6/30/68	7/1/68–11/14/68
Guayaquil	6/17/67–10/24/67	11/30/68–3/30/68	4/1/68–6/30/68	7/1/68–11/14/68
Peru				
Lima	2/15/68–5/14/68	5/15/68–8/14/68	8/15/68–11/14/68	11/15/68–2/15/69
Venezuela				
Caracas	10/15/66–11/15/66	⋯	⋯	⋯
Maracaibo	6/19/67–6/25/67	9/25/67–10/10/67	12/11/67–12/17/67	5/4/68–5/10/68

Source: "Resumen del XIV Seminario del Programa de Estudios Conjuntos sobre Integración Económica Latinoamericana (ECIEL)" (Buenos Aires: June 29–July 3, 1970; processed), pp. 70–71.

sults were not completed as quickly as those for the five Pact countries.[6] Finally, in the case of Uruguay, somewhat more than half the data were received before internal political problems forced the participating institute (the Departamento de Estadística of the Universidad Oriental del Uruguay, Montevideo) to withdraw from the ECIEL program.

Methodology: Sampling and Analysis

The design and conduct of the surveys and the methods by which the data were cleaned and analyzed are described in detail in appendix A and in the sources cited there. A brief summary is given here.

Sample Design

The samples differ among cities in several respects, but they are all variants of the same general design. Its chief features are ex ante stratification of the population, with samples selected randomly and independently in each stratum; nonproportional selection, with deliberate overrepresentation of the high-income stratum; four waves of interviews throughout an interval of a year; and the combination of a panel of households to be interviewed repeatedly, with other groups (subsamples) of households meant to be interviewed only once. The dates of the surveys are shown in table 1-1: the earliest interviews took place in late 1966 and the last near the end of 1969. This design was intended to yield relatively efficient estimates by concentrating observations where the variation in income and consumption is greatest. It was also meant to capture seasonal variation and to rely on relatively short (and therefore more accurate) periods of reference for financial information, while allowing estimates for a full year. The mixture of panel and nonpanel households was designed to retain the advantages of repeated interviewing of some families while protecting the sample against the risk of attrition and conditioning among panel households. Final sample size varies from 636 observations in Cali to 3,377 in Santiago. Because of reinterviewing, the number of different households studied is lower, except in Caracas and Lima; in those cities

6. In Argentina, the Instituto Torcuato Di Tella chose to process its own data using programs developed by the ECIEL Coordination rather than send the data to the Brookings Institution for centralized analysis.

each household was interviewed only once. (In Caracas there was only one wave of interviews, and in Lima the four quarterly samples do not overlap.)

All the features of this design were incorporated in Colombia. The sample for Maracaibo, Venezuela, differs only in being proportional across strata. The Chilean sample departs from the design only in not having the same structure by stratum in the panel and nonpanel subsamples. In Ecuador, the full design was initially followed, but records were not kept of which households were reinterviewed; ex post, therefore, the Ecuadorean sample resembles the one for Peru.

Families were interviewed using questionnaires that follow a common scheme but differ among countries in coverage and detail. There are also some differences in the definition of the household or consuming unit. So far as possible, these differences were removed by converting each country's data to a common format, on which all subsequent cleaning and analysis were based. This involved consolidation of the consuming unit where related units or persons were interviewed separately; aggregation of income and expenditure data to a high level of international uniformity while retaining adequate disaggregation for analysis; and conversion of all financial flows to a common quarterly period of reference. The result is a body of data of much greater comparability across countries than usual, at the cost of some loss of detail or types of information for some countries. Uniformity of the data is best for expenditures, good for nearly all income categories, and relatively poor for wealth and saving variables, for which the national questionnaires differ most.

Quality of Data

Stringent data cleaning techniques were employed to ensure that individual observations were entirely valid, logically and arithmetically consistent, and purged of extreme values likely to be erroneous. Next, the sample as a whole was weighted to make it represent the population from which it was drawn, to expand the sample to the population, and simultaneously to compensate for nonproportionality among strata and for different sample sizes among quarters. Descriptive statistics are always calculated in weighted form, so that they accurately represent the whole population. Regressions, however, were sometimes estimated with weights and sometimes without them: in the latter case, the parameters may be biased toward values appropriate to high-income families. This was the only procedure applied to the Caracas sample. The remaining samples were further tested for internal consistency, using for this purpose the structure of four trimesters and four to eight subsamples. One test compared the distributions of certain variables among quarters and among subsamples: differences were corrected, where appropriate, by modifying the weights of the observations. The other test compared mean values of financial variables, searching for differences that could not be explained by inflation or seasonality and were therefore due to difficulties with the sample. There is no ready adjustment procedure in this case, but the test detected some correctable errors that had escaped previous examination.

The testing procedures just described are certainly the most rigorous ever applied to household data in Latin America, and are believed to be comparable in thoroughness with the best of procedures used to examine such data anywhere else. The principal source of error remaining in the data is undoubtedly neither small sample size nor problems of sample and questionnaire design but possible response errors among the households interviewed. In this respect the ECIEL surveys do not appear to differ appreciably from such surveys in much richer countries, despite the great differences between populations in material well-being and in cultural experience. The tests applied detected and removed the more flagrant errors, and prevented mistakes from being introduced in subsequent manipulation of the data, but no procedure can entirely eliminate or offset response error.

All microeconomic data are subject to error, and macroeconomic information is likely to be equally if not more deficient. Comparisons of the ECIEL survey results with other estimates of (ostensibly) the same information do not necessarily reveal errors in the former. On the contrary, they may show the superiority of the ECIEL data, particularly if alternative sources are scarce and unreliable, as is likely to be the case in the countries studied.[7]

Partly on the basis of the results obtained in this study and partly from experience with similar surveys elsewhere, it is possible to estimate at least

7. See Robert Ferber and Janes A. de Souza, "Problems in the Collection of Micro Data for International Comparisons," paper presented to a conference sponsored by ECIEL and held under the auspices of the Institut für Iberoamerika-Kunde, Hamburg, West Germany, October 1–4, 1973. Specific reference is made to Colombia, and also to Brazil and Paraguay, two countries included in the ECIEL study whose results are not reported here.

the *direction* of bias likely to remain in the data as a result of response error.[8] It is not possible, unfortunately, to estimate reliably the *magnitude* of bias. It is expected that mean values of financial variables are probably somewhat underestimated, although some tendency to overestimation may be introduced in the sample selection. The effect on the dispersion (variance) of values is more difficult to predict, with errors at some stages tending to raise and at others to lower the variability. On the basis both of methodological examination and of subsequent analysis of the results, it seems that the ECIEL data probably suffer the common problem of household survey information: expenditures tend to be underestimated, and income tends to be underestimated proportionately more, so that residual estimates of saving are biased downward.[9] The ECIEL data, however, do not appear to be worse in this regard than is common for household information in other countries.

Sampling or nonresponse errors in general do not introduce bias, but only uncertainty about the true values of population parameters. This measurement error depends on the sample size and on the dispersion of the variable analyzed. The standard error of estimate of mean income in these samples is typically 0.2 to 0.4 percent of the estimate of the mean; the estimation error is smaller for variables such as total spending that have lower variances, and higher for some disaggregated variables for which relatively few households reported values.

Presentation of Results

The ECIEL consumption study consists of a series of uniform statistical results obtained for all countries. Exceptions occur only when a particular variable is missing from a country's questionnaire or is available for so few households that it cannot be used. These results have already formed the basis of several national monographs as well as chapters 2 through 6 of this comparative study.

Also, the data for at least one city in each of the five countries have been used for one or more specialized studies. In some cases, this permits

8. Robert Ferber and Jorge Salazar-Carrillo, "Experience in Generating Micro Data in Latin America," in Eliezer B. Ayal, ed., *Micro Aspects of Development* (Praeger, 1973), pp. 84–100.

9. Robert Ferber, "Research on Household Behavior," *American Economic Review*, vol. 52 (March 1962), pt. 6, pp. 52–54.

us to overcome the limitations of the standard analysis by supplementing it with additional information; in others, it permits a comparison of different models designed to answer essentially the same questions. For these reasons, many of the findings of these specialized analyses are incorporated here.

The area studied is sometimes a country (that is, all the cities surveyed in a country: two each in Ecuador and Venezuela, and four in Colombia) and sometimes an individual city. Descriptive statistics are reported for each city separately as well as for the whole country. However, calculations involving econometric models often pool all cities in a country (with binary variables included to distinguish the cities). Because of the initial difficulties of normalizing financial variables expressed in different currencies, as well as the problems raised by differences in the definition of the consuming unit, observations have not been pooled across countries.[10] It is likely that pooling across the cities within one country introduces some bias, but the effect is presumably slight. There are some differences in prices among cities within a country which ideally should be taken into account, but the variation is not great.[11] It may easily be exceeded by price variation among households within one city.

The choice of information to collect in a household survey, and of the best way to obtain it, is obviously guided by some hypotheses about how consumers behave. Once the data are collected, however, there is a choice betwen analyzing them according to specific models or hypotheses and presenting descriptive statistics that can be calculated without any such restrictions. It was decided to concentrate on the latter in the ECIEL study, largely because of the scarcity of comparable data and the desire to get a general view of income and consumption as quickly as possible. Further, it was not clear, before seeing any results of the investigation, which specific hypotheses or restrictions would be most important to test.

The standard results reported in chapters 2 through 5, therefore, consist largely of descriptive statistics. There are two principal kinds: distributions (either univariate or multivariate) and structural tabulations

10. This does not mean that international pooling of the data would never be appropriate. In particular, parity exchange rates have been estimated to allow normalization of incomes and expenditures, and aggregation or disaggregation of consuming units might remove the problems associated with different definitions.

11. See, for example, the discussion in Rafael Prieto D., "Gasto e Ingreso Familiar Urbano en Colombia," *Ensayos ECIEL,* vol. 4 (August 1977), pp. 45–120.

(involving disaggregation of totals or the comparison of related totals). Comparisons among these results may then be made with test statistics corresponding to precise hypotheses.

One set of econometric estimates is included in the standard results: these are the Engel curves or expenditure functions presented in chapters 3 and 6. A minimum of restrictions was imposed on these estimates. They do not, for example, respect the requirements of utility-maximizing consumer behavior. These regressions were specified to overcome one of the principal limitations of the descriptive tabulations—that the latter cannot, without becoming very cumbersome, take account of a large number of variables simultaneously. The regressions permit some conclusions about the importance of each of several variables when all are considered together, at the cost of limiting the ways in which the variables are presumed to interact. The two kinds of calculations, descriptive statistics and econometric estimates, are complementary.

The previously published specialized studies, as might be expected, focus on specification and tests of econometric models. Only a few of them rely primarily on the interpretation of descriptive statistics. Three of these studies impose assumptions about long-run behavior not directly observable in the survey data, and two impose the full set of restrictions derived from utility theory.

Brief descriptions of the different calculations are given when their results are presented. In the case of econometric models, the interpretation is somewhat more complicated, and a detailed description is given in appendix B. For every set of calculations presented, there are two levels of interpretation. The first involves understanding exactly what the numbers say. This is sometimes easy, but in many cases the numbers do not mean what they might, on a casual inspection, appear to mean; often the computations have been designed to reveal a more complicated or meaningful relation or structure. The second level involves understanding why those structures or relations exist and what their implications are for human welfare and for the public policies that may affect it.

The Economic Setting

Before examining the results of the study, it will be helpful to describe briefly the economic situation in each of the countries studied during the survey period. Of course, it is not possible to analyze exhaustively here any of the national economies; at the level of sectoral aggregates and macroeconomic indicators, these are regularly described in many statistical and analytical publications.[12] Rather, the object of this review is threefold: to give some idea of the importance of the cities studied in their respective national economies; to illustrate some of the principal trends in the years of the surveys; and to evaluate the extent to which the survey period was normal, or representative of conditions in the economy over a longer interval. Since the surveys were not quite simultaneous, the detailed information presented below refers to slightly different periods, and the censuses and other sources refer to different times in different countries.

Population Levels and Growth

At the time of the survey, the five countries included some 56 million people, of whom nearly 32 million lived in Colombia and Peru, the two largest countries (estimates for 1968; see table 1-2). The ten cities include four with populations of 1.9 million or more (all the capitals except Quito) and, at the opposite extreme, three with populations of 0.6 million or less.[13]

As indicated previously, the ten cities include some 24 percent of the total population of the five countries, or 41 percent of the urban population. The percentage shares of total population and of urban population are also shown in table 1-2 (approximately, since there is sometimes a one-year difference between two population estimates).

Growth rates of population are estimated differently for different years or intervals. Some uniformity is possible in the estimates for countries, but

12. Notably the *Economic Survey of Latin America,* published annually by the UN Economic Commission for Latin America. A variety of other material is published by the Organization of American States, the Inter-American Statistical Institute, the Inter-American Development Bank, and the International Bank for Reconstruction and Development/International Monetary Fund, in addition to the publications of national governments and other agencies. A convenient summary for the countries and period studied here is Junta del Acuerdo de Cartegena, Departamento de Programación, "Grupo Andino: Algunos Indicadores Socio-Económicos," Doc. J/PR/50/Rev. 2 (Lima: November 19, 1974; processed). The national monographs for Chile, Colombia, Peru, and Venezuela contain extensive discussion of the demographic and economic conditions at the time of the survey.

13. The population estimates used in the various national monographs sometimes differ markedly from those reported elsewhere. The former have been used whenever they refer to the survey year (1968 or 1969), and other sources were used when the monographs do not include estimates at all, or not for the survey year.

Table 1-2. *Population Data for Time Period of ECIEL Survey, Ten Latin American Cities*

| City | Population | | | | Growth | |
	Time period	Number (thousands)	As percent of total	As percent of urban population	Time period	Yearly rate (percent)
Colombia						
Bogotá	1967	2,050	10.3	17.8	1964–67	6.7
Barranquilla	1967	568	2.9	4.9	1964–67	4.5
Cali	1967	766	3.9	6.7	1964–67	6.3
Medellín	1967	921	4.6	8.0	1964–67	6.0
Total for country	1968	19,830	…	…	1968–72	3.2
Total urban	1968	11,475	57.9	…	1968–72	4.9
Chile						
Santiago	1970	3,045	32.8	47.3	1960–70	3.3
Total for country	1968	9,297	…	…	1968–72	2.1
Total urban	1968	6,447	69.3	…	1968–72	2.9
Ecuador						
Quito	1968–69	513[a]	8.9	22.1	1968–72	3.5[a]
Guayaquil	1968–69	775[a]	13.4	33.3	1968–72	7.5[a]
Total for country	1968	5,776	…	…	1968–72	3.4
Total urban	1968	2,324	40.2	…	1968–72	5.1
Peru						
Lima	1968	2,700[a]	22.4	40.1	1961–72	5.8
Total for country	1968	12,037	…	…	1968–72	3.0
Total urban	1968	6,724	55.9	…	1968–72	5.0
Venezuela						
Caracas	1967	1,911	19.9	26.6	1967	6.2
Maracaibo	1967	603	6.3	8.4	1967	6.1
Total for country	1968	9,622	…	…	1968–72	3.7
Total urban	1968	7,198	74.8	…	1968–72	4.1

Source: Population figures from national monographs cited in the bibliographic note at the end of this chapter.
a. Author's extrapolation.

very little in the case of individual cities. It is evident from the estimates shown in table 1-2 that nearly all the cities were experiencing very rapid growth, faster in most cases than the growth of urban population, which in turn exceeded the increase for the entire country. The very high rates characteristic of Bogotá, Cali, Medellín, Guayaquil, Lima, Caracas, and Maracaibo include much growth resulting from migration. Only Barranquilla, Santiago, and Quito are notable for relatively slow growth, but even their rates of increase are faster than vegetative growth and include some migration. Between 1960 and 1975, Santiago experienced a sharp deceleration in growth because of reductions in births and in mean family size.[14] Elsewhere the rate of population increase appears to have been stable or even slightly accelerating during the 1960s.[15]

Economic Indicators

Of the many possible indicators of economic activity, I consider here only the growth of real per capita product for the countries studied, and the behavior of the consumer price index in the capital city.[16]

Table 1-3 shows the real gross per capita product, in national currency and in U.S. dollars of 1968. The conversion is made by using national price indexes to derive real values for 1968, converting to equivalent Venezuelan bolívars by a purchasing-power-parity exchange rate, and then converting to dollars by an estimated dollar-bolívar rate. (The parity exchange rates are discussed in detail in chapter 2.) At the time of the survey, gross domestic product per capita was just over $1,000 in Venezuela, about $560 in Chile, just under $500 in Colombia and Peru, and about $400 in Ecuador.

As the table indicates, there was an acceleration of economic growth around the time of the survey in Chile, Colombia, and Ecuador. The

14. On this point, see Sergio Chaigneau C., "Resumen de la Situación Económica del País y de las Cuidades Encuestadas," Estudio de Consumo e Ingreso Familiar, Gran Santiago, 1968–1969, Departamento de Economía, Universidad de Chile (Santiago, 1975; processed), pp. 9–10.

15. Appreciably faster growth characterized Cali during 1938–51 (8.3 percent per year) and the Venezuelan cities around 1950 (7.8 and 7.6 percent annually in Caracas and Maracaibo, respectively).

16. In Colombia, indexes are also available for the non-capital cities. This is not the case in Guayaquil and Maracaibo. Estimates of product or income and its rate of growth are not available for individual cities.

Table 1-3. *Per Capita Gross Domestic Product in National Currency and 1968 U.S. Dollars, 1960–69, and Rate of Change, 1961–69, Five Latin American Countries*

Country	1960	1961	1962	1963	1964	1965	1966	1967	1968	1969
					National currency					
Colombia	1,466	1,492	1,524	1,525	1,569	1,579	1,612	1,628	1,673	1,881
Chile	1,796	1,856	1,911	1,935	1,977	2,052	2,206	2,185	2,214	2,289
Ecuador	4,411	4,439	4,434	4,325	4,522	4,587	4,647	4,689	4,742	4,911
Peru	6,338	6,661	7,066	7,117	7,404	7,502	7,699	7,585	7,407	7,285
Venezuela	3,604	3,741	3,948	4,079	4,325	4,364	4,373	4,393	4,467	4,463
					1968 U.S. dollars					
Colombia	441	449	458	458	472	475	485	490	504	566
Chile	451	466	480	486	496	515	554	549	556	575
Ecuador	362	366	365	356	372	377	382	386	390	404
Peru	427	449	477	480	499	506	519	512	499	491
Venezuela	867	900	949	981	1,040	1,049	1,051	1,056	1,074	1,073
					Yearly rate of change (percent)					
Colombia	…	1.9	2.2	0.1	3.0	0.4	2.2	1.0	2.6	3.0
Chile	…	3.3	3.0	1.3	2.2	3.8	7.5	-1.0	1.3	3.4
Ecuador	…	1.4	2.4	-2.5	4.6	1.4	1.3	0.9	1.1	3.6
Peru	…	6.2	0.8	4.1	1.4	2.7	2.6	-1.5	-2.3	-1.6
Venezuela	…	5.5	5.5	3.3	6.0	0.9	0.2	0.4	1.6	-0.1

Sources: UN Economic Commission for Latin America, *Economic Survey of Latin America* (New York: ECLA, 1964–69); Junta del Acuerdo de Cartagena, Departamento de Programación, "Grupo Andino: Algunos Indicadores Socio-Económicos," Doc. J/PR/50/Rev. 2 (Lima: November 19, 1974; processed).
a. Colombia, 1958 peso; Chile, 1965 escudo; Ecuador, 1970 sucre; Peru, 1963 sol; Venezuela, 1957 bolívar.

Table 1-4. *Consumer Price Index, Eight Latin American Cities, 1965–69*
1968 = 100

City	1965	1966	1967	1968	1969
Colombia					
Bogotá	72.28	85.50	93.71	100	107.63
Barranquilla	75.44	86.22	93.50	100	105.79
Cali	74.25	86.53	99.43	100	106.79
Medellín	77.00	83.66	92.00	100	108.08
Chile					
Santiago	54.41	66.84	78.96	100	130.64
Ecuador					
Quito	. . .	92.29	100.95	100	106.37
Peru					
Lima	. . .	. . .	83.95	100	106.23
Venezuela					
Caracas	97.00	98.70	98.70	100	102.40

Source: Organization of American States, *Boletín Estadístico* (Washington, D.C.: OAS, 1967–72).

change was most dramatic in Chile, where the rate of growth of product per capita increased by 4.4 percentage points between the recession year 1967 and 1969. In Peru, gross domestic product per capita actually declined throughout 1967–69. The sol was devalued by 40 percent in September 1967, in response to a foreign exchange crisis brought on by relatively rapid growth in the preceding few years. The ensuing recession was quite sharp.[17] Much smaller changes in gross product occurred in Venezuela.

There was great variation in the rate of price change, from virtual stability in Venezuela to increases in Chile ranging from 18 to 31 percent a year (see table 1-4). The sharp rise in Peru during 1968 reflects the impact of the devaluation in the previous year, after which inflation slowed from about 20 percent to about 6 percent annually during the recession. Inflation was relatively constant at 5 to 7 percent a year in all the Colombian cities.

Representativeness of the Survey Periods

It is possible to characterize the survey period as normal or as exceptional only with respect to the macroeconomic indicators just discussed;

17. On this, see Adolfo Figueroa A., *Estructura del Consumo y Distribución de Ingresos en Lima Metropolitana, 1968–1969* (Lima: Pontificia Universidad Católica del Perú, 1974), pp. 21–26.

the surveys were not repeated annually, so it is impossible to tell how typical was the microeconomic behavior observed. Overall, it appears that the survey year was least normal in Lima, because of the inflation and balance-of-payments pressures that led to devaluation in 1967. One might expect considerable readjustment of relative prices and relative incomes during the ensuing (1968–69) recession. In all other countries, the rate of growth of income was lower than usual when the survey began, but in Chile, Colombia, and Ecuador there was an increase in growth during the interview period. In summary, the data for Colombia, Chile, and Ecuador refer to a (moderately) rising phase of the economic cycle, while the data for Peru and Venezuela refer to a declining phase.

Chile and Peru differ markedly from the other three countries in that they experienced much higher rates of inflation. This inflation may be considered "normal" in Chile, in the sense that it was not appreciably greater in 1968–69 than in other years. The distortions of behavior caused by rapid price change are relatively permanent in Chile. In Peru, however, the 1967 devaluation led to inflation during 1968 that was significantly more rapid than usual. There may therefore have been distortions to which the economy had not become accustomed. Unemployment rates do not seem to furnish any additional information about the representativeness of the survey period, since they follow (or at least are associated with) rates of growth of income. It would be more interesting to know how the survey year compared with other years in the distribution of household incomes, in the composition of the labor force, or in the extent of disguised unemployment or low-productivity employment. Unfortunately, this kind of information is not available at frequent enough intervals for this purpose.

Even if the survey data are representative of the late 1960s, when they were collected, have they become obsolete in the intervening nine to twelve years? Since it is not feasible to repeat such surveys every year because of the costs of interviewing and since, in any case, it takes time to clean and analyze the information, there is no way to have very recent data always available. Yet it is not possible to see how much incomes and consumption patterns have changed until a new—and strictly comparable —survey is taken. One cannot therefore be sure that these data continue to represent the economic behavior of urban households. However, a number of arguments can be made in defense of their continued use, beyond the mere fact that for most countries there are as yet no newer, equally reliable sources.

It is clear that the *money* amounts of income and expenditure change rapidly because of inflation, and less rapidly but still notably because of real income growth. The *relations* between spending and incomes, prices and household characteristics, are much more stable, however, both over time and among countries, because people's tastes are either stable or change only gradually with changes in income and other factors. The whole emphasis of the study is on discovering and quantifying these relations, so that they can be used to describe current patterns of behavior. There is an advantage here in international comparisons, because if a particular parameter is likely to change somewhat over a decade in a given country, examination of other countries may indicate the direction and amount of probable change.

In considering how stable these patterns are likely to be, one should not be misled by the characterization of Latin America as a region of rapid growth or profound change. In economic terms, the region's growth is never so rapid as to destroy or alter household behavior overnight. Many events or changes that seem both rapid and significant—alterations of government, realignments of trade, the creation of new industries, schemes for political or social reform, or the redistribution of income—have little direct or immediate impact on the incomes and spending of most households in the economy.[18] This is even more the case for the psychological or cultural changes that form part of the process of development. To say this is not to say that these phenomena are unimportant, only that household economic behavior responds relatively slowly to other changes in the economy and that we are not studying people's attitudes or aspirations but certain principal aspects of their economic behavior.

Some changes in the organization of the economy are so profound as to alter, radically and immediately, the ways that households receive and spend their incomes. Such instances are rare; they are properly called revolutions whether or not they are carried through to a permanent alteration of the economy. The countries studied here present only one such case: the radical redistribution of consumption attempted by the Allende

18. The part of industrial growth that consists of the replacement of imports affects consumers both through relative price changes and through employment creation. It need not, however, indicate or respond to any change in tastes.

government in Chile in 1972 and 1973.[19] There is no doubt that the patterns of household behavior observed in 1968–69 broke down a few years later and still have not been fully restored. But those patterns may help explain what happened between 1972 and 1975, given the changes in overall income and consumption introduced by the two successive governments. "Normal" behavior could have been used to predict some of the consequences of revolutionary change. Similarly, since the Allende government (unlike the Castro government in Cuba) failed to effect a more permanent transformation of the economy, the information obtained in 1968–69 may very well characterize behavior in Chile in the late 1970s, with suitable allowance for the intervening changes in incomes, prices, and other features. Normal behavior—in the sense of equilibrium, not in any normative sense—is relatively stable. At least over a span of five or ten years, simple obsolescence of the data is probably of less significance than the representativeness of the survey period, the quality of the information obtained, and the care with which conclusions are drawn from it.

Bibliographic Note

Two kinds of analyses have been prepared from the ECIEL survey data. One consists of studies limited to a single country and prepared by the participating institute. The other consists of comparisons of two or more cities in more than one country; these may have been written by researchers in the institutes, members of the coordinating staff, or non-ECIEL investigators. In addition to these two kinds of studies, some investigations used the ECIEL data as well as other information.

National Monographs

National monographs provide part of the economic background material of chapter 1, as well as numerous interpretations of the data and results presented in later chapters. These monographs are limited to the standard ECIEL results except where they report the findings of other

19. For a summary of this redistribution and its consequences, see the annual series published by the Universidad de Chile, Departamento de Economía, *La Economía Chilena.*

surveys undertaken in the same countries for approximately the same purposes. In two countries two or more monographs have been prepared, differing in the degree of completeness or in the quality of the data.

COLOMBIA

Rafael Prieto D., *Estructura del Gasto y Distribución del Ingreso Familiar en Cuatro Ciudades Colombianas* (Bogotá: Universidad de los Andes, 1971). This is a complete three-volume report of the survey methodology and findings, except that the weighted statistics do not include the final sample adjustment and are therefore very slightly biased for all cities except Bogotá. Rafael Prieto D., "El Consumo y el Ahorro Familiar en Cuatro Ciudades Colombianas," in *Necesidades de Movilización de Ahorro para el Desarrollo Colombiano* (Bogotá: Banco de la República, 1971). This is a brief summary of some of the principal results related to total spending and saving. Rafael Prieto D., "Gasto e Ingreso Familiar Urbano en Colombia," *Ensayos ECIEL,* vol. 4 (August 1977), pp. 45–120. This monograph incorporates the final sample adjustments.

CHILE

Dirección de Estadística y Censos, *Encuesta Nacional de Presupuestos Familiares, 1, Distribución del Gasto Familiar en el Gran Santiago* (Santiago, 1970). This is a preliminary summary by the institution that carried out the survey and undertook its own data processing. The results are thus based on data that were not subjected to the ECIEL cleaning and adjustment procedures. These are the data used by Foxley and by Roldán (see below). Since then, several working papers have presented some of the results for Santiago, which did pass through the ECIEL cleaning process. See the series Estudio de Consumo e Ingreso Familiar, Gran Santiago, 1968–1969 (Santiago: Departamento de Economía, Universidad de Chile), of which three papers are available: Sergio Chaigneau C., "Resumen de la Situación Económica del País y de las Ciudades Encuestadas" (1975); Chaigneau and Raquel Szalachman, "Estructura del Gasto" (August 1976), and "Estimaciones de Elasticidades Gasto e Ingreso" (August 1976). These papers correspond respectively to chapters 1, 4, 5, and 6 of this study.

ECUADOR

No national monograph has been written.

Adolfo Figueroa A., *Estructura del Consumo y Distribución de Ingresos en Lima Metropolitana, 1968–1969* (Lima: Pontificia Universidad Católica del Perú, 1974). A document with a similar title, but concerned only with the methodology, was published in 1970; this is its final version and includes all the substantive results.

Antonio Fernández and Beatriz A. de Khan, "ECIEL, Estudio de Consumo: Venezuela" (Caracas: Banco Central de Venezuela, 1974; processed).

Comparative Analyses

A preliminary report, based on both the standard analysis for four countries and on several of the special studies listed below, was prepared in 1974: ECIEL, "Urban Household Income and Consumption Patterns in Latin America: A Comparative Analysis of Colombia, Paraguay, Peru and Venezuela" (Brookings Institution, 1974; processed). Parts 3–6 of that document served as models for portions of chapters 2–6 of this volume.

Five special studies were prepared by ECIEL participants, or by outside scholars invited to use the data, for either four or five countries (or cities in different countries). These are: William R. Cline, "Income Distribution and Economic Development: A Survey, and Tests for Selected Latin American Cities." The empirical part of this paper examines the concentration of total income and several of its components in the cities of Bogotá, Caracas, Lima, Quito, and Asunción, Paraguay. Adolfo Figueroa A. and Richard Weisskoff, "Traversing the Social Pyramid: A Comparative Review of Income Distribution in Latin America." This study includes an examination of the distribution of income (in quartiles), and its relation to several household characteristics, in Colombia, Peru, Venezuela, and Paraguay. Arturo Carlos Meyer, "International Comparison of Consumption Patterns." Expenditure structures are compared in the cities of Bogotá, Caracas, Lima, and Asunción, and both separate and pooled expenditure-share functions are estimated. Philip Musgrove, "Determinants and Distribution of Long Term Income: Estimates for Urban Households in South America." Permanent income and consumption are estimated from household characteristics for Colombia, Ecuador, Peru, and Paraguay. This is a revised version of "Determination and Distribution of Permanent Household Income in Urban South America" (Ph.D. dissertation, Massachusetts Institute of Technology, 1974). These four papers were presented at a conference sponsored by ECIEL and held under the auspices of the Institut für Iberoamerika-Kunde, Hamburg, West Germany, October 1–4, 1973. The papers by Figueroa and Weisskoff and by Meyer were published in *Ensayos ECIEL,* vol. 1 (November 1974), pp. 83–154, 173–213; the paper by Musgrove in *Ensayos ECIEL,* vol. 2 (August 1975), pp. 1–64; and the paper by Cline in *Ensayos ECIEL,* vol. 4 (August 1977), pp. 71–112. A substantially extended version of the survey part of the paper by Cline was also published, without the empirical part, in *Journal of Development Economics,* vol. 1 (February 1975), pp. 359–400, and the paper by Figueroa and Weiskoff appeared in the *Latin American Research Review,* vol. 11, no. 2 (1976), pp. 71–112. The fifth study is Howard Howe and Philip Musgrove, "An Analysis of ECIEL Household Budget Data for Bogotá, Caracas, Guayaquil, and Lima," in Constantino Lluch, Alan A. Powell, and Ross A. Williams, eds., *Patterns in Household Demand and Saving* (New York: Oxford University Press for the World Bank, 1977), pp. 155–98.

Three additional studies were based on the Colombian data and two used the (incompletely cleaned) data for Chile. (One study incorporated some of the results for Peru.) These are: Jean Crockett and Irwin Friend, "Consumption and Saving in Economic Development" (Rodney L. White Center for Financial Research, University of Pennsylvania, Working Paper 22-73, n.d.; processed), also presented at the conference in Hamburg (1973) and published in Spanish in *Ensayos ECIEL,* vol. 4 (August 1977), pp. 121–60. This paper applies a lifetime normal income model of consumption and saving to the Colombian data. Howard J. Howe, "Estimation of the Linear and Quadratic Expenditure Systems: A Cross-Section Case for Colombia" (Ph.D. dissertation, University of Pennsylvania, 1974). The linear, extended linear, and quadratic systems are estimated separately for Bogotá, Barranquilla, Cali, and Medellín, and the extended linear system is based both on current (observed) income and on estimated normal income. Cecilia L. de Rodríguez and Hernando Gómez Buendía, *Familia y Consumo en la Ciudad Colombiana* (Bogotá:

Fundación para la Educación Superior y el Desarollo, 1977). This monograph applies a variety of functional forms to the expenditure data.

The material presented in chapters 3 and 4 served as the basis for two articles by the present author. They are: Philip Musgrove, "Determinants of Urban Household Consumption in Latin America: A Summary of Evidence from the ECIEL Surveys," *Economic Development and Cultural Change,* vol. 26 (April 1978), pp. 441–65; and Musgrove, "The Structure of Household Spending in South American Cities: Indexes of Dissimilarity and Causes of Inter-City Differences," *Review of Income and Wealth,* vol. 23 (December 1977), pp. 365–84.

Finally, several studies used the data for some or all of the Andean cities to examine the distribution of income. Some of these studies consider its relation to regional consumption, and particularly to poverty. Adolfo Figueroa A. and Rubén Suárez, "Características y Determinantes de la Distribución del Ingreso Familiar en Lima Metropolitana, 1968–1969" (Lima: Pontificia Universidad Católica del Perú, 1976; processed). Haroldo Calvo S. and Gary S. Fields, "Distribución de Ingresos Urbanos para Colombia," *Ensayos ECIEL,* vol. 5 (1978). Antonio Fernández and Beatriz A. de Khan, "Distribución del Ingreso Familiar para Caracas y Maracaibo" (Caracas: Banco Central de Venezuela, 1975; processed). András Uthoff B., "La Distribución del Ingreso Familiar Total en el Gran Santiago," *Ensayos ECIEL,* vol. 5 (1978). César Peñaranda C., "Integración Andina: Dimensionamiento del Mercado Subregional y Distribución de Ingresos," *Ensayos ECIEL,* vol. 3 (August 1976), pp. 1–26. Aquiles Arellano V., "La Pobreza en Diez Ciudades Sud-Americanas," *Ensayos ECIEL* (forthcoming). Robert Ferber, "Distribución de Ingreso y Desigualdad de Ingresos en Algunas Areas Urbanas," *Ensayos ECIEL,* vol. 3 (August 1976), pp. 67–125. Philip Musgrove and Robert Ferber, "Identifying the Urban Poor: Characteristics of Poverty Households in Bogotá, Medellín, and Lima," *Latin American Research Review* (forthcoming). Robert Ferber and Philip Musgrove, "Finding the Poor: On the Identification of Poverty Households in Urban Latin America," *Review of Income and Wealth* (forthcoming).

Single Country Special Studies

Three studies were initially presented to the Conference on Income Distribution and Development, Universidad Católica de Chile, Santiago,

March 1973. They are: Alejandro Foxley, "Redistribution of Consumption: Effects on Production and Employment," *Journal of Development Studies,* vol. 12 (April 1976), pp. 171–90; Romualdo Roldán, "Funciones Consumo por Tramos de Ingreso," Centro de Estudios de Planificación Nacional (CEPLAN), documento 38 (Santiago: Universidad Católica de Chile, 1974; processed); and Adolfo Figueroa A., "El Impacto de las Reformas Actuales sobre la Distribución de Ingresos en el Perú (1968–1972)," *Publicaciones CISEPA,* Serie de Documentos de Trabajo no. 8 (Lima: Pontificia Universidad Católica del Perú, 1973). The paper by Roldán most nearly resembles the standard ECIEL analyses, while the others use the ECIEL data (and other information) to analyze quite different questions.

CHAPTER TWO

Household Incomes

THREE ASPECTS of household incomes are considered here. First, I examine the distribution of total income among the populations studied: that is, the level of income in each city or country and the dispersion of incomes around the central value of the distribution. No effort is made to fit specific forms to the observed distributions, although some use is made of the fact that these distributions are approximately lognormal. Second, I examine the composition of income by source, in total and at different income levels. Spending behavior is assumed to depend only on total income, but the way the total is derived from different sources has important implications for welfare and for the impact of different economic policies. Finally, I consider the relations between total income and a variety of characteristics of the household. This investigation shows the degree to which income inequality is related to such factors, and discusses some implications of these relations for public policy. It also permits the effects of those factors to be separated, in subsequent analyses, into direct effects on spending and effects that operate through income.

The Distribution of Income

Three features of the way total income is distributed among households in each of the ten cities studied are examined here.[1] These features are the

1. The analysis of the capital cities is based in part on William R. Cline, "Income Distribution and Economic Development: A Survey, and Tests for Selected Latin American Cities," paper presented at a conference sponsored by ECIEL and held

location or average level of the distribution, its shape, and its degree of concentration or inequality. The latter two are independent of the units in which income is measured, while the first refers to national currency or its equivalent in purchasing power.

Table 2-1 shows the income levels corresponding to the deciles and quartiles, and the ninety-fifth percentile, of the household income distribution. These are shown in national currency per trimester, which is the unit in which all calculations were originally performed. (The samples are too small to investigate the extremes of the distribution, such as the richest or poorest 1 percent. Because high-income households are usually overrepresented, the high end of the distribution can be studied more easily than the low end.) In Colombia and Venezuela, the capital city is uniformly richer than the provincial cities, while the reverse is true in Ecuador. Thus, for example, half the households in the four Colombian cities have incomes below 5,063 pesos per trimester, while in Bogotá the proportion below that level is only 40.6 percent.

Table 2-2 compares the locations of the income distribution among cities in Colombia, Ecuador, and Venezuela in more detail. In Colombia (all four cities), for example, 25 percent of households have incomes below 3,188 pesos per quarter. That interval includes only 18.29 percent of the households in Bogotá, however, but more than one-third of the households in Cali. Conversely, 30 percent of Bogotá households have quarterly incomes in excess of 9,000 pesos, but in the other cities only about 21 percent of all families have incomes that high. In Ecuador, there is no difference between Quito and Guayaquil at high incomes, but the percentage of households with very low incomes—3,465 sucres or less—is much larger in Quito. The greatest difference is observed in Venezuela, where Caracas is much richer than Maracaibo. Fully four-fifths of Caracas households have incomes above the median of 2,370 bolívars.

The distributions are compared across countries, in table 2-3, by first expressing all values in Venezuelan bolívars of equivalent purchasing power, and then converting to U.S. dollars per year. The conversion to bolívars is based on price indices calculated for May 1968 as part of the ECIEL study of prices and purchasing power, adjusted to account for inflation between that date and the time of the household surveys. The parity

---

under the auspices of the Institut für Iberoamerika-Kunde, Hamburg, West Germany, October 1–4, 1973. Similar analyses have not been made in every case for Guayaquil, Maracaibo, and the smaller Colombian cities.

Table 2-1. *Household Income per Trimester, Ten Latin American Cities*
National currency[a]

Income class[b]	Colombia					Chile	Ecuador			Peru	Venezuela		
	Bogotá	Barran- quilla	Cali	Medellín	Mean	Santiago	Quito	Guayaquil	Mean	Lima	Caracas	Mara- caibo	Mean
10	2,434	2,150	1,947	2,010	2,124	1,515	1,924	2,412	2,138	6,868	1,819	1,000	1,513
20	3,372	2,845	2,488	2,698	2,860	2,254	2,738	3,250	2,961	10,624	2,552	1,494	2,055
25	3,808	3,068	2,699	2,985	3,188	2,608	3,094	3,724	3,465	11,952	2,845	1,649	2,369
30	4,236	3,345	3,000	3,231	3,638	2,940	3,506	4,216	3,841	13,375	3,059	1,800	2,699
40	5,203	3,961	3,592	3,895	4,379	3,589	4,411	5,251	4,932	16,656	3,879	2,095	3,183
50	6,106	4,498	4,495	4,618	5,262	4,409	5,685	6,359	6,108	21,357	4,676	2,570	3,986
60	7,330	5,650	5,318	5,689	6,294	5,248	7,631	7,910	7,832	25,050	5,849	3,010	4,943
70	8,870	6,718	6,840	6,881	7,867	6,490	10,671	10,640	10,601	31,443	7,475	3,740	6,304
75	10,349	7,863	7,995	7,778	8,999	7,418	12,386	12,245	12,387	37,050	8,704	4,212	7,452
80	12,433	9,547	9,087	9,250	10,846	8,500	13,883	15,308	14,773	42,633	9,931	4,770	8,965
90	18,466	16,972	14,700	17,860	17,689	12,843	21,545	23,453	22,701	67,424	14,097	7,500	12,942
95	27,224	24,096	21,221	25,000	25,719	19,043	31,875	32,551	32,024	98,665	19,244	10,900	18,048
Mean	9,438	7,534	7,218	7,912	8,433	6,283	9,944	10,594	10,312	32,222	6,729	3,686	5,931

Source: Original ECIEL calculations based on survey data.
a. Colombia, peso; Chile, escudo; Ecuador, sucre; Peru, sol; Venezuela, bolivar.
b. By decile, quartile, and ninety-fifth percentile.

Table 2-2. *Percentage of Households in Each Income Bracket, Eight Latin American Cities*

| City | Income quartile[a] | | | |
	First	Second	Third	Fourth
Colombia				
Bogotá	18.29	22.27	29.31	30.13
Barranquilla	28.79	28.72	21.50	20.99
Cali	34.45	25.29	18.96	21.30
Medellín	29.51	27.49	22.28	20.72
Ecuador				
Quito	30.14	21.75	23.45	24.62
Guayaquil	21.82	26.47	26.70	25.01
Venezuela				
Caracas	17.61	24.35	27.96	30.08
Maracaibo	45.78	26.83	16.68	10.71

Source: Original ECIEL calculations based on the survey data.
a. The first quartile is the lowest income class.

rates are as follows (number of Venezuelan bolívars per unit of national currency):

Colombia	Chile	Ecuador	Peru
0.4800 (pesos)	0.5961 (escudos)	0.4019 (sucres)	0.1593 (soles)

No account is taken of price differences among cities in a country (the price data were collected in both Quito and Guayaquil, but only in Bogotá and Caracas) or of differences in spending patterns among households at different income levels. Assuming prices in non-capital cities to be lower in Colombia and Venezuela than in the capitals, this means the peso is somewhat undervalued relative to the bolívar for all Colombian cities together, while the escudo, sucre, and sol are slightly overvalued. The weights in the price indices reflect the behavior of the middle 60 percent of the population.[2]

2. The price data and the indices derived from them are described in Jorge Salazar-Carrillo, "The Structure and Level of Prices and Purchasing-Power Parities in Latin American Countries" (Brookings Institution, 1977; processed). For Colombia and Peru, the purchasing power parities were adjusted from May 1968 to each trimester of the household survey by Arturo Carlos Meyer, "Diferencias Internacionales en los Patrones de Consumo," *Ensayos ECIEL,* vol. 1 (November 1974), Anexo 2, pp. 211–13. I use arithmetic means of the rate for the four quarters. Meyer's procedure was also applied to the May 1968 parities for Chile and Ecuador.

Table 2-3. *Yearly Household Income, Ten Latin American Cities*
1968 U.S. dollars[a]

Income class[b]	Colombia					Chile	Ecuador			Peru	Venezuela		
	Bogotá	Barran-quilla	Cali	Medellín	Mean	Santiago	Quito	Guayaquil	Mean	Lima	Caracas	Mara-caibo	Mean
10	1,069	945	856	883	933	827	708	887	787	1,001	1,665	915	1,385
20	1,482	1,250	1,093	1,186	1,257	1,230	1,007	1,196	1,089	1,549	2,336	1,367	1,881
25	1,673	1,348	1,186	1,312	1,401	1,423	1,138	1,370	1,275	1,743	2,604	1,509	2,168
30	1,861	1,470	1,318	1,420	1,599	1,604	1,290	1,551	1,413	1,950	2,800	1,648	2,470
40	2,286	1,740	1,578	1,711	1,924	1,958	1,623	1,932	1,814	2,428	3,550	1,918	2,913
50	2,683	1,976	1,975	2,029	2,312	2,406	2,092	2,339	2,247	3,114	4,280	2,352	3,648
60	3,221	2,483	2,337	2,500	2,766	2,863	2,807	2,910	2,881	3,652	5,354	2,755	4,524
70	3,897	2,952	3,005	3,024	3,457	3,541	3,926	3,914	3,900	4,584	6,842	3,423	5,770
75	4,547	3,455	3,513	3,418	3,954	4,047	4,557	4,505	4,557	5,402	7,967	3,855	6,821
80	5,463	4,195	3,993	4,064	4,766	4,638	5,108	5,632	5,435	6,216	9,090	4,366	8,206
90	8,114	7,457	6,459	7,848	7,773	7,007	7,926	8,628	8,352	9,830	12,903	6,865	11,846
95	11,962	10,588	9,325	10,985	11,301	10,390	11,727	11,976	11,782	14,385	17,614	9,977	16,519
Mean	4,147	3,310	3,172	3,477	3,705	3,428	3,658	3,898	3,794	4,698	6,159	3,374	5,429

Source: Table 2-1.
a. National currency per trimester converted to 1968 U.S. dollars per year by the following exchange rates: Colombia, 0.4394; Chile, 0.5456; Ecuador, 0.3679; Peru, 0.1458; and Venezuela, 0.9153.
b. By decile, quartile, and ninety-fifth percentile.

There are two bases, neither of which is entirely satisfactory, for converting Venezuelan bolívars to U.S. dollars. One is an extrapolation to 1968 of parities derived by the UN Economic Commission for Latin America (ECLA) for 1960, allowing for differential inflation in the interval and for changes in the relative importance of private consumption, investment, and government in gross product.[3] The U.S. price data refer only to the cities of Houston and Los Angeles; the extrapolation yields an estimated parity rate for private consumption of 4.76 bolívars per dollar.

The second approach is the direct comparison of Colombian and U.S. prices undertaken as part of the International Comparison Project of the World Bank and the United Nations.[4] This yields an estimated parity rate for private consumption in 1970 of 8.3 Colombian pesos per dollar, equivalent—at 0.48 bolívars per peso—to 3.98 bolívars per dollar. The Colombian prices refer to seven cities (including the four studied here) and their adjacent rural areas; the U.S. prices are national averages.

Vega's estimate probably undervalues the bolívar, because it does not allow for detailed changes in consumption baskets between 1960 and 1968. The estimates of Kravis and others, in addition to referring to a later date, probably overvalue the Colombian peso in the major cities because of the inclusion of data for smaller cities and rural areas, where prices are presumably lower. An error of only 5 percent from this source, together with a 5 percent undervaluation of the peso relative to the bolívar, yields a parity rate of 4.37 bolívars per dollar, which is also the average of the two estimates. I therefore adopt this as "the" bolívar-dollar exchange rate in this study; it is only slightly below the free rate of 4.50 prevailing in 1968. The conversion rates from national currency per trimester to equivalent dollars per year are then as follows:

Colombia	Chile	Ecuador	Peru	Venezuela
0.4394	0.5456	0.3679	0.1458	0.9153

These rates probably understate real values slightly in Barranquilla, Cali, Medellín, and Maracaibo, and may overstate them slightly in Santiago,

3. Máximo Vega-Centeno, "Tipos de Cambio, Paridades y Poder Adquisitivo en el Grupo Andino," *Ensayos ECIEL,* vol. 2 (August 1975), pp. 182–200. See particularly Cuadro 12, p. 189, and Cuadro 17, p. 199.

4. Irving B. Kravis, Zoltan Kenessey, Alan Heston, and Robert Summers, *A System of International Comparisons of Gross Product and Purchasing Power* (Johns Hopkins University Press for the World Bank, 1975). See especially table 13.1, p. 170, and table 13.19, p. 191; pp. 81–82 on Colombia and pp. 83–84 on the United States.

Quito, Guayaquil, and Lima. In any case, the dollar estimates should be regarded as approximations; changing the bolívar-dollar rate would not alter the relative real incomes of the cities and countries studied.

The comparison in table 2-3 shows that in income per household Caracas is the richest city and Cali the poorest, with Lima and Bogotá the next richest and Barranquilla and Maracaibo the next poorest. Santiago appears to be the poorest of the capital cities. When differences in household size are taken into account, however, Santiago and Lima are seen to be equally rich, followed by Bogotá and then by Quito and Guayaquil. (The relation between income and family size is discussed more fully below.) Median household income in Caracas is more than double that in Quito; mean income is almost 70 percent higher. The ranking of countries is less clear, because of income differences among cities within a country. Venezuela is uniformly richer than Peru (Lima), which in turn is richer than the group of four cities in Colombia or two cities in Ecuador. If the poorest half of the population is examined, Colombia appears richer than Ecuador, but the reverse is true at higher incomes.

The Shape of the Income Distribution

The content of table 2-3 is reproduced in figure 2-1, with the addition of points corresponding approximately to 3, 5, 8, 15, 85, 93, and 97 percent of the population. Only the capital cities are examined. The vertical axis measures income, in U.S. dollars per year, on a logarithmic scale; thus a given vertical distance represents a constant proportional difference in income. The horizontal axis measures the share of all households whose income is less than the indicated amounts. Equal horizontal distances correspond to equal numbers of standard deviations of the frequency distribution function, and the percentages are those of the cumulative normal distribution. When the logarithmic and normal-probability scales are combined in this way, a straight line on the graph represents a lognormal distribution function; that is, the logarithm of income has a normal probability distribution. The modal or mean value of the logarithm is then the logarithm of median income, which is less than mean income since the distribution is positively skewed.[5]

5. See J. Aitchison and J. A. C. Brown, *The Lognormal Distribution, with Special Reference to Its Use in Economics* (Cambridge University Press, 1963), especially pp. 116–19.

Figure 2-1. *Household Income Distribution, Five Capital Cities*

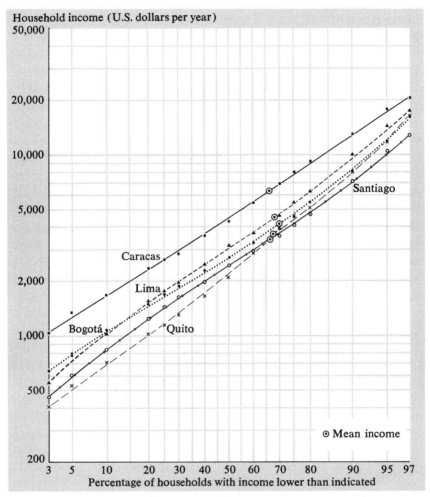

In each of the capital cities the distribution of income is approximately lognormal over considerable ranges of income, but a single straight line does not fit well over the entire income range. There seem instead to be two overlapping lognormal distributions, as indicated by the change of slope in the line somewhere between the fortieth and the seventy-fifth percentiles of the population. (This is also the case for the non-capital cities, which are not shown.) It appears that the incomes of the rich may be generated by a slightly different process than the incomes of the poor, perhaps because they consist of different forms (more capital and relatively less of wages, for example).[6] This distinction is most pronounced in Quito and least notable in Caracas, but appears in the distributions for all the cities in Colombia, in Ecuador, and in Venezuela.

It is also clear from the figure that in relative or proportional income, poor households differ more among cities than do rich households. A family at the ninetieth percentile in Caracas has an annual income $4,977 higher than that of a family at that percentile in Quito, but the proportional difference is only 63 percent. By contrast, at the tenth percentile the absolute difference is only $957 a year, but the proportional difference is 136 percent. Up to about the sixtieth percentile, there is a large proportional difference between Quito and Bogotá, but beyond the eightieth percentile there is little difference. The difference between a richer and a poorer city might be expected to be due largely to the higher incomes of the rich households in the wealthier city, with the poor households in both cities living at or near a uniform subsistence level. In absolute terms this is the case, but it is not always true in relative terms. It is true when Caracas, Bogotá, or Lima is compared to Quito, or Bogotá or Lima to Caracas, although it is not the case when Bogotá is compared to Lima. Differences among cities or countries in the composition of expenditure may therefore be due, more than might be expected, to differences in real income levels among the poor.

The same comparison can be made among cities within a country. In the case of Colombia, Cali appears to be uniformly poorer than Bogotá: the two lines are parallel, incomes in Cali at each percentile being 75 to 80 percent of those in Bogotá. In Barranquilla, however, and even more notably in Medellín, there is a sharp upward bend at the eightieth percentile. The very rich in those two cities have incomes comparable to those of rich

6. The incomes of the rich are often found to fit the Pareto distribution, which has the form $N = AY^{-\alpha}$, N being the share of recipients with incomes higher than Y, and α the parameter describing the concentration of incomes (α is larger as income is less concentrated). The Pareto distribution is a straight line on log-log, rather than lognormal paper. See Martin Bronfenbrenner, *Income Distribution Theory* (Aldine-Atherton, 1971), pp. 43–54.

The distributions shown in table 2-3 may fit the Pareto "law" quite well, although they seem to be well described by a lognormal distribution, provided the *same* distribution is not applied to all income levels. These results do not support the view that a single lognormal distribution will fit well at all but the highest incomes, where the Pareto distribution becomes appropriate, because the change in slope sometimes occurs at or below median income.

households in the capital, although at the fiftieth percentile incomes are only three-quarters as high.

Caracas and Maracaibo show the same relation as Bogotá and Cali, except that the disparity is even wider: incomes in Maracaibo are about 60 percent of those in Caracas, at every percentile. In Ecuador, the two cities are quite similar beyond the fiftieth percentile, where incomes in Quito are about 90 percent of those in Guayaquil. The disparity is much wider at low incomes. Except for Cali and Maracaibo, the comparison of cities within a country confirms the result of comparing only capital cities; in relative terms, the poor tend to differ more among cities than do the rich.

The Concentration of Income

Figure 2-1 also indicates something about the concentration of income, or the degree to which income is distributed unequally among households. Shifting a line up or down on the figure corresponds to an equiproportional change in all incomes and therefore has no effect on the concentration; changing the slope does, however, change the concentration, higher slopes corresponding to more unequal distributions. It appears that the concentration of income does not differ much among the cities studied, but that income is distributed most evenly in Caracas and least evenly in Quito.

These impressions are confirmed by table 2-4, which shows the shares of total income accruing to households in each decile and quartile of the income distribution.[7] In every country and city, the poorest half of the population receives 21 percent or less of the total income, while the top quartile receives a share between 55 and 63 percent. The share of the richest 5 percent ranges from ten (in Caracas) to almost twenty (in Quito) times the share received by the poorest 10 percent. These figures, it must be remembered, refer to only one or a few cities, which include most of the high-income households in a country. The nationwide inequality of income may be substantially higher because of the preponder-

---

7. The table shows cumulated income shares, but the share corresponding to a particular decile or quartile may be found by subtraction. Mean income in a given interval is simply mean total income, from table 2-1, multiplied by the ratio of income share to population share. Thus the second decile of the population in Colombia, for example, receives 3.01 percent of total income, and has a mean income of 2,540 ($= 8,433 \times 0.0301/0.10$) pesos per trimester.

Table 2-4. *Cumulative Percentage of Household Income, by Income Class, Ten Latin American Cities*

Income class[a]	Colombia					Chile	Ecuador			Peru	Venezuela		
	Bogotá	Barranquilla	Cali	Medellín	Mean	Santiago	Quito	Guayaquil	Mean	Lima	Caracas	Maracaibo	Mean
10	1.81	2.35	2.12	1.82	1.87	1.64	1.36	1.62	1.45	1.46	1.99	1.82	1.77
20	4.83	5.73	5.08	4.84	4.88	4.61	3.67	4.07	3.98	4.25	5.24	5.22	4.80
25	6.74	7.70	6.58	6.36	6.68	6.52	5.15	5.89	5.53	6.00	7.25	7.41	6.71
30	8.86	9.82	9.14	8.55	8.69	8.50	6.79	8.02	7.32	7.95	9.44	10.02	8.79
40	13.82	14.68	13.45	12.84	13.40	13.68	10.78	12.38	11.57	12.58	14.58	15.12	13.74
50	19.88	20.27	18.91	18.52	19.09	20.24	15.87	17.76	16.89	18.36	20.91	21.32	19.80
60	27.03	26.98	25.82	25.00	25.99	27.98	22.55	23.97	23.70	25.58	28.76	28.95	27.28
70	35.58	35.12	34.14	32.91	34.34	37.18	31.55	33.12	32.36	34.34	38.48	37.94	36.80
75	40.59	40.00	39.27	37.40	39.32	42.58	37.38	38.60	38.03	39.62	44.64	43.40	42.52
80	46.64	45.74	45.58	43.30	45.10	49.09	43.97	45.31	44.62	45.83	51.39	49.37	49.38
90	62.41	62.74	61.37	58.21	61.21	65.64	60.96	63.15	62.31	62.11	69.01	65.19	67.43
95	74.36	75.65	74.08	71.03	73.51	77.71	73.86	76.32	75.30	75.11	81.16	78.51	79.83
Gini index	0.472	0.463	0.479	0.499	0.473	0.451	0.518	0.489	0.495	0.487	0.429	0.437	0.443

Source: Original ECIEL calculations based on the survey data.
a. By decile, quartile, and ninety-fifth percentile.

ance of low-income households in small towns and rural areas, even if income is not highly concentrated within the rural or agricultural sector.[8]

The values in table 2-4 correspond to points on a Lorenz curve. The diagonal in such a diagram is a line of perfect equality of income for all households; incomes are unequal or concentrated to the extent that the Lorenz curve lies below the diagonal. The degree of inequality can be measured by the ratio of the area between the Lorenz curve and the diagonal to the total area below the diagonal; this ratio is the Gini index, ranging from 0 for perfect equality to 1.0 when all the income accrues to one recipient.[9] This index, ranging from 0.429 to 0.518, is also shown in table 2-4. The differences among Gini coefficients are not very large, but they are all statistically significant despite the rather small samples from which they were calculated.[10]

Among the capital cities, Lorenz curves unambiguously show income to be concentrated most in Quito and least in Caracas, and to be more nearly equal in Santiago than in Lima. The curve for Bogotá, however, crosses those for Santiago (at about the fortieth percentile) and for Lima (at the ninety-second percentile), so the ordering is not uniform. The same problem arises when comparing countries in which two or more cities

8. For an extensive comparison of mean incomes, income shares, and income concentrations between urban and rural areas in Latin America, see Adolfo Figueroa A. and Richard Weisskoff, "Traversing the Social Pyramid: A Comparative Review of Income Distribution in Latin America," *Latin American Research Review*, vol. 11, no. 2 (1976), pp. 76–81 and tables 3, 4, and 5. A further comparison for Peru appears in Adolfo Figueroa A., *Estructura del Consumo y Distribución de Ingresos en Lima Metropolitana, 1968–1969* (Lima: Pontificia Universidad Católica del Perú, 1974), p. 99.

9. This measure is commonly used to describe the concentration of income; in practice, it is estimated on the assumption that the Lorenz curve is linear between points. This lower bound approximation is quite accurate when many points are known; the estimates in table 2-4 are based on 100 or more points distributed through the entire range of income. For discussions of income distribution statistics, see Bronfenbrenner, *Income Distribution Theory;* Richard Weisskoff, "Income Distribution and Economic Growth in Puerto Rico, Argentina and Mexico," *Review of Income and Wealth*, vol. 16 (December 1970), pp. 303–32; Aitchison and Brown, *The Lognormal Distribution*, pp. 111–15; and D. G. Champernowne, "A Comparison of Measures of Inequality of Income Distribution," *Economic Journal*, vol. 84 (December 1974), pp. 787–816.

10. Comparisons of concentration among capital cities, except for Santiago, were made using a Kolmogorov-Smirnov test with Lima as the base city. See Cline, "Income Distribution and Economic Development," table 5. Differences among countries may be presumed to be significant, given the values of the Gini coefficient and the larger samples involved.

were surveyed: the curve for Colombia crosses those for both Ecuador and Venezuela. The Gini coefficient differs less among countries than among the capital cities. If all ten cities are compared, income in Barranquilla is less concentrated than in Caracas, up to median income, and the curve for Maracaibo lies above that for Caracas between the twenty-fifth and sixtieth percentiles. At the other extreme, the curve for Medellín lies below that for Quito, beyond the eightieth percentile; the richest two deciles of households receive a larger share of total income in Medellín than in any other city studied.

Compared to the worldwide variation in real income levels among countries, these ten cities are all at about the same level of income. It is therefore not surprising that there does not seem to be any relation between the average income in a city (measured by the mean or median of household income or by the mean of consumption per person) and the degree of income concentration (measured by the Gini coefficient or by the income share of the poorest 40 percent or the richest 20 percent of the population). The results in tables 2-3 and 2-4 provide no evidence concerning the "Kuznets hypothesis" that income inequality should be expected initially to increase as income rises, and then to decline. When such a relation is estimated from data for a large number of countries, nine of these cities cluster near the turning point, at relatively high levels of income concentration and at per capita income levels of about $500 to $750 a year. (Caracas has appreciably higher income and the lowest degree of inequality.)[11]

Differences among cities or countries in the concentration of pretax income might of course be reduced by direct taxation if taxes were most progressive where incomes were most unequal. Even if this were not the case, taxes might significantly reduce the concentration of income in some or all of the cities studied. This possibility was examined for the capital cities (except Santiago), comparing the concentration of total income, income net of direct taxes, and disposable income (net of taxes and social security payments). Gini coefficients for these concepts are as follows:[12]

	Bogotá	Quito	Lima	Caracas
Total income	0.472	0.518	0.487	0.429
Income after taxes	0.468	0.516	0.485	0.427
Disposable income	0.468	0.518	0.486	0.428

11. The most extensive investigation of the relation between income level and concentration is Montek Ahluwalia, "Inequality, Poverty and Development," *Journal of Development Economics,* vol. 3 (December 1976), pp. 307–42.

12. Cline, "Income Distribution and Economic Development," table 2.

After-tax inequality is slightly less than for pretax income, but the change in the Gini coefficient is negligible. Moreover, social security taxes seem to be regressive, causing the index to rise again in three cities. The analysis here and in the remainder of this volume is therefore based on total rather than disposable income, which permits income to be divided by source. It is not clear whether total or disposable income is more accurately estimated, but the difference is likely to be slight.

The Composition of Income

In all the analyses of the ECIEL budget data, it is assumed that a household's behavior depends on the amount of its income but is independent of the source. A unit of income is saved or spent in the same way whether it is received by the head of the household or by another member, and whether it comes as payment for labor, return on capital, or in another form.[13] Nonetheless it is of interest to examine the composition of income, because payments from different sources may be taxed at different rates, respond differently to changes in economic conditions or policies, and be more or less stable over time. Public policies intended to change the distribution of income affect different kinds of income quite differently. Moreover, total income as defined here includes some estimated, nonmonetary items—imputed rent to owned dwellings, domestic production, and income in kind—and it is important to know what shares these are of the total.

Global and Individual Composition

Total income is divided into six classes for this analysis, as follows:

—wages and salaries (including income in kind but excluding bonuses);
—self-employment income (including income in kind and the returns to capital used in family enterprises);
—returns on other capital (including imputed rents, without deduction for interest paid on mortgages);
—transfers (both public and private, including transfers in kind);

13. The only exception to this assumption is introduced in the analyses of normal or permanent income, which, it is assumed, may be spent differently from transitory or from residual income.

—transitory or windfall income (including inheritances, lottery winnings, and bonuses);[14]

—unclassified income (residual).

The first two classes together are called labor income (although some returns to capital are included). The last two classes are generally extremely small or are received by very few families, so they are not further considered.

The share of one income class in total income is usually measured, as in the national accounts, by the ratio of mean income in that class to mean total income. These mean values, in national currency per trimester and then in dollars per year, are shown in table 2-5 along with the corresponding global shares. Labor income always forms the largest share, but its importance varies considerably among countries and even among cities. Of every hundred units of income received, eighty-three or more accrue to labor in Venezuela, eighty in Peru, seventy-one in Colombia, sixty-four in Santiago, and only fifty-nine in Quito. If wages and salaries alone are considered, the share is over 63 percent in Venezuela, 54 percent in Peru, and about 44 percent or less in Colombia, Chile, and Ecuador.[15] The variation in self-employment income—including the receipts of street vendors with those of educated professionals—is proportionally wider, from less than 20 percent in Caracas and Quito to 38 percent in Barranquilla.

Capital income accounts for about 15 percent of income in Peru and Venezuela and close to 20 percent in Colombia and Ecuador, being notably high only in Medellín and Quito. Transfer income forms about 7 to 9 percent of the total in Colombia and Ecuador; within a country, the transfer share is, to some extent, inversely related to mean real income, being relatively high in Quito and low in Bogotá. In Peru and Venezuela, the transfer share is much lower, partly because incomes are higher in those countries (particularly in Venezuela), but it is also likely that the

14. This is an a priori classification and does not correspond to transitory or residual income as defined in the analysis of permanent income.

15. This result is consistent with the ranking of real wages and salaries across countries, for identical occupations in selected industries. See Jorge Salazar-Carrillo, with the assistance of Juan J. Buttari, "The Structure of Wages in LAFTA Countries" (Brookings Institution, 1977; processed), especially chaps. 5 and 7. Venezuela and Peru are found to have much higher real wages than Colombia, Chile, or Ecuador. Of course, income shares also depend on the occupational structure of the population.

Table 2-5. *Household Income per Trimester by Source, Ten Latin American Cities*

City and income source	Global share[a] (*percent*)	Individual share[a] (*percent*)	Mean value[b] (*national currency and U.S. dollars*)
Colombia			
Bogotá			
Wages and salaries[c]	43.57	47.83	4,112 (1,807)
Self-employment	28.51	25.81	2,691 (1,182)
Total labor	72.08	73.64	6,802 (2,989)
Capital	19.61	17.84	1,851 (813)
Transfers	7.21	7.62	680 (299)
Barranquilla			
Wages and salaries[c]	37.24	37.99	2,806 (1,233)
Self-employment	38.33	34.98	2,888 (1,269)
Total labor	75.57	72.97	5,964 (2,502)
Capital	11.62	9.90	875 (385)
Transfers	10.46	14.86	788 (346)
Cali			
Wages and salaries[c]	40.31	48.45	2,910 (1,279)
Self-employment	32.38	26.73	2,337 (1,027)
Total labor	72.69	75.18	5,247 (2,306)
Capital	18.90	13.90	1,364 (599)
Transfers	7.20	9.85	520 (228)
Medellín			
Wages and salaries[c]	36.54	46.63	2,891 (1,270)
Self-employment	28.80	20.73	2,279 (1,001)
Total labor	65.34	67.36	5,170 (2,272)

Footnotes to table 2-5 on page 44.

Table 2-5 *(continued)*

City and income source	Global share[a] (percent)	Individual share[a] (percent)	Mean value[b] (national currency and U.S. dollars)
Capital	21.66	16.26	1,714 (753)
Transfers	10.78	13.66	853 (375)
All urban			
Wages and salaries[c]	40.76	46.34	3,437 (1,510)
Self-employment	30.32	25.99	2,557 (1,124)
Total labor	71.08	72.33	5,994 (2,634)
Capital	19.01	15.71	1,603 (704)
Transfers	8.39	10.41	708 (311)
Chile			
Santiago			
Wages and salaries[c]	43.99	46.57	2,764 (1,508)
Self-employment	20.51	17.81	1,289 (703)
Total labor[d]	64.50	64.38	4,052 (2,211)
Capital	13.67	12.07	859 (469)
Transfers	8.90	11.15	559 (305)
Ecuador			
Quito			
Wages and salaries[c]	40.47	45.77	4,024 (1,480)
Self-employment	18.62	25.50	1,852 (681)
Total labor	59.09	71.27	5,876 (2,162)
Capital	23.35	12.09	2,322 (854)
Transfers	9.16	10.00	911 (335)
Guayaquil			
Wages and salaries[c]	46.57	46.62	4,934 (1,815)

Table 2-5 *(continued)*

City and income source	Global share[a] *(percent)*	Individual share[a] *(percent)*	Mean value[b] *(national currency and U.S. dollars)*
Self-employment	25.57	31.66	2,709
			(998)
Total labor	72.14	78.28	7,643
			(2,812)
Capital	15.10	7.64	1,600
			(589)
Transfers	6.42	6.63	679
			(250)
All urban			
Wages and salaries[c]	44.06	46.26	4,543
			(1,672)
Self-employment	22.71	29.02	2,342
			(862)
Total labor	66.77	75.28	6,885
			(2,533)
Capital	18.50	9.54	1,908
			(702)
Transfers	7.55	8.07	779
			(287)
Peru			
Lima			
Wages and salaries[c]	54.09	57.14	17,429
			(2,541)
Self-employment	25.54	25.00	8,229
			(1,200)
Total labor	79.63	82.14	26,659
			(3,741)
Capital	14.51	10.51	4,676
			(682)
Transfers	4.13	5.13	1,331
			(194)
Venezuela			
Caracas			
Wages and salaries[c]	64.43	67.33	4,335
			(3,968)
Self-employment	19.24	19.27	1,295
			(1,185)
Total labor	83.67	86.60	5,630
			(5,153)
Capital	14.44	11.05	972
			(890)
Transfers	2.11	2.80	141
			(129)

Table 2-5 (*continued*)

City and income source	Global share[a] (percent)	Individual share[a] (percent)	Mean value[b] (national currency and U.S. dollars)
Maracaibo			
Wages and salaries[c]	58.01	49.41	2,138 (1,957)
Self-employment	26.96	32.99	994 (910)
Total labor	84.97	82.40	3,132 (2,867)
Capital	7.56	10.18	279 (255)
Transfers	3.58	5.60	132 (121)
All urban			
Wages and salaries[c]	63.38	62.64	3,759 (3,441)
Self-employment	20.49	22.87	1,215 (1,112)
Total labor	83.87	85.51	4,974 (4,553)
Capital	13.33	10.83	790 (723)
Transfers	2.35	3.54	139 (127)

Source: Original ECIEL calculations based on the survey data.

a. Global and individual shares are calculated thus: let Y_{rh} be income of type r received by household h; Y_h that household's total income; and W_h its weight in the sample. Then the global share of type r income in total income is defined as $\Sigma_h W_h Y_{rh}/\Sigma_h W_h Y_h$ (the ratio of means of Y_{rh} and Y_h). The individual share is defined as $\Sigma_h W_h (Y_{rh}/Y_h)/\Sigma_h W_h$ (the mean of the individual ratios Y_{rh}/Y_h).

b. Colombia, peso; Chile, escudo; Ecuador, sucre; Peru, sol; Venezuela, bolivar. Dollar amounts are shown in parentheses. Figures are dollars per year and national currency per trimester.

c. Includes transitory income related to wage and salary income such as bonuses, thirteenth-month pay, and so on, since these are anticipated by employees.

d. Includes only monetary income. Income in kind, virtually all derived from labor, forms an additional 11.99 percent individual mean share of total income.

low share in Peru is partly a consequence of the household definition used.[16] The share in Caracas is lower than in Maracaibo, reflecting the much higher mean income in the capital.

16. Transfers between related primary and secondary consuming units were merged in defining the household. Such payments appear in the data for Colombia and Ecuador. The definition of the household probably also accounts for the low labor share in Colombia: supplementary members, whose income is likely to consist almost entirely of labor receipts, were excluded from the sample.

Table 2-5 also shows the individual mean shares: these are defined as means of ratios rather than as ratios of means; thus,

$$y_r = \Sigma_h W_h (Y_{rh}/Y_h)/\Sigma_h W_h,$$

where Y_{rh} is household h's income in class r, Y_h is its total income, and W_h is its weight in the population. If income of type r is more important to low-income households than to richer households, the individual share y_r will exceed the global share $\overline{Y}_r/\overline{Y}$. A comparison of the two measures therefore indicates how different kinds of income are distributed among levels of total income.

Table 2-5 shows that wages and salaries, total labor income, and transfers are slightly concentrated among low-income households (Maracaibo is a striking exception). Capital is slightly more important to high-income households, and no pattern can be discerned in self-employment income because of the heterogeneity of occupations represented. The finding that labor income is somewhat more important at low incomes and capital receipts at high incomes may help account for the change of slope in the income distributions portrayed in figure 2-1; it is necessary only that capital income be more concentrated among families owning some capital than labor income is concentrated among families with employed members. The case of Quito is particularly notable: the ratio of y_r to $\overline{Y}_r/\overline{Y}$ is much lower for capital income than in any other city, and much higher for labor income.

Individual Income Composition by Quartile

The concentration of different types of income at different levels of total income can be examined by calculating the individual mean shares y_r separately for each quartile and each income source. This is done in tables 2-6 through 2-11; in Colombia and Ecuador, national quartiles were used. (See table 2-2 for the shares of population in these groups in each city.)

Table 2-6 shows labor income as a share of total income in each quartile in each city. There is no general tendency for the share to rise or to fall with increasing total income, but it tends to rise in relatively small and poor cities such as Barranquilla and Maracaibo. In larger cities, particularly in those with a large industrial work force such as Bogotá, Medellín, Santiago, Lima, and Caracas, the share tends to decline. Sometimes the decline is evident only from the first to the second quartile, as in Colom-

Table 2-6. *Labor Income as Individual Mean Share of Household Income, Ten Latin American Cities*
Percent

City	Income quartile				Mean
	First	Second	Third	Fourth	
Colombia					
Bogotá	81.79	71.53	71.04	72.79	73.64
Barranquilla	68.30	74.46	71.56	78.82	72.97
Cali	78.27	74.78	71.76	73.71	75.18
Medellín	72.77	64.39	66.21	64.85	67.16
Mean	76.36	70.69	70.17	72.05	72.33
Chile					
Santiago[a]	65.89	66.92	61.59	63.20	64.38
Ecuador					
Quito	84.86	76.07	65.53	55.96	71.27
Guayaquil	84.17	82.49	76.95	70.22	78.28
Mean	84.52	80.04	72.47	64.17	75.29
Peru					
Lima	83.67	82.37	82.62	79.87	82.14
Venezuela[b]					
Caracas	86.99	89.39	88.31	81.75	86.60
Maracaibo	73.50	83.47	85.59	86.23	82.40

Source: Original ECIEL calculations based on the survey data.
a. Monetary labor income. If all income in kind is attributed to labor, the quartile shares are 75.18, 78.63, 75.25, and 76.40 percent, and the mean is 76.37 percent.
b. Mean of totals not calculated, since income distributions in Caracas and Maracaibo have differing quartile levels.

bia. A marked, consistent decline occurs only in Ecuador, and this is largely due to the opposite trend in capital income. It does not appear that the labor share is much more uniform across cities within any one quartile than over the whole distribution, although there may be a greater uniformity at some range of real income.

Table 2-7 shows the share of labor income received as wages and salaries.[17] It is difficult to draw any general pattern from these shares, but an interesting relation emerges if they are considered together with the real income levels of table 2-3 and the comparison of distributions across cities in table 2-2. Briefly, it appears that wages and salaries increase relative to total labor receipts up to some level of real total income and thereafter

17. This share is calculated as y_r (wages)/y_r (labor). It is not the same thing as the mean of the individual ratios of wages and salaries to labor income.

Table 2-7. *Wages and Salaries as Individual Mean Share of Labor Income, Ten Latin American Cities*
Percent

| City | Income quartile | | | | |
	First	Second	Third	Fourth	Mean
Colombia					
Bogotá	63.46	77.94	60.39	60.87	64.95
Barranquilla	49.80	55.65	56.08	46.37	52.06
Cali	61.22	78.34	67.24	50.83	64.45
Medellín	72.08	77.11	69.97	53.49	69.43
Mean	63.32	74.20	62.75	56.28	64.07
Chile					
Santiago	74.85	74.36	73.21	66.84	72.34
Ecuador					
Quito	57.40	64.99	68.66	70.94	64.22
Guayaquil	50.67	57.38	63.96	66.16	59.56
Mean	54.13	60.13	65.63	67.93	61.45
Peru					
Lima	72.39	63.83	69.64	72.10	69.56
Venezuela[a]					
Caracas	77.68	74.09	81.77	77.38	77.75
Maracaibo	42.39	59.46	62.34	71.30	59.96
Mean	...	...	...	...	73.25

Source: Original ECIEL calculations based on the survey data.
a. Mean of totals not calculated, since income distributions in Caracas and Maracaibo have differing quartile levels.

decline. In Colombia, the peak share is reached in the second quartile in Bogotá, Cali, and Medellín, and is spread over the second and third quartiles in Barranquilla. The real income level at which wages and salaries are relatively most important may be about the same in all four cities. For both Quito and Guayaquil, the peak occurs in the top quartile, with the share increasing very rapidly from the first to the second quartile and then more slowly.[18] The range of real incomes in the second quartile in Colombia corresponds to the third quartile in Ecuador (see figure 2-1). Similarly, the peak share occurs in the third quartile in Caracas, but not until the fourth quartile in the much poorer city of Maracaibo. In Chile the

18. The presence of government employment probably accounts for the consistently higher share in Quito than in Guayaquil.

Table 2-8. *Distribution of Major Income Source, Three Latin American Countries*
Percent

Income source	Income quartile				Total
	First	Second	Third	Fourth	
Colombia (four cities)					
Wages and salaries	13.30	14.35	11.46	9.54	48.65
Self-employment	7.25	4.53	6.89	8.40	27.07
Capital	0.88	0.98	1.19	1.85	4.91
Peru (Lima)					
Wages and salaries	15.18	13.67	14.73	14.21	57.80
Self-employment	5.14	6.80	6.19	5.12	23.25
Capital	0.93	0.50	1.03	1.52	3.98
Venezuela (two cities)					
Wages and salaries	15.69	15.88	18.17	17.25	66.99
Self-employment	6.82	5.76	4.72	4.87	22.17
Capital	0.58	0.44	0.37	1.11	2.51

Source: Original ECIEL calculations based on the survey data.

share is nearly constant over the first three quartiles.[19] Thus the real income level at which the peak occurs differs, but not too greatly, among countries.

This kind of relation has both a price and a quantity component. That is, wage and salary income may vary, relative to self-employment earnings, either because wages vary or because the number of households earning wages varies. Table 2-8 shows the fraction of all households in each quartile that obtain half or more of their total income from wages and salaries, self-employment, or capital.[20] The calculation is limited to Colombia, Peru, and Venezuela, but it shows that the peak in the labor income share occurs in the same quartile as the peak in the share of households depending chiefly on wages and salaries. The comparison is inexact, since households earning a majority of their income from one source may also have other sources of income. Differences in real incomes among

19. The comparison for Chile is based only on monetary income, without attributing income in kind to different kinds of labor income.

20. These shares are derived from the calculations summarized by Figueroa and Weisskoff, "Traversing the Social Pyramid," table 8. Multiplication of the percentages by four yields the shares of households in a category *within* a quartile.

Table 2-9. *Income from Capital as Individual Mean Share of Household Income, Ten Latin American Cities*
Percent

City	Income quartile				Mean
	First	Second	Third	Fourth	
Colombia					
Bogotá	10.60	18.95	21.04	18.27	17.84
Barranquilla	10.92	7.45	8.40	13.40	9.90
Cali	10.15	13.59	13.59	20.60	13.90
Medellín	10.14	16.83	17.37	22.97	16.26
Mean	10.41	15.67	17.80	18.99	15.71
Chile					
Santiago	8.70	11.32	13.57	14.56	12.07
Ecuador					
Quito	1.92	6.67	13.59	27.82	12.09
Guayaquil	1.75	3.73	6.82	17.70	7.64
Mean	1.83	4.85	9.48	22.00	9.54
Peru					
Lima	7.20	9.70	9.61	15.58	10.51
Venezuela[a]					
Caracas	9.06	9.11	9.37	16.71	11.05
Maracaibo	16.26	9.56	8.94	6.63	10.18
Mean	. . .	. . .	. . .	. . .	10.83

Source: Original ECIEL calculations based on the survey data.

a. Mean of totals not calculated, since income distributions in Caracas and Maracaibo have differing quartile levels.

countries correspond to the differences in wages and salaries noted earlier: wages may be particularly high relative to self-employment earnings in Venezuela.

Wage and salary income is most important in the middle-income quartiles because wage jobs are concentrated in the modern sector and are relatively well paid. Self-employment is more common at both ends of the income distribution, but it consists of two very different kinds of jobs. The poorest households are employed in the informal sector, particularly in services, while self-employment among the richest households is associated either with professional jobs requiring high levels of education or with ownership of unincorporated businesses.

Table 2-9 shows capital income as a share of total income in each city and quartile. (As table 2-8 shows, few families in any quartile receive a majority of their income from capital, although the fraction is always highest in the richest quartile.) Three general patterns may be observed. In Bogotá, Cali, Medellín, Santiago, Lima, and Caracas, the capital share approximately doubles between the first and fourth quartiles, and the largest increase usually occurs between the third and fourth quartiles. (Bogotá is a conspicuous exception to the latter occurrence.) There is a much smaller increase in Barranquilla, but the share rises monotonically—approximately doubling—between the second and fourth quartiles. The reverse pattern appears in Maracaibo, where the share declines steadily and sharply. Finally, in Quito and Guayaquil, the capital income share starts very low and increases rapidly. This accords with the high concentration of capital income in Ecuador noted earlier.

It may not seem plausible that the poorest households in a city could obtain 10 percent of their incomes from capital or—as in Maracaibo— that poor households could depend more on capital earnings than do rich households. It is also difficult to reconcile the results of Ecuador with those for other countries. However, the bulk of capital income for nearly all households consists of imputed rent on owned (or occupied) dwellings.[21] Table 2-10 therefore shows the share of imputed rent in total income. This share follows that for total capital income closely, except (sometimes) in the fourth quartile: nonrent capital income is clearly concentrated among high-income households.[22] The peculiar results for Ecuador may now be explained by the shares in each quartile of households that own (or occupy without renting) their dwellings:

	Quartile			
	1	2	3	4
Quito	5.96	18.73	45.39	75.09
Guayaquil	16.16	22.15	36.70	63.97

Homeownership is infrequent among the poor in Ecuador, but predominates at high incomes, whereas in Colombia, Chile, and Peru the proportion of homeowners does not vary much from one quartile to another. For households receiving imputed rent in Ecuador, the share that it forms of total income is relatively stable and resembles more closely the shares

---

21. Most families appear not to own other income-producing assets; see chapter 3.

22. Almost no such income is reported for Ecuador because the questionnaire included only dividends and interest, taking no account of rents received (paid by tenants) and capital gains.

Table 2-10. *Imputed Rent as Individual Mean Share of Household Income, Ten Latin American Cities*
Percent

| City | Income quartile | | | | Mean |
	First	Second	Third	Fourth	
Colombia					
Bogotá	7.96	14.67	15.52	11.81	12.84
Barranquilla	9.86	5.91	7.51	9.35	8.12
Cali	8.77	11.50	11.13	10.80	10.34
Medellín	8.35	12.45	11.80	13.23	11.26
Mean	7.96	14.67	15.52	11.81	12.84
Chile					
Santiago	7.59	10.36	12.65	12.68	10.85
Ecuador					
Quito	1.77	6.40	13.56	26.77	11.72
Guayaquil	1.75	3.73	6.82	17.02	7.47
Mean	1.76	4.75	9.44	21.16	9.29
Peru					
Lima	6.66	8.26	8.05	11.50	8.64
Venezuela[a]					
Caracas	8.91	8.56	8.13	13.80	9.84
Maracaibo	16.08	9.45	8.18	6.16	9.80

Source: Original ECIEL calculations based on the survey data.
a. Mean of totals not calculated, since income distributions in Caracas and Maracaibo have differing quartile levels.

for other countries. The same explanation serves for Maracaibo, except that in that city homeownership is more common at low than at high incomes. (Mean total expenditure of homeowners is only two-thirds as high as for families who rent.)

The share of total income provided by transfers, both private and public, appears in table 2-11. Within a country, the share varies inversely with the location of the income distribution, being higher in the poorer cities. (A partial exception occurs for Medellín, but that may be because it has a large industrial labor force and therefore relatively large pension payments.) Except in Chile and Venezuela, the share is always highest in the second or third quartile, and there is—except in Ecuador—not much variation in the share among the first three quartiles. In most but not all cities the share is lowest in the richest quartile, but even at high incomes the absolute amount of transfer income may be quite large.

Table 2-11. *Transfer Income as Individual Mean Share of Household Income, Ten Latin American Cities*
Percent

| City | Income quartile | | | | Mean |
	First	Second	Third	Fourth	
Colombia					
Bogotá	6.38	8.40	7.25	8.15	7.62
Barranquilla	17.33	16.19	18.73	5.66	14.86
Cali	10.56	10.90	12.47	5.11	9.85
Medellín	13.14	15.87	14.77	10.26	13.66
Mean	10.94	12.01	10.89	7.84	10.41
Chile					
Santiago	15.59	9.65	11.00	8.51	11.15
Ecuador					
Quito	7.28	12.48	13.38	7.93	10.00
Guayaquil	5.65	5.24	9.22	6.15	6.63
Mean	6.48	7.99	10.85	6.90	8.07
Peru					
Lima	5.91	4.65	6.43	3.53	5.13
Venezuela[a]					
Caracas	4.64	2.54	2.46	1.53	2.80
Maracaibo	10.11	6.26	3.54	2.89	5.60
Mean	...	...	...	...	3.54

Source: Original ECIEL calculations based on the survey data.
a. Mean of totals not calculated, since income distributions in Caracas and Maracaibo have differing quartile levels.

It therefore does not seem that transfers make incomes significantly more nearly equal.[23] Government transfers appear to have no effect at all on income concentration; private transfers do serve to reduce slightly the concentration, as measured by the Gini index:

	Bogotá	*Quito*	*Lima*	*Caracas*
Total income	0.472	0.518	0.487	0.429
Less government transfers	0.472	0.518	0.487	0.429
Less private transfers	0.486	0.541	0.503	0.429

For the poorest decile of the population, however, private transfers make a substantial difference in raising mean incomes and income shares. The total amount of income transferred to the very poor is small but represents a large share of their pretransfer income. Most of it appears to come from households (presumably of relatives) within the poorest 40 percent of

23. Since pensions are a large part of transfers, they may equalize incomes among age groups without affecting the wide income disparities within each age group.

the income distribution and not from the rich.[24] However, not more than
2 percent of households in the bottom quartile in Caracas, 2.75 percent in
Peru, and 3.57 percent in Colombia can depend primarily on transfer income (see table 2-8); most poor households receiving transfers are probably not retired but have some labor income. The share of households
depending on transfers for a majority of income may be larger at high
incomes.

GLOBAL INCOME COMPOSITION BY INCOME LEVEL. The analysis of individual shares of each type of income in the total, presented in tables 2-6,
2-7, and 2-9 through 2-11, could be repeated for the global shares. Instead the same information is presented in a different way, by showing, in
table 2-12, the global share of each type of income that is received in each
quartile.[25] (For comparison, the shares of total income received in each
quartile are repeated from table 2-4.) The quartiles are those defined in
table 2-4 for the individual cities in Colombia and Ecuador (not the
national quartiles used in tables 2-6 through 2-11).

The general pattern is for the shares of the different types of income in
each quartile not to differ greatly from that quartile's share of total income, except at the extremes of the distribution and then only for capital
and transfer income. Compared with the share that each quartile receives
of total income, the share for wages and salaries is usually high in the
poorest quartile and low in the richest quartile. Barranquilla and Maracaibo are the only exceptions; both are relatively small, poor cities in
which wage or salary income is low relative to self-employment or irregular income. Capital income is concentrated heavily in the top quartile (except in Maracaibo, where imputed rent is concentrated at low incomes);
the poorest quartile usually gets only a very small share of this type of income. Transfer income usually shows the reverse concentration. The top

24. See Cline, "Income Distribution and Economic Development," table 4 and
subsequent discussion. Chile was not included in this analysis; it appears from table
2-11 that transfers may do more to equalize incomes in Santiago than in other cities,
since the share of transfers in the total is quite high in the poorest quartile.

25. The shares in table 2-12, for quartile q and type of income r, are $N_q \bar{Y}_{qr}/N\bar{Y}_r$,
where $\bar{Y}$ is mean income and N is population: for quartiles, $N_q/N = \frac{1}{4}$. For total income (the last line for each city), the share is $\bar{Y}_q/4\bar{Y}$. These shares are related to the
global shares within quartiles ($\bar{Y}_{qr}/\bar{Y}_q$) by

$$\frac{\bar{Y}_{qr}}{4\bar{Y}_r} = \frac{\bar{Y}_{qr}}{\bar{Y}_q} \frac{\bar{Y}_q}{\bar{Y}} \bigg/ \frac{\bar{Y}_r}{\bar{Y}}.$$

The second term is the total income share, shown in the table, and the third term ($\bar{Y}_r/\bar{Y}$)
is the global share, over all quartiles, shown in table 2-5.

Table 2-12. *Distribution of Income by Income Source, Ten Latin American Cities*
Percent

City and income source	Income quartile			
	First	Second	Third	Fourth
Bogotá				
Wages and salaries	8.36	15.51	20.30	55.85
Self-employment	5.86	9.46	20.50	64.16
Capital	4.04	13.80	21.95	60.00
Transfers	7.55	12.88	22.37	57.03
Mean	6.74	13.14	20.71	59.41
Barranquilla				
Wages and salaries	6.93	14.96	20.52	57.60
Self-employment	7.24	9.93	16.57	66.00
Capital	7.32	8.04	14.01	70.80
Transfers	11.86	19.61	35.91	32.40
Mean	7.70	12.57	19.73	60.00
Cali				
Wages and salaries	8.03	15.66	27.28	48.58
Self-employment	5.33	10.11	11.81	72.88
Capital	3.82	7.64	14.86	73.48
Transfers	11.58	15.78	32.37	40.08
Mean	6.58	12.33	20.36	60.73
Medellín				
Wages and salaries	8.97	15.81	27.43	49.45
Self-employment	4.45	7.54	11.73	77.00
Capital	3.43	8.63	15.51	73.24
Transfers	7.95	18.24	25.65	49.45
Mean	6.36	12.16	18.88	62.60
Total, urban Colombia				
Wages and salaries	8.02	15.88	22.25	54.01
Self-employment	6.01	7.69	16.59	69.18
Capital	3.74	9.93	19.22	66.75
Transfers	8.95	17.87	26.91	46.72
Mean	6.68	12.41	20.23	70.68
Santiago, Chile				
Wages and salaries	7.63	15.64	22.79	53.97
Self-employment	5.02	11.52	17.65	65.46
Capital	4.17	11.52	22.56	62.01
Transfers	11.15	14.54	27.70	46.51
Mean	6.52	13.72	22.34	57.42
Quito				
Wages and salaries	6.44	13.40	22.80	57.61
Self-employment	9.73	15.44	25.17	49.47

Table 2-12 (*continued*)

City and income source	Income quartile			
	First	*Second*	*Third*	*Fourth*
Capital	0.41	3.00	12.69	83.91
Transfers	4.22	12.22	34.20	48.84
Mean	5.15	10.72	21.51	62.62
Guayaquil				
Wages and salaries	6.01	11.75	21.88	60.17
Self-employment	8.36	16.14	22.72	52.80
Capital	0.71	3.09	10.00	85.96
Transfers	5.24	12.11	28.13	54.65
Mean	5.89	11.87	20.84	61.40
Total, urban Ecuador				
Wages and salaries	5.81	12.38	22.41	59.49
Self-employment	9.18	15.90	23.04	52.05
Capital	0.66	2.95	11.42	84.90
Transfers	4.92	12.27	30.86	52.05
Mean	5.53	11.36	21.14	61.97
Lima, Peru				
Wages and salaries	6.96	12.11	22.96	57.96
Self-employment	4.74	14.46	20.41	60.38
Capital	3.30	8.16	14.24	74.27
Transfers	9.66	14.21	30.19	46.49
Mean	6.00	12.36	21.26	60.38
Caracas				
Wages and salaries	7.83	14.07	26.34	52.04
Self-employment	7.25	16.53	20.17	55.91
Capital	3.92	8.88	16.14	72.45
Transfers	13.49	15.30	28.48	42.63
Mean	7.25	13.66	23.73	55.36
Maracaibo				
Wages and salaries	4.67	12.24	20.31	62.83
Self-employment	11.56	17.11	26.50	44.71
Capital	13.19	17.80	25.39	43.58
Transfers	16.08	21.70	23.40	38.49
Mean	7.41	13.91	22.08	56.60
Total, urban Venezuela				
Wages and salaries	6.04	12.96	25.67	55.18
Self-employment	8.45	16.36	20.45	54.61
Capital	5.30	8.51	13.18	73.00
Transfers	17.85	16.62	19.08	46.56
Mean	6.71	13.09	22.72	57.48

Source: Original ECIEL calculations based on the survey data.

quartile in all cities gets a substantial share of all transfers (from 32 to 57 percent, and typically somewhat less than half); but this is less than its share of total income, which is usually about 60 percent. The bottom quartile receives between 8 and 13 percent of all transfers in most cities. Quito and Guayaquil, however, are rather startling exceptions; there the poorest quartile gets a smaller share of transfers than it does of total income, and transfers are largest relative to the total in the third quartile. The fact that transfers hardly reach the poorest households at all explains part of the great difference between Ecuador and the other countries at low incomes (see figure 2-1 and the accompanying discussion).

Self-employment income displays less of a pattern than other types, probably because of the great variety of occupations represented. In Bogotá, Barranquilla, Cali, Medellín, Santiago, Lima, and Caracas, the share is relatively low in the first quartile and high in the fourth. In Quito, Guayaquil, and Maracaibo the reverse is true. The difference is probably due mainly to occupational structure, and also reflects the peculiar distributions of transfers in Ecuador and of capital income in Maracaibo.

In summary, at all income levels, labor income predominates. It is slightly more important at low than at high incomes, although at very low incomes transfers may reduce the labor share of total income somewhat. The extremes of the labor income distribution usually represent self-employment, while wages and salaries are more important in the middle quartiles. Except in the top quartile, capital income consists almost entirely of imputed rent. This kind of income is slightly concentrated at high incomes, and the receipts from other forms of capital are highly concentrated there. Transfers are distributed throughout the range of incomes but are usually most important for very poor families and least important for rich households. Few households at any income level depend on either capital or transfers for a major portion of their income; half or more depend on wages and salaries, and about another fourth on self-employment income. Relatively few households appear not to obtain a majority of their income from a single source.

Characteristics Associated with Income

The principal objective of this study is to explain the level and structure of household spending. Many characteristics of a family that affect its spending directly, by influencing its tastes or needs, also have an indirect effect by way of income. Before examining the relation between spending and household characteristics, it is necessary to consider the relation between some of those characteristics and total family income. The characteristics are sometimes regarded as *causes* of income and sometimes merely as variables *associated* with income.

This analysis suffers from two limitations. First, the characteristics examined here are probably related most strongly to labor income, and no effort has been made to explain other forms of income. However, labor receipts are the major source of income for most families; capital income, the next largest category, consists mostly of imputed rent and may therefore be strongly associated with past labor income; and transfer income is likely to be related (perhaps in opposite directions) to present and to past labor income, at least if age is taken into account. The second limitation is that households are usually classified according to one or more characteristics of the head, so it is his or her labor income that is most readily explained. The head is nearly always the chief—and often the only—income earner, but there may be other employed members whose characteristics are not taken into account. (The same household classification, according to the head, is used in subsequent chapters also.)

Effects of Education, Occupation, Age, and Household Size

Tables 2-13, 2-14, and 2-16 show the joint distribution of households among income quartiles and among classes of education, occupation, and household size. (The association between income and each of these characteristics is tested by the χ^2 statistic, applied to joint frequencies.) Table 2-15 gives the same information for age classes, but it is limited to Colombia, Peru, and Venezuela.[26]

26. A more complete description of these joint distributions for Colombia, Peru, and Venezuela (and Paraguay) is given in ECIEL, "Urban Household Income and Consumption Patterns in Latin America: A Comparative Analysis of Colombia, Paraguay, Peru, and Venezuela" (Brookings Institution, 1974; processed). These distributions were originally calculated for Colombia only, using eleven income classes and a large number of classes for each of the associated variables: nine household size groups, five age classes, eleven occupational categories, and five classes of employment status. See Rafael Prieto D., *Estructura del Gasto y Distribución del Ingreso Familiar en Cuatro Ciudades Colombianas, 1967–1968, Parte Tercera* (Bogotá: Universidad de los Andes, 1971), pp. 200–19. The number of classes was reduced in subsequent analyses because some of the cells contained too few observations for analysis.

Table 2-13. *Distribution of Households by Educational Level of Head,*
Ten Latin American Cities
Percent

City and educational level[a]	Income quartile				
	First	Second	Third	Fourth	Mean
Bogotá					
None	2.85	2.22	1.57	0.38	7.02
Primary	13.07	16.18	15.19	7.11	51.55
Secondary	2.37	3.92	11.56	14.98	32.82
Higher	0.04	0.00	0.84	7.73	8.61
Barranquilla					
None	4.83	2.52	0.59	0.36	8.29
Primary	21.09	18.92	11.77	3.35	55.13
Secondary	2.88	7.28	9.14	13.06	32.35
Higher	0.00	0.00	0.00	4.22	4.22
Cali					
None	3.24	0.94	0.09	0.07	4.34
Primary	28.91	17.39	10.55	5.97	62.83
Secondary	2.21	6.97	8.14	11.65	28.97
Higher	0.08	0.00	0.17	3.61	3.86
Medellín					
None	1.59	0.82	1.17	0.23	3.80
Primary	24.90	18.74	14.18	5.46	63.28
Secondary	3.02	7.86	6.50	9.75	27.13
Higher	0.00	0.07	0.44	5.28	5.78
Total, urban Colombia					
None	2.88	1.71	1.08	0.28	5.96
Primary	19.73	17.37	13.68	6.02	56.79
Secondary	2.56	5.84	9.43	12.90	30.73
Higher	0.03	0.02	0.52	5.96	6.52
Santiago, Chile					
None	0.96	0.75	0.43	0.10	2.24
Primary	17.14	14.86	11.49	3.53	47.03
Secondary	6.29	9.00	12.33	14.35	41.97
Higher	0.28	0.36	0.80	7.32	8.76
Quito					
None	3.06	0.31	0.17	0.00	3.53
Primary	23.61	13.42	9.74	4.34	51.11
Secondary	3.42	7.69	11.89	13.66	36.66
Higher	0.05	0.35	1.67	6.62	8.69
Guayaquil					
None	0.80	0.98	1.23	0.11	3.12
Primary	17.85	19.69	14.36	6.74	58.63
Secondary	3.18	5.33	9.10	11.73	29.34
Higher	0.00	0.48	2.01	6.42	8.91

Table 2-13 (*continued*)

City and educational level[a]	Income quartile				
	First	Second	Third	Fourth	Mean
Total, urban Ecuador					
None	1.76	0.69	0.77	0.06	3.30
Primary	20.31	17.01	12.38	5.71	55.41
Secondary	3.28	6.34	10.29	12.56	32.47
Higher	0.02	0.42	1.87	6.51	8.82
Lima, Peru					
None	0.58	0.27	0.26	0.31	1.42
Primary	16.34	15.67	10.29	4.49	46.78
Secondary	6.54	6.77	10.49	9.46	33.26
Higher	0.96	2.08	4.83	10.67	18.54
Caracas					
None	4.03	2.72	0.87	0.21	7.84
Primary	17.70	14.22	9.48	4.85	46.25
Secondary	3.44	7.18	12.47	11.42	34.51
Higher	0.21	0.43	2.37	8.40	11.40
Maracaibo					
None	11.71	6.57	4.91	3.26	26.45
Primary	10.66	17.05	13.90	12.41	54.02
Secondary	0.87	2.31	4.65	7.35	15.18
Higher	0.00	0.00	0.60	3.75	4.34
Total, urban Venezuela					
None	7.45	2.95	1.89	0.43	12.72
Primary	17.22	13.95	11.48	5.63	48.28
Secondary	1.92	5.31	8.51	9.89	25.63
Higher	0.18	1.04	2.99	9.15	13.36

Source: Original ECIEL calculations based on the survey data.
a. The association between education and income is tested by the χ^2 statistic. On the null hypothesis of no association, the percentage in each cell should be one-fourth the total percentage in the corresponding row. All χ^2 statistics are significant (show an association) at the 99 percent confidence level.

In every city about half the household heads have some primary schooling: the share is lower in Lima and Caracas, and above 60 percent in Cali and Medellín. Capital cities are usually better educated than noncapital cities, if measured by the proportions of household heads with some primary and some secondary schooling.[27] The disparity is most striking in Venezuela, where differences in incomes are also most pronounced.

27. However, university (or postsecondary) schooling is more common in Guayaquil than in Quito, and heads of household with no formal education are more common in Bogotá than in Cali or Medellín.

The share of uneducated family heads varies widely, from only 1.42 percent in Lima to more than 25 percent in Maracaibo.[28]

Education is quite strongly associated with income. Except in Lima, more than 70 percent of the highly educated in every city are found in the top income quartile, while those with no formal schooling are concentrated in the bottom two quartiles. Households with primary or secondary education are common in all quartiles, but the share with primary schooling falls across at least three consecutive quartiles in all cities. The share with secondary education rises across quartiles everywhere except in Medellín, Lima, and Caracas; the latter two cities have large university-educated shares, which may explain the smaller participation of secondary schooling in the top quartile. Similarly, relatively few families with primary education are found in the bottom quartile in Maracaibo, where many household heads have no formal schooling.

Occupation (shown in table 2-14) also shows a marked association with income. Four occupational classes are distinguished:

professional, technical, and managerial;

clerical and sales (nontechnical and nonmanagerial white-collar occupations);

artisans and operatives (blue-collar occupations);

all other occupations (including mining, agricultural, and a variety of service occupations).[29]

The first occupational class is highly concentrated in the top quartile. About one-fourth of households in this class are found in the third quartile only in Quito and Caracas, where professional and related occupations are relatively common. The association with income is less pronounced for other occupations, but the share in white-collar jobs tends to increase with income while that in blue-collar occupations tends to decline. The "other" class is usually concentrated in the poorest quartile, although Bogotá is an exception to this rule.

28. Household definitions partly explain this variation. In Lima, heads of secondary units are absorbed into primary households, so the reported heads tend to be older and better educated than in other countries.

29. Information was also collected on the sector of employment, but this has been used to classify households in only two studies: Figueroa and Weisskoff, "Traversing the Social Pyramid"; and Philip Musgrove and Robert Ferber, "Identifying the Urban Poor: Characteristics of Poverty Households in Bogotá, Medellín, and Lima," *Latin American Research Review* (forthcoming). A large number of households in Ecuador did not report the occupation of the head; this inflates the group classified as "other."

Table 2-14. *Distribution of Households by Occupational Class of Head,*
Ten Latin American Cities
Percent

City and occupational class[a]	Income quartile				Mean
	First	Second	Third	Fourth	
Bogotá					
1	0.78	0.49	1.42	8.92	11.61
2	3.52	4.90	10.86	10.93	30.21
3	8.53	11.01	11.88	5.68	37.10
4	5.45	5.87	5.16	4.61	21.08
Barranquilla					
1	0.00	1.00	1.11	7.13	9.24
2	6.51	7.05	7.55	7.62	28.73
3	8.32	14.49	9.17	4.20	36.18
4	13.96	6.19	3.67	2.03	25.85
Cali					
1	0.50	1.03	1.28	5.32	8.14
2	6.12	7.34	5.87	8.69	28.03
3	16.56	11.13	8.81	3.70	40.21
4	11.27	5.79	2.99	3.58	23.63
Medellín					
1	0.21	0.94	0.37	6.83	8.35
2	5.23	6.96	10.07	5.65	27.91
3	12.50	11.51	7.21	3.18	34.40
4	11.58	8.08	4.63	5.06	29.34
Total, urban Colombia					
1	0.49	0.76	1.10	7.56	9.91
2	4.78	6.11	9.36	8.84	29.08
3	10.85	11.62	9.87	4.54	36.88
4	9.06	6.42	4.45	4.19	24.13
Santiago, Chile					
1	0.36	0.50	1.95	9.36	12.17
2	3.50	6.03	6.96	10.29	26.78
3	12.82	13.51	12.20	4.50	43.02
4	6.96	6.12	3.41	1.54	18.03
Quito					
1	0.32	0.95	3.41	7.84	12.52
2	3.38	3.07	6.20	9.67	22.32
3	17.70	11.93	11.41	3.03	44.07
4	11.25	5.60	1.65	2.58	21.08
Guayaquil					
1	0.10	0.93	1.97	6.23	9.24
2	5.68	8.68	8.81	9.77	32.94
3	7.67	9.22	11.68	4.46	33.03
4	8.39	8.09	4.28	4.02	24.78

Table 2-14 (*continued*)

City and occupational class[a]	Income quartile				
	First	Second	Third	Fourth	Mean
Total, urban Ecuador					
1	0.19	0.94	2.55	6.89	10.59
2	4.73	6.37	7.74	9.72	28.56
3	11.81	10.34	11.57	3.87	37.59
4	9.57	7.06	3.20	3.43	23.26
Lima, Peru					
1	1.44	2.45	3.79	12.17	19.84
2	5.74	5.27	8.70	6.61	26.32
3	13.59	13.87	7.01	4.25	38.73
4	3.77	4.19	4.36	2.79	15.11
Caracas					
1	0.97	2.58	5.16	13.46	22.18
2	6.48	8.55	12.14	6.35	33.52
3	7.90	8.20	4.76	1.94	22.80
4	10.04	5.21	3.13	3.12	21.50
Maracaibo					
1	0.68	1.01	1.19	5.72	8.61
2	3.91	4.69	6.87	9.92	25.40
3	5.96	10.37	10.78	6.33	33.44
4	12.68	9.86	5.21	4.80	32.55
Total, urban Venezuela[b]					
1	1.21	1.37	4.38	11.66	18.62
2	7.40	5.66	10.43	7.90	31.39
3	10.74	6.51	5.94	2.40	25.59
4	13.91	3.15	4.24	3.10	24.40

Source: Original ECIEL calculations based on the survey data.

a. The four occupational classes are (1) professional, technical, and managerial; (2) clerical and sales; (3) artisans and operatives; and (4) all other (mining, agricultural, service, and so on). All χ^2 statistics show an association significant at the 95 percent confidence level.

b. Caracas quartiles are used.

At least for Colombia and Venezuela (all cities together) and Peru, the age of the household head is not strongly associated with income, as indicated by table 2-15. Families with young heads (between twelve and thirty-four years old) tend to be concentrated in the bottom quartile—or at least not to be found in the richest quartile—but otherwise there is no pattern to the distribution. It might be supposed that the incomes of all households start low, rise as the head ages, and then decline in retirement. Much of the observed inequality of income in the population might then

Table 2-15. *Distribution of Households by Age of Head of Household and Income Quartile, Three Latin American Countries*
Percent

Country and age of head	Income quartile				
	First	Second	Third	Fourth	Mean
Colombia					
Under 35	10.29	6.91	6.94	6.76	30.90
35–49	9.36	11.69	11.98	11.69	44.72
50–64	4.19	5.62	4.75	5.25	19.81
Over 64	1.34	0.68	1.12	1.44	4.57
Peru					
Under 35	8.54	7.06	5.14	3.13	23.87
35–49	9.73	10.83	11.68	11.84	44.08
50–64	4.93	4.43	7.30	7.73	24.39
Over 64	1.29	2.32	1.80	2.24	7.65
Venezuela					
Under 35	11.15	10.20	10.33	7.01	38.68
35–49	9.77	8.39	10.23	10.76	39.15
50–64	4.44	3.88	3.73	6.23	18.28
Over 64	1.42	0.79	0.57	1.10	3.88

Source: Original ECIEL calculations based on the survey data. All χ^2 statistics are significant at the 90 percent confidence level.

be due to the age distribution and would not represent a problem in terms of welfare or equity. When age alone is related to income, as in table 2-15, there is not much evidence for this conjecture. It may be that families' incomes vary systematically with age, but if so, the age-income profile must not be the same for all families. Other characteristics must be taken into account simultaneously with age.

Another relation between the concentration of income and its implications for welfare involves the association of income with household size. If low-income families have few members and rich families have many members, income per person may vary much less than household income.[30] Table 2-16 shows the association between income quartile and size of household. Households of one to three members become less fre-

30. Comparisons of income per person are complicated by the fact that people of different ages, sex, and occupation may have different needs for income, and also by the possible existence of economies of scale in consumption by the household. These problems are considered briefly in chapter 5.

Table 2-16. *Distribution of Households by Size of Household,*
Ten Latin American Cities
Percent

City and household size	Income quartile				Mean
	First	Second	Third	Fourth	
Bogotá					
1–3	5.90	3.60	3.00	3.40	15.91
4–5	5.98	4.99	8.40	8.99	28.35
6–8	5.15	8.75	11.42	12.99	38.32
9 or more	1.25	4.93	6.48	4.75	17.42
Barranquilla					
1–3	6.05	3.39	1.15	1.84	12.43
4–5	7.77	8.56	5.18	4.60	26.10
6–8	9.72	10.25	9.13	8.97	38.06
9 or more	5.25	6.52	6.04	5.58	23.40
Cali					
1–3	7.62	4.64	2.22	1.99	16.47
4–5	11.55	7.74	4.75	6.06	29.80
6–8	12.08	9.41	8.80	10.11	40.40
9 or more	3.50	3.51	3.19	3.13	13.33
Medellín					
1–3	6.96	4.31	2.48	2.11	15.86
4–5	7.92	7.02	6.42	4.72	26.08
6–8	8.83	7.26	5.31	8.83	30.23
9 or more	5.79	8.91	8.07	5.06	27.83
Total, urban Colombia					
1–3	6.47	3.92	2.50	2.64	15.53
4–5	7.60	6.43	6.86	6.87	27.76
6–8	7.85	8.71	9.20	10.96	36.73
9 or more	3.26	5.84	6.23	4.65	19.98
Santiago, Chile					
1–3	10.95	7.69	6.80	8.13	33.56
4–5	7.33	8.80	8.19	9.21	33.53
6–8	5.22	6.89	7.43	6.12	25.66
9 or more	1.46	1.55	2.57	1.66	7.25
Quito					
1–3	12.27	4.94	3.69	3.67	24.57
4–5	6.72	5.42	7.15	6.12	25.40
6–8	8.39	8.25	9.75	9.67	36.07
9 or more	2.76	3.14	2.86	5.20	13.95
Guayaquil					
1–3	7.59	5.76	3.56	2.63	19.55
4–5	5.71	6.07	7.10	6.92	25.80
6–8	5.71	10.79	10.59	10.51	37.60
9 or more	2.75	3.78	5.64	4.88	17.05

Table 2-16 (*continued*)

City and household size	Income quartile				Mean
	First	Second	Third	Fourth	
Total, urban Ecuador					
1–3	9.59	5.41	3.62	3.08	21.70
4–5	6.14	5.79	7.12	6.58	25.63
6–8	6.86	9.71	10.23	10.15	36.95
9 or more	2.75	3.51	4.45	5.01	15.73
Lima, Peru					
1–3	3.87	2.27	3.18	1.78	11.10
4–5	7.91	8.64	6.03	5.24	27.81
6–8	10.17	9.71	9.51	12.54	41.93
9 or more	2.91	5.30	5.50	5.45	19.16
Caracas					
1–3	8.45	6.89	5.48	4.09	24.91
4–5	7.24	8.49	9.14	8.07	32.94
6–8	7.61	5.82	7.85	9.69	30.96
9 or more	2.08	3.36	2.72	3.02	11.19
Maracaibo					
1–3	7.03	4.60	3.49	1.76	16.88
4–5	5.93	7.61	5.86	9.79	29.19
6–8	7.32	8.77	9.15	9.81	35.06
9 or more	2.95	4.97	5.54	5.41	18.87
Total, urban Venezuela[a]					
1–3	9.60	4.73	4.78	3.69	22.80
4–5	9.22	4.81	9.12	8.81	31.96
6–8	10.49	4.29	7.69	9.58	32.04
9 or more	3.96	2.87	3.40	2.98	13.20

Source: Original ECIEL calculations based on the survey data. All χ^2 statistics are significant at the 99 percent confidence level.

a. Caracas quartiles are used.

quent at higher incomes in all cities, as might be expected. Large households (nine or more members) become more frequent, in most cities, between the first and third quartiles but are usually rarer in the richest quartile. Many large families have low total incomes, and therefore low incomes per person. Households of intermediate size—four to eight members—are found at all income levels.

The strength of each characteristic's association with income can be measured by the χ^2 statistic calculated from the joint distribution: this measure is zero when the two variables are distributed independently and rises as they are more closely associated. Calculation of the statistic for

Table 2-17. Mean Household Income by Education of Head of Household and Income Quartile, in National Currency[a] per Trimester and Dollars per Year, Three Latin American Countries

Country and educational level	Income quartile									
	First		Second		Third		Fourth		Mean	
	National currency	Dollars	National currency	Dollars	National currency	Dollars	National currency	Dollars	National currency	Dollars
Colombia										
None	2,045	899	4,122	1,811	6,618	2,908	13,574	5,964	4,022	1,767
Primary	2,272	998	4,166	1,831	6,646	2,920	15,035	6,606	5,257	2,310
Secondary	2,347	1,031	4,342	1,908	7,076	3,109	19,289	8,476	11,305	4,967
Higher	2,760	1,213	4,075	1,791	7,222	3,173	26,517	11,651	20,666	9,081
Peru										
None	3,416	498	18,316[b]	2,670	28,665[b]	4,179	54,653	7,968	21,988	3,206
Primary	7,804	1,138	15,492[b]	2,259	26,839[b]	3,913	70,229	10,239	20,554	2,997
Secondary	8,067	1,176	16,063[b]	2,342	26,470[b]	3,859	75,636	11,028	34,714	5,061
Higher	4,422	695	16,231[b]	2,366	28,981[b]	4,225	84,159	12,270	58,031	8,461
Venezuela										
None	1,395	1,277	3,144[b]	2,878	5,046	4,619	10,221	9,355	2,644	2,420
Primary	1,720	1,574	3,153[b]	2,886	5,248	4,803	12,047	11,027	4,178	3,824
Secondary	1,835	1,680	3,200[b]	2,929	5,546	5,076	12,436	11,383	7,439	6,809
Higher	1,745	1,597	3,298[b]	3,019	5,704	5,221	15,988	14,634	12,503	11,444

Source: Original ECIEL calculations based on the survey data. Differences among mean values significant at the 99 percent confidence level except where otherwise noted.
a. Colombia, peso; Peru, sol; Venezuela, bolivar.
b. Differences among mean values not significant at the 90 percent level.

each city and country in tables 2-13 through 2-16 shows that all the associations are statistically significant. Moreover, the ranking is always the same: the strongest association is found for education, followed by occupation, household size, and age. For each variable, the χ^2 statistic is higher for a country than for any single city in the country, reflecting differences among cities in the distribution of household characteristics as well as the larger sample size.[31]

Mean Incomes and Income Differences

Another way to measure the association between income and a household characteristic is to compare mean incomes across classes of that variable. The significance of differences in mean income can then be established by an F-test.[32] Table 2-17 compares mean incomes by quartile and educational class, for Colombia, Peru, and Venezuela. There are evidently large differences among educational classes, when all quartiles are considered together; the group with the highest education has a mean income some three to five times as high as that with the lowest. In Peru, where household heads with no formal schooling are quite rare, there is no difference between their incomes and those with primary education only.

More strikingly, there are also usually significant income differences by education within each quartile. In the middle quartiles the income distributions may overlap too much to detect any effect, but in the highest and lowest quartiles the means can be distinguished. Some households with little or no education have incomes in the top quartile, but they tend to have much lower incomes than the better-educated families in the same

31. Figueroa and Weisskoff, in "Traversing the Social Pyramid," conclude that none of the variables studied—including the number of income earners, the principal income source, and the sector of employment, in addition to those considered here—distinguishes among households sharply enough to associate different groups with different income quartiles. If a group is defined as poor (rich) whenever two-thirds of the households in it lie in the lower (upper) half of the income distribution, then the poor are less educated and the rich are more educated and have professional, technical, or managerial occupations. These two characteristics of the rich are highly correlated. Poor households tend also to be small and to have occupations in the third and fourth categories (blue collar and other). The remaining variables have much less discriminating effect.

32. This requires a one-dimensional analysis of variance. Analysis in two dimensions is of no value when the second dimension is income quartiles, since the means are known to differ among quartiles.

Table 2-18. *Mean Household Income by Household Size and Income Quartile, in National Currency[a] per Trimester and Dollars per Year, Three Latin American Countries*

Country and household size	First		Second		Third		Fourth		Mean	
	National currency	Dollars	National currency	Dollars	National currency	Dollars	National currency	Dollars	National currency	Dollars
Colombia										
1–2	2,030	892	4,207[b]	1,849	6,535[c]	2,871	18,722	8,226	5,370	2,360
3–5	2,241	985	4,173[b]	1,834	6,733[c]	2,958	18,604	8,175	7,551	3,318
6–8	2,286	1,004	4,175[b]	1,834	6,943[c]	3,051	20,173	8,864	9,240	4,060
9 or more	2,245	986	4,257[b]	1,871	6,828[c]	3,000	24,614	10,815	9,503	4,176
Peru										
1–2	7,145[b]	1,042	16,122[b]	2,351	28,129[b]	4,101	61,247	8,930	17,379	2,534
3–5	7,609[b]	1,109	16,011[b]	2,334	27,470[b]	4,005	70,240	10,240	26,690	3,891
6–8	7,716[b]	1,125	15,258[b]	2,225	27,195[b]	3,965	78,465	11,440	35,295	5,146
9 or more	7,745[b]	1,129	16,058[b]	2,341	26,227[b]	3,824	86,284	12,580	38,038	5,546
Venezuela										
1–2	1,495	1,368	3,179[c]	2,910	5,542[b]	5,073	10,729	9,820	3,490	3,194
3–5	1,621	1,484	3,182[c]	2,912	5,351[b]	4,898	12,726	11,648	5,864	5,367
6–8	1,687	1,544	3,107[c]	2,844	5,440[b]	4,979	14,688	13,444	6,779	6,205
9 or more	1,753	1,605	3,240[c]	2,966	5,328[b]	4,877	14,303	13,092	5,901	5,401

Source: Original calculations undertaken for the ECIEL study by Adolfo Figueroa and Richard Weisskoff and published in "Traversing the Social Pyramid: A Comparative Review of Income Distribution in Latin America," *Latin American Research Review*, vol. 11, no. 2 (1976), pp. 71–112. Differences among mean values significant at the 99 percent confidence level except where otherwise noted.

a. Colombia, peso; Peru, sol; Venezuela, bolivar.

b. Differences among mean values not significant at the 90 percent level.

c. Differences among mean values not significant at the 95 percent level.

quartile. In the poorest quartile, education, at least up to the secondary level, raises income; there are few university-educated households with very low incomes, and their incomes may be relatively high or low. Overall, the analysis of mean incomes shows education to be even more strongly associated with income than appears from the joint frequency distribution.

Table 2-18 applies the same analysis to household size. Here also the effect is to show a stronger association with income than appears in the frequency distributions. Families of all sizes are found in the richest quartile, for example, but mean income usually increases with the number of members. This tendency also exists, but is less pronounced, in the bottom quartile. Overall, income increases with family size (except for very large families in Venezuela), but less rapidly. Assuming average sizes in the four size classes to be 1.8, 4.0, 6.7, and 10.0 members, mean income per person declines steadily in all three countries as size increases (dollars per year in parentheses):

	1–2	3–5	6–8	9 or more
Colombia	2,983	1,888	1,379	950
	(1,311)	(830)	(606)	(417)
Peru	9,655	6,673	5,268	3,804
	(1,408)	(973)	(768)	(555)
Venezuela	1,939	1,466	1,012	590
	(1,775)	(1,342)	(926)	(540)

Even allowing for more children per adult in larger families, it is clear that larger households tend to have lower incomes per person. Large families in the lower half of the income distribution are extremely poor, while small families in even the bottom quartile are about as well off as the average for all large households.[33]

Table 2-19 explores this relation between income and family size further for the ten cities (results are not shown by country). For each income quartile, the table shows mean household income $\overline{Y}$, mean household size $\overline{N}$, and the ratio $\overline{Y}/\overline{N}$, or mean income per capita. This is a global mean and does not necessarily equal the mean of the individual ratios, Y_h/N_h; it says nothing about variation in per capita income within quartiles.

These averages suggest three conclusions. First, there is substantial

---

33. The mean is a poor measure of central tendency for distributions with much positive skewness. The ranking would probably be the same, however, if comparisons were based on the median or some other measure.

Table 2-19. *Mean Household Size and Mean Income in National Currency[a] per Trimester for Each Household and for Each Person, and in Dollars per Year for Each Person, by Income Quartile, Ten Latin American Cities*

Income quartile and item	Bogotá	Barran-quilla	Cali	Medellín	Santiago	Quito	Guayaquil	Lima	Caracas	Mara-caibo
First quartile										
Household size	5.50	5.69	5.27	5.59	4.21	4.51	5.12	5.89	4.94	5.35
National currency, per household	2,545	2,320	1,900	2,014	1,639	2,049	2,496	7,733	1,951	1,093
National currency, per person	463	408	361	360	389	454	488	1,313	395	204
Dollars, per person	203	179	159	158	212	167	180	191	362	187
Second quartile										
Household size	5.95	6.48	5.89	6.43	4.80	5.74	5.83	6.34	5.29	6.12
National currency, per household	4,961	3,788	3,560	3,848	3,448	4,264	5,030	15,931	3,677	2,051
National currency, per person	834	585	605	598	718	743	863	2,513	695	335
Dollars, per person	366	257	266	263	392	273	317	366	636	307

Third quartile

Household size	6.65	7.22	6.19	7.82	5.22	5.94	6.50	6.71	5.38	6.68
National currency, per household	7,818	5,946	5,877	5,975	5,615	8,556	8,831	27,402	6,387	3,255
National currency, per person	1,176	826	949	764	1,076	1,440	1,359	4,084	1,187	487
Dollars, per person	517	363	417	336	587	530	500	595	1,086	446

Fourth quartile

Household size	6.39	7.05	6.33	6.86	4.69	6.34	6.55	6.92	5.91	6.47
National currency, per household	22,429	18,082	17,535	19,812	14,431	24,908	26,019	77,823	14,901	8,345
National currency, per person	3,510	2,565	2,770	2,888	3,077	3,929	3,972	11,246	2,521	1,290
Dollars, per person	1,542	1,127	1,217	1,269	1,679	1,445	1,461	1,640	2,307	1,181

Mean

Household size	6.13	6.62	5.94	6.68	4.73	5.63	6.00	6.46	5.38	6.16
National currency, per household	9,438	7,534	7,218	7,912	6,283	9,944	10,594	32,222	6,729	3,686
National currency, per person	1,540	1,138	1,215	1,184	1,328	1,766	1,766	4,987	1,251	598
Dollars, per person	677	500	534	520	725	650	650	727	1,145	547

Source: Same as table 2-18.

a. Colombia, peso; Chile, escudo; Peru, sol; Ecuador, sucre; Venezuela, bolivar.

variation in mean household size among cities and particularly among countries; the extremes are represented by Chile and Peru. Part of this variation is undoubtedly due to differences in the definition of the household (see appendix A), but part of it is real and represents differences in population growth rates, migration patterns, and living habits. When these differences are taken into account, the results shown in table 2-3 must be modified. In per capita terms, Caracas is still the richest city, but Barranquilla is the poorest and Santiago has a mean income 12 percent higher than Quito rather than 6 percent lower. Santiago and Lima have very different mean household incomes but almost identical incomes per person, in real terms.

Second, households typically have more members in the non-capital cities. In Colombia (except for Cali) and in Venezuela, this means the capital cities are relatively richer in per capita income than in absolute income; the reverse is true in Ecuador, however, where there is no difference between Quito and Guayaquil in average income per person.

Finally, average household size rises, in all cities, between the first and third income quartiles, although much less rapidly than income. At least over this range, income per person is somewhat less concentrated than income per family, although the difference is not very large. Furthermore, the mean obscures the considerable variation in household size in each quartile that is apparent in table 2-17. (The standard deviation of size is typically between two and three members.) In the fourth quartile, mean size continues to increase slightly in five cities but declines in the other cities, leading to a sharper concentration of per capita income.[34] This concentration is particularly sharp in Medellín and Santiago. These per capita measures do not allow for differences between adults and children, or among different kinds of adults: domestic servants, for example, do not share equally with other adults in household income. (Servants are included with the household in Chile, Peru, and Venezuela, but not in Colombia and Ecuador.)

Mean income also increases with the age of the household head, at least

34. The same pattern emerges, but with more variation, if household size is compared across the deciles of the income distribution. In the top three deciles there is usually a decline in the average number of members, but this may not lower the mean for the entire upper quartile. The variability of size is about equally great at all deciles.

up until about sixty-five; thereafter it may decline. The differences are not usually significant, since there is a great dispersion of incomes within each age group, according to other family characteristics. Comparisons of mean income by age within quartiles do not show any significant differences.

The Determinants of Income

In three investigations, functions have been estimated relating income to a series of variables that may be considered to determine the income of a household or to be systematically associated with it.[35] The simplest such model relates disposable income to mean incomes in classes defined by education, occupation, housing tenancy, and expenditure on housing. For Colombia the following equation was obtained (incomes in pesos):

$$Y_d = -1499.96 + 0.67212 \ \bar{Y} \text{ (education class)}$$
$$+ 0.35337 \ \bar{Y} \text{ (occupation class)}$$
$$+ 0.58986 \ \bar{Y} \text{ (housing expenditure class)}$$
$$+ 1.23329 \ \bar{Y} \text{ (housing tenancy class)} - 58.502 \ BAR$$
$$- 116.17 \ CAL - 39.209 \ MED.$$

BAR, CAL, and MED are dummy variables indicating the different non-capital cities. Use of income means by class for the other variables is equivalent to dummy variables, except that fewer coefficients must be estimated. All variables except BAR and MED were significant.[36]

35. Throughout this study, functions estimated by regression methods are reported with standard errors rather than *t*-statistics or other indications of statistical significance. In this I follow the argument of G. S. Maddala, *Econometrics* (McGraw-Hill, 1977), that standard errors or confidence intervals are more illuminating than tests of whether a coefficient is zero; see "Some Comments on Significance Levels," pp. 45–46. In addition to the regression parameters reported here and in chapters 3, 4, and 6 and appendix C, some other statistics are reported with standard errors; see the individual consumption shares in chapter 3. Standard errors are also used in the tests of equality of mean incomes; see tables 2-17 and 2-18. The proportions of income from different sources in this chapter and the budget shares analyzed in chapters 4 and 5 are calculated without standard errors.

36. Jean Crockett and Irwin Friend, "Consumption and Saving in Economic Development" (Rodney L. White Center for Financial Research, University of Pennsylvania, Working Paper 22-73, n.d.; processed). The unpublished regression coefficients were supplied (without standard errors) by Jean Crockett.

The same procedure was applied to Venezuela, except that city and mean income by level of housing expenditure were omitted. The income equation (in bolívars) is:

$$Y_d = -8666 + 0.823 \; \bar{Y} \text{ (education class)}$$
$$(1155) \quad (0.048)$$
$$+ 0.464 \; \bar{Y} \text{ (occupation class)} + 1.2546 \; \bar{Y} \text{ (tenancy class).}$$
$$(0.050) \qquad\qquad\qquad (0.191)$$
$$\bar{R}^2 = 0.321$$

All variables are significant, but education has a greater impact on income than occupation.

Normal income was also estimated for each of the four cities in Colombia, using a large number of dummy variables for education, occupation, socioeconomic stratum, and trimester, and either dummy or continuous variables for age.[37] In every specification tested, the logarithm of income gave better results than the linear form.[38] The coefficients and standard errors of the income equations are shown in table 2-20. All variables included in an equation are statistically significant, the others having been eliminated from the specification.

Clearly, education always acts to raise income. Income initially rises with age but may then decline, as indicated by the negative effect of age squared. Incomes differ somewhat among occupations, but not all classes differ significantly. Other things being equal, households in the middle stratum have higher incomes than those in the low stratum, and incomes in the high stratum are larger still. The classification by stratum presumably captures effects left out of the other variables, such as discrimination in hiring, quality of education, and—perhaps most important—nonlabor income.

All the analyses described so far consider either a single variable or a series of variables that do not interact. For example, the effect of age on income is presumed not to depend on the level of education. An interactive model of income determination has also been estimated for Colombia,

37. Howard J. Howe, "Estimation of the Linear and Quadratic Expenditure Systems: A Cross-Section Case for Colombia" (Ph.D. dissertation, University of Pennsylvania, 1974), pp. 189–98. Age was omitted from the Crockett and Friend specification in order to approximate (undiscounted) lifetime income.

38. The regression passes through the mean of the logarithms rather than through mean income. If the distribution of income is lognormal, this is equivalent to explaining the median rather than the mean of income, since log (median income) = mean (log income).

Table 2-20. *Coefficients of Logarithmic Income Equations as Functions of Sociodemographic Variables, Urban Colombia*[a]

Variable	Bogotá	Barranquilla	Cali	Medellín
Age				
Years	0.0429	0.0355	...	0.0411
	(0.0099)	(0.0106)		(0.0100)
Years^2	−0.0037	−0.00035	...	−0.00037
	(0.00001)	(0.00001)		(0.00001)
50–64 years	...	...	0.1237	...
			(0.0474)	
65 years and over	...	...	0.2487	...
			(0.0902)	
Educational level				
Primary	0.4044	0.1643	0.3885	...
	(0.0875)	(0.0867)	(0.1300)	
Secondary	0.8495	0.5611	0.6228	0.4247
	(0.0922)	(0.0987)	(0.1364)	(0.0576)
Higher	1.3510	1.0635	0.9666	0.9680
	(0.1109)	(0.1254)	(0.1606)	(0.1099)
Occupation				
Professional, technical	...	...	...	0.2917
				(0.1101)
Managerial	0.4243	0.5578	0.4513	0.7378
	(0.1106)	(0.0975)	(0.1277)	(0.1130)
Clerical	...	...	0.2001	...
			(0.0703)	
Agricultural	...	...	0.7344	...
			(0.1531)	
Skilled labor	−0.1798	...	...	−0.1361
	(0.0539)			(0.0631)
Unskilled labor	−0.5219	...	...	−0.4462
	(0.1500)			(0.1453)
Personal service	−0.2277	−0.2123	−0.3374	−0.3299
	(0.0857)	(0.0950)	(0.0984)	(0.0972)
Stratum[b]				
High	1.0254	0.9850	1.1952	0.7410
	(0.0732)	(0.0723)	(0.0734)	(0.0735)
Middle	0.3068	0.4317	0.6731	0.3631
	(0.0464)	(0.0584)	(0.0594)	(0.0572)
Trimester				
Interval 3	0.1711	...	...	...
	(0.0506)			
Interval 4	0.2707	0.1386	...	...
	(0.0509)	(0.0506)		
$\bar{R}^2$	0.363	0.385	0.384	0.285

Source: Howard J. Howe, "Estimation of the Linear and Quadratic Expenditure Systems: A Cross-Section Case for Colombia" (Ph.D. dissertation, University of Pennsylvania, 1974), pp. 196–97.

a. Standard errors are in parentheses.

b. This classification captures effects not included among other variables, such as discrimination in hiring, quality of education, and nonlabor income.

Table 2-21. *Coefficients of Logarithmic Income Equations as a Function of Sociodemographic Variables, Three Latin American Countries*[a]

Variable[b]	Colombia	Ecuador	Peru
Age and education of head			
All ages, no education	−0.151	−0.350	−0.172
	(0.057)	(0.091)	(0.179)
35–49, primary education	0.089	0.080	0.153
	(0.038)	(0.050)	(0.081)
50–64, primary education	0.123	0.055	0.373
	(0.049)	(0.061)	(0.093)
65 and over, primary education	0.349	−0.101	0.232
	(0.084)	(0.090)	(0.132)
12–34, secondary education	0.527	0.406	0.447
	(0.045)	(0.059)	(0.091)
35–49, secondary education	0.650	0.629	0.613
	(0.045)	(0.059)	(0.087)
50–64, secondary education	0.731	0.676	0.662
	(0.064)	(0.075)	(0.105)
65 and over, secondary education	1.152	0.525	0.914
	(0.123)	(0.130)	(0.166)
12–34, higher education	1.189	0.823	0.641
	(0.082)	(0.095)	(0.115)
35–49, higher education	1.414	1.049	1.115
	(0.086)	(0.099)	(0.104)
50–64, higher education	1.508	0.953	1.125
	(0.108)	(0.133)	(0.135)
65 and over, higher education	2.001	1.043	1.254
	(0.267)	(0.183)	(0.209)
Occupation of head			
Professional	0.284	0.178	0.342
	(0.047)	(0.062)	(0.069)
Blue collar	−0.156	−0.137	−0.149
	(0.029)	(0.040)	(0.055)
Other	−0.246	−0.303	−0.025
	(0.037)	(0.044)	(0.068)
Life cycle of head			
Unmarried	−0.184	−0.267	−0.106
	(0.041)	(0.052)	(0.108)
Married, no children	−0.087	−0.074	−0.025
	(0.066)	(0.095)	(0.131)
Married, children 8–18	0.158	0.057	0.038
	(0.030)	(0.040)	(0.055)
Married, children 19 and over	0.135	−0.002	0.024
	(0.056)	(0.066)	(0.082)

Table 2-21 (*continued*)

Variable[b]	Colombia	Ecuador	Peru
Retired	−0.148	−0.309	−0.263)
	(0.088)	(0.121)	(0.180)
Employment			
Head unemployed	−0.058	0.028	−0.158
	(0.049)	(0.059)	(0.079)
Two or more household			
members employed	0.197	0.453	0.344
	(0.030)	(0.031)	(0.041)
Other			
Capital share of income			
(percent)	0.007	0.020	0.006
	(0.001)	(0.001)	(0.001)
$\bar{R}^2$	0.452	0.526	0.326

Source: Original calculations undertaken for the ECIEL study by Philip Musgrove and used in "Determination and Distribution of Permanent Household Income in Urban South America" (Ph.D. dissertation, Massachusetts Institute of Technology, 1974).

a. The numbers in parentheses are standard errors.

b. The base classes of the variables with zero coefficients are age twelve to thirty-four, primary education; white-collar occupation; married, children seven years old or less; head employed; and only one or no member employed.

Ecuador, and Peru. Occupation, life cycle stage, employment status of the head, presence of additional employed members, and the share of income derived from capital all enter the specification independently; age and education interact, however, except for the group with no formal education. The coefficients of the income equations appear in table 2-21.[39] Life cycle effects are often insignificant, after taking account of age; the former refers to family composition and thus is distinct from age though associated with it. It also does not matter whether the head of the household is employed, although the possession of capital and the presence of additional earners both raise income. Income rises with age or with education, but the higher the level of schooling, the greater is the effect of age. Age-income profiles are not the same for all households, even in general shape, but differ markedly by education. Occupational differences in income are almost always significant. Finally, there are differences between

39. The coefficients shown relate *observed* income to the independent variables, so that the equations are comparable to those of Howe and of Crockett and Friend. They are not the permanent income coefficients reported in Philip Musgrove, "Determination and Distribution of Permanent Household Income" (Ph.D. dissertation, Massachusetts Institute of Technology, 1974), tables 4 and 5, which include the relation of consumption to income.

Quito and Guayaquil (income is higher in the latter city) and much smaller differences among the Colombian cities.

In summary, there are some clear and stable relations between income and several socioeconomic variables. None of these differentiates among households so sharply as to group them in small intervals of the total income distribution, but several of them are strongly associated both with the frequency distribution of households and with their mean (or possibly median) incomes. The most powerful variable explaining income is education, even at a rather high level of aggregation. Occupational differences are also important; much higher incomes are associated with professional, technical, and managerial jobs than with other jobs. Income differences are less marked among the other aggregate occupational categories; within-category variation may be much more important.

In general, age does not appear to have a strong influence on income, but definite patterns emerge when age and education are considered simultaneously. At high educational levels, income rises with age and eventually declines; but income is rather age-insensitive for the less-educated. Other variables such as life cycle stage and current employment status are much less strongly associated with income. Household size is also less strongly related to income. Total income rises when there are more members (and more rapidly if only earning members are considered), but income per person declines steadily, in total and in income quartiles, as family size increases. These findings indicate that the observed inequality of household incomes is real and that it has fairly clear implications for welfare and for consumer behavior. Income concentration is not due, to a significant degree, to the age distribution of the population, and different groups have different income experience with increasing age. Neither is the concentration due to the size distribution of households: income per person appears to be about as unequally distributed as income per family.

CHAPTER THREE

Total Consumption and Saving

IN THIS CHAPTER I review the results relating to the determinants of total spending or total saving by households, and discuss the distribution of a given level of saving among various assets. A comparable analysis for spending—how a given amount of consumption is divided among different goods and services—is presented in chapters 4 through 6.

Strikingly few studies have been made of the determinants of total spending or saving at the household level in Latin America. Nearly all studies of consumption or saving have drawn on national accounts aggregates, whether for time-series or cross-section analysis.[1] In less developed countries, such aggregates often show inexplicable or dubious year-to-year changes, and they may yield negative estimates of personal saving over

1. Raymond F. Mikesell and James E. Zinser, "The Nature of the Savings Function in Developing Countries: A Survey of the Theoretical and Empirical Literature," *Journal of Economic Literature,* vol. 11 (March 1973), pp. 1–26, surveys 134 studies of consumption or saving, of which only two are based on household information in Latin America. A more recent survey by Donald W. Snyder, "Econometric Studies of Household Saving Behavior in Developing Countries: A Survey," *Journal of Development Studies,* vol. 10 (January 1974), pp. 139–53, restricted to household data, covers seventy-one sources, of which only one refers to Latin America. See also Pedro Jeftanovic P., "Estudio sobre el Ahorro Familiar en el Gran Santiago," *Cuadernos de Economía,* vol. 8 (August 1971), pp. 73–104; and Rafael Prieto D., "El Consumo y el Ahorro Familiar en Cuatro Ciudades Colombianas," in *Necesidades de Movilización de Ahorro para el Desarrollo Colombiano* (Bogotá: Banco de la República, 1971).

relatively long intervals.[2] Moreover, even if national accounts analyses accurately relate total consumption or saving to total income and other macroeconomic variables, they cannot show how these variables depend on the distribution of income and other characteristics among households. Some consideration of household consumption or saving functions is an essential step between the description of income distribution and population characteristics, and the analysis of the household budget.

After a brief discussion of the variables to be studied and the approaches used, I examine, first, the average propensity to consume, variously measured, and next, the determinants of total consumption or saving, with income analyzed separately from household characteristics. Finally, I consider briefly the demand for specific forms of saving.

With one exception, all the various analyses described at the end of chapter 1 yield some information on total spending or saving. Because these analyses are based on different models and use different concepts, the results will not all coincide; still less will they identify the "true" saving or consumption function. The intention is to examine the effects of a number of variables rather than decide among competing specifications or hypotheses. Given the scarcity of previous studies, such an approach, which provides an opportunity for comparison among cities and countries and among various forms of analysis, seems appropriate and likely to be most useful.

Clearly, the different approaches measure different things. In the case of income, the one determinant of consumption and saving examined by all methods, the result is variously an average propensity, a marginal propensity, or an elasticity. Comparability of results depends, among other things, on the concept of income used and the level at which it is evaluated.

The independent variables considered in one or more of the analyses as possible determinants of saving are: income (current, normal, permanent); housing characteristics (size, tenure, quality); employment (of the household head, of spouse, number of members employed); education (of the head); household size (total, number of adults, number of children); age (of the head); life cycle stage; wealth; and city of residence. These

2. See Markos Mamalakis, "Negative Personal Savings in the Chilean National Accounts: An Artifact or Reality" (Yale University Economic Growth Center, Discussion Paper 36, August 24, 1967; processed); and Lester D. Taylor, "Personal Saving in Colombia," *Estadística* (June 1969), pt. 2, pp. 236–41.

variables are taken from the individual household observations. In addition, some account is taken of possible macroeconomic influences, particularly the rate of inflation and the degree of disequilibrium of the economy. The more speculative analyses, which employ the latter variables, are based on international comparisons of the results, particularly those that expressly incorporate effects related to prices or to transitory incomes.

The dependent variable is usually a measure of consumption. This is partly because the data were collected primarily in order to study expenditures, and partly because of the difficulty of estimating saving directly by measuring changes in assets.[3] When saving must be estimated residually, it is simpler and more accurate to work with consumption. However, certain categories of saving, for which the data are fairly complete, can also be analyzed.[4]

Several different measures of consumption are employed:

C = total expenditure including tax and social security payments; includes imputed or paid rent rather than mortgage payments on a dwelling, total expenditure on vehicles, and total value of household durables purchased

C_d = expenditure less tax and social security payments; includes purchases of durables

C_e = expenditure less purchases of durables; includes only purchases (or imputed value) of nondurable goods and services

C_a = C_d except that imputed rent is replaced by half of mortgage payments (amortization and interest are not separated)

C_m = C_e except that imputed rent is replaced by half of mortgage payments

C_f = $0.5 (C_d + C_e)$; includes half of purchases of durables

When the object is to relate total consumption to total income (or disposable income), it does not seem to matter much how durables are

3. The standard code for the data defines saving as net total asset transactions (not including the purchase of a vehicle or increased equity in the family dwelling), adjusted for capital gains so as to yield net increase in wealth. In every country, however, one or more of the elements of this total are missing, and even when the items are included in the questionnaire there are many nonresponses.

4. Regression analysis with saving as the dependent variable is included only in Jean Crockett and Irwin Friend, "Consumption and Saving in Economic Development" (Rodney L. White Center for Financial Research, University of Pennsylvania, Working Paper 22-73, n.d.; processed), who employ two measures of total saving and five components (including purchases of durables as one form of saving).

treated or which measure of housing consumption is used. However, these choices do matter when age or life cycle variables are also analyzed because there are marked age variations in durables and housing purchases; there are also considerable differences among countries in the importance of purchases of durables.

Corresponding to the concepts C and C_d are total income Y and disposable income Y_d. They differ only in the exclusion from Y_d of tax and social security payments. Both include imputed rent as a component of income from capital, and also include realized capital gains, income in kind, and bonuses, lottery winnings, inheritances, and other irregular sources of income.

Both $Y - C$ and $Y_d - C_d$ are lower-bound estimates of current saving, since whatever is not included in C or C_d is clearly saved. True saving is higher than these estimates by the amount of unrealized capital gains, the increase in housing equity, and the proportion of purchases of durables that may be considered as saving rather than consumption. Some part or some function of social security payments and private life insurance premiums should also be treated as saving, but it is not clear how to relate these payments to the future income of the household or to their beneficiaries, so they have not been analyzed.

Average Propensities to Consume

Because income occupies a central place in the determination of consumption and saving, all the results pertaining to income are considered together in this and the following section. This is a somewhat artificial distinction, because relations estimated with income as an independent variable often include other variables, whose degree of correlation with income affects the coefficient(s) of the latter. Nonetheless, it seems most convenient to separate all these other variables and their effects for later consideration. This section summarizes a number of estimates of the average propensity to consume or save and relates them to the level, concentration, and composition of income.

Global Average Consumption Propensities

Part of the interest in household data on consumption and saving derives from the inadequacies of national accounts estimates. Although household and national accounts data are not strictly comparable (if only because of the limited geographic coverage of the former), it is interesting to calculate the global mean propensity to consume, which is conceptually similar to the propensity estimated from aggregate data. If this is defined by $\overline{C}/\overline{Y}$, including tax and social security payments in both concepts, the following results are obtained:[5]

Colombia		*Chile*	*Ecuador*		*Peru*	*Venezuela*	
Total	0.945	0.906	Total	0.976	0.980	Total	0.913
Bogotá	0.965		Quito	1.032		Caracas	0.924
Barranquilla	0.999		Guayaquil	0.937		Maracaibo	0.857
Cali	0.985						
Medellín	0.843						

For most cities, these ratios are close to 1.0 and show a low, but positive, average propensity to save. Quito is an exception, but here $\overline{C}$ and $\overline{Y}$ are indistinguishable on the basis of their standard errors of measurement.[6] The only strikingly low estimates of the consumption propensity are for Medellín and Maracaibo; that for Santiago is also rather low despite the high propensity recorded in national accounts data.

If the mean propensity is estimated as $\overline{C}_f/\overline{Y}_d$, excluding taxes and social security and also half of expenditure on durables (on the assumption that half of purchases of durables are for saving), the results are:

Colombia	*Chile*	*Ecuador*	*Peru*	*Venezuela*
0.970	0.873	0.969	0.986	0.902

Differences between these and the previous estimates reflect the importance of taxes and social security ($\overline{C}_d/\overline{C}$ does not equal $\overline{Y}_d/\overline{Y}$ in general) and the share of the budget devoted to durables. This share is particularly high in Peru.

The mean propensity was also estimated from estimates of permanent consumption and permanent income corresponding to the observed vari-

---

5. Slightly different values are obtained by Howard J. Howe, "Estimation of the Linear and Quadratic Expenditure Systems: A Cross-Section Case for Colombia" (Ph.D. dissertation, University of Pennsylvania, 1974), p. 82, for Colombia, using C_d for consumption and Y for income: Bogotá, 0.9137, Barranquilla, 0.9502, Cali, 0.9076, and Medellín, 0.7634.

6. The estimates of $\overline{C}$ and $\overline{Y}$ differ by less than one standard error also in Bogotá, Barranquilla, Cali, Guayaquil, and Lima.

ables C_f and Y_d.[7] Since the model was estimated in logarithmic form, the assumption of zero mean transitory income does not guarantee that the permanent mean propensity equals the observed propensity. In one calculation, the logarithmic error of estimation is assumed to be normally distributed, although the true values of permanent income may not be distributed lognormally; in the other, *total* permanent income is assumed to be distributed lognormally. The resulting propensities are:

	Colombia	Ecuador	Peru
Permanent	0.997	0.939	0.924
Lognormal	1.003	0.959	0.950

The assumption of lognormality implies somewhat more households at low incomes and fewer at high incomes than the data show, so the estimated propensity to consume rises. Comparison of these results with those given above suggests that the distribution of transitory income in the survey year favored saving in Colombia and Peru, and favored consumption in Ecuador; that is, mean transitory income in *additive* terms was positive in Colombia and Peru but negative in Ecuador. This conclusion cannot be trusted in the case of Peru, where the economy was still recovering from the effects of the devaluation in the previous year.

Individual Average Consumption Propensities

The average propensity to consume for a household, h, is C_h/Y_h; and the mean of these is another measure of average propensity over the population. The global measure $\overline{C}/\overline{Y}$ discussed above is a weighted mean of these individual ratios, with weights defined by relative incomes or income shares:

$$\overline{C}/\overline{Y} = (1/N) \sum_h (C_h/Y_h)(Y_h/\overline{Y}).$$

If households with relatively low incomes have high propensities, as might be expected, then the mean of the C_h/Y_h will exceed $\overline{C}/\overline{Y}$. The discrepancy between the two measures depends on the variability of $Y_h/\overline{Y}$ and hence on the concentration of income as well as on the variation in C_h/Y_h.

7. The estimates that follow are from Philip Musgrove, "Determination and Distribution of Permanent Household Income in Urban South America" (Ph.D. dissertation, Massachusetts Institute of Technology, 1974), pp. 108–10. See appendix B for a brief explanation of the model and its estimation.

The values of mean C_h/Y_h obtained are (standard errors in parentheses):[8]

Colombia		Chile	Ecuador		Peru	Venezuela
Total	1.092	1.150	Total	0.987	1.250 Total	1.096
	(0.008)	(0.025)		(0.010)	(0.031)	(0.015)
Bogotá	1.095		Quito	1.045	Caracas	1.085
	(0.015)			(0.012)		(0.021)
Barranquilla	1.222		Guayaquil	0.944	Maracaibo	1.126
	(0.021)			(0.015)		(0.024)
Cali	1.124					
	(0.014)					
Medellín	0.990					
	(0.010)					

The ratio of these two measures in the capital cities is inversely related to the concentration of income, measured by the Gini coefficient (the rank correlation is -0.3). If only variations in income concentration were involved, the association would be positive; however, this effect is clearly outweighed by the effect of variations in the propensity to consume, as shown below (numbers in parentheses indicate rank within row):

	Bogotá	Santiago	Quito	Lima	Caracas
Ratio	1.135 (4)	1.270 (2)	1.013 (5)	1.276 (1)	1.174 (3)
Gini index	0.472 (3)	0.451 (4)	0.518 (1)	0.487 (2)	0.429 (5)

Part of this concentration is due to transitory income. If it is assumed that the variance of transitory income is proportional to the level of permanent income, the following estimates are obtained for the share that the logarithmic variance of transitory income is of the logarithmic variance of observed income: Colombia, 0.078; Ecuador, 0.088; and Peru, 0.315.[9]

Since the estimation assumes zero expected transitory income, the variance of (logarithmic) transitory income is overestimated when there is a nonzero mean either of transitory income or of the error of observation of income. This is probably the case in Peru. When the survey data are more accurate and refer to a more nearly normal period, transitory variation accounts for less than 10 percent of income variance and therefore probably does not account for much of the interhousehold variation in the observed propensity to consume.

8. Howe's estimates, again using C_d and Y, are: Bogotá, 1.0578; Barranquilla, 1.1682; Cali, 1.0591; and Medellín, 0.9089. See Howe, "Linear and Quadratic Expenditure Systems," p. 79.

9. Musgrove, "Determination and Distribution," p. 92, table 8.

In summary, then, the global average propensity to save is positive (but not clearly distinguishable from zero simply because the samples are small and income and consumption are highly variable) in five cities and negative but not significant in two more. Some underreporting of income probably occurs in all cities. The estimated propensity exceeds 5 percent in two others. Durables account for a relatively large share of expenditure and therefore affect estimates of saving in Lima and have rather little effect elsewhere.

The individual mean propensity to save is negative in all but two cities (Medellín and Guayaquil). Most households appear to save little or nothing, and the concentration of saving is strongly related to the concentration of income, of which only a small part is due to transitory income. Removing the transitory component and estimating a global mean on the basis of permanent income and consumption gives mixed results; generally, the propensity to save declines slightly. This is indirect evidence for a higher propensity to save out of transitory income than out of permanent income.[10]

Mean Individual Propensities by Income Quartile

The effects of transitory income are stronger when individual propensity is computed within income quartiles. Transitory income shifts many households to a quartile different from the one appropriate to their permanent income.[11] Table 3-1 shows the mean of C_h/Y_h in each quartile for each city, with standard errors in parentheses. Income means by quartile are not equidistant between quartiles or comparably distant among cities, so these values do not translate directly into a consumption function. The mean expenditure propensities shown in table 3-1 reinforce the evidence that relatively few families save. The mean saving propensity is always positive in the highest quartile and positive for six out of ten cities in the third quartile. Notice also the great variation of interquartile differences among cities: the apparent relation is very steep in Santiago, Lima, and Maracaibo, and very slight in Quito.

10. The results are, of course, sensitive to the assumption of a normal distribution for the error term that accounts for roughly half the variance of permanent income (or 40 percent of observed income).

11. The variance of transitory income may also be a different share of total income variance in different quartiles, probably being highest in the bottom quartile.

Table 3-1. *Individual Mean Expenditure Propensity by Income Quartile, Ten Latin American Cities*[a]

| City | Income quartile | | | |
	First	Second	Third	Fourth
Colombia				
Bogotá	1.338	1.181	1.047	0.932
	(0.065)	(0.023)	(0.018)	(0.017)
Barranquilla	1.515	1.264	1.090	0.895
	(0.061)	(0.030)	(0.019)	(0.019)
Cali	1.262	1.142	1.077	0.924
	(0.032)	(0.024)	(0.028)	(0.021)
Medellín	1.112	1.036	0.962	0.786
	(0.025)	(0.019)	(0.016)	(0.015)
Mean	1.284	1.149	1.038	0.898
	(0.024)	(0.012)	(0.010)	(0.009)
Chile				
Santiago	1.703	1.145	0.962	0.811
	(0.011)	(0.024)	(0.016)	(0.009)
Ecuador				
Quito	1.170	1.105	0.975	0.908
	(0.030)	(0.031)	(0.014)	(0.012)
Guayaquil	1.099	0.963	0.904	0.835
	(0.032)	(0.015)	(0.014)	(0.044)
Mean	1.135	1.017	0.931	0.866
	(0.022)	(0.015)	(0.010)	(0.024)
Peru				
Lima	1.678	1.083	0.887	0.664
	(0.086)	(0.032)	(0.024)	(0.024)
Venezuela[b]				
Caracas	1.461	1.120	0.942	0.814
	(0.054)	(0.035)	(0.030)	(0.027)
Maracaibo	1.744	1.128	0.971	0.727
	(0.083)	(0.024)	(0.021)	(0.022)

Source: Original ECIEL calculations based on the survey data.
a. The numbers in parentheses are standard errors.
b. Means of totals not calculated, since income distributions in Caracas and Maracaibo have differing quartile levels.

Consumption and Saving Functions: Income Effects

This section considers together all the functions estimated of the form

$$C = \mu_o + \mu Y + \ldots + e,$$

where C is any of the several measures of consumption described above, or the logarithm of consumption, and Y is an income concept or its logarithm. A few functions have also been estimated as

$$S = \mu_o + \mu Y + \ldots + e,$$

where S is a direct or residual measure of total saving (or something as close to total saving as can be measured). The coefficient μ is either an elasticity or a marginal propensity to consume or to save. Other variables may be included in the equations; their coefficients are considered later in this chapter.

Consumption as a Function of Current Income

Five sets of estimates relate consumption to current income. Three are in logarithmic and two in linear form, the latter being estimates of the extended linear expenditure system (ELES).[12] The elasticities μ were estimated from the logarithmic form by country and are as follows:

	Colombia	Chile	Ecuador	Peru	Venezuela
(1)	C_f against Y_d: no other variables (weighted)				
	0.813	...	0.812	0.555	...
	(0.007)		(0.009)	(0.016)	
(2)	C against Y: city dummies included (unweighted)				
	0.814	0.713	0.893	0.677	0.701
	(0.006)	(0.008)	(0.007)	(0.014)	(0.011)
(3)	C against Y: many other variables included (unweighted)				
	0.702	0.549	0.772	0.435	0.578
	(0.010)	(0.012)	(0.011)	(0.019)	(0.016)

The additional variables—age, education. household size, dwelling characteristics, employment, and so forth—are sufficiently correlated with income, or at least with its permanent component (see chapter 2), that the estimated elasticity falls (between specifications 2 and 3) when they are included in the regression. To the extent that these variables explain permanent income, μ may be biased toward the elasticity with respect to tran-

12. The ELES was developed by Constantino Lluch, "The Extended Linear Expenditure System," *European Economic Review,* vol. 4 (April 1973), pp. 21–32, using a concept of permanent labor income plus a (constant) return on wealth. Howe, "Linear and Quadratic Expenditure Systems," reformulated the system in current income, and this formulation is used by Howard Howe and Philip Musgrove, "An Analysis of ECIEL Household Budget Data for Bogotá, Caracas, Guayaquil, and Lima," in Constantino Lluch, Alan A. Powell, and Ross A. Williams, eds., *Patterns in Household Demand and Saving* (New York: Oxford University Press for the World Bank, 1977), pp. 155–98. For the interpretation of the parameters, see appendix B.

sitory income. Since C includes tax and social security payments and durables, it is not to be expected that this elasticity will be zero even if the true propensity to consume transitory income is zero. The difference between specifications 1 and 2 to some extent reflects the increasing importance of durables, taxes, and social security payments as incomes rise.[13]

The linear results for the marginal propensity to consume are as follows:[14]

(4)

	C_d against Y		
Bogotá	*Barranquilla*	*Cali*	*Medellín*
0.850	0.711	0.873	0.736
(0.023)	(0.023)	(0.020)	(0.014)

(5)

	C against Y		
Bogotá	*Caracas*	*Guayaquil*	*Lima*
0.931	0.743	0.799	0.757
(0.017)	(0.022)	(0.023)	(0.026)

(Both sets of estimates are weighted and include family-size variables in the estimating equation.) For a rough comparison to specification 5, marginal consumption propensities are calculated from expression 2 at *median* income. The inclusion of city dummies in 2 makes it possible to select results that correspond approximately to Bogotá, Caracas, and Guayaquil. The estimated propensities (standard errors not calculated) are:

(6)

Bogotá	*Santiago*	*Guayaquil*	*Lima*	*Caracas*
0.583	0.712	0.844	0.665	0.645

It is difficult to compare constant-elasticity and constant-marginal-propensity models. Moreover, the results of the comparison are not entirely plausible, since each model estimates consumption to be larger than income, over a range that may easily include most of the households in the sample. To a great extent, this is because current income is a poor explanatory variable since it contains transitory elements. However, it may also be the case that the specifications are simply too rigid. For this reason, the ELES was estimated separately for each of three socioeconomic strata in each of four cities. The strata are defined ex ante by neighborhood, not

13. Social security contributions are a regressive tax in the United States, and may also be regressive in Latin American countries, for those workers covered. However, a much smaller share of the population pays these contributions, and they have, on average, higher incomes than those who do not pay because they are not in covered occupations.

14. Estimates in specification 4 are from Howe, "Linear and Quadratic Expenditure Systems," pp. 176, 178, 181, 183; those in specification 5 from Howe and Musgrove, "Analysis of ECIEL Household Budget Data," p. 164.

by observed income. Separate estimates were made for young and old households (heads under or over forty-five years of age), and family size was retained in the estimating equation. The object is to obtain a piecewise linear consumption function that will show curvature but not be forced into logarithmic shape; the expectation is that the marginal propensity μ will decline in going from the low to the high stratum for each age class. The results are as follows (6):[15]

Stratum	Age	Bogotá	Caracas	Guayaquil	Lima
Low	Young	0.970	0.388	0.681	0.791
		(0.032)	(0.066)	(0.033)	(0.050)
	Old	0.939	0.337	0.809	0.289
		(0.048)	(0.128)	(0.040)	(0.091)
Middle	Young	0.914	0.714	0.998	0.910
		(0.035)	(0.043)	(0.081)	(0.054)
	Old	0.855	0.679	0.859	0.244
		(0.055)	(0.045)	(0.036)	(0.057)
High	Young	0.860	0.711	0.860	0.149
		(0.046)	(0.043)	(0.049)	(0.083)
	Old	0.554	0.747	0.874	0.654
		(0.070)	(0.075)	(0.104)	(0.045)

The estimates for Bogotá are fairly plausible, and most of those for Guayaquil are reasonable; but some very low values appear for Caracas and Lima (five estimates are below 0.5). Moreover, μ does not, except in Bogotá, decline as income rises. Very low values are found in the lowest stratum. If the linear form of the permanent income hypothesis is correct, μ is related to the true propensity (k) to consume permanent income (Y^*) by

$$\mu = k \text{ var } (Y^*)/\text{var } (Y).$$

Then if k is constant or declines as income rises, a low value of μ at low income implies a relatively low variance of permanent income or a relatively high variance of transitory income. It appears that transitory income forms a larger share of total income in some cities than in others and, further, that it is often a larger share in the low-income stratum than in other strata.[16]

15. Howe and Musgrove, "Analysis of ECIEL Household Budget Data," p. 164.
16. Milton Friedman, *A Theory of the Consumption Function* (Princeton University Press, 1957), pp. 21–37. The first implication is tested above; but the assumption of a constant transitory variance makes it impossible to test the second implication unless the model is reestimated separately by stratum.

Consumption as a Function of Normal or Permanent Income

Although the estimates based on current income may be appropriate for relating short-run changes in income and consumption, the inclusion of transitory income in the model renders them unsuitable for characterizing long-run behavior, particularly in extremely high- or low-income groups. Moreover, if consumption or saving reacts differently to different kinds of income, it is appropriate to estimate these reactions directly. Three sets of functions have been estimated from the ECIEL data, using long-run income concepts. Two refer only to Colombia; the other refers to Ecuador and Peru also. The first two use normal income, Y_N, which is distinguished both from transitory income, Y_T (composed of ex ante transitory elements such as bonuses and lottery winnings, although bonuses are likely to be anticipated and so are not transitory in the sense of unexpected), and from residual income, $Y - Y_N - Y_T$. The third set of estimates is based on permanent income, Y^*, which is distinguished only from transitory income, Y^{**}.[17] Roughly, Y_N and Y^* are comparable, so that Y^{**} includes residual income as well as income classifiable ex ante as transitory. Strictly, Y_N is comparable to $\hat{Y}^*$, the estimator of permanent income; the latter model also allows for an error, ϵ, which is conceptually distinct from Y^{**}.[18]

The variable Y_N is estimated by regressing Y or its logarithm on $X_1, \ldots, X_n$, and only later is consumption related to Y_N, while Y^* is estimated by the simultaneous regression of $\log C$ and $\log Y$ on $X_1, \ldots, X_n$, subject to the relation of $\log C^* = WK + \mu^* \log Y^*$. Crockett and Friend base Y_N on mean incomes in classes of the population defined by education, occupation, tenure of dwelling, and level of housing expenditure, as well as city dummies; the other analyses base Y_N and Y^* on dummy variables for age, educational class, occupation, life cycle stage, city, employment, type of household, and relative importance of income

17. See Crockett and Friend, "Consumption and Saving," and Howe, "Linear and Quadratic Expenditure Systems." Howe estimates propensities to consume out of Y_N only; Crockett and Friend also estimate the propensities to consume or save Y_T and residual income. The third analysis is Musgrove, "Determination and Distribution."

18. Because $Y = \hat{Y}^* + \epsilon + Y^{**}$, individual values of ϵ and Y^{**}, or of Y^* and Y^{**}, cannot be estimated; there is no ex ante identification, as in the normal income model. See appendix B for other conceptual differences between Y_N and Y^*.

from capital. Because the treatment of age differs among these models, the horizon is longer for one concept of Y_N than for the other measure or for Y^*.

Crockett and Friend obtain the following marginal propensities to consume, for normal, transitory, and residual income, using a linear specification with three of the measures of consumption defined earlier (each regression also includes family size, age, and a wealth-related variable, which is considered later):[19]

	Consumption	Y_N	Y_T	$Y - Y_N - Y_T$
(7)	C_d	0.791	0.110	0.545
		(0.010)	(0.079)	(0.008)
(8)	C_a	0.735	0.186	0.463
		(0.013)	(0.103)	(0.010)
(9)	C_m	0.662	0.127	0.412
		(0.009)	(0.071)	(0.007)

The elasticities with respect to Y_N, estimated at the mean, are, respectively, 0.84, 0.88, and 0.82, somewhat higher than the constant-elasticity results reported above in specifications 1 and 2—although the latter may be biased downward because they are unweighted and overrepresent the high-income stratum. The marginal consumption propensities for Y_N are significantly below those obtained for Bogotá alone, using total Y, in the ELES model (4 and 5). This may be at least partially due to the exclusion of households headed by retired persons from the normal income calculations. A further reason is the treatment of housing expenditure: the result for C_d exceeds that for C_a or C_m because the inclusion of imputed rent in both C_d and Y spuriously raises the estimate of μ.

These results coincide with the difference noted above between specifications 2 and 3. Both sets of results indicate a much lower consumption propensity for transitory or windfall income than for normal income. The propensity to consume residual income is intermediate, as one might expect. As income rises, an increasing share of total consumption is devoted to durables.

Two linear functions for total saving were estimated against the three classes of income: S_1 is monetary saving plus social security payments, plus half of mortgage payments (half is assumed to be increase in equity and half interest charges); S_2 is monetary saving, social security payments,

19. "Consumption and Saving," p. 65, table 1.

major home improvements, down payments on a house or car, and expenditures on durables. The results are:[20]

	Saving	Y_N	Y_T	$Y - Y_N - Y_T$
(10)	S_1	0.265	0.840	0.541
		(0.011)	(0.082)	(0.008)
(11)	S_2	0.323	0.892	0.572
		(0.009)	(0.071)	(0.007)

The elasticities with respect to Y_N (again, estimated at the mean) are 1.53 and 1.54, respectively. The results closely complement those obtained for C_a and C_m, and show saving to be most sensitive to windfall income.

Howe's results relate C_d to Y_N, and may be compared to the current income version (4) of the ELES:[21]

	Bogotá	Barranquilla	Cali	Medellín
(12)	0.847	0.898	0.886	0.783
	(0.033)	(0.037)	(0.040)	(0.038)

The effect of using Y_N instead of Y is to raise the propensities to consume (except that for Bogotá, which is unchanged) and to narrow their dispersion.[22] The estimate for Barranquilla in particular becomes much more reasonable, since that city has the highest average consumption propensity. These estimates exceed the Crockett-Friend estimate of 0.791 for Colombia (except in Medellín), which uses the same definition of consumption; the difference is probably due to the different estimation of Y_N, a logarithmic function giving a better fit to Y over its entire range (see chapter 2).[23]

20. Crockett and Friend, "Consumption and Saving," p. 65, table 1.
21. "Linear and Quadratic Expenditure Systems," pp. 203–04, 206.
22. This is to be expected if the permanent propensities are nearly equal in the four cities, but there are different amounts of transitory variation in income.
23. Estimates of Y_N were also made for Venezuela, and different measures of consumption and saving were then regressed on Y_N and on residual income $Y_R = Y - Y_N$. These results are not strictly comparable to those obtained for Colombia, because of differences in the data, and are less satisfactory; they were therefore not reported by Crockett and Friend. Family size and age were included in the regressions; the wealth-related variable used in Colombia was omitted. The following marginal propensities to spend or save were obtained:

	Y_N	Y_R
C_d (excludes taxes and social security)	0.818	0.704
	(0.025)	(0.018)
C_e (C_d − durables)	0.795	0.705
	(0.024)	(0.017)
S_f (financial saving)	0.174	0.288
	(0.026)	(0.018)

Finally, the estimates of the elasticity of consumption, C_f, out of permanent income, Y^*, are as follows:[24]

	Colombia	Ecuador	Peru
(13)	0.881	0.896	0.776
	(0.015)	(0.013)	(0.023)

These values are clearly distinguishable from the current income elasticities reported in specification 1. As before, the estimates for Colombia and Ecuador are almost identical (although more different for Y^* than for Y), while the Peruvian value is notably lower.[25] In none of these countries is the permanent elasticity unitary, as required by the Friedman hypothesis. Neither are unitary elasticities found for normal income, since the constant terms μ_0 are not zero. Those found by Howe are much larger than those found by Crockett and Friend, whose estimates yield elasticities appreciably below 1.0 only at fairly high incomes. Either a linear or a logarithmic function with less than unit elasticity and a positive μ_0 implies that at sufficiently low income levels, dissaving occurs, which implies a threshold at which the household begins to save. The concept and estimation of this threshold are briefly discussed in the following section.

The Shape of the Consumption Function

Given the results reported so far, it seems possible to obtain reasonable estimates of the (average or constant) elasticity or marginal propensity of consumption with respect to income. Comparably good estimates of the level at which households begin to save are much harder to obtain. Numerous efforts have been made to estimate the threshold level of saving, but with unsatisfactory results both for individual countries and across countries. The estimates differ greatly, in real terms, from one country to another for the same kind of household. In part, this is because the zero saving level depends heavily on household size and other household characteristics, and is extremely sensitive to transitory income and expenditures. There is a further difficulty in that the shape of the long-run or normal or permanent consumption function is surely neither linear nor logarithmic but something more complicated. Assuming that a family cannot accumulate debts or consume assets in order to live beyond its means

24. Musgrove, "Determination and Distribution," p. 70.
25. As indicated above, the assumption of zero mean transitory income may not be valid in Peru; therefore, μ^* may be biased downward even after the transitory component has supposedly been removed.

for long intervals (since this is very difficult for low-income households to do, given their low initial wealth and the difficulty of borrowing at reasonable rates of interest), consumption must be less than or equal to income at all income levels. At very low income levels, subsistence requirements absorb all of income, and at sufficiently low levels everything must be spent on food. But the fact that it is hard to estimate these levels does not make them any less real.

The true long-run function must therefore have consumption equal to income over some range, after which income exceeds consumption and the household begins to save. At high incomes, the marginal propensity to consume may again be constant (but less than one) or it may continue to fall: hence, either a linear or a logarithmic specification may become appropriate. In a transitional range of incomes, there will be a decline in the marginal propensity and in the elasticity, both starting from 1.0. This shape has been proposed to explain saving as a function of income in cross-section analysis of national accounts data. Saving, initially zero, rises at an accelerating rate and then approaches a constant share of income.[26]

The ELES was estimated by stratum in order to better describe the shape of the consumption function. As noted above, satisfactory results were obtained for Bogotá but not for any other city. The Bogotá results suggest a steadily declining marginal consumption propensity, perhaps leveling off at about 0.85. Some other results also bear on this question. The permanent income model for Ecuador (13) was estimated in both weighted and unweighted form. Each elasticity estimate is then a linear combination of the elasticities for the three strata, with different coefficients in the two cases. Since the coefficients are known (shares of the sample or shares of the population), if one elasticity is assumed known, the other two can be calculated. The assumption that $\mu = 1.0$ for the low-income stratum gives estimates of 0.88 for the middle stratum and 0.89 for the high stratum. This corresponds to a function with all (or a constant share) of income consumed up to some level, beyond which there is a constant elasticity of about 0.9.

26. Luis Landau, "Saving Functions for Latin America," in Hollis B. Chenery, ed., *Studies in Development Planning* (Harvard University Press, 1971), pp. 299–321. A function with this shape is $(C/Y) = k + (1 - k) \exp (- \delta Y^m)$, or $(S/Y) = (1 - k) [1 - \exp(- \delta Y^m)]$; k is the average propensity to consume, which is approached asymptotically as income rises; m and δ are parameters determining the speed of the transition to this propensity and the income level at which the transition occurs.

Consumption and Saving Functions:
Household Characteristics

In this section, I consider the effects on consumption and saving of the household characteristics described earlier. While a few of the results reported here do not control for income, the principal focus is on the propensity to consume or save out of a given income.

Characteristics of the Dwelling

The logarithmic regressions of C on Y, reported in specification 3 above, include among the independent variables three characteristics of the dwelling: type (single-family house, multifamily house, apartment, room, tenement); principal construction material (brick, cement, wood, adobe); and total number of rooms (one to two, three to four, five, six, seven, and eight or more, including kitchens and bathrooms).[27] These variables are included on the assumption that the size and quality of the dwelling are proxies for permanent or normal income, so that part of the income effect in the regression is due to consumption out of transitory income. (This is why the elasticity μ is uniformly lower in specification 3 than in specification 2, which does not include dwelling variables.)

Neither the type of dwelling nor the construction material systematically affects the propensity to consume. Tenement, rooming house, and slum dwellers tend to spend less of a given income than households in other types of housing, but the coefficients are not always distinct from zero. Households living in buildings that also house commercial enterprises tend to spend more, but this effect is not statistically significant. Given the difficulty of estimating imputed rents for these types of dwellings, the results may be unreliable. Construction material is even less significant.

27. Tenure (owned, rented, other) is also included, but is not considered here. Since consumption includes total paid or imputed rent, rather than mortgage payments, the saving represented by increased equity is disregarded. The apparent propensity to consume may therefore be expected to differ spuriously among tenure classes. In fact, in all five countries, consumption is higher, given income, for families who rent than for families who own their dwellings.

Size of dwelling, however, is important: the propensity to consume rises almost uniformly in every country as the number of rooms increases. (Dwelling size is not simply a proxy for the number of members of the household, which is separately included in these regressions.) The coefficients and their standard errors are shown below. The base class for comparison consists of dwellings of eight or more rooms. (This variable is not available for Venezuela.)

Number of rooms	Colombia	Chile	Ecuador	Peru
1–2	−0.072	−0.218	−0.250	−0.478
	(0.027)	(0.038)	(0.033)	(0.063)
3–4	−0.085	−0.161	−0.170	−0.401
	(0.018)	(0.034)	(0.030)	(0.051)
5	−0.052	−0.025	−0.146	−0.252
	(0.018)	(0.037)	(0.033)	(0.050)
6	−0.056	0.073	−0.093	−0.190
	(0.018)	(0.039)	(0.034)	(0.051)
7	−0.042	0.077	−0.046	−0.162
	(0.019)	(0.047)	(0.039)	(0.056)

Employment of Household Members

The employment status of the members of the household is characterized in three ways: whether the head is employed;[28] whether the spouse is employed; and the total number of employed members.

The logarithmic relation of C to Y (specification 3) includes as independent variables both the number of employed household members (none, one, two, three or more) and the employment of the spouse (usually the wife) of the household head. It is then possible to test whether it matters which members are employed—specifically whether the spouse works—and to abstract from his or her contribution to the number who work. Only in Ecuador does the employment of the spouse make a difference: for a given income, expenditure is reduced by 6.1 percent. In no other country is the coefficient distinguishable from zero: it is positive in Colombia, Peru, and Venezuela, and negative in Chile.[29]

28. The not-employed include the unemployed, retired, disabled, students, and those living off nonlabor income. The particular case of retired heads of households is considered later, in a life cycle model.

29. These differences do not coincide with differences among countries in the definition of the consuming unit.

In the estimation of permanent income and consumption, a variable indicating that the household head was not employed at the time of the survey was included to explain both permanent income and the propensity to consume. The first effect is insignificant in all three countries examined, with a negative coefficient. The effect on the propensity to consume is always positive; coefficients and standard errors are:[30]

Colombia	Ecuador	Peru
0.067	0.180	0.039
(0.020)	(0.029)	(0.049)

Provided most nonemployment is transitory, these results are compatible with the permanent income hypothesis. When the head is not working, there is negative transitory income but no change in permanent income, so the propensity to consume appears to rise. The effect is significant in Colombia and Ecuador, where the head is defined as the chief income earner, and insignificant in Peru, where a "social" definition was used: the head can be permanently not employed even if not retired, so there may be no effect on consumption.

Finally, the effect of having different numbers of members employed was examined in both the current income and the permanent income models, with generally compatible results. In the first specification, households are classified as having no, one, two, or three or more members employed. For a given income, consumption declines steadily as the number who are working increases in Colombia, Peru, and Venezuela. The propensity initially rises in Chile, but no coefficients are significant. The base class is three or more employed.

Number employed	Colombia	Chile	Ecuador	Peru	Venezuela
0	0.180	0.015	−0.007	0.191	0.161
	(0.045)	(0.038)	(0.036)	(0.084)	(0.057)
1	0.124	0.040	−0.077	0.126	0.160
	(0.042)	(0.029)	(0.024)	(0.049)	(0.039)
2	0.071	0.033	−0.047	0.011	0.086
	(0.042)	(0.030)	(0.021)	(0.046)	(0.036)

At least in the countries where the head is defined in economic rather than social terms (Colombia, Ecuador, and Venezuela), zero employment often represents unemployment, probably transitory, for the head. It can therefore be expected to raise the propensity to consume. Similarly, it

30. Musgrove, "Determination and Distribution," p. 85.

might be argued that in all countries employment is likely to be transitory for members other than the principal income earner. The income of such members would therefore be largely transitory. At least, the share of transitory income in total income rises as more members are employed, so that the propensity to consume should appear to fall—as it does in the majority of cases. However, the data do not indicate how stable the employment of each member is or how normal the income received.

To remove these transitory effects as far as possible, households were classified as having one or no member employed or more than one member employed, and this dichotomous variable was introduced for three countries to determine permanent income and the propensity to consume it. The results are as follows:[31]

Effect of more than one employed	*Colombia*	*Ecuador*	*Peru*
On permanent income	0.195	0.436	0.356
	(0.030)	(0.031)	(0.040)
On consumption	−0.039	−0.003	−0.105
	(0.014)	(0.017)	(0.030)

These estimates suggest that much of the additional employment is in fact permanent, so that having more members employed not only increases a household's transitory receipts, but also substantially raises its permanent income. There is a slight, but sometimes significant, tendency to consume a smaller share of permanent income when it is earned by two or more members together than when it is all received by one member. This suggests that additional members seek employment, not only in order to increase consumption, but at least partly so that the household can regularly save more. Creating more employment opportunities in these countries might raise the rate of saving, apart from the direct effect on incomes, at least so long as the newly employed remain in their original households. A large enough increase in income might lead some of these people to form new households, where their propensity to save would presumably be lower.

Education of the Head of Household

The effect of education on the household's consumption can be briefly summarized. As the head's schooling increases beyond the primary level,

31. Ibid., pp. 82, 85.

Table 3-2. *Individual Mean Expenditure Propensity by Educational Level of Head of Household, Ten Latin American Cities*[a]

City	Education			
	None	Primary	Secondary	Higher
Colombia				
Bogotá	1.061	1.130	1.089	0.941
	(0.035)	(0.017)	(0.035)	(0.027)
Barranquilla	1.232	1.306	1.127	0.820
	(0.059)	(0.035)	(0.024)	(0.033)
Cali	1.216	1.164	1.053	0.921
	(0.037)	(0.020)	(0.023)	(0.047)
Medellín	0.990	1.021	0.958	0.796
	(0.047)	(0.013)	(0.020)	(0.028)
Mean	1.102	1.131	1.061	0.898
	(0.024)	(0.010)	(0.015)	(0.016)
Chile				
Santiago	0.925	1.213	1.096	1.100
	(0.045)	(0.047)	(0.018)	(0.012)
Ecuador				
Quito	1.280	1.084	0.995	0.944
	(0.151)	(0.018)	(0.016)	(0.022)
Guayaquil	0.930	0.961	0.940	0.839
	(0.054)	(0.014)	(0.039)	(0.024)
Mean	1.087	1.009	0.966	0.884
	(0.084)	(0.011)	(0.022)	(0.017)
Peru				
Lima	1.499	1.302	1.199	1.194
	(0.385)	(0.071)	(0.039)	(0.043)
Venezuela				
Caracas	1.251	1.131	1.042	0.921
	(0.098)	(0.031)	(0.033)	(0.047)
Maracaibo	1.233	1.153	0.973	0.675
	(0.035)	(0.039)	(0.047)	(0.059)
Mean	1.241	1.137	1.032	0.892
	(0.037)	(0.023)	(0.027)	(0.039)

Source: Original ECIEL calculations based on the survey data.
a. The numbers in parentheses are standard errors.

the mean of the individual propensities, C_h/Y_h, falls uniformly. At a given income level, however, consumption rises uniformly as education increases beyond the primary level. The first result is evident from the means of C_h/Y_h shown in table 3-2 by city and country. The second result emerges from the logarithmic relation of C to Y (specification 3), which includes the same four levels of education as independent variables (proportional differences in consumption are estimated relative to the class with no formal education):

	Primary	Secondary	Higher
Colombia	0.087	0.142	0.161
	(0.025)	(0.027)	(0.033)
Chile	0.077	0.248	0.387
	(0.042)	(0.042)	(0.047)
Ecuador	−0.018	0.036	0.090
	(0.037)	(0.039)	(0.043)
Peru	−0.032	0.103	0.343
	(0.121)	(0.121)	(0.123)
Venezuela	0.037	0.149	0.214
	(0.027)	(0.035)	(0.049)

Neither of these findings necessarily shows that education has any effect on the propensity to consume. The first simply reflects the fact that higher education usually means higher income and that therefore a lower share of income is consumed. Education appears, in fact, to be the single most powerful variable in explaining household incomes, whether the analysis refers to current income or to normal or permanent income.[32]

The second result is compatible with the first. Since income usually rises with education, if households with different levels of schooling have equal incomes, it is likely that the less educated household has a higher transitory income than the more educated household. Since less of transitory than of permanent income is consumed, the less educated household has the lower observed propensity to consume.

Unfortunately for this analysis, education was not included among the determinants of consumption in any of the models based on normal or permanent income. It is therefore not possible to test the hypothesis that better educated households have a higher permanent propensity to consume because they have a higher level of wealth in the form of human capital and thus less need to accumulate nonhuman wealth. The only evidence bearing on this hypothesis is that in five of the ten cities studied the mean of C_h/Y_h is lower for uneducated households than for those whose head has at least one year of primary schooling. In only two cases, however, is the difference statistically significant. The negative coefficients for primary education, in the regressions for Ecuador and Peru, are not significantly different from zero.

32. See the results in chapter 2, especially tables 2-12, 2-16, 2-18, and 2-19.

Occupation of the Head of Household

The means of the ratios C_h/Y_h were also calculated for four large occupational groupings, and the results are shown in table 3-3. Much of the variation in spending propensity among occupational groups is probably

Table 3-3. *Individual Mean Expenditure Propensity by Occupation of Head of Household, Ten Latin American Cities*[a]

| City | Occupation | | | |
	Professional, technical, managerial	White collar	Blue collar	Other
Colombia				
Bogotá	1.010	1.054	1.124	1.149
	(0.031)	(0.021)	(0.021)	(0.053)
Barranquilla	0.951	1.218	1.213	1.335
	(0.036)	(0.029)	(0.030)	(0.060)
Cali	1.069	1.081	1.159	1.135
	(0.043)	(0.033)	(0.022)	(0.023)
Medellín	0.810	0.966	1.027	1.021
	(0.023)	(0.017)	(0.021)	(0.019)
Mean	0.971	1.060	1.121	1.136
	(0.017)	(0.012)	(0.012)	(0.021)
Chile				
Santiago	0.930	1.060	1.173	1.194
	(0.026)	(0.022)	(0.029)	(0.036)
Ecuador				
Quito	0.963	0.979	1.067	1.111
	(0.021)	(0.019)	(0.019)	(0.043)
Guayaquil	0.860	0.930	0.909	1.044
	(0.023)	(0.016)	(0.016)	(0.060)
Mean	0.910	0.946	0.986	1.069
	(0.016)	(0.012)	(0.013)	(0.040)
Peru				
Lima	1.172	1.171	1.244	1.288
	(0.042)	(0.068)	(0.038)	(0.116)
Venezuela				
Caracas	0.957	1.104	1.083	1.192
	(0.033)	(0.035)	(0.046)	(0.052)
Maracaibo	0.816	1.169	1.048	1.254
	(0.045)	(0.062)	(0.028)	(0.047)
Mean	0.940	1.118	1.071	1.213
	(0.027)	(0.030)	(0.026)	(0.033)

Source: Original ECIEL calculations based on the survey data.
a. The numbers in parentheses are standard errors.

due to differences in income. (Occupation was not included in any of the consumption functions estimated, so it is impossible to tell how spending varies among occupational groups, given income.) As chapter 2 shows, some occupational differences are strongly associated with income differences: professional, technical, and managerial jobs, for example, are concentrated in the upper quartile or half of the income distribution. White-collar (clerical, sales, and related) occupations are slightly higher than blue-collar jobs in the income distribution, with marked differences in only the highest and lowest quartiles.

The pattern in most cities is for the mean individual spending propensity to fall as the mean income of the occupational group rises, but the differences are often insignificant between adjacent groups. There are marked differences among cities in the variation of the propensity. It is similar for all groups in Lima, for example, but differs by as much as 0.4 in Maracaibo and 0.2 in Medellín, Santiago, and Caracas. Except in Cali, Quito, and Lima, the propensity is clearly lowest for the professional group. The heterogeneous "other" occupational category has the highest propensity, except in Cali. There is no strong systematic difference between white-collar and blue-collar workers.

There is considerable variation in income, consumption, and their ratio within each occupational group because of large differences in education and sector of employment. If all these factors were taken into account simultaneously, one might discern an effect of occupation on the propensity to consume that could be related to specific job characteristics. There may also be differences, related to occupation, in the form that saving takes. However, neither of these effects can be tested with the simple analysis given here.

Household Size and Composition

The size of the household may be expected to influence consumption more than any variable except income, so it should have a significant effect on the propensity to consume. All the analyses of the ECIEL data (except the permanent income model) take some account of the size, and sometimes of the composition, of the household. None of the linear relations estimated allows the marginal propensity to consume to depend on household size, although such an effect would be plausible. Instead, size and composition affect only the intercept of the consumption or saving function and thus only the average propensity. In other words, size determines the household's subsistence needs or its threshold level of saving, but not its behavior beyond that point. In a logarithmic formulation, the elasticity is not determined by household size; but since the marginal propensity is the product of the elasticity and the average propensity, it does depend on size.

There is surprisingly little variation by household size in the mean individual propensity to spend (C_h/Y_h), and what variation there is shows different patterns in different countries and cities. The propensity tends to rise with increasing size in Colombia, but this is probably because the sample excludes supplementary (income-earning) members—large households therefore include more children in Colombia than elsewhere. The reverse pattern is found in Venezuela.

	Number of members			
	1–3	*4–5*	*6–8*	*9 or more*
Colombia	1.061	1.061	1.125	1.100
	(0.021)	(0.012)	(0.014)	(0.015)
Chile	1.200	1.111	1.121	1.203
	(0.058)	(0.023)	(0.050)	(0.064)
Ecuador	0.994	0.948	0.992	1.032
	(0.018)	(0.012)	(0.012)	(0.047)
Peru	1.503	1.229	1.176	1.296
	(0.160)	(0.048)	(0.029)	(0.093)
Venezuela	1.120	1.124	1.095	0.991
	(0.033)	(0.026)	(0.029)	(0.032)

The normal income model of Crockett and Friend includes the number of members, N, without differentiation of age or allowance for nonlinear effects, in the several consumption and saving functions estimated for Colombia (specifications 7–11). Household size is always significant, and at mean size (about six persons) a difference of one member means a difference of about 2 percent in consumption (at the mean) or about 10 percent in saving (also at the mean). Coefficients are given in pesos in the following table:[33]

	C_d	C_a	C_m	S_1	S_2
Coefficient of N	184	141	159	−149	−154
	(23.6)	(31.3)	(21.5)	(24.8)	(21.7)
Mean of C or S	7,778	6,984	6,627	1,353	1,637

33. Crockett and Friend, "Consumption and Saving," p. 65, table 1.

Table 3-4. *Coefficients of Household Size in Equations for Propensity to Consume, Five Latin American Countries*[a]

Number in household	Colombia	Chile	Ecuador	Peru	Venezuela
Adults					
1	−0.220	−0.452	−0.114	−0.456	−0.319
	(0.063)	(0.078)	(0.048)	(0.250)	(0.085)
2	−0.225	−0.296	−0.041	−0.310	−0.215
	(0.058)	(0.073)	(0.041)	(0.070)	(0.068)
3	−0.175	−0.211	−0.021	−0.196	−0.169
	(0.059)	(0.073)	(0.040)	(0.064)	(0.067)
4–5	−0.115	−0.173	−0.013	−0.166	−0.079
	(0.058)	(0.071)	(0.040)	(0.057)	(0.065)
6–7	−0.098	−0.052	0.004	−0.137	−0.074
	(0.060)	(0.074)	(0.040)	(0.056)	(0.066)
Children					
0	−0.107	−0.075	−0.099	−0.000	−0.010
	(0.039)	(0.133)	(0.076)	(0.185)	(0.068)
1	−0.062	−0.068	−0.085	0.034	0.017
	(0.039)	(0.132)	(0.077)	(0.185)	(0.069)
2	−0.061	−0.062	−0.071	0.046	0.090
	(0.039)	(0.133)	(0.077)	(0.185)	(0.069)
3	−0.054	0.001	−0.035	0.023	0.052
	(0.039)	(0.133)	(0.077)	(0.185)	(0.070)
4–5	−0.027	−0.001	−0.050	0.091	0.130
	(0.038)	(0.133)	(0.076)	(0.185)	(0.069)
6–7	−0.010	−0.015	−0.028	0.144	...
	(0.041)	(0.139)	(0.079)	(0.193)	

Source: Original ECIEL calculations based on the survey data.
a. The numbers in parentheses are standard errors.

Although income is distinguished as normal, transitory, or residual, the effect of N is not separately estimated for each type of income. The results are therefore comparable to those obtained in specification 3 for consumption as a function of current income, when household size is introduced by a set of dummy variables for the number of adults (over fourteen years of age) and another set for the number of children. Size effects are measured relative to the presence of eight or more adults and eight or more children. The results are shown in table 3-4.

In general, the propensity to consume seems to depend markedly on the number of adults in the household and somewhat less on the number of children. Only one coefficient is significant for this variable, and for Peru and Venezuela the propensities decrease with size. It is not surprising that children should have less effect than adults on consumption, since their needs are smaller, but it is surprising that the effect should be so slight. However, the lack of statistical significance of the coefficients may be due to the very small number of households with large numbers of children. If the standard errors are ignored, the coefficients show a reasonable and consistent pattern. At a given income level and for a given number of adults, the household will spend between 6.0 percent (Chile) and 14.4 percent (Peru) more when there are six or seven children in the household than when there are none at all. A difference of one child means, typically, a difference in total spending of between 1 and 2 percent. A difference of one adult typically raises total spending by 3 or 4 percent.

Since the regression includes the number of people employed, the results offer some support to the argument that the propensity to consume rises with the number of dependents in the household (children or adults who are not employed).[34] The test is inexact to the extent that nonemployed adults have income from capital or transfers and therefore are not dependents, but the evidence is fairly clear in the case of children.

As noted earlier, it is extremely difficult to obtain plausible estimates of the zero saving or threshold income level. In both ELES formulations estimated, the threshold value is a function of household size. Howe and Musgrove estimated subsistence expenditures separately for large (more than four members) and small households in each stratum and age class in each of four cities, as well as for the whole population of each city. Their estimates of subsistence income by household size and city are as follows (in national currencies):[35]

Household size	Bogotá	Caracas	Guayaquil	Lima
Small	5,469	5,543	2,206	23,547
Large	14,580	4,116	4,411	33,170

These results may be plausible for mean household size, but they are too highly aggregated to take account of nonlinearities or of differences in household composition. The ELES estimates made by Howe for Colombia attempt to include some of these effects by computing the threshold separately for each of several types of members: the head, other adults (eigh-

34. See Nathaniel H. Leff, "Dependency Rates and Savings Rates," *American Economic Review*, vol. 59 (December 1969), pp. 886–96.

35. "Analysis of ECIEL Household Budget Data," pp. 168–75.

teen years old and over), adolescents (eight to seventeen), and children (seven and under).

When the estimation is based on current income, the results are unsatisfactory at the level of individual household members, even though they explain well the expenditure of a "typical" household consisting of 4 adults, 1.5 children, and 1.5 adolescents. In Barranquilla, Cali, and Medellín, subsistence expenditure is much larger for the head than for other adults; even the estimates for food differ by a factor of seven or more.[36] The needs of adults cannot possibly differ by so much simply because one is the head of the household; the difficulty arises because the head represents the intercept (one-person household) of a function that is nonlinear but must be estimated linearly. (A possible solution to this problem is discussed below.) In Bogotá, the threshold is much lower for the head than for other adults. When the estimation is based on normal income, the threshold is negative for the head in all four cities.

Finally, Howe's results include estimates of the threshold level as a function of the number of members (without taking account of age differences), allowing for nonlinearities or economies of scale in consumption. The levels (in pesos) are given here for Bogotá:[37]

Number of members

	2	3	4	5	6	7	8	9	10	11 or more
Income	539	3,747	6,369	3,979	3,866	11,549	8,677	8,986	9,923	6,731

The estimate rises steadily, as it should, except for households of five to seven or eleven or more members. Households of different sizes have different incomes and sufficiently different behavior that their "needs" may appear lower at lower incomes. The result for two-person households is implausibly low, but at least some of the difficulty with the intercept of the function is alleviated. No estimates were made for one-person households comparable with the estimates for the head alone.

As far as it is possible to summarize these diverse calculations, at a given level of income consumption seems to rise steadily as the number of household members increases. Very approximately, an extra adult adds twice as much to consumption as a young child, with intermediate increments for older children and adolescents. An additional child appears to cause an increase on the order of 2 percent in total household spending;

36. Howe, "Linear and Quadratic Expenditure Systems," pp. 126–83.
37. Ibid., pp. 298–99.

an adult causes a change of about 4 percent. The corresponding reductions in saving are approximately 10 percent at mean income and saving levels, and perhaps larger at lower incomes. The effect of household size on saving depends, of course, on its effect on purchases of durable goods. Different concepts of consumption or spending, of which expenditure on durables is a fairly small share, give generally consistent results, but the same may not be true of different measures of saving.

Age and Life Cycle

These two variables are often regarded as synonymous, but here they are treated as distinct because, while age indicates approximately where an individual is in his life cycle, the cycle itself varies according to whether and when he marries, has children, retires, and so on. Six life cycle stages are defined in the ECIEL data. The head of the household may be unmarried (single); married but with no children; married with children of seven or less; with children of eight to eighteen, with children nineteen or older living at home; or retired. (The age classes correspond closely to the child-adolescent-adult distinction described above.) The age of the head is classified as twelve to thirty-four; thirty-five to forty-nine; fifty to sixty-four; or sixty-five and over. The age and life cycle classes are correlated, but not so closely that they cannot be used in the same analysis. (For example, income is explained better by age than by life cycle, but the reverse is true of consumption.)[38] All the analyses reported here use an age classification, except the permanent income model, which allows income to depend on age but makes propensity to consume a function of life cycle stage. (This model does not include household size and composition, which are also correlated with the life cycle.)

The object in these analyses is to determine how the propensity to consume current income (or permanent income) varies over the life cycle or with age. It is expected that the household's propensity to consume will initially rise, both because consumption needs increase as children grow up and because saving in the form of durable goods is largely completed in the early years. Thereafter, as consumption needs decline and saving for retirement and estate building becomes important, the propensity to consume should fall. Because saving in different forms (durables, housing

38. These conclusions derive from experiments, in both linear and logarithmic specifications, with the Colombian data; Musgrove, "Determination and Distribution," pp. 60–64.

equity, financial assets) is concentrated at different ages, the observed pattern may be fairly sensitive to the definition of consumption or saving.[39]

Age variables, using twelve to thirty-four as the base class, are included in the regressions of log C on log Y (specification 3), with these results:

Age	Colombia	Chile	Ecuador	Peru	Venezuela
35–49	0.014	−0.025	0.016	0.046	0.062
	(0.013)	(0.019)	(0.016)	(0.038)	(0.022)
50–64	0.038	−0.059	0.029	0.005	0.090
	(0.016)	(0.023)	(0.020)	(0.045)	(0.030)
65 and	−0.010	−0.103	−0.040	−0.056	0.048
over	(0.026)	(0.030)	(0.028)	(0.059)	(0.051)

In Colombia, Ecuador, and Venezuela, the highest propensity to consume is observed for the group aged fifty to sixty-four, with a sharp subsequent decline. (In Peru, the peak occurs earlier, with a steady decline after forty-nine). Households do not appear to save heavily relative to income in the years immediately preceding retirement, as might be expected, and thereafter to dissave; only in Chile is the first effect observed. This result may reflect the difficulties of saving for retirement in conditions of inflation, uncertainty, and poor capital markets, particularly for low-income households. Also, retirement does not necessarily occur at sixty-five, especially for the poor. The result may also reflect the definition of C, which includes tax and social security payments and imputed rent.

The linear model based on normal income for Colombia shows that changes in the concept of consumption or saving affect the age pattern to some extent. The oldest group, however, continues to have a relatively high rate of saving (coefficients in pesos):

Age	Consumption			Saving	
	C_d	C_a	C_m	S_1	S_2
35–49	17.5	8.8	−0.5	8.5	1.3
	(14.6)	(22.0)	(12.5 or more)	(17.0)	(13.0)
50–64	38.1	−9.7	24.6	4.0	−28.7
	(18.0)	(24.3)	(16.4)	(20.0)	(16.9)
65 and	−11.3	−124.7	−81.4	129.7	85.7
over	(28.3)	(41.6)	(29.1)	(34.1)	(29.6)

39. See Albert Ando and Franco Modigliani, "The 'Life Cycle' Hypothesis of Saving: Aggregate Implications and Tests," *American Economic Review*, vol. 53 (March 1963), pp. 55–84; Lester C. Thurow, "The Optimum Lifetime Distribution of Consumption Expenditures," *American Economic Review*, vol. 59 (June 1969), pp. 324–30; and Crockett and Friend, "Consumption and Saving," pp. 3–21.

Most coefficients are not statistically significant. Up to the age of sixty-four, saving appears to consist largely of increased equity in residences: S_1 includes this component, while S_2, which does not, declines in the group aged fifty to sixty-four. Similarly, C_d, which includes imputed rent, rises after the age of fifty, while C_a, which includes half of mortgage payments, does not. (The results for C_d are most closely comparable to those reported above, using C, for Colombia).

A cruder distinction is used in the current-income extended linear model, where young households are analyzed separately from old households. Given the evidence reported above, in particular, the change in behavior at about the age of sixty-five, it would have been preferable to distinguish three or four age classes; but the samples are too small to permit separate analyses of so many classes. The model gives estimates of the threshold saving level and the marginal propensity to consume for each combination of age group and stratum. Here I consider only the estimates of the marginal propensity to consume, μ, because of the difficulty of estimating the threshold and its evident dependence on household size and composition. The average propensity to consume, to which the theories of household behavior refer, depends of course on both the threshold and μ, and it is not clear that μ should be expected to vary with age.

I assume that all estimates below 0.67 are too severely biased by transitory components to be considered. Values of μ (young) and μ (old) are compared in the following table for the cases where both estimates exceed 0.8, and (in brackets) where one or both estimates lie between 0.67 and 0.8:[40]

Stratum	Bogotá	Caracas	Guayaquil
Low	μ(young)>μ(old)	. . .	[μ(young)<μ(old)]
Middle	μ(young)>μ(old)	[μ(young)>μ(old)]	μ(young)>μ(old)
High	. . .	μ(young)<μ(old)	μ(young)<μ(old)

Young households tend to consume a higher share of marginal income than older households, but the differences are almost never significant. Moreover, μ is a weighted mean estimate over large and small households, and the average size varies with age. Hence, it does not seem possible to draw any firm conclusions about how *marginal* saving behavior varies with age.

Finally, I consider the life cycle effect in the permanent income model.

40. Howe and Musgrove, "Analysis of ECIEL Household Budget Data," p. 164.

Propensities to consume are estimated relative to the class of households with young children (which corresponds most closely to the group aged twelve to thirty-four) :[41]

Life cycle stage	Colombia	Ecuador	Peru
Unmarried	−0.064	0.058	−0.062
	(0.019)	(0.028)	(0.080)
No children	−0.052	0.007	0.139
	(0.031)	(0.053)	(0.096)
Children under 7	0	0	0
Children 8–18	0.006	0.070	0.037
	(0.012)	(0.019)	(0.034)
Children over 18	−0.031	0.068	−0.015
	(0.024)	(0.032)	(0.051)
Retired	−0.071	0.012	−0.005
	(0.037)	(0.058)	(0.123)

The results for Colombia conform fairly well to expectations, with the propensity to consume rising steadily until the household includes adolescent children, and then declining rapidly. A somewhat similar pattern is found in Peru, but consumption appears to be highest for households with no children. (Part of this difference is undoubtedly due to the much greater spending on durables in Peru.) The Ecuadorean results fit this pattern approximately, but they show the *lowest* propensity for families with small children and a very high propensity to spend among the unmarried.

Overall, these results show a variation in consumption over the life cycle, given income, of about 7 percent in Colombia and Ecuador (and 14 percent in Peru, or 6 percent if the class of childless households is ignored). Since permanent income in this model is not a lifetime concept, but depends on age, this is a reasonable amount of variation, which roughly shows the expected pattern over time. Most of the coefficients, however, are not statistically significant. The results for Colombia are compatible with those obtained using a normal income concept that does not depend on age and that therefore takes an average over a household's earning lifetime. The consistency of these findings suggests that the household's planning horizon in these countries is considerably less than its expected lifetime, so that reestimating its normal or permanent income every decade or so does not seriously misrepresent its behavior. In general, and for comparable definitions of consumption, all the different results agree

41. Musgrove, "Determination and Distribution," p. 85.

fairly well, with a variation over age or over the life cycle on the order of some 6 to 10 percent in consumption, given income. Agreement among estimating methods and countries is least at the ends of the cycle, where differences in the definition of consumption, saving, or the household are most important.

Wealth

As indicated previously, the ECIEL data do not include information on household wealth, except for the estimated value of owned dwellings and the possession of a vehicle, bank accounts, and a few other assets. However, if income by source is known, the share of total income derived from nonhuman wealth is a crude proxy for the share of total wealth in non-human form, or for the ratio of nonhuman to human wealth. The propensity to consume is expected to be higher as this share is higher because the need to save is reduced as assets are accumulated.[42] When the ratio is calculated from observed income, it is, of course, sensitive to transitory influences.

The analysis of Crockett and Friend for Colombia includes the share of income derived from dividends and interest, Y_I/Y. The following coefficients (in pesos) are obtained:[43]

C_d	C_a	C_m	S_1	S_2
423.3	259.9	238.9	−246.2	−226.1
(103.2)	(144.4)	(91.9)	(107.0)	(94.2)

These results clearly support the expectation of a higher propensity to consume for households with greater financial assets. This expectation is not generally satisfied when Y_I is replaced by Y_w, total income from capital including imputed rent. Inclusion of the share Y_w/Y in the permanent income model gives the following effects on the propensity to spend:

Colombia	Ecuador	Peru
−0.000	−0.001	0.005
(0.000)	(0.001)	(0.001)

For a given level of permanent income, consumption rises by at most 0.5 percent when Y_w/Y increases by one percentage point. The only coeffi-

42. Friedman, *Theory of the Consumption Function*, pp. 16–17.
43. "Consumption and Saving," p. 65, table 1.

cient that is significant is positive, as expected; but this occurs for Peru, where the mean of transitory income plus reporting errors in income was almost certainly negative in the sample data. When the income data are more nearly normal (in Colombia and Ecuador), Y_w/Y appears to have no effect on the propensity to consume. It seems reasonable to conclude from this that, when income is abnormal, consumption can be better explained with the aid of some information on wealth. The difference between the results for Y_w/Y and Y_I/Y simply reflects the fact that imputed rent, although a major component of capital income, has little or no effect on the propensity to consume. Presumably, the equity the household has in its dwelling is important in this respect, but the value of the service provided by the dwelling is not important.

City of Residence

Of the forty-five binary comparisons among the ten cities studied, thirty-seven involve comparisons between countries. In three countries, however (Colombia, Ecuador, and Venezuela), two or more cities were surveyed, so that comparisons are possible within a single economy. Striking intercity differences have been noted in the global average consumption propensity and in the individual average propensity. Howe's results for Colombia show differences of 16.2 percent in the marginal propensity to consume out of current income, and of 11.5 percent in the marginal propensity to consume normal income.

The coefficients of the city variables in the regressions of log C on log Y (specification 3) and in the permanent income model (specification 13) are as follows (comparison is always made with the capital city):

Coefficient of	*Current income*	*Permanent income*
Barranquilla	0.045	0.072
	(0.015)	(0.017)
Cali	−0.005	−0.011
	(0.015)	(0.015)
Medellín	−0.139	−0.133
	(0.017)	(0.014)
Guayaquil	−0.108	−0.166
	(0.014)	(0.014)
Maracaibo	−0.239	. . .
	(0.028)	

With the exception of the individual average propensity, which is higher for Maracaibo than for Caracas, all the analyses coincide in showing a low propensity to consume in Medellín, Guayaquil, and Maracaibo, and a high propensity in Barranquilla. (There is little difference in this respect between Bogotá and Cali.) These differences may arise from a great variety of differences among the cities compared—in mean income, concentration of income, occupational structure, historical or cultural traits—some of which are outside the scope of this analysis. A few regularities and possible explanations may, however, be noted.

First, the propensity to consume is usually higher in the capital than in other cities. Second, these differences cannot be attributed to differences in mean income.[44] The capital is usually the highest-income city, or else there is no difference (as in Ecuador). Third, it is striking that the city with the lower propensity to consume is always more of an industrial center than the capital. It may be that the rich in these cities are typically industrialists who save a large share of their incomes, while the rich in the capital cities include a higher proportion of landowners and other classes who save relatively little. (This question has not been investigated, partly because the samples are rather small for examining the behavior of a particular income and occupation class.) There may also be differences in the saving behavior of low-income households.[45] Such differences could arise in the occupational structure, the dependency rate, or the ties to rural areas.[46] There do not seem to be significant differences among cities in other household characteristics, such as age and size. Clearly, there is scope for more detailed analysis than has been conducted so far, since

44. The case of Barranquilla, the lowest-income city surveyed in Colombia, can perhaps be explained in this way.

45. Alfonso Aulestia of the Central Bank of Ecuador has suggested that the high saving rate in Guayaquil may be due to the tendency of migrants to the city to save a large share of their incomes to remit to their families in the countryside. This is particularly true of migrants seeking work during only part of the year, who leave the city when they cannot earn enough to save this way. This behavior is less common in Quito.

46. Rafael Prieto D., "Gasto e Ingreso Familiar Urbano en Colombia," *Ensayos ECIEL*, vol. 4 (August 1977), notes that there is considerable variation among Colombian cities in average labor income and output–labor and capital–labor ratios attributable to differences in industrial structure and in the industrial share of total employment. (The propensities to consume by occupation, described above, do not relate these differences to variation in average propensities among cities, since they do not control for income.) Caracas and Maracaibo also differ markedly in employment and occupational structures, as do Quito and Guayaquil.

large intercity differences remain even when a host of relevant variables are taken into account.

Demands for Specific Assets

So far, there has been little examination of demands for specific assets or of the determinants of the composition of total saving. This is principally because the ECIEL study was directed toward the composition of consumption. Moreover, the saving data are incomplete in all countries, so that comparisons among them are difficult. Nonetheless, some analyses have been made and are briefly reviewed here.[47]

Acquisition of Durables

Household durable goods (furniture and appliances) are particularly difficult to analyze since they can be purchased both for consumption and as substitutes for other forms of saving. This problem also arises with housing, but it can be dealt with conceptually by distinguishing imputed rent, a measure of consumption, from the equity component of mortgage payments, a measure of saving. (The data do not always permit equity and interest to be separated, so the empirical problem may still be severe.) Conceptually, durables also produce an imputed "rent," which is the value of their consumption services, but this is difficult, if not impossible, to measure. There is no way to measure amortization, except to regard the initial purchase as an act of saving and subsequent use as consumption or depreciation of the asset. For this reason, the purchase of durables has been treated, in most of the ECIEL analysis, as spending or consumption rather than saving, and is included in the measures C and C_d. The data give the total price of durables bought in the period of reference, not the amount actually spent at that time when goods are bought on credit. Data on purchases of vehicles are so sparse that they can be related to total income or expenditure only in Colombia and Peru, and the regressions are not significant (at the 95 percent confidence level of the F-test).

47. The only study of demands for specific categories of saving, as functions of income and other variables, is that of Crockett and Friend for Colombia. Descriptive material is also found in the preliminary saving study "Un Estudio del Ahorro Familiar," ECIEL, "Resumen del Decimonoveno Seminario del Programa de Estudios Conjuntos sobre Integración Económica Latinoamericana (ECIEL)" (Quito: January 15–19, 1973; processed), pp. 24–88.

Engel curves for durable goods are estimated in several functional forms in chapter 6. A brief review of the findings that bear on the importance of durables as a form of saving and their relation to other assets is useful at this point. For all five countries, Engel curves were estimated between log D (durables) and log C, so that only households that purchased durables are included.[48] Age of head and household size are included; the results are shown in table 3-5. The concentration of purchases of durables among young households is evident, with declines of 25 to 30 percent in the group aged thirty-five to forty-nine and of 30 to 60 percent in the group aged fifty to sixty-four. This confirms the expectation "that accumulation of service generating assets will tend to precede accumulation of assets for retirement and estate purposes."[49] The dependence on household size is somewhat less regular, but in Colombia, Chile, Peru, and Venezuela durables are purchased primarily by newly formed (two-person) households.

The other estimates of spending on durables are linear in income (current or normal). Crockett and Friend obtain the following marginal propensities: for normal income Y_N, 0.048 (0.003); for windfall or transitory income Y_T, 0.009 (0.022); and for residual income $Y - Y_N - Y_T$, 0.025 (0.002). Windfall income does not go to purchase durables; in this respect they resemble consumption rather than saving. The usual age pattern is found, with coefficients (in pesos) for thirty-five to forty-nine years, −11.9 (4.4); fifty to sixty-four years, −25.7 (5.4); and sixty-five years and over, −36.6 (9.5). The coefficient of household size is negative but not quite significant, and that of Y_I/Y (wealth) is positive but not significant.

Howe's results, also for Colombia, relate D to both current income Y and normal income Y_N. The marginal propensities to spend on durables, estimated as the marginal consumption propensity times the marginal budget share, are as follows (standard errors are quite small):[50]

	Bogotá	Barranquilla	Cali	Medellín
Y	0.028	0.028	0.035	0.017
Y_N	0.042	0.031	0.053	0.033

48. Elasticities for durables are likely to be overestimated relative to long-run Engel curves based on normal or permanent income (see chapter 6).

49. Crockett and Friend, "Consumption and Saving," p. 24.

50. "Linear and Quadratic Expenditure Systems," pp. 176, 181, 183, 202, 204, 206.

Table 3-5. *Coefficients of Equations for Two Determinants of Expenditure on Durables, Double-Log Model, Five Latin American Countries*[a]

Variable	Colombia	Chile	Ecuador	Peru	Venezuela
Age of head of household					
35–49	−0.278	−0.443	−0.251	−0.288	−0.302
	(0.107)	(0.143)	(0.129)	(0.177)	(0.126)
50–64	−0.483	−0.592	−0.238	−0.364	−0.330
	(0.136)	(0.162)	(0.157)	(0.202)	(0.163)
65 and over	−0.888	−0.783	−0.137	−0.570	−0.076
	(0.233)	(0.237)	(0.000)	(0.284)	(0.375)
Number in household					
1	−0.074	. . .	0.669	. . .	−0.743
	(0.642)		(0.406)		(0.598)
2	0.666	0.220	0.294	0.691	0.604
	(0.275)	(0.261)	(0.282)	(0.539)	(0.281)
3	0.309	−0.228	0.694	0.276	0.210
	(0.200)	(0.247)	(0.243)	(0.319)	(0.251)
4–5	0.272	−0.158	0.593	0.078	−0.137
	(0.160)	(0.232)	(0.204)	(0.235)	(0.198)
6–7	0.028	−0.049	0.409	0.156	−0.156
	(0.154)	(0.246)	(0.196)	(0.218)	(0.203)
8–9	−0.000	−0.038	0.335	−0.320	−0.185
	(0.165)	(0.302)	(0.216)	(0.232)	(0.217)
Elasticity[b]	1.475	1.717	1.380	1.496	1.308
	(0.076)	(0.098)	(0.092)	(0.111)	(0.090)

Source: Original ECIEL calculations based on the survey data.
a. The numbers in parentheses are standard errors.
b. Expenditures on durables with respect to total expenditure.

The normal income propensities systematically exceed those for current income and are comparable to the Crockett-Friend estimate. Household size effects are not very satisfactorily estimated: subsistence expenditures are often implausible for the household head and do not show a consistent pattern with increasing numbers of members.

Howe and Musgrove obtain the following estimates of the marginal budget share for durables, by stratum and age group:[51]

51. "Analysis of ECIEL Household Budget Data," pp. 168–74. Estimates of the marginal propensity to consume, $\mu\beta_r$, by stratum are not reliable because of the biases in μ discussed previously: $\mu\beta_r$ for the total population in each city can be estimated as 0.030 for Bogotá, 0.021 for Caracas, 0.038 for Guayaquil, and 0.075 for Lima.

Stratum	Age group	Bogotá	Guayaquil	Lima	Caracas
Low	Young	0.046	0.074	0.144	−0.011
		(0.002)	(0.004)	(0.010)	(0.002)
	Old	−0.000	0.028	−0.402	0.023
		(0.000)	(0.001)	(0.155)	(0.009)
Middle	Young	0.059	0.049	0.168	0.047
		(0.002)	(0.004)	(0.011)	(0.003)
	Old	0.032	0.051	0.220	0.015
		(0.002)	(0.002)	(0.054)	(0.001)
High	Young	0.075	0.049	0.219	0.045
		(0.004)	(0.003)	(0.132)	(0.003)
	Old	0.057	0.030	0.088	0.017
		(0.007)	(0.004)	(0.006)	(0.002)

These estimates generally show a higher propensity to acquire durables among young households, a propensity that tends to rise with income level. Most striking is the very high propensity to spend on durables in Lima. It appears that the most important determinants of spending on durables are normal income (propensities being quite low for transitory income), age, and household size. These variables may be expected to affect chiefly the consumption demand for durables. Durables (and also housing) are also traditional hedges against inflation, so there is also an investment demand for them.

Financial Saving

Crockett and Friend estimated financial saving—defined as disposable income less all purchases for consumption or real assets—as a function of income and other variables. The results are, not surprisingly, very different from those obtained for durables; they closely resemble the results for total saving S_1 and S_2, reported earlier. The marginal propensity to save is 0.252 (0.011) for Y_N; 0.675 (0.080) for Y_T; and 0.520 (0.009) for residual income $Y - Y_N - Y_T$. Saving increases with age, rising sharply after sixty-five, and decreases significantly with increasing household size. The financial wealth variable Y_I/Y has the expected negative effect, of −213.5 (118.6) pesos per 1 percent increase in the share of dividends and interest in income. For Colombia, financial saving accounts for about three-quarters of total saving S_2, partly because errors in income and expenditure appear in both (the share may of course be much lower for the typical low- or middle-income family).

Equity and Improvements in Housing

Housing expenditure is regressed on total expenditure for all the ECIEL data, but the results, which are based on imputed rent, do not describe asset accumulation. Crockett and Friend have estimated functions for increases in equity—defined as half of mortgage payments—and for major improvements (adding rooms, and so forth) in residences, for Colombia. Marginal propensities for both forms of saving are highest for windfall income Y_T. Saving in these forms increases slightly for larger families (but less proportionally than that for housing) and is highest in the group aged thirty-five to forty-nine, declining steadily at higher ages. Relative to age, acquisition of housing equity follows purchases of durables and precedes financial saving, but the effect is not pronounced. Moreover, with increasing age, mortgage payments are likely to consist more of amortization and less of interest, rather than maintaining the equal division assumed in the regression (the data do not separate these components). Equity is therefore likely to increase more with age than these estimates indicate, perhaps enough to nullify the apparent age pattern. Older households' mortgage payments may also be low simply because they bought their houses earlier, when all prices were lower. (This argument does not apply to residential improvements.)

Asset Choices

From the above, it appears that increased financial wealth reduces all forms of saving except (possibly) the acquisition of durables. There is also a fairly clear age pattern to asset choices—durables, followed by housing, followed by financial saving. Finally, I consider some findings of the preliminary analysis of the data on total spending (C_d) and asset possession for Colombia (Bogotá and Barranquilla only) and Peru (Lima).[52] The data on financial assets are much more complete for Colombia; only the presence of dividend or interest income is reported in Peru.

In Colombia, the great majority of households do not seem to hold any of the following assets: bank accounts, stocks, bonds, rent-producing

52. ECIEL, "Un Estudio del Ahorro Familiar," pp. 73–74. Since the purpose of this analysis was partly to check the frequency in the sample of various types of households, the data are unweighted. This means upper incomes are overrepresented, especially in Peru.

property, or shares in unincorporated business. By far the most commonly held asset is a dwelling; households that own rent-producing property tend to own their dwellings also. Second in importance (frequency) are vehicle ownership and the possession of interest- or dividend-paying securities or bank accounts. Both these assets are only slightly concentrated among homeowners. There is no discernible difference in total spending between homeowners and renters, but spending increases dramatically with the number of different assets held. It appears, in other words, that there is a kind of natural order of asset acquisition with increasing income or spending and that only at high incomes do households face a choice among several different assets. Houses are acquired first, then bank accounts, then vehicles, and then securities and income-producing property. A roughly similar pattern is found in Peru, except that fewer households own only a dwelling and rather more have rental property. Again, spending rises rapidly with the number of different assets held.

Summary

The results presented in this chapter come from so many different specifications, and provide such a variety of parameter estimates, that it may be useful to summarize the principal findings briefly. The object, as was indicated at the outset, is not so much to determine the best estimate of any particular measure as to assess the shape of the relation between income and consumption, the level of saving and spending rates, and the importance of factors other than income.

At the time of the surveys, transitory income variation appears to have been greater in some cities or countries than in others, and this accounts for some of the diversity in elasticities and marginal propensities: the propensity to consume transitory income is low, possibly even zero, and such income tends to be used to accumulate financial wealth and residences. The low propensity to spend transitory income on consumption may also explain why less of income is spent as more members of a household take employment.

The importance of the distinction between transitory, or irregular, and permanent, or normal, income gives some support to the permanent income hypothesis, but the results do not uphold the view that the propensity to consume is independent of the level of permanent income. The elasticity of consumption out of permanent income clearly exceeds the elasticity with respect to current income, but it is still less than one, except perhaps at very low or very high incomes.

A reasonable specification of the income-consumption relation is that at low enough incomes there is no saving, so that the average and marginal propensities and the elasticity are all unitary. Saving begins above some threshold that depends on household size and composition and possibly on several other factors, after which there is a transition to a nonzero saving propensity. It is, however, difficult to estimate the threshold level, and it is not clear whether the marginal propensity is asymptotically constant or continues to decline. Overall, the long-run consumption elasticity is close to 0.9 in the range of incomes observed, but it may be somewhat lower in the transition region and as high as 1.0 at the extremes of income. The average saving rate over all families is quite low, typically 5 percent or less, but it is higher than sometimes appears from national accounts estimates. At high incomes it rises to about 15 percent. The majority of families appear to dissave, but this results only partly from low permanent incomes; there are also reporting errors that lead to underestimates of savings, and many households are affected by transitory variation. Such variation is probably more important to low and high incomes than to median income, chiefly because of differences in occupational structure.

For these reasons, the relation between income distribution and the propensity to consume is quite complex. Redistribution of income toward greater equality might significantly lower saving rates in some income ranges but have little or no effect at other income levels. It is also clear that consumption depends not only on income but also on households' characteristics and the opportunities they have for employment and for acquiring assets. The possible effects of changes in income distribution cannot be evaluated without taking these factors into account, despite the general conclusion that the saving rate is positively but weakly related to the level of inequality.[53]

Consumption rises as there are more adults in the family, each additional adult increasing expenditure by about 4 percent on average. An additional child adds only about half as much to consumption. Spending out of a given income therefore tends to increase until the household in-

53. For a careful discussion of these points and an analysis of United States aggregate data, see Alan S. Blinder, "Distribution Effects and the Aggregate Consumption Function," *Journal of Political Economy,* vol. 83 (June 1975), pp. 447–75.

cludes adolescent children, and thereafter to decline. This pattern is observed both with current income and with estimated permanent income; the only surprising life cycle result is that elderly households save at high rates rather than dissaving. This behavior presumably reflects household definition and composition in part, but it is particularly related to the difficulty of long-term planning when capital markets are imperfect and inflation high and variable. Age, considered apart from family composition, has little effect on total consumption or saving but is associated with demands for particular assets. Durables are usually acquired first, followed by dwellings and vehicles and then by financial savings. Most families, however, own none but the first two kinds of assets.

Finally, there is some evidence that increased wealth raises the propensity to consume, which supports the notion that saving is undertaken to achieve a desired stock of wealth. The data do not, however, cover all the assets a family may own or acquire, and in particular there is no analysis of the relative importance of human and nonhuman wealth.

CHAPTER FOUR

The Structure of the Budget

HAVING discussed the generation and distribution of household incomes and the relation between total consumption and income, I consider, in this and the next two chapters, how spending is allocated among different categories of goods and services. In chapters 4 and 5 the emphasis is on the shares of the household budget devoted to these categories, and the total budget is defined as total expenditure less tax and social security payments (or C_d, in the notation of the previous chapter). These budget shares are first analyzed for the entire population, and then for subgroups, defined according to eleven variables or characteristics.[1] These variables, and the number of classes associated with each, are as follows: income level (four); education (four); occupation (four); employment status of the household head (two); employment status of the spouse (two); tenure of dwelling (three); age (four); stage of life cycle (six); number of members (four); number of children (four); and trimester (four).

Each of these characteristics except trimester was used in one or more of the analyses presented earlier. Here, however, the analysis is almost uniform across all variables and is conducted for each of the ten cities as well as, or instead of, each of the five countries.[2] First, I consider the entire

---

1. Stratum was also used to classify households in some countries, but these results are not reported here because of the difficulty of comparing strata among countries. Analyses by stratum for Peru are reported in Adolfo Figueroa A., *Estructura del Consumo y Distribución de Ingresos en Lima Metropolitana, 1968–1969* (Lima: Pontificia Universidad Católica del Perú, 1974), pp. 35–38.

2. The only exceptions are caused by the absence of data on life cycle and trimester in the study of Caracas.

budget in each city and country and the degree to which these budgets differ. Next, the variation of individual budget shares among household groups is examined to see which spending categories are most variable and which characteristics are most strongly associated with budget differences. Finally, I analyze a few factors presumed to affect some specific expenditure categories.

Table 4-1 gives the mean value of C_d (household expenditure less tax and social security payments) for each of the cells defined by the classifying variables. The means are shown in national currency, since the object is to compare families in different groups within each city or country. The results conform to those associated with the distribution of income: $\bar{C}_d$ rises with the education of the household head and, generally, with his or her age. Spending also increases with family size, although less than proportionately, and often decreases as the number of children increases. The other variables show less uniform patterns both within and among cities.

Global and Individual Budget Shares

For this analysis the household budget is divided into fifteen categories. Six of them (food and beverages, housing, household furnishings and operation, clothing, recreation and culture, and other consumption expenditures) are further divided into twenty-eight components. Altogether, forty-three categories are studied. (With a few exceptions, these are the same categories for which Engel curves are estimated in chapter 6.)

The simplest measure of the share of the household budget devoted to a particular category, r, is the ratio of weighted mean C_r to weighted mean C_d. This ratio is denoted by $G_r = \bar{C}_r / \bar{C}_d$, and is shown in table 4-2 for all categories in each of the ten cities and the mean across cities in each of the five countries. The value of $\bar{C}_r$ in national currency can be found from G_r and the value of $\bar{C}_d$ in the first line of table 4-1. For example, households in Santiago, Chile, spend an average of 5,302 escudos per quarter, and 34.03 percent of this, or 1,804 escudos per quarter, goes for food and beverages. The shares G_r add to 100 percent (except for rounding errors and a few items that enter the total without being assigned to any of the components) and translate into monetary amounts comparable to elements of national product. They have the great disadvantage, however, of effectively representing each family in the population according to its total spending, C_d, without taking any account of the distribution of total expenditure among households. The shares G_r are analogous in this respect to the consumption propensities $\overline{C}/\overline{Y}$ discussed in chapter 3; hence, it seems appropriate to define an individual budget share g_r to contrast with the global share G_r, analogous to the mean of the individual ratios (C_h/Y_h). I define g_r as the (weighted) mean of the individual shares (C_{rh}/C_{dh}), so that each family is represented in the statistic according to its frequency in the population rather than according to its (weighted) income.[3]

Individual Shares and Income Concentration

Table 4-3 presents the shares g_r for each of the five countries and each of the ten cities. When tables 4-2 and 4-3 are compared, it is apparent that g_r and G_r give very different pictures of the way households allocate their consumption budgets. In the case of food, for example, G_r for Ecuador is only 38 percent, whereas g_r is exactly 50 percent. The difference results from the considerable concentration of income and consumption in Ecuador and because at lower incomes families spend larger shares of the budget on food. The typical household in Quito or Guayaquil has to spend half its discretionary consumption on food and beverages and is therefore considerably worse off than appears from the statistic G_r. Because this analysis is concerned with the spending and welfare of individual families, it seems appropriate to work with the shares g_r, and the rest of this chapter is devoted primarily to these measures. They have the advantage of conforming more closely to differences in real incomes among cities and countries. Thus, for example, G_r (food) gives the impression that urban Colombia is appreciably poorer, in real terms, than urban Ecuador, and that there is virtually no difference between Chile and Peru. The values of g_r (food), however, show Colombia and Ecuador to be virtually indistinguishable in this respect, and show Peru to be poorer than Chile, which is only slightly poorer than Venezuela. The G_r values continue to be useful primarily for translating effects at the level of individual

3. That is, $g_r = \sum_h W_h (C_{rh}/C_{dh})/ \sum_h W_h$. Of course, the entire distribution of the shares C_{rh}/C_{dh} is of interest; the mean is adopted as a convenient summary statistic, although it has the disadvantage of being sensitive to extremely high or low values.

Table 4-1. *Mean Household Expenditure in National Currency,*[a] *by Household Characteristic, Ten Latin American Cities*

Household characteristic	Colombia					Chile
	Bogotá	Barranquilla	Cali	Medellín	Mean	Santiago
Number of members						
1–2	4,920	5,550[b]	4,260[b]	4,700	4,820	4,319
3–5	8,340	6,210	6,410	6,020	7,220	5,562
6–8	9,690	8,440	7,860	7,400	8,730	5,536
9 and over	10,730	8,880	8,240	7,250	8,990	5,073
Age of head						
13–34	8,540	7,060	6,140	5,580	7,290	4,693
35–49	8,840	7,930	7,080	7,090	8,010	5,430
50–64	10,640	8,030	7,910	7,120	8,920	5,874
65 and over	8,540[b]	7,270[b]	11,640	8,370	8,860	4,919
Life cycle of head						
Unmarried	6,200	5,960	6,210	4,850	5,740	4,212
Married, no children	11,000[b]	7,190[b]	7,120[b]	5,990[b]	8,320	5,172
Children under 8	8,220	7,580	6,220	6,060	7,260	4,662
Children 8–18	10,070	8,060	8,010	7,660	8,950	5,858
Children 19 and over	11,360	7,460	7,620	8,130	9,260	5,629
Retired	5,930[b]	9,800[b]	8,770[b]	8,670[b]	7,370	5,188
Education of head						
No education	4,330	4,170	3,370[b]	4,150[b]	4,150	2,819
Primary	6,020	5,470	5,130	4,990	5,510	3,528
Secondary	10,840	10,720	10,690	8,450	10,300	6,133
Higher	24,670	19,250	17,820	18,390	22,120	11,787
Number of children						
0	10,620	7,430	8,750	6,330	8,630	5,641
1–2	9,770	7,730	7,420	6,630	8,480	5,269
3–5	8,130	7,820	6,460	7,660	7,700	5,084
6 and over	7,420	7,280	5,280	5,910	6,580	4,041
Occupation of head						
Professional	19,300	16,550	15,250	16,960	17,940	10,816
White collar	9,470	8,390	8,030	6,530	8,420	6,363
Blue collar	6,470	6,290	5,320	5,160	5,950	3,936
Other	7,370	5,430	6,400	5,840	6,500	3,852
Employment status, head						
Employed	9,150	7,980	7,170	6,750	8,130	5,447
Not employed	8,440	5,420	7,370	6,650	7,180	4,746
Employment status, spouse						
Employed	11,050	7,220	7,550	7,350[b]	9,620	5,995
Not employed	8,770	7,730	7,160	6,710	7,840	5,209
Dwelling tenure						
Owned	9,350	7,560	6,660	7,680	8,200	5,701
Rented	9,130	8,240	8,290	5,640	8,040	5,063
Other	4,760[b]	5,110[b]	6,740[b]	4,510[b]	5,060	3,280
Income quartile						
First	2,930	3,520	2,850	2,600	2,920	2,412
Second	4,880	5,290	4,840	4,290	4,770	3,723
Third	7,150	7,370	7,290	6,420	7,030	4,964
Fourth	17,440	16,250	15,740	15,300	16,640	10,124
Mean	9,090	7,680	7,190	6,740	8,030	5,302

Source: Original ECIEL calculations based on the survey data.
n.a. Not available.
a. Colombia, peso; Chile, escudo; Ecuador, sucre; Peru, sol; Venezuela, bolívar.
b. Estimate based on 40 or fewer observations.

	Ecuador			Peru	Venezuela		
Quito	*Guayaquil*	*Mean*		*Lima*	*Caracas*	*Maracaibo*	*Mean*
4,372	4,311	4,342		23,430	3,657	1,948	3,247
8,609	7,991	8,261		24,760	5,949	3,078	5,327
9,526	10,042	9,827		30,350	7,176	3,298	6,063
13,123	10,491	11,496		35,810	6,285	3,346	5,186
6,133	6,704	6,478		22,490	4,847	2,915	4,394
9,339	9,614	9,488		31,630	7,102	3,274	5,945
11,691	10,071	10,753		30,170	6,935	3,274	6,126
10,752	10,850	10,807		33,150	6,309	2,342	5,016
6,231	7,783	7,056		20,260	n.a.	2,502	n.a.
7,620[b]	7,027[b]	7,271		29,270	n.a.	2,608	n.a.
6,591	7,245	6,969		27,840	n.a.	3,092	n.a.
10,734	9,445	10,004		30,470	n.a.	3,430	n.a.
14,635	13,094	13,633		29,880	n.a.	2,540	n.a.
8,559[b]	7,092[b]	7,884		32,940[b]	n.a.	2,943[b]	n.a.
2,534	5,171[b]	3,962		17,530	3,056	2,215	2,597
5,038	5,605	5,381		18,980	4,307	3,026	3,932
12,390	12,447	12,420		30,860	7,303	4,288	6,895
20,694	19,271	19,871		54,490	12,141	5,363	11,333
8,758	9,429	9,137		28,270	5,936	2,686	5,291
9,286	9,611	9,473		31,830	6,338	3,460	5,565
9,463	8,371	8,833		27,700	6,399	2,970	5,212
7,018	6,379	6,662		26,660	4,233[b]	2,135[b]	4,163
19,254	20,150	19,714		54,540	10,130	5,243	9,537
11,529	9,643	10,253		26,350	5,886	4,026	5,491
5,601	6,220	5,921		19,740	3,884	2,648	3,461
5,344	6,196	5,877		28,730	4,798	2,288	3,919
8,573	8,636	8,609		29,570	6,104	3,196	5,375
12,410	10,859	11,629		26,450	6,925[b]	2,246	4,767
7,765	10,012	8,660		28,750	7,133	3,530	6,445
9,415	8,679	8,968		29,320	6,024	3,074	5,229
14,879	12,578	13,486		36,200	7,070	2,816	5,514
5,945	6,692	6,340		26,250	5,435	4,111	5,256
5,754	4,921	5,173		21,230	4,234[b]	2,652	3,735
2,466	2,514	2,489		14,210	2,661	1,703	n.a.
4,955	4,461	4,649		19,730	4,025	2,230	n.a.
8,289	7,595	7,868		27,570	5,945	3,040	n.a.
21,330	20,239	20,702		55,670	11,961	5,234	n.a.
9,025	8,834	8,916		29,220	6,137	3,104	5,341

Table 4-2. *Global Mean Expenditure Shares by Spending Category,*
Ten Latin American Cities
Percent

Spending category	Bogotá	Barranquilla	Cali	Medellín	Urban Colombia
Food and beverages	39.27	49.29	47.40	44.17	42.74
Dairy products and eggs	5.59	6.12	6.76	7.02	6.12
Cereals	6.50	9.12	7.11	6.50	6.92
Meat and poultry	7.76	12.78	12.31	11.33	9.79
Seafood	0.25	0.97	0.29	0.14	0.32
Vegetables and tubers	5.52	5.15	6.05	5.81	5.61
Fruits	2.30	2.70	2.91	1.75	2.33
Fats and oils	1.51	2.20	2.22	1.75	1.75
Sugar and sweets	1.27	1.70	2.11	2.77	1.75
Hot beverages	1.63	0.99	1.78	1.96	1.64
Alcoholic beverages	0.67	1.13	0.54	0.39	0.65
Other beverages	0.23	0.61	0.29	0.24	0.29
Other foods	0.43	0.83	0.50	0.45	0.50
Meals away from home	5.58	4.98	4.51	4.05	5.04
Housing	25.21	18.86	20.00	24.60	23.50
Principal dwelling	24.09	17.44	19.03	22.89	22.25
Other	0.12	0.05	0.14	0.95	0.28
Maintenance	1.00	1.37	0.83	0.76	0.97
Furnishings and operation	7.00	6.14	7.60	5.37	6.66
Furniture and durable goods	3.28	2.28	3.42	2.02	2.92
Nondurable goods	1.52	1.80	1.59	1.19	1.50
Services	2.20	2.07	2.60	2.15	2.24
Clothing	8.78	6.93	7.28	5.61	7.69
Men's ready-made	2.75	2.15	2.53	1.42	2.38
Women's ready-made	3.77	2.80	3.02	2.46	3.28
Children's ready-made	1.98	1.63	1.44	1.23	1.71
Other	0.27	0.36	0.30	0.49	0.33
Medical care	2.55	3.19	1.81	2.50	2.51
Education	6.04	4.94	3.40	4.51	5.20
Recreation and culture	2.74	2.09	2.46	2.01	2.47
Recreation	2.03	1.35	1.64	1.39	1.76
Reading and culture	0.71	0.74	0.82	0.62	0.71
Vehicle operation and maintenance	1.37	1.61	1.48	0.93	1.33
Public transportation	2.17	1.83	1.64	1.46	1.91
Telephone and other communication	0.59	0.53	0.66	0.13	0.50
Vehicle purchase	0.04	0.00	0.04	0.26	0.08
Other consumption	2.17	3.15	2.65	2.50	2.43
Tobacco	0.27	0.62	0.48	0.65	0.42
Personal care	1.81	2.26	2.02	1.46	1.83
Ceremonies	0.08	0.27	0.15	0.39	0.18
Insurance	0.39	0.15	0.28	0.34	0.35
Gifts and transfers	1.46	1.10	1.43	1.50	1.42
Other nonconsumption	0.21	0.18	0.29	0.34	0.25
Unspecified or rounding error	0.01	0.01	1.58	3.77	0.98

Source: Original ECIEL calculations based on the survey data.
n.a. Not available.

Santiago	Quito	Guayaquil	Urban Ecuador	Lima	Caracas	Maracaibo	Urban Venezuela
34.03	34.36	41.02	38.14	33.66	27.93	46.71	30.80
3.75	5.35	5.73	5.56	4.76	4.41	9.33	5.16
5.96	6.87	7.70	7.34	5.38	2.82	5.96	3.30
7.54	5.93	9.09	7.72	8.51	6.15	10.31	6.78
0.88	0.55	1.47	1.07	1.14	0.69	0.86	0.72
4.70	4.09	4.30	4.21	4.06	2.79	3.18	2.85
2.18	1.98	2.04	2.02	2.22	1.79	3.34	2.02
1.51	1.72	2.06	1.91	0.97	1.10	1.97	1.23
1.67	1.93	2.28	2.13	1.03	0.96	1.52	1.05
1.10	0.97	0.98	0.98	0.49	0.80	1.59	0.92
0.87	0.48	0.69	0.60	0.39	1.07	1.22	1.09
0.62	0.53	0.95	0.77	0.11	0.77	1.00	0.81
0.72	0.57	0.60	0.58	0.92	0.88	1.22	0.93
2.53	3.13	3.04	3.08	3.57	3.14	4.78	3.39
26.24	33.72	27.82	30.37	23.71	26.48	18.60	25.71
25.32	29.15	25.32	26.98	19.30	26.94	18.56	25.66
n.a.	3.90	1.74	2.67	2.25	n.a.	n.a.	n.a.
0.92	0.66	0.76	0.72	2.17	0.05	0.04	0.05
10.21	7.23	7.87	7.59	12.33	6.93	8.94	7.23
5.88	3.92	4.12	4.03	8.02	1.82	5.23	2.34
1.30	1.47	1.17	1.30	1.59	1.56	1.79	1.60
3.04	1.84	2.58	2.26	2.72	3.50	1.92	3.26
12.67	9.71	7.18	8.28	8.57	6.83	4.24	6.44
6.26	4.00	3.13	3.50	3.69	1.70	1.62	1.69
4.78	4.74	3.14	3.84	3.53	2.57	1.35	2.38
0.25	0.17	0.16	0.17	0.29	1.44	0.99	1.37
1.38	0.79	0.75	0.77	1.05	1.13	0.27	1.00
1.62	2.94	2.11	2.47	2.21	5.53	1.61	4.93
1.17	1.80	2.31	2.09	2.20	4.40	2.24	4.07
3.78	1.86	1.96	1.92	2.90	3.90	3.53	3.85
3.48	1.33	1.29	1.31	1.80	3.17	2.89	3.13
1.40	0.53	0.67	0.61	1.10	0.73	0.64	0.71
1.58	0.85	0.64	0.73	2.66	5.01	2.39	4.61
2.58	n.a.	n.a.	n.a.	2.75	2.35	3.06	2.46
0.70	0.64	0.41	0.51	0.36	0.88	0.26	0.79
n.a.	n.a.	n.a.	n.a.	1.65	0.21	2.77	0.60
4.43	2.93	3.19	3.07	4.22	3.33	4.40	3.50
1.60	0.61	0.69	0.66	0.69	1.16	1.28	1.18
2.39	1.92	2.28	2.13	3.07	2.17	3.11	2.32
0.44	0.40	0.21	0.29	0.47	0.00	0.00	0.00
n.a.	0.11	0.66	0.42	1.47	0.37	0.18	0.34
0.48	2.55	4.30	3.54	0.64	1.37	0.49	1.24
0.45	0.70	0.21	0.42	0.59	0.17	0.13	0.16
0.06	0.55	0.31	0.43	0.08	3.81	0.45	3.27

Table 4-3. *Individual Mean Expenditure Shares by Spending Category, Ten Latin American Cities*
Percent

Spending category	Bogotá	Barranquilla	Cali	Medellín	Urban Colombia
Food and beverages	46.60	56.77	56.32	51.72	50.79
Dairy products and eggs	6.14	6.72	6.81	7.57	6.67
Cereals	8.66	11.36	9.18	8.22	9.00
Meat and poultry	9.09	14.20	14.60	12.74	11.56
Seafood	0.17	1.15	0.23	0.08	0.29
Vegetables and tubers	7.59	6.08	8.16	7.45	7.45
Fruits	2.34	3.04	3.38	1.79	2.48
Fats and oils	2.12	2.66	3.13	2.20	2.38
Sugar and sweets	1.71	2.20	2.93	3.86	2.49
Hot beverages	2.35	1.27	2.40	2.73	2.30
Alcoholic beverages	0.46	1.20	0.40	0.31	0.51
Other beverages	0.21	0.64	0.21	0.15	0.25
Other foods	0.44	0.94	0.58	0.44	0.53
Meals away from home	5.33	5.31	4.30	4.20	4.89
Housing	26.01	17.52	18.73	23.75	23.12
Principal dwelling	25.25	16.59	18.18	23.14	22.41
Other	0.06	0.03	0.03	0.26	0.10
Maintenance	0.71	0.90	0.52	0.34	0.61
Furnishings and operation	4.87	4.77	4.94	3.56	4.56
Furniture and durable goods	1.86	1.68	1.77	1.06	1.63
Nondurable goods	1.63	2.01	1.80	1.36	1.65
Services	1.38	1.07	1.37	1.14	1.28
Clothing	7.31	5.96	6.11	4.36	6.23
Men's ready-made	2.24	1.90	2.09	1.11	1.90
Women's ready-made	2.87	2.35	2.44	1.81	2.48
Children's ready-made	2.04	1.45	1.39	1.07	1.63
Other	0.16	0.25	0.19	0.37	0.22
Medical care	1.87	2.36	1.31	1.79	1.82
Education	4.93	3.57	2.62	3.45	4.01
Recreation and culture	1.81	1.71	1.86	1.45	1.72
Recreation	1.24	1.07	1.19	0.97	1.14
Reading and culture	0.57	0.65	0.67	0.48	0.58
Vehicle operation and maintenance	0.46	0.69	0.38	0.38	0.46
Public transportation	2.49	2.08	1.95	1.69	2.16
Telephone and other communication	0.36	0.28	0.36	0.10	0.29
Vehicle purchase	0.03	0.00	0.01	0.06	0.03
Other consumption	2.15	3.44	2.69	2.34	2.46
Tobacco	0.27	0.76	0.52	0.80	0.50
Personal care	1.78	2.41	2.08	1.41	1.83
Ceremonies	0.09	0.27	0.09	0.13	0.13
Insurance	0.13	0.05	0.10	0.11	0.11
Gifts and transfers	0.82	0.68	0.84	0.93	0.83
Other nonconsumption	0.15	0.12	0.13	0.23	0.16
Unspecified or rounding error	0.01	0.00	1.65	4.08	1.25

Source: Original ECIEL calculations based on the survey data.
n.a. Not available.

Santiago	Quito	Guayaquil	Urban Ecuador	Lima	Caracas	Maracaibo	Urban Venezuela
40.81	45.68	53.23	50.00	43.36	35.55	52.37	39.96
4.25	5.93	6.48	6.24	6.01	5.63	10.57	6.93
8.35	10.29	11.81	11.16	7.75	4.14	7.43	5.00
8.12	6.68	10.85	9.07	11.01	7.70	10.90	8.54
1.00	0.59	2.13	1.47	1.45	0.94	1.03	0.97
6.21	6.02	6.22	6.14	5.90	3.93	3.69	3.87
2.28	2.26	2.31	2.29	2.34	2.18	3.82	2.61
2.00	2.48	3.08	2.82	1.39	1.58	2.24	1.76
2.21	2.66	2.80	2.74	1.35	1.23	1.80	1.38
1.41	1.37	1.48	1.43	0.66	1.16	1.87	1.35
0.90	0.42	0.50	0.47	0.36	1.14	1.15	1.14
0.67	0.47	0.99	0.77	0.12	1.02	1.13	1.05
0.84	0.56	0.57	0.57	1.18	1.07	1.37	1.14
2.59	5.60	3.90	4.63	3.81	3.67	5.13	4.05
26.22	25.96	21.81	23.58	20.04	27.71	19.16	25.47
25.51	24.15	20.82	22.25	18.11	27.68	19.14	25.44
n.a.	1.35	0.51	0.87	0.48	n.a.	n.a.	n.a.
0.71	0.45	0.48	0.47	1.45	0.03	0.02	0.03
6.95	5.57	5.57	5.57	9.47	5.62	6.88	5.95
3.93	2.83	2.54	2.66	5.86	1.22	3.88	1.92
1.42	1.68	1.58	1.62	1.89	1.74	1.93	1.79
1.60	1.06	1.45	1.29	1.73	2.64	1.07	2.23
11.68	10.21	6.51	8.10	7.88	6.36	3.66	5.65
5.68	4.30	2.90	3.50	3.48	1.56	1.36	1.50
4.38	4.75	2.76	3.61	3.25	2.37	1.11	2.04
0.29	0.23	0.19	0.21	0.32	1.52	0.90	1.36
1.33	0.94	0.67	0.78	0.82	0.91	0.28	0.75
1.30	2.94	2.00	2.40	2.12	3.65	1.20	3.01
0.73	1.40	1.79	1.62	1.69	3.27	1.55	2.82
3.06	1.57	1.73	1.66	2.61	3.20	2.96	3.14
1.81	1.08	1.01	1.04	1.40	2.65	2.50	2.61
1.26	0.49	0.73	0.62	1.21	0.55	0.46	0.53
0.69	0.25	0.31	0.28	1.91	3.64	1.52	3.08
3.07	0.05	n.a.	0.02	3.05	3.20	3.91	3.39
0.43	0.44	0.20	0.31	0.27	0.72	0.16	0.57
n.a.	n.a.	n.a.	n.a.	0.56	0.36	0.74	0.46
4.40	2.99	3.27	3.15	4.40	3.96	5.04	4.24
1.75	0.68	0.67	0.67	0.68	1.50	1.47	1.49
2.35	2.00	2.53	2.31	3.36	2.45	3.57	2.75
0.30	0.30	0.07	0.17	0.36	0.00	0.00	0.00
0.30	0.05	0.14	0.10	1.58	0.22	0.14	0.20
n.a.	1.95	2.99	2.55	0.45	0.94	0.32	0.77
0.29	0.58	0.19	0.36	0.55	0.14	0.12	0.14
0.07	0.36	0.26	0.30	0.06	1.46	0.27	1.15

families into monetary totals, which are important for estimates of aggregate demand.[4]

Budget Shares and Expenditure Elasticities

In general, G_r can be expected to exceed g_r for categories that take a larger share of the budget of rich households than of poor ones, and to be less than g_r for categories of greater importance to poor households. The ratio G_r/g_r might therefore be related to the elasticity β_r of expenditure C_r, relative to total expenditure C. This association can be tested by computing rank correlation coefficients for G_r/g_r and β_r in each country, for nine categories (excluding insurance, transport, and communication), with the following results:[5]

Colombia	Chile	Ecuador	Peru	Venezuela
0.633	0.733	0.100	0.667	0.783

Estimated for eight categories (excluding gifts and transfers):

Colombia	Chile	Ecuador	Peru	Venezuela
0.833	0.905	0.381	0.548	0.833

The expected relation is discernible in Colombia, Chile, Peru, and Venezuela when the calculation is limited to nine aggregated categories that are identical in the two kinds of estimates. Nothing seems to explain the almost complete lack of association in the case of Ecuador; the correlation remains low even when the gifts and transfers category is removed.[6]

Intercity Differences in Budget Structure

Of the fifteen aggregated categories, twelve are comparable across all ten cities (public transportation, vehicle purchase, and insurance are not comparable). Among these twelve, food always has the largest share of

4. The shares G_r were also computed by stratum everywhere except in Venezuela. See the national monographs cited in the bibliographical note, chapter 1, for these results and their analysis.

5. In the standard ECIEL analyses, β_r was computed by country only, not by city. See table 6.1.

6. There are, of course, three other differences between the budget shares and the elasticities. First, the former do, and the latter do not, respect the budget constraint. Second, the elasticities are estimated in regression equations that simultaneously take account of a number of other variables that may not be independent of income. Finally, the β_r are based only on households that actually spent something in the category, although for large aggregates this is a minor restriction.

the budget and housing the second largest. Clothing is third everywhere except in Lima and Maracaibo; in those cities household furnishing and operation, normally fourth in importance, is third. The other consumption category (personal care, tobacco, and ceremonial expenditures) is always either fifth or sixth. There is more variety in the ranking of the other categories, each of which accounts for less than 5 percent of the budget in every city.

There are a few striking differences among cities and countries in the relative importance of different categories. Gifts and transfers account for a large share of household budgets in Quito and Guayaquil, apparently because urban households send substantial amounts to relatives in smaller cities or rural areas. The share devoted to educational expenditures is low in the cities in Ecuador and in Lima and Caracas, but is exceptionally high in Bogotá. Vehicle operation and maintenance are most important in Caracas, large also in Lima and Maracaibo, and very low in Quito. The fact that expenditure on vehicles is high in both Caracas and Maracaibo, despite the large income differences between these cities, is probably due to the lower price of cars in Venezuela than in other countries.[7]

The differences in budget structure evident in table 4-3 can be crudely summarized by the index of dissimilarity, defined as the sum of the absolute values of the differences of budget shares between two cities:

$$\Delta(c, c') = \sum_r |g_{rc} - g_{rc'}|,$$

where c and c' are the cities being compared, and the sum is over the categories r. The index ranges from zero to a maximum of 200, and is clearly quite sensitive to the level of disaggregation. (Disaggregating any category can raise, but cannot lower, the index.) No test of statistical significance exists for comparing values of Δ.[8]

Table 4-4 presents values of Δ based on twenty-nine expenditure categories (thirteen food and sixteen nonfood categories).[9] Expenditures on

---

7. Relative to the general price level, cars cost only one-third as much in Venezuela as in Colombia, 0.41 compared to Chile, 0.48 to Ecuador, and 0.68 to Peru.

8. The Δ is the same as the index of similarity first defined and used by Irving Kravis. See "International and Intertemporal Comparisons of the Structure of Consumption," in Lincoln H. Clark and J. B. Carney, eds., *Consumer Behavior: Research on Consumer Reactions* (Harper, 1958), pp. 308–54. Here, Δ is referred to as an index of *dis*similarity since it increases when two structures are more unlike.

9. Arturo Carlos Meyer, "Diferencias Internacionales en los Patrones de Consumo," *Ensayos ECIEL,* vol. 1 (November 1974), pp. 173–213, computed this index

Table 4-4. Indexes[a] of Dissimilarity in Total Spending and Food Spending among Ten Latin American Cities

City and spending category	Bogotá	Barranquilla	Cali	Medellín	Santiago	Quito	Guayaquil	Lima	Caracas
Barranquilla									
Total	30.07	...	...	...	...	...	...	...	...
Food	20.34	...	...	...	...	...	...	...	...
Cali									
Total	24.80	16.55	...	...	...	...	...	...	...
Food	19.44	0.90	...	...	...	...	...	...	...
Medellín									
Total	20.26	28.29	19.58	...	...	...	...	...	...
Food	10.24	10.10	9.20	...	...	...	...	...	...
Santiago									
Total	28.09	42.20	42.34	39.95	...	...	...	...	...
Food	11.58	31.92	31.02	21.82	...	...	...	...	...
Quito									
Total	23.72	34.56	37.13	34.92	24.93	...	...	...	...
Food	1.84	22.18	21.28	12.08	9.74	...	...	...	...
Guayaquil									
Total	29.36	23.33	25.22	28.26	36.04	23.24	...	...	...
Food	13.26	7.08	6.18	3.02	24.84	15.10	...	...	...
Lima									
Total	33.70	32.85	34.00	38.12	29.18	38.16	29.48	...	...
Food	6.48	26.82	25.92	16.72	5.10	4.64	19.74	...	...
Caracas									
Total	33.10	44.21	47.04	42.82	30.38	38.83	43.74	36.50	...
Food	22.10	42.44	41.54	32.34	10.52	20.26	35.36	15.62	...
Maracaibo									
Total	42.29	33.16	35.41	39.31	39.84	48.19	39.03	28.33	42.87
Food	11.54	8.80	7.90	1.30	23.12	13.38	1.72	18.02	33.64

Source: Calculated from the individual mean budget shares in table 4-3.

a. No adjustments were made for missing categories, so the values slightly overstate the true dissimilarity. This problem is most severe where the category of unspecified expenditures and rounding errors is large.

housing, clothing, recreation and culture, and other consumption are not disaggregated for this analysis (although their components appear in table 4-3), because differences in allocation within those categories are not very important or informative. To show how much of the total index depends only on the difference in food budget shares, table 4-4 also shows an index ($\Delta_{f,n}$) based only on the disaggregation into food and nonfood categories.

One would expect that the principal source of dissimilarity is differences in real income levels and, to some extent, differences in the relative prices of food versus nonfood items. By this measure, Bogotá and Quito are very similar, as are Cali and Barranquilla and Medellín, Guayaquil, and Maracaibo. Caracas is quite different from all other cities but it resembles the other capital cities, especially Santiago and Lima, more than any of the non-capital cities. The overall index Δ incorporates $\Delta_{f,n}$ (that is, $\Delta \geq \Delta_{f,n}$) and adds the effect of differences at lower levels of aggregation. The pairs of cities that are most similar are Barranquilla-Cali, Cali-Medellín, Bogotá-Medellín, Guayaquil-Barranquilla, and Guayaquil-Quito. Santiago is fairly similar to Quito; otherwise, Santiago, Lima, Caracas, and Maracaibo differ considerably among themselves and also from each of the six cities in Colombia and Ecuador.

Three factors appear to have the greatest influence on the degree of similarity in budget structures: real income level, relative prices (as suggested by the tendency of cities in the same country to be similar), and location, which is associated with climate. The ten cities include four in the interior, at altitudes above 3,000 feet (Bogotá, Cali, Medellín, and Quito), and six at lower altitudes which are on the seacoast (Barranquilla, Guayaquil, Lima, and Maracaibo) or are separated from it only by a low, narrow mountain range (Santiago and Caracas). To separate the effects of these three factors, Δ and $\Delta_{f,n}$ were regressed on income differences between pairs of cities (the variable $\Delta \log Y$ is the absolute value of the difference in the logarithms of median real income, from table 2-3) and on dummy variables indicating whether the two cities are in different coun-

---

for comparisons of Bogotá, Caracas, Lima, and Asunción, Paraguay. The categories were slightly redefined for this comparison and do not correspond exactly to those in table 4-3; in particular, food and beverages was not disaggregated. More important, the household was redefined to incorporate secondary units and supplementary members.

tries (D) or in different geographic groups (G). The results of the analysis are as follows (standard errors of regression coefficients in parentheses):

$$\Delta = 23.13 + 7.73\ D + 1.54\ G + 11.46\ \Delta \log\ Y;$$
$$\quad\ \ (2.67)\quad(2.55)\qquad(1.94)\qquad(4.45)$$
$$R^2 \text{ adjusted} = 0.264$$

$$\Delta_{f,n} = \quad 9.87 + 0.11\ D - 2.35\ G + 29.79\ \Delta \log\ Y.$$
$$\qquad\quad(3.64)\quad(3.48)\qquad(2.65)\qquad(6.08)$$
$$R^2 \text{ adjusted} = 0.338$$

Geographic location does not affect either index significantly, but country differences are important for the overall dissimilarity. The effect of real income differences is most apparent in the index $\Delta_{f,n}$. This index contributes little to total dissimilarity between some cities, but it accounts for more than three-quarters of the total index Δ, for ten of the forty-five pairs of cities (including Bogotá-Cali and Caracas-Maracaibo, pairs in the same country).

Indexes of dissimilarity can be computed not only for any desired disaggregation of the total budget, but also for any portion of the budget. It is particularly interesting to measure the dissimilarity among cities in the composition of the food and nonfood budgets. Since income differences show up most strongly in the food-nonfood index, $\Delta_{f,n}$, the indexes for the different parts of the budget might be expected to be more sensitive to differences in location. This turns out to be the case: income differences are insignificant, while the variable D (country differences) is significant for both partial indexes. Geographic location (seacoast or interior) is never significant, but there is a marked tendency for housing to take a larger share of the nonfood budget in interior cities than on the coast.[10]

Variability of Budget Shares

The combination of forty-three expenditure categories and eleven classifying variables produces an enormous number of individual budget shares g_r.[11] The complete set for each country is presented in the corre-

10. This analysis is extended in Philip Musgrove, "The Structure of Household Spending in South American Cities: Indexes of Dissimilarity and Causes of Inter-City Differences," *Review of Income and Wealth*, vol. 23 (December 1977), pp. 365–84.

11. Altogether there are 21,669 shares by household group, or 1,763 per city or country when all categories and variables are defined. The initial analysis for Colom-

sponding national monograph; here only some of the results are considered.

The budget shares have two chief analytical uses. One is to show which factors or characteristics have the greatest influence on the distribution of the household budget—that is, for which classifying variables the greatest differences exist among classes in the way households allocate spending. The other use is to show which categories of expenditure are most sensitive to differences among households. These two approaches are combined in the analysis that follows.

An Index of Variation

The set of values g_r are of interest here to the extent that they vary appreciably among classes in the population. When there is little difference among household groups, it is enough to know the aggregate shares presented in table 4-3. The variability of the budget share for category r, among classes k of the classifying variable v, can be measured by the percentage relative mean deviation from the overall share g_r. This statistic is

$$\xi_{rvc} = (100/n_v g_{rc}) \sum_{k=1}^{n_v} |g_{rcvk} - g_{rc}|,$$

where c indicates the city or country and n_v is the number of classes defined by the variable v. The share g_{rcvk} refers only to households in class k. The relative mean deviation resembles the index of dissimilarity in using absolute values of differences in budget shares, but it is summed across household groups rather than across expenditure categories, and the comparison is made for one city or country rather than between pairs. (There is, of course, no upper bound to the statistic, nor does it give a measure of statistical significance.) Although g_{rc} and g_{rcvk} are weighted shares, no further use is made of the weights in calculating ξ_{rvc}. A large difference between the budget share in the population and the corresponding share in some group of households is regarded as important even if there are few households in that group.

The logic of this index is as follows: if a variable v is associated with large differences in the budget share allocated to category r, then the

---

bia had many more values, since there were ten income groups, nine household size classes, eleven occupational groups, and so on. See Rafael Prieto D., *Estructura del Gasto y Distribución del Ingreso Familiar en Cuatro Ciudades Colombianas, 1967–1968*, Parte Tercera, Anexo A Estadístico (Bogotá: Universidad de los Andes, 1971).

shares g_{rcvk} should differ substantially among the different classes k. Therefore, at least some classes will show large differences from the mean share g_{rc} taken over all households. If a variable has no influence on how spending is allocated to category r, g_{rcvk} should equal g_{rc} for all classes k, and the index will be zero. Dividing the sum of absolute differences by g_{rc} simply takes account of the fact that the budget share is systematically much larger for some categories than for others, and it is variation relative to the mean share that is of interest. Dividing by n_v is necessary because some variables define more different classes than others.

The statistic ξ_{rvc} measures variation among classes in much the same way as a regression equation with dummy variables identifying the different classes, but with some important differences: only one variable at a time is considered, and all comparisons are made to the mean budget share rather than to the share in a "base" class. The index is an overall measure of variation; it does not indicate *which* classes differ most from the mean, just as the index Δ discussed earlier does not show which categories contribute most to the total dissimilarity.

If the analysis is limited to twenty-six expenditure categories (thirteen food and thirteen nonfood), there are between 234 and 286 values of ξ_{rvc} in each city or country. Since the index is computed only to identify which categories and variables require analysis, it is not necessary to evaluate them for all ten cities. The relative mean deviations are computed only for Bogotá, Santiago, Quito, Lima, and Maracaibo (Caracas is omitted because trimester and life cycle data are not available). Table 4-5 presents the (unweighted) averages ξ_{rv}, which summarize the variability of each category r according to each classifying variable v.[12] Quito is omitted from the average for public transport expenditures.

The highly aggregated results shown in table 4-5 condense the information on budget structures so much that they must be interpreted with cau-

---

12. Averaging over all ten cities would overrepresent Colombia and underrepresent Chile and Peru. The indexes could be computed for each country, but some effects might be lost in the aggregation. This would occur if g_{rcvk} exceeds g_{rc} for one city in a country, while for the same r, v, and k, g_{rcvk} is less than g_{rc} in another city. It would also occur if the relation between the variable v and some other important variable, such as income, differed between the two cities. The five cities studied include the extremes of altitude and (almost) of latitude in the sample; two are interior cities, and three are on or near the coast. The chief respect in which they do not represent the entire group of ten cities is size: none of the three smallest cities, all in Colombia, is included.

tion. There is no a priori distribution of the statistic ξ_{rv}: the distribution obtained for the 286 values in the table has a median of 15 percent, with the first and third quartiles at about 9 and 25 percent, respectively. I consider, somewhat arbitrarily, that any variation over 20 percent is large enough to examine, and any statistic over 50 percent is very large. A few expenditure categories—dairy products, meat, fruits, other foods, nondurables, clothing, and other consumption items—show very stable shares; ξ_{rv} does not exceed 20 percent for any of these variables.[13] At the other extreme, ξ_{rv} frequently exceeds 50 percent for spending on services, vehicle operation, communication, and gifts and transfers. There is less, though still considerable, variation in the shares devoted to alcoholic beverages, meals away from home, durable goods, and education.

Factors Associated with Variation

When ξ_{rv} is high for most or all variables v, for a category r, there is probably a great deal of essentially random variation among households. The more interesting cases are those in which the variation is large for some variables, which may be presumed to cause or account for the differences in budget shares, and small for unrelated variables. In some cases, of course, there are interactions among the variables analyzed; the cause of variability may best be represented by a combination of several characteristics, rather than by one of them alone.

If 20 percent is taken as a threshold, the most powerful explanatory or discriminatory variables are education and income. Life cycle, occupation, housing tenure, and number of children are slightly less powerful. Employment status, age, household size, and trimester are associated with high variability in only a few expenditure categories.

Household income is considered first here, since, together with prices, it determines what the household can buy. There are actually four income-related variables in table 4-5; besides current income quartile, families are classified according to the education, occupation, and age of the head. All these are significantly associated with income, and the extent to which they explain variation in the size of budget shares is directly related to the strength of their association with income, an association that is more

---

13. The variability for housing exceeds 20 percent only when households are classified by tenure.

Table 4-5. *Variability in Individual Mean Expenditure Shares, by Spending Category, Eleven Variables*[a]
Percent

Spending category	Income	Education	Occu-pation	Head employed	Spouse employed	Dwelling tenure	Age	Life cycle	Household size	Number of children	Trimester
Dairy products and eggs	9.9	11.3	8.0	3.2	3.9	8.6	5.6	13.3	7.6	6.7	3.8
Cereals	26.0[b]	31.4[b]	22.8[b]	5.7	5.2	12.3	4.6	18.1	16.3	24.1[b]	4.8
Meat and poultry	11.3	13.9	9.0	3.6	4.0	4.9	5.5	7.5	6.9	6.2	5.9
Seafood	21.7	24.5	19.8	25.3	5.9	17.1	13.1	15.6	14.5	21.0	20.2
Vegetables and tubers	25.4[b]	31.6[b]	22.2[b]	3.4	5.0	13.7	5.4	11.7	11.1	23.0	6.0
Fruits	6.1	9.4	8.7	3.4	2.8	8.2	6.3	10.0	8.6	9.9	8.7
Fats and oils	23.7[b]	26.6[b]	21.1[b]	3.7	4.7	11.1	4.6	9.6	5.7	14.2	6.1
Sugar and sweets	23.3[b]	27.7[b]	20.0	4.2	6.1	13.2	5.2	13.7	12.9	20.6	4.7
Hot beverages	23.0[b]	29.6[b]	19.3[b]	2.4	5.9	12.0	6.2	10.5	7.5	7.3	6.7
Alcoholic beverages	24.7[b]	28.0[b]	18.0	12.6	12.3	28.0	24.0[b]	33.7[b]	19.8	27.6	15.1
Other beverages	13.5	23.8	17.3	12.4	10.2	22.0	13.8	23.2[b]	14.4	20.9[b]	21.8
Other foods	18.3	14.5	14.6	5.8	7.3	12.7	14.8	16.2	9.6	14.2	9.9
Meals away from home	**18.3**	28.2	15.7	19.3	9.5	30.8[b]	16.5	34.8[b]	25.8	25.9[b]	12.7
Housing	**12.1**	15.7	13.7	16.5	5.4	24.6	15.5	19.0	13.8	12.0	4.8
Durable goods	33.9[b]	31.8[b]	17.7	13.3	15.6	20.5	36.3[b]	39.8[b]	14.2	19.6	19.9[b]

Nondurables	3.3	9.9	7.6	13.3	7.6	11.2	2.2	6.2	8.6	15.4	12.1
Services	10.5	33.0[b]	22.4	30.7[b]	16.2	32.9	19.3	11.4	72.9[b]	100.9	66.0
Clothing	17.7	8.8	8.4	15.1	13.2	11.2	9.3	10.3	5.9	13.7	14.4
Medical care	15.6	16.4	17.8	26.9[b]	17.1	17.0	17.9	16.2	22.4[b]	26.8	17.3
Education	21.5[b]	19.0	32.7[b]	54.7[b]	30.8[b]	12.8	11.2	14.3	32.4[b]	38.7[b]	32.5[b]
Recreation and culture	9.0	19.6[b]	13.9	24.1	14.8	12.4	4.9	12.9	24.5[b]	31.9[b]	27.8[b]
Vehicle operation	19.4[b]	38.1[b]	32.4[b]	52.3[b]	31.3	38.2[b]	33.2[b]	28.2[b]	91.0[b]	126.6[b]	89.3[b]
Public transportation	14.2	10.3	18.8	20.1	18.9	21.2	14.1	15.1	13.1	24.5	23.6
Communication	10.5	47.8[b]	26.2[b]	55.9[b]	39.5[b]	31.3[b]	14.9	31.5[b]	70.5[b]	92.6[b]	66.6[b]
Other consumption	6.9	7.4	10.4	15.3	7.0	7.6	4.6	8.5	7.0	12.4	9.4
Gifts and transfers	30.0	33.3[b]	30.6[b]	49.0[b]	22.5[b]	23.4[b]	20.3[b]	18.7	47.5[b]	67.1[b]	54.8[b]

Source: Calculated from the individual mean budget shares in table 4-3; original ECIEL calculations.
a. Average for Bogotá, Santiago, Quito, Lima, and Maracaibo.
b. Variation exceeds 20.0 in three of the five cities.

powerful than any independent effect these variables may have on spending.

Educational level explains more variability than income quartile, except for expenditure on other foods and durables. Education classes are of unequal size, which allows for a sharper separation of income levels. The exception for durables may be due to purchases related to transitory incomes; education is a better measure of permanent than of current income and does not account for transitory effects.[14] Income, in turn, is a more powerful variable than occupation, except for seven categories, and three of these are among the four most variable types of spending. Age is associated with more variation than income only for housing and durable goods; both the latter are categories in which a pure age effect, unrelated to income, might be expected. The fact that occupation and age generally explain less variation than income does suggests that, with few exceptions, these variables do not account for large differences in tastes or needs. (The case of education is perhaps more complicated.)

There are some significant economies of scale in household consumption, particularly for housing, housing services, and durable and semidurable goods. The level of welfare attained therefore depends on both total income and the size of the household. Because of the scale effects, income per person is an imperfect measure of welfare, but it is undoubtedly preferable to total income. Consequently, it is surprising that household size (total number of members) appears to account for so little variation in budget shares; ξ_{rv} exceeds 20 percent only six times, nearly always for nonfood categories (meals away from home, the only food category, includes a large component of services).[15]

When ξ_{rv} is compared for the variables number of members and number of children, some rather surprising results emerge. In eighteen out of twenty-six categories, the number of children explains spending variation better than total family size, which appears to be more important only for dairy products, meat, housing, medical care, education, and other items of consumption. The latter tend to be categories with relatively high expenditure elasticities (see chapter 6, table 6-1). Although size is impor-

14. Note, however, that the marginal spending on durables out of transitory or windfall income is low; see chapter 3.

15. This is also the only category for which ξ_r (size) is appreciably larger than ξ_r (income).

tant only for nonfood spending, the number of children leads to a high ξ_{rv} for seven out of thirteen food categories and for only four nonfood categories. It is particularly striking that household size seems more important than number of children for spending on medical care, education, and milk products, categories for which children might be expected to account for most of a family's needs. What these results appear to demonstrate is the importance of income per capita. Children (fourteen or younger) in general add little to household income, while adults are likely to have some employment (or capital or transfer income in the case of older adults). Thus, unless they include many adults, households with large numbers of children will have lower per capita incomes than large households generally. Children generate needs, but these needs are not translated into effective demand unless income is high enough. The allocation of the budget varies with household size even if income per person is constant, but it varies more with income per capita than with size alone.

As noted earlier, age and life cycle are treated as equivalent in many studies, although they differ in that life cycle is based on household composition and is not strictly associated with age. In the results shown in table 4-5, life cycle accounts for more variability than age in every expenditure category. Of course, there are exceptions, which the averages given in this table do not show. In each city analyzed, the effects of age exceed those of life cycle on certain expenditure items. There is no pattern to these exceptions; only meat, other food, housing, and clothing are affected more than once. The larger number of classes for life cycle than for age (six versus four) makes it easier to isolate differences among households for this variable, even though the measure of variability is normalized for the number of classes. The major influence, however, is probably the inclusion of family composition.

For neither classifying variable does ξ_r exceed 20 percent for any category of food expenditure (as distinct from alcoholic and other beverages and meals away from home). Excluding a few highly variable categories— services, communication, and transfers—the substantial age or life cycle effects are limited to relatively long-lived purchases: durable goods, education, and private vehicles. For some categories (medical care and recreation), which are dependent on household composition or on the ages of members other than the head, life cycle is important but age is not. This suggests that life cycle is a more valuable criterion by which to classify households than age, and it will be analyzed more fully later in this chapter. Age is more strongly associated with income, but not necessarily with income per person.[16]

The two factors that emerge as most important in this comparison are the income of the household and its composition, where composition includes size and the proportions of adults and children. Life cycle combines household composition and age effects, since it is defined by the age of the oldest child in the family. Chapter 5 discusses the effects of these variables in some detail. The remaining variables are discussed below.

Seasonal Effects

Of the variables examined in table 4-5, ten characterize individual households and one, trimester, is a feature of the sample. The surveys were taken at quarterly intervals throughout twelve months or longer (in every city except Caracas) to capture seasonal or temporal effects.[17] Analysis of budget shares rather than of absolute expenditures should detect mostly seasonal variation or changes caused by large shifts in relative prices; homogeneous changes in all prices and incomes resulting from inflation should have no effect. Trimester appears, in table 4-5, to be associated with significant variation in budget shares for no more than seven categories: seafood, other beverages, durables, clothing, education, vehicle operation, and gifts and transfers.[18] For private transport, ξ_{rv} is lower for trimester than for any other classifying variable, so this category can be ignored. The apparent seasonal variation for seafood and beverages is probably also random, and is limited to just a few cities. At most, four

16. The Engel curve analysis in chapter 6 is based on age because that variable is available for all cities and countries and because fewer variables are required in the regressions. Age rather than life cycle is also examined for Colombia, Peru, and Venezuela (with no distinction by city) in ECIEL, "Urban Household Income and Consumption Patterns in Latin America: A Comparative Analysis of Colombia, Paraguay, Peru and Venezuela" (Brookings Institution, 1974; processed), pp. V-24–V-34. The results by city can be found in the national monographs for Colombia and Venezuela.

17. This is important to obtain representative annual or quarterly spending estimates, even if seasonal analysis is of limited interest.

18. At a sufficiently disaggregated level there are undoubtedly seasonal differences in spending on some food categories, but these differences are lost in the present analysis, where all fruits are combined, as are all vegetables.

categories show the seasonal differences one might expect: durables, clothing, education, and transfers.

This variation is difficult to compare across cities, because the "quarters" during which interviews were taken fall at different times of the year and differ greatly in length. Interviewing was continuous or even overlapping among quarters in Chile, Peru, and Ecuador, but was confined to intervals of one month in Colombia and one week in Maracaibo. Account must also be taken of the different reference periods for different expenditures in deciding when to expect a seasonal increase or decrease.[19]

First, do gifts and transfers increase in the quarter(s) including Christmas? These expenditures should rise if they consist largely of gifts, but not if they consist of transfers that are made regularly. The following table compares the mean budget share in the Christmas quarter(s) with the mean of the shares in the remaining quarters for each city, and shows the standard deviation for the other quarters:

	Christmas quarter(s)		*Other quarters*
Bogotá	4th	1.35	0.64 (0.07)
Barranquilla	4th	0.62	0.70 (0.26)
Cali	4th	1.32	0.70 (0.19)
Medellín	4th	1.16	0.85 (0.37)
Santiago	1st and 2d	0.46	0.14 (0.01)
Quito	2d	2.02	1.93 (0.36)
Guayaquil	2d	2.56	3.13 (0.66)
Lima	4th	0.27	0.51 (0.07)
Maracaibo	3d	0.37	0.30 (0.11)

Evidently, there is a holiday effect in Bogotá, Cali, Santiago, and perhaps Medellín, but not elsewhere. In Ecuador, transfers are much more important than gifts and show no seasonal pattern. In Lima, these expenditures are relatively lowest around Christmas, perhaps in response to an increase in the share devoted to food. This may be largely a relative price effect.

There are fairly pronounced seasonal variations in educational spending, although these differ in form among countries. In Colombia, the share is high in the first and fourth quarters (winter and spring) and low in the

19. Trimester presents less of an analytic problem than some other variables, however, because it is not correlated with such factors as age, income, household size, or employment status. The samples were tested, and adjusted as necessary, for such associations. See appendix A.

second and third (summer and fall). It is high in the third quarter only (spring) in Santiago, in the second quarter (autumn) in Maracaibo, and in the second quarter also (winter) in Quito, and in Lima, there is one particularly low quarter (the fourth, including winter holidays). In Guayaquil, spending is high in the fourth quarter (summer and early fall) and low in the second (winter)—just when it is highest in Quito. The timing of vacations, the proportions of children attending public versus private schools, and the schedule for paying fees all affect how these expenditures are distributed through the year. Typically, in Colombia, Santiago, and Maracaibo, the highest share is about double the lowest; it is slightly less than double the lowest share in Quito and Lima.

Table 4-6 shows the budget shares devoted to durables and clothing, arranged in calendar order from approximately midwinter to autumn. (In Colombia, the spring quarter is actually the fourth survey interval and came in the year after the winter, summer, and autumn surveys.)[20]

There appears to be a striking seasonal pattern for expenditure on clothing in Ecuador, but this may be spurious. The period of reference was changed (from annual to quarterly) after the first survey interval (the autumn quarter), and, despite efforts to adjust for this change, the first trimester expenditures may still be overstated. The same problem occurs for purchases of durables, particularly in Guayaquil. In Lima, both durables and clothing were purchased in relatively large amounts in the first (winter) quarter, but this is probably not a seasonal effect but a reflection of a peak of purchases of such goods in response to a surge of inflation following the devaluation of September 1967.[21] Durables and semidurables appear to have been bought as saving substitutes and not simply for consumption. Colombia shows a concentration of clothing expenditure in the fourth (spring) quarter, which may be primarily seasonal since durables are not similarly affected. Santiago and Maracaibo show no particular pattern. Overall, at the level of aggregation used here, there are seldom large differences among trimesters. Hence, the procedure of averaging estimates across the survey year, which is followed in most of this analysis, does not seriously misrepresent spending behavior.

20. Winter always implies the northern hemisphere definition, December to February, although this is the warmer season in Lima and Santiago.

21. See Howard Howe and Philip Musgrove, "An Analysis of ECIEL Household Budget Data for Bogotá, Caracas, Guayaquil, and Lima," in Constantino Lluch, Alan A. Powell, and Ross A. Williams, eds., *Patterns in Household Demand and Saving* (New York: Oxford University Press for the World Bank, 1977), pp. 187–91.

Table 4-6. *Individual Budget Shares for Durables and Clothing as a Function of Season,*[a] *Nine Latin American Cities*
Percent

City and spending category	Winter	Spring	Summer	Autumn
Bogotá				
Durables	2.02	2.21	1.17	2.25
Clothing	6.73	11.45	4.90	6.22
Barranquilla				
Durables	1.96	1.31	1.59	1.68
Clothing	5.56	9.56	4.78	3.68
Cali				
Durables	2.06	1.45	1.49	1.58
Clothing	5.33	10.31	5.02	4.99
Medellín				
Durables	1.16	1.02	1.07	0.95
Clothing	5.05	5.06	4.02	3.28
Santiago				
Durables	4.13	2.84	3.45	5.32
Clothing	10.86	11.60	12.58	11.67
Quito				
Durables	3.61	3.10	2.20	2.40
Clothing	9.37	8.14	9.19	14.17
Guayaquil				
Durables	3.10	1.57	0.84	4.66
Clothing	5.00	6.00	5.17	9.86
Lima				
Durables	7.27	6.90	4.59	4.68
Clothing	9.97	6.99	6.98	7.57
Maracaibo				
Durables	4.55	3.82	4.43	2.73
Clothing	5.50	3.79	2.65	2.69

Source: Original ECIEL calculations based on the survey data.
a. The survey trimesters corresponding to the seasons are: Colombia: 1, 4, 2, 3; Chile and Ecuador: 2, 3, 4, 1; Peru: 1, 2, 3, 4; and Venezuela: 3, 4, 1, 2.

Household Characteristics and Budget Allocation

The household characteristics discussed here are educational level, employment status, and housing tenure. Each of these variables appears to affect only certain kinds of expenditures. Education, of course, affects the total budget through increased income, but has an additional effect on spending patterns for educational or quasi-educational items. The employment status of neither the household head nor of the spouse appreciably affects budget allocation, though a few expenditure items are affected. Housing tenure (owned, rented, or other) affects many more budget categories, but this effect is primarily a function of income. Households that neither own nor rent have much lower incomes than owners or renters in Colombia, Chile, Peru, and Caracas, but there are large differences in income between owners and renters in Ecuador and in Maracaibo.

Schooling Level and Educational and Cultural Spending

One expects that educated parents will devote a larger share of their resources to educating their children than will less educated parents, because schooling creates or changes tastes.[22] Similarly, more educated households might spend larger shares on quasi-educational materials and activities—books, magazines, newspapers, and cultural events, excluding sports. Table 4-7 shows the individual budget shares for these two categories—education and cultural items—at each educational level and in each city.

For both categories, budget shares rise as schooling increases, often doubling or tripling. Otherwise, there is no particular pattern. Educational spending is always high relative to quasi-educational spending in Colombia and Ecuador, slightly less high in Peru and Venezuela, and of comparable size or even smaller in Chile.[23] The educational share rises faster than the quasi-educational share across schooling classes in five cities, and the reverse is true in the other five. There is some indication that educational spending expands more rapidly when real incomes are low (as in Ecuador) and that at higher incomes schooling is complemented by a rapid increase of quasi education (as in Venezuela). Colombia, Chile, and Peru fit neither of these patterns.[24] Expenditure on cultural goods tends to

22. This effect can be observed, of course, only if account is also taken of income and of the number and ages of children in the family. Also, it may be that the education of the mother—or even perhaps of an older sibling—is more important in this respect than the schooling of the household head, who is usually the father. Since level of education is divided into only four classes, it seems reasonable to suppose that the levels of schooling of spouses are highly correlated.

23. The educational share is of course very sensitive to the price of private schooling and the ratio of public to private school enrollment.

24. Cali is a conspicuous exception. Spending on cultural items is comparable at every level to that in the other Colombian cities, but spending on education is always lower than elsewhere in Colombia and rises much less than in the other cities.

Table 4-7. *Educational and Cultural Individual Budget Shares as a Function of Educational Level of the Head of Household, Ten Latin American Cities*

Percent

City and spending category	Education			
	None	*Primary*	*Secondary*	*Higher*
Bogotá				
Education	2.49	4.75	5.51	5.91
Reading and culture	0.31	0.41	0.66	1.39
Barranquilla				
Education	1.20	3.07	4.65	6.34
Reading and culture	0.25	0.54	0.85	1.20
Cali				
Education	1.18	2.42	3.26	2.77
Reading and culture	0.16	0.60	0.83	1.22
Medellín				
Education	1.81	3.17	3.86	5.43
Reading and culture	0.16	0.33	0.72	1.10
Santiago				
Education	0.58	0.47	0.81	1.83
Reading and culture	1.11	1.17	1.23	1.90
Quito				
Education	0.31	1.00	1.84	2.27
Reading and culture	0.28	0.39	0.58	0.82
Guayaquil				
Education	0.82	1.63	2.11	2.18
Reading and culture	0.53	0.66	0.83	0.87
Lima				
Education	1.14	1.25	1.76	2.82
Reading and culture	1.10	1.15	1.24	1.34
Caracas				
Education	2.81	2.40	3.92	5.15
Reading and culture	0.43	0.46	0.59	0.86
Maracaibo				
Education	1.05	1.53	2.13	2.72
Reading and culture	0.23	0.42	0.82	1.13

Source: Original ECIEL calculations based on the survey data.

Table 4-8. *Ratios Comparing Individual Mean Expenditure Shares, Employed Spouse and Spouse Not Employed, Various Spending Categories, Ten Latin American Cities*

Spending category	Bogotá	Barranquilla	Cali	Medellin	Santiago	Quito	Guayaquil	Lima	Caracas	Maracaibo
Food and beverages	0.97	1.02	0.97	1.06	0.90	1.06	0.95	0.97	0.93	0.94
Meals away from home	1.24	1.41	1.63	1.18	1.15	1.27	1.24	1.19	0.87	0.87
All housing	0.78	0.77	0.96	0.83	0.91	0.91	0.99	0.88	0.86	0.99
Furnishings and operation	1.54	1.06	1.23	1.26	1.36	0.94	1.25	1.02	1.26	1.03
Durable goods	2.15	1.10	1.33	0.84	1.25	0.89	1.48	1.05	0.89	1.17
Nondurables	0.95	0.94	1.01	1.21	1.02	1.01	0.93	1.09	1.15	0.96
Services	1.52	1.23	1.40	1.73	2.01	1.09	1.20	0.88	1.54	0.67
All clothing	1.17	1.22	1.33	1.33	1.19	1.05	1.20	1.20	1.24	1.34
Women's clothing	1.17	1.36	1.06	1.47	1.26	1.01	1.39	1.51	1.28	1.65
Recreation and culture	1.35	1.01	1.06	1.16	1.06	1.04	0.94	1.02	1.05	0.96
Vehicle operation	2.55	0.65	0.30	0.10	1.54	0.59	1.27	1.38	1.08	1.72
Public transportation	1.27	1.72	1.05	1.11	1.11	n.a.	n.a.	1.10	1.14	0.86
Other consumption	1.00	0.95	1.19	1.00	1.12	0.75	1.05	0.96	0.99	1.08
Total expenditure	1.26	0.93	1.05	1.10	1.15	0.82	1.15	0.98	1.18	1.15

Source: Original ECIEL calculations based on the survey data.
n.a. Not available.

level off at around 1 percent of the budget, whereas educational spending rises to between 2 and 6 percent of the budget for the most educated households.

Employment Status

Table 4-8 compares the budget structures of households in which the spouse is employed with those in which he or she is not working[25] for thirteen of the twenty-six expenditure categories. (Because the classifying variable has only two classes, ratios rather than individual values are shown.) In most cities the employment status of the spouse is not associated with large differences in total spending (Bogotá, Quito, and Caracas show the greatest differences), so income effects are probably slight. Households in which the spouse works systematically spend a smaller share only on one expenditure category—housing.[26] This is probably because such households are usually formed of young adults with no children.

This same feature, age and household composition, may account for the systematically higher budget share for clothing, particularly for women's clothing, in such households. (Actually, two factors are at work: women who work need more clothing because they are in public more, and they also tend to be in the age groups with a high marginal propensity to spend on clothing and accessories.)[27]

It might also be expected that if the spouse is employed, the household will spend more on meals away from home and on transportation (particularly public transport to and from work). Both effects are found everywhere except in Venezuela; there, meals away from home decline in importance even as a share of the food budget, which is difficult to explain.

There is less of a pattern for other expenditures. Life cycle effects probably account for the tendency to spend more on durables when the spouse

25. The comparison here is not between employment and unemployment but between employment and nonemployment; the latter includes both the unemployed and people not in the labor market.

26. Guayaquil and Maracaibo appear to be exceptions, but these are cities in which households with an employed spouse spend an average of 15 percent more than other families (see table 4-1), and the housing share of the budget tends to rise slightly with total income or expenditure.

27. In seven of the nine cities where life cycle is defined, the clothing share of the budget is highest for households composed of a young married couple with no children.

is employed, although appliances may be bought specifically to compensate for the spouse having less time for housework. More also tends to be spent on services when the spouse is employed, which may be related both to having more durable goods and to such households' lower spending on housing; durable goods and services are to some extent substitutes in yielding domestic comfort.

The employment status of the household head appears to matter appreciably more than that of the spouse only for meals away from home, housing, recreation and culture, and public transport. These categories are examined in table 4-9. Relatively more is always spent on recreation and on meals away from home, and relatively less on housing when the head is employed. Transportation is quite variable. Income differences between households whose head is employed and those whose head is not employed are sometimes very large (over 30 percent in Barranquilla, Quito, and Maracaibo, all of which are relatively poor cities), and there are also marked differences in age and in sources of income. The nonemployed class includes many retired heads of households and, in general, has lower mean total spending. (In Ecuador, however, this class has higher expenditures on average, perhaps because relatively many families obtain all their income from capital.) The age effect creates sizable differences in such categories as clothing and durable goods, and also in educational spending.

Housing Tenure

Finally, there are some notable differences in budget allocation between households that rent and those that own their homes. Households that neither own nor rent are excluded from this comparison because they are relatively few in number and may differ greatly in income from other families. Of particular interest here are housing expenditure and the housing-related categories of furnishings and operation. Transportation is also of interest because it is related to location, which may be associated with tenure, and because owning a car may be either more or less likely for a family that owns its dwelling.[28] Expenditure on meals away from home is also likely to be related to location, as well as to household age

28. The evidence reviewed in chapter 3 suggests that homeowners are slightly more likely to own vehicles than nonowners, but no comparison is made specifically to renters; and the observed concentration (in Bogotá, Barranquilla, and Lima only) may be due primarily to income differences.

and size (and these factors in turn affect the probability of homeowner-ship).

As table 4-10 indicates, homeowning families tend to devote a large budget share to housing unless (as in Cali and Maracaibo) they are appreciably poorer on the average than renters.[29] But even then, the drop in housing's share of the total budget is less sharp than the drop in total spending observed between the two classes. It is not clear, since tenure and household size are not examined simultaneously, whether per person expenditure on housing also differs according to tenure. Homeowners tend to spend less on durables and—somewhat surprisingly—less on services, while there is little variation in expenditure on nondurables. This suggests that the additional outlay on housing is partly offset by decreased consumption of services within the dwelling (although in the case of durables, differences in age or length of tenure may be more important). If families buy most of their durables while young, only recent home buyers will be observed spending much in this category; older households are likely to have owned their dwellings longer and to have acquired most of their durables earlier. Owners tend also to eat out less, which again may be primarily an age effect.

It appears that owners spend less on private transport (operation only, not including vehicle purchases) in the largest cities, even when their incomes are higher, although the pattern is less clear for the smaller cities. There is some evidence that families paying for dwellings are less likely also to be paying to operate a car, but the evidence is slight. In any case, since these comparisons are based on imputed rent, they do not answer the question of how families finance the purchase of a home; such an analysis would be based on cash flows and would have to consider the entire budget.

Another way to examine the effect of housing tenure is to compare shares of the nonhousing budget. The comparison shows that owners and renters differ little in the budget shares spent on food and on other consumption items. With some exceptions, owners tend to spend less on furnishings and home operation, clothing, and recreation and culture, and more on education. Again, it is not clear how much difference would re-

29. Expenditure for homeowners is imputed rent, not mortgage payments. Households that own may have lower cash outlays on housing because many have paid off their mortgages; the ratio of cash housing expenditures between owners and renters probably is high for young families and declines with age.

Table 4-9. *Ratios Comparing Individual Expenditure Shares, Employed Head and Head Not Employed, Various Spending Categories, Ten Latin American Cities*

Spending category	Bogotá	Barranquilla	Cali	Medellín	Santiago	Quito	Guayaquil	Lima	Caracas	Maracaibo
Meals away from home	2.81	2.51	2.74	2.49	1.03	2.51	1.26	1.53	2.87	1.28
Housing	0.63	0.77	0.70	0.77	0.79	0.74	0.72	0.84	0.70	0.74
Recreation and culture	1.51	2.10	1.64	1.63	1.11	1.18	1.10	1.31	1.61	1.78
Public transportation	1.64	1.29	1.55	1.36	0.92	n.a.	n.a.	0.74	1.19	1.09
Total expenditure	1.06	1.45	0.96	1.00	1.15	0.69	0.80	1.12	0.88	1.42

Source: Original ECIEL calculations based on the survey data.
n.a. Not available.

Table 4-10. *Ratios Comparing Individual Expenditure Shares, Owned Dwelling and Rented Dwelling, Various Spending Categories, Ten Latin American Cities*

Spending category	Bogotá	Barranquilla	Cali	Medellín	Santiago	Quito	Guayaquil	Lima	Caracas	Maracaibo
Meals away from home	0.76	0.96	0.81	0.82	0.63	0.21	0.48	1.04	1.03	1.27
Housing	1.30	1.18	1.01	1.12	1.30	2.10	1.31	1.52	1.04	0.88
Durables	0.57	0.55	0.79	0.71	0.90	0.67	1.15	0.69	0.56	0.83
Nondurables	0.93	0.97	1.22	0.83	1.05	0.69	0.92	0.91	1.03	1.09
Services	0.82	0.66	0.62	1.17	0.87	1.09	1.05	1.09	1.18	0.29
Vehicle operation	0.50	1.14	1.19	1.11	1.10	2.73	0.90	0.91	0.86	0.63
Public transportation	0.88	1.16	1.23	0.76	0.94	n.a.	n.a.	1.14	1.02	1.32
Total expenditure	1.05	0.94	0.86	1.39	1.13	2.50	1.88	1.38	1.30	0.69

Source: Original ECIEL calculations based on the survey data.
n.a. Not available.

main after taking account of the effects of age, life cycle, and family size. At this level of aggregation, tenure does not explain the allocation of the budget well, except for the few categories closely related to housing.

The analysis in this chapter is in large measure exploratory, being designed to focus attention on a small number of variables that explain much of the variation in budget structure. The principal finding is that the allocation of the budget, at this level of aggregation, depends primarily on income and on the size and composition of the household. This can be interpreted to mean that spending is chiefly a function of income and of needs, both of which are relatively easy to define and measure, and that "tastes" unrelated to either of these factors are of little importance. This means, in turn, that to understand spending patterns it is necessary to take account of only a few variables, and that the most important of these are those traditionally regarded as fundamental (prices being the only basic variables not included in the analysis).[30]

For several reasons, this insistence on the primacy of incomes and needs should not be stressed. First, more subtle effects of cultural and personal preferences may be important at finer levels of disaggregation. Second, "needs" are not well defined except for basic categories such as food, and many households spend far in excess of needs even on those categories. The strong association between budget structure and household composition means that needs are defined socially rather than biologically and therefore incorporate some measure of preferences. What is important is that these preferences are relatively stable in each country and quite similar among countries. Third, variables other than income and family composition clearly are significant determinants of spending on some categories, although they affect most categories very little. The clearest examples are age patterns in spending on durables and clothing and the effects of employment on clothing and some smaller categories. Finally, there is clear evidence that budget structures are more alike between cities in the same country or in the same geographic location. Both effects could be the result more of similarity of relative prices than of basic cultural distinctions—although, of course, cultural preferences help shape prices through public decisions on taxes, subsidies, tariffs, and other measures.

---

30. A similar effort to classify households by a small number of variables so as to explain the allocation of the budget is presented in Lluch and others, *Patterns in Household Demand and Saving,* especially pp. xxi–xxxi and 240–47. This study considers fewer categories of expenditure but introduces price effects.

Much of what might appear to be differences among groups of families by social class or cultural factors is interpreted here as corresponding to differences in income, particularly permanent income: education, occupation, and age are all variables that may be associated with different tastes but that seem more important as determinants of income. The great importance of family size, and particularly of the number of children in the household, indicates that it is income per person and not total income that matters. Several otherwise paradoxical results become clear once this interaction is taken into account. These two features—income and household composition—are analyzed extensively in chapter 5 for their impact on spending in all categories of expenditure.

CHAPTER FIVE

Income, Household Composition, and Budget Structure

IN THIS CHAPTER, the effects of total income and family composition on the allocation of household budgets are considered. The analysis covers all categories of expenditure listed in tables 4-2 and 4-3. Income effects are treated first, followed by household composition effects. Finally, some methods of combining information about income and household composition are discussed. Since there are four variables related to income (education, income quartile, occupation, and age) and four variables related to family structure (size, number of children, life cycle, and age), not all the budget structures actually computed can be discussed here. Instead, one or more variables in each group have been selected for analysis.

Income and the Allocation of Spending

The choice of which variable to analyze depends on whether it is more valuable to study income directly or to study one or more of the household characteristics that appear to determine income. Age is a difficult variable to use, since it is associated with family composition as well as with income. Also, while income is related to the age of the household head, the relation varies among education levels. Education and occupation, the other two income-related variables, appear to have little associa-

157

tion with family structure and therefore seem reasonable alternatives to measured income as explanatory factors. However, occupation usually explains less of the variation in spending shares than does current income. Some kinds of expenditure, such as those for particular types of clothing, tools and equipment, and some education, are undoubtedly work-related, but at this level of aggregation they are unimportant. Education of the head is systematically more powerful than current income in explaining expenditure patterns, both because it separates income classes more clearly and because it removes much of the transitory variance of income. Nonetheless, current income quartile rather than schooling is analyzed here, for three reasons.

First, it is traditional to classify households by current income level, regardless of life cycle or family size. The use of this variable, despite its drawbacks, makes the ECIEL results more nearly comparable to those obtained from other surveys.[1] Second, income quartiles are somewhat easier to compare across cities and countries than are household variables and for a given country are all the same size. Third, global budget shares have been calculated for current income but not for any other classifying variable. These shares cannot be compared to the individual budget shares, except in Santiago and Lima, because they are based on quartiles defined for the individual cities.[2] They can, however, be used to describe the proportion of the demand for each category generated in each of the quartiles. In both cases, only city totals are examined, not country totals.

Individual Budget Structure by Income Quartile

Appendix tables C-1 through C-10 show the individual household budget shares g_{rcq} for each of forty-two categories in each of the ten cities.

1. It is increasingly recognized that current income should be adjusted for life cycle effects, or perhaps replaced altogether by estimated lifetime income, when describing income distribution. See Vladimir Stoikov, "How Misleading Are Income Distributions?" *Review of Income and Wealth,* vol. 21 (June 1975), pp. 239–50, and Morton Paglin, "The Measurement and Trend of Inequality: A Basic Revision," *American Economic Review,* vol. 65 (September 1975), pp. 598–609. It is less reasonable to try to apply such adjustments to expenditure analysis, because a large share of the family budget is spent on items such as food, which are always financed out of current income and meet current (short-run) demand.

2. This discrepancy exists because the two sets of budget structures were computed at different times and for different purposes. The global expenditure structures parallel the global income structures described in chapter 2.

The shares are exactly comparable to the averages over all income levels shown in table 4-3. It is hardly possible to analyze all these percentages; only certain expenditure categories and certain trends or patterns across income levels are considered here. The proportion of the budget spent on food always declines as income rises (except in Maracaibo), as do the components cereals and vegetables. Similarly, the budget share devoted to nondurables always falls, while that for household services always rises. The share for housing tends to rise with income, sometimes increasing sharply in the richest quartile. Transfers almost always account for a larger share of spending as income increases, and public transportation almost always takes a smaller share. Other categories of expenditure show less regular behavior. There are upward trends, for example, in spending on both durables and clothing, though with exceptions in one or both categories in Barranquilla, Cali, Quito, Lima, and Caracas. Expenditure on a few categories, such as insurance and private vehicles, is concentrated in the top quartile, with not much pattern at lower income levels.

It is somewhat difficult to evaluate the expenditure shares shown in tables C-1 through C-10 because the quartiles do not correspond to equal income intervals. It is not immediately clear, for instance, whether the decline in the food share from 47 to 36 percent between the third and fourth quartiles in Bogotá is a large or a small decrease. The income range defining each quartile also differs among countries in real terms, and in Colombia, Ecuador, and Venezuela the proportions of the population found in each quartile also differ among cities.

To aid comparison among cities and to allow for the "stretching" of quartiles in each city, median income is calculated within each quartile in each city. These values are given in table 5-1 in national currency and (using the parity exchange rates explained in chapter 2) in U.S. dollars. These levels do not correspond to comparable points in the overall income distribution of each city.[3] Rather, they are computed in order to relate budget shares to specific income levels, wherever these may occur in the

3. For example, the first quartile median in Maracaibo is nearly as high as that in Caracas, which is a much richer city. However, the first quartile in Venezuela contains 45.78 percent of the population of households in Maracaibo while the same income range in Caracas includes only 17.61 percent of the households there. Households with incomes below 1,750 bolívars per trimester are then only 8.8 percent of the population of Caracas (half of 17.61 percent, since the median is defined as the level with half the population below it), whereas in Maracaibo fully 22.89 percent of all households have incomes below 1,586 bolívars per trimester.

Table 5-1. *Median Household Income in National Currency per Trimester and U.S. Dollars per Year, by Income Quartile, Ten Latin American Cities*

City and currency	Income quartile			
	First	Second	Third	Fourth
Bogotá				
Pesos	2,360	3,936	6,748	14,245
Dollars	1,037	1,729	2,965	6,259
Barranquilla				
Pesos	2,504	4,096	6,490	15,370
Dollars	1,100	1,800	2,852	6,754
Cali				
Pesos	2,341	4,327	6,748	13,795
Dollars	1,029	1,901	2,965	6,062
Medellín				
Pesos	2,402	4,192	6,577	17,030
Dollars	1,055	1,842	2,890	7,483
Santiago				
Escudos	1,726	3,430	5,474	11,390
Dollars	942	1,871	2,987	6,214
Quito				
Sucres	2,297	4,514	8,533	18,406
Dollars	845	1,661	3,139	6,772
Guayaquil				
Sucres	2,435	4,726	8,250	20,730
Dollars	896	1,739	3,035	7,627
Lima				
Soles	7,960	15,189	26,725	57,605
Dollars	1,161	2,215	3,897	8,399
Caracas				
Bolívars	1,750	3,051	5,423	11,806
Dollars	1,602	2,793	4,964	10,806
Maracaibo				
Bolívars	1,586	2,991	4,943	10,553
Dollars	1,452	2,738	4,524	9,659

Sources: Interpolated from the data in table 2-1 (for national currency per trimester) and table 2-3 (for U.S. dollars per year).

distribution. The median is chosen as the best measure of the midpoint of a quartile, to which an average budget share might correspond.

Figure 5-1 relates quartile median incomes, in U.S. dollars, to quartile mean budget shares for food and beverages. While this relation differs in height (that is, percentage of expenditure) among cities, it is nearly al-

Figure 5-1. *Food Budget Shares by Median Income in Each Quartile*

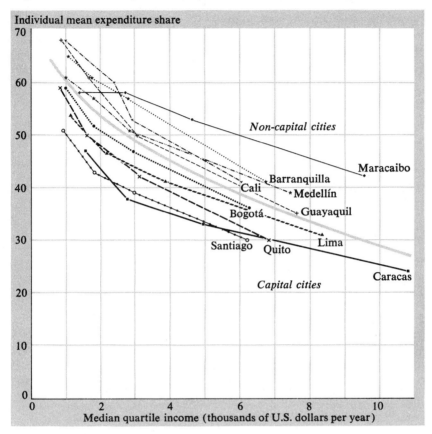

ways strikingly similar in shape. Only Maracaibo is an exception. The portion of the budget devoted to food drops about 6 percentage points as annual income rises from $1,000 to $2,000; drops another 8 points at $4,000; and then another 8 points to $8,000. The curves for Santiago and Caracas or for Cali and Medellín are almost indistinguishable. The whole curve is lower for all capital cities than for all non-capital cities, probably because of the higher incomes in the former. There is also a slight tendency for the range of shares to shrink as income rises (and price differences presumably become less important).

Figures 5-2 and 5-3 depict the same sort of relation between income level and budget share for two major components of the food budget:

Figure 5-2. *Cereal Budget Shares by Median Income in Each Quartile*

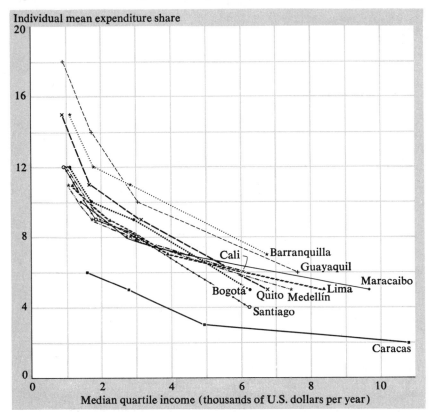

cereals, and meat and poultry. (These, together with vegetables and tubers, are usually the largest components of the food budget at low incomes; at higher incomes dairy products and eggs are often the second or third largest category.) There is a very similar pattern for spending on cereals in every city except Caracas; the share falls from a median of about 12 percent at an income of $1,000 a year to about 5 percent at $8,000. There is no clear difference between capital and non-capital or rich and poor cities in this budget pattern. In the case of meat and poultry, the pattern is much less regular, both within and among cities.[4] As income

4. The curves for meat and poultry may differ more among cities than those for cereals, because relative prices have much more effect on the budget share for meat. When the share of the budget is expressed as a function of the logarithm of consump-

Figure 5-3. *Meat and Poultry Budget Shares by Median Income in Each Quartile*

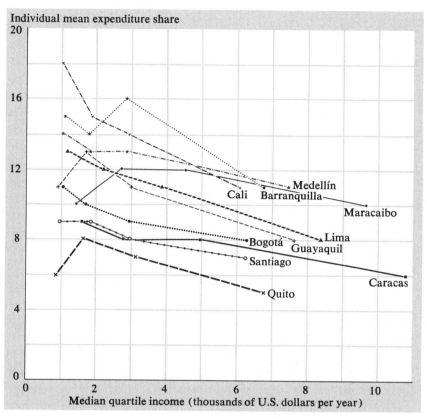

rises, the budget share devoted to meat and poultry decreases. However, in Quito, Guayaquil, and Maracaibo—all rather poor cities—the share rises between the first and second quartiles and then drops. Evidently there is an income level below which meat is not only a declining share of the diet but a declining fraction of total spending as well. The median budget share allocated to meat falls from about 11 percent at $1,000 to 8

tion per person and the logarithm of relative price, there is only an income effect for cereals but a smaller income effect and a very large price effect for meat and poultry. See Philip Musgrove, "Price and Income Effects on Budget Allocation: Comparisons Among and Within Latin American Cities" (Brookings Institution, January 1978; processed), table 2.

percent at $8,000; this is a change only from about 18 percent to about 23 percent of the median budget share for total food and beverages.

This analysis can be extended to other categories of spending, but a less consistent pattern is found among cities. The pattern for clothing is quite similar for five of the ten cities (Bogotá, Barranquilla, Cali, Guayaquil, and Lima), with an initial rise from roughly 5 to 7 percent of expenditure, followed by only a slight further increase as income rises beyond $3,000 a year.

The relation between income and budget share devoted to housing is extremely varied. The extremes are represented by Quito and Maracaibo, but (as discussed in chapter 2) these are cities in which the proportion of households owning their dwellings changes markedly as income rises, rising in Quito and falling in Maracaibo. Even in the remaining eight cities there is little pattern, except for similarities between Santiago and Caracas and between Cali and Lima. The share tends to be higher in the capital cities, which are usually larger and have higher rents, but the tendency is not very strong. The median share is about 20 percent at an income of $1,000 and about 25 percent at an income of $8,000.

Household furnishings and operation appear to increase their share of the budget fairly systematically as income rises. Durables tend to rise irregularly, services always rise, and nondurables always decline. The aggregate rises with income beyond a level of $4,000 a year; at lower incomes there are sharp variations in Santiago, Quito, and Lima, caused entirely by differences in expenditures on durables. This pattern may be an artifact of the sample, since it is somewhat difficult to get good estimates of infrequent large purchases and since these may be related to variations in transitory income.

It is difficult to extract any pattern for expenditure on durables, but it appears that such expenditures may increase only slightly relative to total spending at very low incomes ($1,000 to $2,000), then rise rather sharply in an intermediate range (up to $6,000 or $7,000), and thereafter level off or at least increase more slowly.

The budget shares for education show even more variation among cities, although there is a somewhat more consistent upward trend within each city. The most striking trend is the more than fourfold difference between the highest and the lowest share, at each income level. The intercity differences seem to be largely differences among countries, since the shares for different cities in one country lie relatively close together (although there is a large separation between Caracas and Maracaibo). This phenomenon is related to differences in what families must pay for schooling, which reflect international differences in the proportions of public and private schools and in national policies regarding the private cost of public schooling.[5]

While not an exhaustive analysis of the relation between income and budget structure, the preceding discussion, together with appendix tables C-1 to C-10, is as detailed as such highly aggregated information permits. The following section considers another facet of this relation: how total demand in each expenditure category is divided among income quartiles.

Global Expenditure Shares and Concentration by Income Level

The analysis of budget structure by income quartile can be repeated using global rather than individual mean shares: each share G_{rcq} would show the percentage of total spending by all the households in quartile q, in city c, devoted to category r. However, the procedure used in chapter 2 seems preferable, whereby these shares are transformed to show the proportion of total spending on category r in the city c, which is accounted for by the households in quartile q. These shares G^o_{rcq} are given in appendix tables C-11 through C-20. Both G_{rcq} and G^o_{rcq} can be thought of as fractions in which the numerator is actual spending on category r by the households in quartile q in city c. The denominator of G_{rcq} is total spending on all categories by those same households, whereas the denominator of G^o_{rcq} is total spending on category r only by all the households in all four quartiles in city c. The quartiles are defined for individual cities, not, as in tables C-1 through C-10, for countries. This makes the shares comparable among cities with respect to fractions of the population, although, of course, the income levels corresponding to the quartiles differ in real

5. This point is considered again later, in connection with the relation between educational expenditure and family size. Note that, for this purpose, differences in what it costs society to provide schooling are irrelevant; what matters is how much expenditure is required directly of households. The relation between schooling expenditure and total expenditure and family composition in these cities is analyzed more fully in Philip Musgrove, "La Contribución Familiar al Financiamiento de la Educación," paper presented to the Inter-American Development Bank Seminar on the Financing of Education in Latin America, Washington, D.C., November 15–19, 1976.

terms among cities. (The boundaries of the quartiles are compared, in U.S. dollars, in table 2-3.)[6]

The distribution of total expenditure on a particular category among the quartile groups depends on two factors: the relation between spending on that category and household income, and the distribution of income among all the households in the population. If income were distributed equally, and if the category budget shares were the same for all households, then the values of G^o_{rcq} in tables C-11 through C-20 would all be exactly 25 percent. If budget shares were similar among all households but incomes were unequal among households, then all the shares for a given quartile would be equal across categories, and would be equal to the proportion of total income obtained by the households in that quartile (shown in table 2-12).[7] Thus variations in G^o_{rcq} over categories (r) for a given quartile (q) reflect only the reallocation of the budget as income rises; variations among quartiles for a given category reflect both their reallocation and the fact that income is unequally distributed.

One other factor may have an important influence on these shares: this is the existence of different prices for what are ostensibly the same goods or services at different income levels. For example, if the poor are provided with medical care free or at very low cost, while richer households pay the full cost of private physicians and hospitals, the top quartile will account for a larger share of total spending than if all households pay the same prices. The same is true of educational spending if the children in poorer households attend public schools while the rich send their children to private schools. Subsidies or differential prices may also be available for housing.[8] However, differential prices are unlikely to be important for any of the other categories of expenditure analyzed here.

6. The global shares G_{rcq} (and decile shares G_{rcd} also) are presented in Junta del Acuerdo de Cartagena, "Grupo Andino: Distribución de Ingresos y Estructura del Consumo (Area Urbana)," Doc. J/PR/68 (Lima: March 15, 1976; processed).

7. Assuming, of course, a constant ratio of total spending to income. Allowing for an increasing tendency to save as income rises would lead to the shares all being equal within a quartile, but no longer equal to the quartile's share of total income.

8. A subsidy to a particular category of expenditure—cereal products, for example—does not by itself produce the shift in market shares just described *within* a category. Some income groups need to be subsidized more than others. A subsidy for cereals will, however, raise the share(s) of the top quartile(s) in total expenditure on *all* foods and beverages, and lower the share(s) of the lower quartile(s), since the latter households devote a larger share of their food budget to cereals.

The shares G^o_{rcq} indicate which households constitute the market for particular categories of goods and services, and especially whether demand is generated over the entire range of incomes or is highly concentrated among high-income households. With a few exceptions—always for categories constituting rather small shares of the total budget, and usually in comparisons between the first and second quartiles—G^o_{rcq} always rises with income. That is, each quartile accounts for a larger share of the market than any lower-income quartile. The shares vary greatly among categories and also, in some categories, among cities.

The richest quartile always accounts for the largest market share, ranging from about 30 percent for some food categories to 100 percent for private automobiles and insurance. The various expenditure categories can be classified by comparing G^o_{rc4} (the market share for the top quartile) with the income share for that quartile (from table 2-12). For the following categories, G^o_{rc4} is smaller than the income share, and is always below 50 percent: food and beverages (and their components, cereals, meat and poultry, vegetables and tubers, fats and oils, sugar and sweets, hot beverages), nondurable goods, and (except in Caracas) public transportation.

Other consumption (tobacco, personal care, and ceremonies) is alway consumed by the top quartile less than in proportion to their income share, but the market share sometimes exceeds 50 percent.

For the following categories, G^o_{rc4} exceeds the corresponding income share: furnishings and operation (except in Santiago and Lima); services; education (Lima is just barely an exception); vehicle operation (except in Caracas); communication (except in Caracas); insurance (except in Lima); and transfers (except in Quito). In addition, half or more of total spending for housing is nearly always generated in the richest quartile but, except in Quito and Guayaquil, the market share is less than the corresponding income share.

The market for durable goods is concentrated in the top quartile in Colombia and Ecuador, but the richest quartile of households account for only 53 percent of total demand in Caracas and 55 percent in Maracaibo, and for only 41–47 percent in Santiago and Lima. In the latter two cities this rather low concentration is probably due to purchases of durables by middle-income households as a form of saving in response to rapid or accelerated inflation. (The market share is 10 percent or less in the poorest quartile and rises to 20 percent or more in higher quartiles.) In Caracas

Table 5-2. *Income in National Currency per Trimester and U.S. Dollars per Year for Households in Tenth Expenditure Percentile, Various Spending Categories*

Spending category	Bogotá		Santiago		Quito		Lima		Caracas	
	Pesos	Dollars	Escudos	Dollars	Sucres	Dollars	Soles	Dollars	Bolivars	Dollars
Food	2,885	1,268	1,673	913	2,819	1,037	6,610	964	1,687	1,544
Housing	4,117	1,809	2,652	1,447	5,412	1,991	13,051	1,903	2,931	2,683
Durables	6,750	2,966	2,854	1,557	3,964	1,458	11,952	1,743	3,330	3,048
Nondurables	3,260	1,432	1,815	990	3,195	1,175	7,351	1,072	1,988	1,820
Services	6,725	2,955	5,315	2,900	7,405	2,724	17,979	2,621	3,843	3,517
Clothing	4,602	2,022	2,699	1,473	3,834	1,410	9,856	1,437	2,627	2,404
Medical care	5,127	2,253	2,431	1,326	3,630	1,335	7,809	1,139	3,401	3,113
Education	4,552	2,000	3,926	2,142	5,290	1,946	13,685	1,995	3,560	3,258
Vehicle operation	14,173	6,227	7,475	4,079	16,696	6,142	15,549	2,267	2,987	2,734
Public transport	2,996	1,316	1,768	965	n.a.	n.a.	9,178	1,338	3,517	3,219
Other	3,781	1,661	2,607	1,422	4,150	1,527	10,226	1,491	1,830	1,675

Source: Interpolated from data in tables C-11 through C-20.
n.a. Not available.

and perhaps also in Maracaibo, the low concentration of expenditure on durables reflects the low concentration, and high level, of income.

Another way to describe the concentration of the market is to estimate the income level $Y_r(90)$ such that 90 percent of all purchases are made by households with incomes above that level. (This is the tenth percentile of the distribution of purchases, measured from low to high incomes.) A precise estimate would require either computing the global budget structure for a large number of income classes or estimating both the income distribution and the relation between spending and income, so as to derive the income level analytically. The level is estimated here from information given by quartile in appendix tables C-11 to C-20 by linear interpolation. At low incomes this gives a systematic underestimate of the level desired, since below modal income the number of households decreases as income falls. At higher incomes, the estimate can be either too high or too low, depending on the shapes of the frequency distribution of income and of the Engel curve for the category analyzed.[9] Since the estimates are merely illustrative, only eleven expenditure categories are analyzed in table 5-2, and only for the five capital cities. For comparison among cities, the values are also converted to U.S. dollars.

It is immediately apparent that $Y_r(90)$ tends to be higher for a given category when the city is richer. The value is always highest in Caracas, except for expenditure on private vehicles. The richest 5 percent of all households account for 71 percent of spending on automobiles in Quito, 61 percent in Bogotá, 47 percent in Santiago, but only 20 percent in Lima and 15 percent in Caracas; automobile ownership penetrates to much lower income levels in the last two cities than in the first three. It is also evident, from the table and from the fourth-quartile expenditure shares shown in tables C-11 through C-20, that the market extends down to fairly low incomes, or encompasses the bulk of the population, only in "traditional" goods and services such as food, housing, clothing, nondurable goods, public transport, and other consumption. The more "modern" categories of expenditure toward which industrial development is oriented, particularly durable goods, vehicles, and services such as electricity, are

9. The city income distributions are all approximately lognormal, and double-logarithmic Engel curves were estimated for all the expenditure categories studied here (see chapter 6). These two functions could be combined analytically, but the double-log curve represents expenditure poorly at the extremes of income: interpolation is much easier and may not be much less accurate.

generally much more concentrated among the rich. These markets may completely exclude the poorest 30 to 60 percent of the population.[10] However, certain services, particularly medical care and education, do not fit the traditional-modern distinction well. They are also likely to be subject to differential prices.

Clearly, the degree of concentration of the market for an expenditure category depends on many factors. If the degree of market concentration is measured by the fourth-quartile share G^o_{r4}, it is positively correlated (among cities) with the concentration of income, as measured by the Gini coefficient.[11] Moreover, the correlation tends to decline toward zero as the income or expenditure elasticity of the category increases. That is, the market for luxuries is always concentrated in the richest quartile, almost by definition, while for necessities the degree of concentration depends very much on how income is distributed. The top-quartile share is negatively associated with the level of income, as measured by the median income in dollars. This correlation tends toward zero as the elasticity *decreases:* the negative association is in general stronger for luxuries than for necessities.[12]

Combining these results shows that the market concentration for necessities, which may be roughly identified with traditional expenditure categories, depends greatly on the concentration of income and not so much on the level of income. For luxury categories, which may be classed as modern, the concentration is more sensitive to income level and less to income concentration. This means that a more equitable distribution of income might, surprisingly, have a greater impact on market concentration in traditional than in modern goods. This does not mean that demand

10. For a further analysis, see César Peñaranda C., "Integración Andina: Dimensionamiento del Mercado Subregional y Distribución de Ingresos," *Ensayos ECIEL,* vol. 3 (August 1976), pp. 1–26. The analysis is based on the individual mean expenditure shares reported in ECIEL, "Urban Household Income and Consumption Patterns in Latin America: A Comparative Analysis of Colombia, Paraguay, Peru and Venezuela" (Brookings Institution, 1974; processed), pt. 5, and in Arturo Carlos Meyer, "Diferencias Internacionales en los Patrones de Consumo," *Ensayos ECIEL,* vol. 1 (November 1974), pp. 173–214, as well as on material in this chapter.

11. Rank correlation coefficients between the share G^o_{r4} and the Gini index of household income (table 2-4) are, for example, 0.770 (food), 0.770 (housing), 0.588 (clothing), 0.576 (durables), 0.818 (other consumption), and −0.097 (services).

12. Values of the rank correlation coefficient between G^o_{r4} and median Y are −0.479 (food), −0.648 (housing), −0.709 (clothing), −0.273 (other consumption), −0.636 (durables), and −0.879 (services).

for traditional goods would be reduced, only that it would be more widely distributed among households.

In conclusion, note that all this analysis has been conducted in terms of total income, without allowance for the effects of household size and composition. These factors are considered next.[13]

Household Composition and Expenditure Structure

Four variables are associated with household composition—number of members, number of children, age of the head, and stage in the life cycle—and it is more difficult than in the case of income to select any one of these as the best characterization of the household. Life cycle is associated with the highest value of the statistic ξ_{rv} (see table 4-5), except in six food categories, where the number of children is slightly more important. Altogether, life cycle and number of children are first and second in importance for fourteen of the twenty-six expenditure categories; life cycle and household size for seven categories; and life cycle and age for five categories (but for only two of these five, durables and clothing, is age significantly more powerful than size as an explanatory variable).

It appears, then, that only durables and clothing need be analyzed in purely life cycle terms, without taking any account of household size. As a first approximation, household size best explains the following expenditure categories: dairy products, meat, fruit, meals away from home, medical care, education, public transportation, and other consumption; while number of children best explains the remaining fifteen categories, excluding expenditures on housing.

In general, total household size can be expected to be associated with total income, while the number of children tends to be more strongly associated with income per person. This may explain the fact that, among food categories, those with high expenditure elasticities vary among households according to their total number of members, and those with low elasticities vary among households according to their number of children.[14] For non-

13. The question of how the market for a particular category of goods or services would be affected by a redistribution of income is surveyed by D. Morawetz, "Employment Implications of Industrialization in Developing Countries: A Survey," *Economic Journal*, vol. 84 (September 1974), pp. 503–07.

14. These elasticities are estimated allowing for nonproportional household size effects.

food spending there is no apparent association with such elasticities. Instead, it seems that number of members is the relevant variable for items that must be purchased for individual members and that are associated with no significant economies of scale; these are medical care, education, public transport, and other consumption. The number of children matters more when economies of scale exist, that is, for nondurables, services, recreation, private transport, communication, and transfers. There are definite economies of scale for housing, but these may be offset by differences in quality, so that ξ_{rv}^* is about equal for total size and for number of children; for durables (more for appliances than for furniture); and for children's, though not adults', clothing. These economies are reflected in the values of the index of variability of budget shares.

No one variable is ideal for describing household composition effects on expenditure. Life cycle is always important, but it has the disadvantage—apart from not being available for Caracas—that some of the classes are often very small.[15] There is therefore much random variation among households, which exaggerates the statistic. Number of members and number of children are both often important, but they seem—because of the effects of income per person and economies of scale—to be best suited to explaining different groups of expenditures.[16] All three classifying variables should be examined at least for some categories but age can be considered only together with life cycle.

Household Size

It is traditional in socioeconomic analyses to classify households according to size, or number of members. It was previously argued that it is not a particularly illuminating variable unless considered jointly with total income or expenditure. Nevertheless, it is used here to complement the discussion of the relation between budget structure and income and to

15. The "married without children" and "retired" classes each have fewer than forty observations in six of the nine cities, and the retired group is also small in two other cities; only in Santiago, where the sample is largest, are all classes sufficiently large for analysis (see table 4-1). Note also that life cycle stage—unlike age and size—was not tested across trimesters in the sample analysis (see appendix A).

16. The zero class for number of children includes single people, young couples who do not yet have children, and retired people who no longer have children living at home. This has the effect of combining the groups at the extremes of the age or life cycle distribution. The same is true of the size variable, although less markedly, where the smallest class is one- or two-member households.

make the ECIEL findings comparable to those of other studies. Appendix tables C-21 to C-30 show the budget shares for all expenditure categories, for each of four household sizes (one to two, three to five, six to eight, and nine or more) in the ten cities.[17]

I consider first expenditures on food, which tend to increase slightly with household size, as a share of total spending. In a few cases—Cali, Guayaquil, Lima, and Caracas—the share declines between very small households and those with between three and five members. This is always due to high expenditures on meals away from home by single people and two-person households (nearly always married couples without children). If the comparison is confined to food and drink consumed at home, the food share almost always increases with household size, but is inversely related to real income. The values for the capital cities cluster together, particularly those for large households; and those for non-capital cities are also clustered. This is largely but perhaps not entirely an income effect: Quito and Guayaquil are both relatively poor and have high concentrations of income, but they are clearly separated by the capital–non-capital distinction.

Table 4-5 and appendix tables C-21 to C-30 show very little variation among households of different sizes in budget shares for fruits, hot beverages, dairy products, meat, and fats and oils. These categories therefore tend to decline as a portion of total food spending. At the other extreme, there is great variability for meals away from home and for alcoholic beverages (usually highest for one- to two-person units) and for cereals (where the share tends to increase sharply with size). Apart from apparent household size effects that are actually due more to life cycle differences, the principal change in the diet as household size increases is a shift away from animal protein and fat (except for the rather small share for seafood) and an increase in the consumption of cereals, both measured as shares of total food expenditure excluding alcoholic beverages and meals away from home. The same pattern is visible in all cities, with a few exceptions for very small households. In most cases, however, the shares do not change dramatically: the largest variation for cereals is from 21 to 32 percent of the food budget (Quito), and for protein and fats, from 54 to 44 percent (Lima) or from 40 to 31 percent (Santiago).

17. The same information for all cities together in Colombia, Ecuador, and Venezuela appears in the national monographs. See also ECIEL, "Urban Household Income and Consumption Patterns," pt. 5, sec. 4, for Colombia and Venezuela.

A few other consistent relations may be noted between budget shares and household size. The proportion of the budget devoted to housing tends always to decrease as household size increases, because of the considerable economies of scale for this category, except in Quito. This decrease is sharpest in the capital cities, probably in consequence of higher rents there than in non-capital cities. Clothing takes a remarkably constant share of the budget; although the level differs notably between Quito or Santiago and the remaining eight cities, there is never much variation among household size classes. There are essentially no economies of scale for spending on education. The budget share tends almost always to rise as the household is larger, at least up to eight members. Households larger than that tend to be notably poorer and therefore in some cities spend relatively less on schooling.

Number of Adults and Children

The number of adults in the household is of course known, but this variable was not used to classify families for this analysis. Neither were families classified according to the dependency ratio or the proportions of adults and children; only the number of children was used. The number of members and the number of children are correlated, although as table 4-5 indicates, they yield rather different descriptions of the variability of budget shares and the causes of that variation.

The ECIEL survey data have only begun to be used to analyze explicitly the cost that households incur by having children; this requires assigning some costs directly to children and apportioning others to reflect additional needs and economies of scale.[18] Research on this question in the United States appears to have established the following relations between income, spending, and number of children:[19] (1) household income per capita declines (even if total income rises), until the oldest child is eighteen; the decline is steeper and more prolonged the more children there are in the family; (2) expenditures on children rise with income, but less than

18. The Colombian data have been used to investigate child-related costs or the relation of spending to population composition and growth. See Cecilia L. de Rodríguez and Hernando Gómez Buendía, *Familia y Consumo en la Ciudad Colombiana* (Bogotá: Fundación para la Educación Superior y el Desarrollo, 1977). See also Howard J. Howe, "Estimation of the Linear and Quadratic Expenditure Systems: A Cross-Section Case for Colombia" (Ph.D. dissertation, University of Pennsylvania, 1974).

19. Thomas J. Espenshade, *The Cost of Children in Urban United States,* Population Monograph Series, no. 14 (University of California Press, 1973), pp. 78–79.

proportionally, with elasticities in the range of 0.3 to 0.5; and (3) expenditures on food, housing, and clothing are most affected and the marginal cost of a first child is much higher than that of later children—as much as twice that of a second child.[20]

These findings may not hold for Latin America but the general pattern should be similar. Table 5-3 shows the behavior of budget shares for food, housing, and clothing (generally the three largest spending categories) and for three categories that might be expected to vary appreciably with the number of children: education, medical care, and children's clothing.

The budget share for food and beverages always rises with an increase in the number of children, both because of reduced income per capita and increased needs. Typically, an additional 12 percent of total spending is devoted to this category as households go from having no children to having six or more. Most of the increase is due to food and beverages that do not contain animal protein and are not considered luxuries. Cereals account for a large part of the increase. The totals for meat, poultry, seafood, dairy products, and eggs form fairly constant shares of the budget and therefore decline as a share of the total food budget; the same is true of spending on fruit. The share for cereals always rises. On average, the protein share drops about 8 percent and the cereal share rises 6 percent. The effect is more pronounced than the comparable effect noted for total household size because the income effect is stronger. The comparison is made after eliminating alcoholic beverages and meals away from home.

Except in Bogotá, the budget share devoted to housing always falls as there are more children: the average decline is about 8 percent of total spending, or about two-thirds of the increase in the food share. In the case of clothing, the total share tends to be stable or to decline slightly; this is partly an income effect and may also include a life cycle effect. The share spent for children's clothing usually rises with more children, at least up to four or five in the family. Beyond that point, declining income per person and economies of scale may cause the share to drop. Clearly, expenditures on children's clothing displace expenditures on adults' clothing in the budget, but the effect is usually slight.[21]

20. Costs also rise sharply with age, an adolescent being three times as expensive as a child of five or less. The ages of children are not taken into account simultaneously with their number in this analysis.

21. Large differences among cities in the share of expenditure on children reflect different age limits and classifications in the surveys: boys' and girls' clothing, after infancy, is sometimes included with men's and women's clothing. Colombia and Venezuela use an age classification; Chile, Ecuador, and Peru use a sex classification.

Table 5-3. *Individual Mean Expenditure Shares in Six Spending Categories, by Number of Children in Household, Ten Latin American Cities*
Percentage

City and spending category	Number of children			
	None	1–2	3–5	6 or more
Bogotá				
Food and beverages	40.76	45.71	49.52	50.00
Housing	31.11	24.62	24.83	25.38
All clothing	7.46	7.99	6.93	6.11
Children's clothing	0.51	2.05	2.51	3.22
Education	3.89	4.91	5.19	6.06
Medical care	2.32	1.98	1.64	1.47
Barranquilla				
Food and beverages	53.52	56.30	57.27	64.25
Housing	21.04	18.24	15.93	14.56
All clothing	5.30	5.62	6.63	5.21
Children's clothing	0.29	1.22	2.02	2.15
Education	1.94	3.49	4.35	3.52
Medical care	3.38	1.87	2.42	1.68
Cali				
Food and beverages	50.28	56.16	58.67	63.36
Housing	23.46	19.21	16.58	13.30
All clothing	5.02	6.57	6.64	5.35
Children's clothing	0.11	1.26	2.29	1.58
Education	1.86	2.45	2.96	3.84
Medical care	2.23	1.02	0.93	1.32
Medellín				
Food and beverages	49.69	50.95	52.02	56.20
Housing	26.49	24.63	21.66	21.19
All clothing	4.01	4.95	4.58	3.56
Children's clothing	0.16	0.99	1.76	1.54
Education	2.27	3.19	4.21	4.60
Medical care	1.80	1.67	2.19	1.23
Santiago				
Food and beverages	36.46	40.48	45.23	52.70
Housing	30.44	25.74	22.41	19.33
All clothing	10.50	12.52	11.93	12.35
Children's clothing	0.02	0.46	0.33	0.73
Education	0.50	0.87	0.82	0.74
Medical care	1.43	1.34	1.20	0.46
Quito				
Food and beverages	42.21	45.20	47.15	50.16
Housing	29.99	25.21	25.02	22.21
All clothing	9.87	10.26	10.36	10.34
Children's clothing	0.01	0.24	0.32	0.38
Education	0.84	1.43	1.59	1.91
Medical care	2.91	3.00	2.72	3.70

Table 5-3 (*continued*)

City and spending category	Number of children			
	None	*1–2*	*3–5*	*6 or more*
Guayaquil				
Food and beverages	49.02	50.66	56.01	61.73
Housing	26.17	23.02	19.09	17.80
All clothing	6.51	6.34	6.90	5.47
Children's clothing	0.04	0.27	0.20	0.22
Education	1.33	1.83	2.01	1.90
Medical care	2.30	2.16	1.74	1.76
Lima				
Food and beverages	39.78	40.75	46.52	50.79
Housing	24.21	20.27	18.12	16.44
All clothing	8.26	8.53	7.45	5.65
Children's clothing	0.22	0.36	0.34	0.31
Education	1.62	2.01	1.54	1.11
Medical care	2.04	2.44	1.83	2.31
Caracas				
Food and beverages	32.40	34.51	39.11	47.97
Housing	31.08	27.78	24.23	22.11
All clothing	6.45	6.24	6.49	5.97
Children's clothing	0.72	1.60	2.17	3.01
Education	2.13	3.30	4.62	3.54
Medical care	3.77	4.00	3.28	1.67
Maracaibo				
Food and beverages	48.64	50.24	56.84	65.99
Housing	23.40	19.92	15.80	15.50
All clothing	3.88	3.52	3.70	1.68
Children's clothing	0.22	0.85	1.37	0.44
Education	1.16	1.81	1.49	0.58
Medical care	1.30	1.38	0.94	0.52

Source: Original ECIEL calculations based on the survey data.

In all ten cities, the total budget share devoted to food, housing, and clothing is remarkably stable up to households with five children. The combined share is about 80 percent in Colombia, 76 or 77 percent in Santiago and Maracaibo, 82 percent in Ecuador, and 70 to 72 percent in Lima and Caracas. This stability continues in most cities even for households with six or more children, but in Cali, Santiago, Caracas, and Maracaibo there is an increase after the sixth child of 5 to 7 percent of the budget devoted to these three categories of necessities. In any case, most of the adjustment in spending occasioned by the presence of children occurs among these three categories, rather than between them and the remaining 20 or 25 percent of the household budget.

Medical expenditure seems to show no pattern, except that in some cities there is a slight concentration of such expenditure among childless households, which include a disproportionate share of the elderly. As noted earlier, medical needs occur randomly and may not be reflected in spending. There is a clearer pattern for education, where the share rises through the first three classes (except in Santiago, Lima, and Maracaibo) but may decline as income effects begin to outweigh any specific demands created by more children.

Age and Life Cycle

Analysis of these variables is limited to five spending categories: durables, clothing, medical care, education, and transfers. Life cycle effects are less pronounced for housing, nondurables, and vehicle operation.[22] Table 5-4 shows the budget shares by life cycle and age for the five categories analyzed (for Caracas, only age is available).

The most pronounced pattern is that for durables: there is always a peak for recently formed households or for families whose head is under fifty years of age, and usually under thirty-five. This pattern is observed independent of the average share of durables in total household expenditure, which is very high in Lima but low in Colombia and in Caracas. Clothing shows a similar, but less pronounced, life cycle pattern. Purchases are concentrated among young households and decline with age; there is less variation between one age class and the next. This is undoubtedly because children create demands for clothing to a much greater extent than for durables, and economies of scale are smaller.

There is a very sharp life cycle effect on educational spending. In every city, the educational budget share is much higher for households with children of school age (eight to eighteen years) than for any other group.[23] There is usually, though not always, an increase for households

22. Among other categories, only dairy products show a fairly large variation with life cycle, the budget share generally being highest for households with small children (in six of nine cities); in some cities, it is fairly high for the retired as well. Dairy products as a share of total food spending is highest for families with young children in Barranquilla, Cali, Santiago, and Lima. In Bogotá, Medellín, Quito, Guayaquil, and Maracaibo this ratio is as high or higher for households whose head is retired, or (in Guayaquil only) where there are grown children at home.

23. This effect is even more striking in the Engel curve analysis of chapter 6,

with young children (aged seven or less), but since most children in this class are too young to attend school, the effect is slight. Age is a less helpful explanatory variable than life cycle for this category, as it merely shows a broad peak in spending when the head is between thirty-five and sixty-four years old.

There is often considerable variation in budget shares devoted to medical expenditure among age groups within each city, but no consistent pattern emerges across cities. Such expenditures might be expected to be highest for the elderly and for families with young children. However, whether medical needs result in expenditures depends both on the severity of illnesses and accidents and on the family's financial situation, so that the spending pattern is not always closely linked to medical need. In any case, illnesses and accidents are sufficiently random occurrences that samples like these probably do not represent their occurrence in the population very well.[24] The most that is evident in the budget shares is a tendency for spending to be slightly lower in one or both of the middle age groups than at the extremes. In four cities, the medical budget share is higher for retired households; in five cities, it is relatively high for families with older children at home, but these households may also include some young children and may be larger than average.[25]

Life cycle effects are clear and consistent for expenditure on transfers. (This category includes gifts, though these are probably less important than other transfers and show little variation with age.) The share is low for unmarried people and for families with children under eighteen, who are dependents rather than significant income earners. The share is high for households that either have no children or have children old enough to contribute to income. Transfers therefore appear to originate in households with low dependency ratios and presumably go to households with more dependents per earner. In seven cities, transfers are highest or nearly highest for families whose head is fifty to sixty-four; these are likely to be families with several earners. The age effect is much less pronounced than the life cycle variation, however.

---

which takes account of the number of children in each age group, and where the age groups correspond to school levels.

24. This analysis does not separate emergency expenditures—particularly hospitalization—from routine purchases of medicine and supplies or medical examinations.

25. Life cycle is defined by the age of the oldest child, so the age distribution of children gets wider as life cycle is more advanced.

Table 5-4. Individual Mean Expenditure Shares in Five Spending Categories, by Life Cycle and Age of Head, Ten Latin American Cities

Percent

City and spending category	Unmarried	Married, no children	Children			Retired	Age of head			
			Under 8	8–18	Over 18		Under 35	35–49	50–64	Over 64
Bogotá										
Durables	1.02	7.67	2.85	1.35	1.49	0.10	3.64	1.31	0.84	0.27
Clothing	5.84	8.75	7.93	7.43	6.66	3.88	7.84	7.51	6.87	3.66
Medical care	0.82	1.82	2.32	1.47	3.47	4.80	2.42	1.31	2.18	2.41
Education	2.99	1.20	2.11	7.75	1.98	0.87	2.54	6.37	5.49	3.54
Transfers	1.33	2.07	0.68	0.74	0.93	0.71	0.82	0.74	1.03	0.69
Barranquilla										
Durables	1.43	2.62	2.48	1.11	1.34	0.01	2.39	1.43	1.20	0.78
Clothing	3.61	8.47	6.36	5.99	4.86	4.19	7.65	5.51	4.94	3.47
Medical care	1.94	6.05	2.76	1.85	2.49	1.87	3.19	2.11	2.05	1.95
Education	1.78	0.48	1.95	5.44	1.74	0.40	1.68	4.31	4.19	2.99
Transfers	0.64	1.50	0.68	0.62	0.59	0.40	0.51	0.73	0.83	0.54
Cali										
Durables	1.04	2.20	1.64	2.01	0.21	0.36	1.72	2.06	0.66	0.38
Clothing	4.92	6.95	7.18	6.56	4.72	2.31	7.24	6.63	4.92	3.99
Medical care	1.83	0.91	1.26	1.09	2.95	1.52	0.99	1.07	2.43	2.51
Education	1.57	0.24	1.40	4.17	1.51	0.43	1.26	3.24	3.02	1.01
Transfers	0.64	2.09	0.78	1.67	1.60	2.53	0.88	0.80	0.77	2.04
Medellín										
Durables	0.52	3.13	1.27	1.01	0.69	0.24	1.02	1.27	0.84	0.43
Clothing	3.29	6.66	4.68	4.51	3.29	4.17	4.80	4.55	3.69	3.17
Medical care	1.03	1.14	1.88	1.84	2.66	1.31	1.74	1.73	1.46	3.27
Education	1.90	1.18	1.64	5.69	0.93	1.00	1.44	4.38	3.89	1.64
Transfers	0.72	0.58	0.68	1.08	1.03	1.30	0.70	0.78	1.30	0.87
Santiago										
Durables	3.43	7.85	4.41	3.82	2.82	2.36	5.73	3.85	3.05	1.91
Clothing	9.02	11.80	12.52	12.36	10.75	8.18	12.25	12.36	10.88	9.32

Medical care	1.56	1.27	1.41	1.12	1.53	1.32	1.41	1.06	1.46	1.63
Education	0.23	0.33	0.49	1.12	0.55	0.09	0.49	0.95	0.80	0.26
Transfers	0.64	0.70	0.18	0.23	0.31	0.22	0.29	0.32	0.30	0.19
Quito										
Durables	2.33	2.95	3.69	2.66	1.67	0.81	3.82	2.93	1.98	0.89
Clothing	10.90	10.09	10.37	10.23	9.60	6.85	11.33	10.21	10.12	6.23
Medical care	3.01	2.80	3.97	2.20	2.73	3.24	3.59	2.96	2.06	2.84
Education	0.85	0.53	0.94	2.12	0.81	0.06	0.75	1.58	2.09	0.93
Transfers	1.73	2.33	1.24	2.15	4.30	1.15	1.25	1.85	3.20	1.69
Guayaquil										
Durables	0.97	5.02	3.71	2.27	1.41	0.00	3.13	2.68	1.66	0.73
Clothing	6.94	7.46	6.74	6.42	6.29	1.90	6.81	6.32	6.94	5.05
Medical care	1.99	2.27	2.08	1.68	2.84	2.92	2.04	1.93	2.07	2.04
Education	1.21	0.01	1.22	2.71	1.04	0.69	1.08	2.41	1.90	1.51
Transfers	3.49	2.83	2.11	2.75	6.64	0.59	2.31	2.47	4.39	4.75
Lima										
Durables	6.51	8.15	7.10	5.87	2.97	1.08	7.80	5.88	4.98	2.49
Clothing	10.56	8.65	7.67	8.18	6.83	3.38	8.66	7.91	7.22	7.23
Medical care	2.38	1.40	2.05	2.01	2.67	3.21	2.10	1.99	2.04	3.24
Education	0.59	1.17	1.00	2.48	0.99	0.03	0.75	2.13	1.89	1.27
Transfers	0.33	0.28	0.33	0.39	0.99	0.12	0.30	2.42	0.65	0.40
Caracas										
Durables	n.a.	n.a.	n.a.	n.a.	n.a.	n.a.	1.52	1.10	0.77	1.55
Clothing	n.a.	n.a.	n.a.	n.a.	n.a.	n.a.	7.41	5.98	5.23	4.62
Medical care	n.a.	n.a.	n.a.	n.a.	n.a.	n.a.	2.94	4.05	4.21	4.41
Education	n.a.	n.a.	n.a.	n.a.	n.a.	n.a.	2.30	4.56	2.94	2.49
Transfers	n.a.	n.a.	n.a.	n.a.	n.a.	n.a.	0.78	1.03	1.14	0.62
Maracaibo										
Durables	4.22	6.47	4.10	3.51	3.10	2.13	4.89	3.40	3.74	1.59
Clothing	3.38	4.19	4.07	3.57	3.54	3.52	4.23	3.57	3.26	1.69
Medical care	0.97	1.28	1.51	1.05	1.10	2.11	1.33	1.09	1.12	1.53
Education	0.92	0.36	0.93	2.35	1.01	0.78	0.89	2.07	1.59	1.19
Transfers	0.33	0.04	0.30	0.30	0.91	0.26	0.29	0.33	0.24	0.64

Source: Original ECIEL calculations based on the survey data.
n.a. Not available.

Expenditure per Person

So far, income and household composition have been considered separately, although some classifying variables such as age are associated with both effects, and the allocation of spending seems clearly to depend on both variables. It is not easy to take both factors into account simultaneously in analyzing expenditure, since the response of the budget to a change in one variable is likely to depend on the level(s) of the other variable(s). The problem is greatly simplified, however, if the analyses are based on average expenditure per household member, regardless of differences in types of members or interactions between income and household size.

Two sorts of averages are analyzed here. First, estimates of specific per person expenditures are presented, with household size used as a classifying variable and budget shares translated into monetary amounts. Next, the analysis returns to budget shares, but the classifying variable is the average total expenditure per person, with households grouped into quartiles. Average total expenditure per person was not included in the initial standard ECIEL analysis and was not used to compute indexes of variation for table 4-5. It is included here since both income and household size have been shown to be important determinants of the allocation of expenditure.

Spending per Household Member

The preceding analysis was based on the individual expenditure shares g_{rcvk} (where v refers to household size, number of children, age, or life cycle). Since total spending also varies among the constituent classes of each of these variables, actual expenditure on a category need not move in the same way as the budget share. This section examines estimates of actual spending per person, in different household-size classes, for the three principal categories of food and beverages, housing, and clothing. Other expenditure categories are not considered, partly because they take smaller shares of the budget, and partly because many of them either show strong life cycle patterns (for example, durables) or are purchased only for particular members of the household (for example, education), so that per capita measures are not very meaningful.

Per capita consumption of category r (food, housing, or clothing) in size class k is estimated by

$$v_{rk} = \frac{g_{rk}\bar{G}_k}{N_k},$$

where g_{rk} is the budget share, $\bar{G}_k$ is mean total expenditure in size class k, and N_k is the number of members per family in that class. This estimate differs in three ways from a direct measure of expenditure where the households could be grouped in size classes: g_{rk} is a mean rather than a value for an individual household; $\bar{G}_k$ is likely to be higher than the expenditure of a typical family whose budget share approximately equals g_{rk}; and N_k is only an average of family size.

For these reasons, v_{rk} is only a crude index of per capita expenditure. Nonetheless, it may be instructive in showing how consumption per person is related to household size and to possible scale effects. The typical size N_k is not estimated separately for each city but is taken to be 1.7 members in the one-to-two-member class (except in Lima, Caracas, and Maracaibo, where only two-member households are included), four members in the three-to-five-member class, seven in the six-to-eight-member class, and ten in the class of nine members or more.

Table 5-5 shows the resulting values of v_{rk}, in national currency, for each city in each size class for the three expenditure categories. Were it not for variations in mean total spending $\bar{G}_k$, per capita consumption would decline as household size increased, for all three categories. The decline would be least for food (where economies of scale are least) and sharpest for housing (where such economies are largest). However, as indicated in table 4-1, in most cities $\bar{G}$ almost doubles between very small and very large households (Santiago and Lima are notable exceptions). The increase is often particularly marked between the first two size classes (Lima again being an exception). Therefore, v_{rk} can initially rise but must eventually decline. Table 5-5 shows, however, that this initial rise never occurs: spending per person falls in all three categories in every city when household size increases, with the sole exception of clothing expenditure in Quito.

Because of all the approximations involved in estimating v_{rk} and the fact that no account is taken of differences among cities in the composition of the food and clothing budgets, these estimates of expenditure per person cannot be given great weight. Nonetheless, they appear to show that spend-

Table 5-5. *Spending per Person per Trimester, in National Currency, for Food, Housing, and Clothing, by Size of Household, Ten Latin American Cities*

City and spending category	Number of members			
	1–2	*3–5*	*6–8*	*9 or more*
Bogotá (pesos)				
Food and beverages	1,266	928	668	500
Housing	1,030	517	332	271
Clothing	128	161	100	74
Barranquilla (pesos)				
Food and beverages	1,667	861	669	525
Housing	559	257	205	136
Clothing	176	94	68	50
Cali (pesos)				
Food and beverages	1,430	850	618	496
Housing	433	286	194	129
Clothing	147	96	79	35
Medellín (pesos)				
Food and beverages	1,286	756	532	390
Housing	611	331	245	152
Clothing	119	66	43	29
Santiago (escudos)				
Food and beverages	944	551	348	233
Housing	848	368	182	96
Clothing	230	170	95	69
Quito (sucres)				
Food and beverages	1,219	996	610	589
Housing	663	560	357	334
Clothing	280	208	140	142
Guayaquil (sucres)				
Food and beverages	1,343	1,043	765	581
Housing	677	459	288	215
Clothing	167	116	103	67
Lima (soles)				
Food and beverages	4,117	2,617	1,912	1,608
Housing	3,944	1,310	820	664
Clothing	712	501	337	283
Caracas (bolívars)				
Food and beverages	647	499	369	270
Housing	585	431	263	148
Clothing	118	89	69	40
Maracaibo (bolívars)				
Food and beverages	473	385	252	191
Housing	244	162	82	54
Clothing	29	26	19	13

Sources: Calculated from the values of mean total expenditure by household size, table 4-1, and the values of individual mean expenditure shares by household size, appendix tables C-21 to C-30.

ing on necessities per household member falls, and falls fairly uniformly among cities, as household size increases. For food, expenditure is around $500 per person per year in small households (with a range of $430 to $660) and declines to around $380, $250, and $200 per person in successive size classes. This sharp drop is associated with the shift from expensive high-protein foods to low-cost cereals.

Expenditure per person varies much more widely among cities for housing than it does for food. Lima, Caracas, and Bogotá show the highest spending levels and also the sharpest decreases as household size increases. In capital cities, the decline in housing expenditure is sharper than that for food, whereas for non-capital cities the reverse is true. This must result from differences in the structure of rents and in the geographic distributions of households of different sizes, but it is not clear how this occurs. The median expenditure per person is about $340 a year for small households, and falls to about $90 for the largest households, a greater decline on average than for food, as is to be expected.

There is relatively little variation in per person spending on clothing among size classes, though there is a decline from about $65 to about $27 a year in the median.

Total Consumption per Person

The best single measure of a household's welfare appears to be the level of consumption expenditure per person. Consumption is subject to somewhat less transitory variation than income; and division by household size, while it leaves the shape of the income distribution essentially unchanged, rearranges families within the distribution so that a household is not likely to appear rich simply because it is large, or poor because it is small.[26] Adjustments for economies of scale, or for differences among household members of different ages, are of some importance but can be ignored at least for a first approximation.

Classifying households by consumption per person instead of by total income or consumption has two important effects. First, differences be-

26. The choice of consumption per person as a welfare indicator follows from comparisons with other possible measures, in a study for Bogotá, Medellín, and Lima. See Philip Musgrove and Robert Ferber, "Identifying the Urban Poor: Characteristics of Poverty Households in Bogotá, Medellín and Lima," *Latin American Research Review*, forthcoming. Some of this research has been extended to all ten of the cities studied here.

tween quartiles in the composition of spending are accentuated, because each quartile no longer mixes together families at very different levels of welfare. The second effect is that one source of differences among cities—variation in the distribution of household sizes—is removed (see table 2-17). Any remaining differences can then be more securely attributed to differences in relative prices or in preferences. Both these effects can be observed in the behavior of budget shares.

Appendix tables C-31 to C-40 show the individual mean budget structure in each quartile of the distribution of consumption per person. These tables resemble tables C-1 to C-10, except that the income quartiles in tables C-1 to C-10 are defined for all the cities in a country together, whereas the quartiles of consumption per person in tables C-31 to C-40 are defined for each city separately. As with the tables based on income, the median value for per person expenditure in each quartile is first estimated and then related to the percentage shares of the budget. Median values are estimated by interpolation and are shown in table 5-6, in national currency and in U.S. dollars of equivalent purchasing power, as in table 5-1.

Figure 5-4 shows the behavior of the share of the budget devoted to food; the analysis is repeated in figure 5-5 for the share spent on cereal products. When figure 5-4 is compared to figure 5-1, the shape of the curve for each city is similar, declining from, at most, 70 percent of the budget in the poorest quartile to at least 20 percent in the richest quartile. Further, there continues to be a fairly marked separation between capital and non-capital cities, but the curves for Maracaibo and Medellín meet those for the capital cities at low levels of consumption per person. The chief difference is that when households are classified by consumption per person all the curves lie much closer together; the range across cities at a given level of expenditure per person is typically only 10 percentage points rather than 20. The share of the budget devoted to food is about 60 percent in the capital cities, at a level of welfare corresponding to some $200 per person per year; it falls to 50 percent at $400 and to 30 percent at about $1,200 with only a slight further decline at higher welfare levels.

The budget share spent on cereal products varies greatly among cities at low levels of consumption per person, as prices differ and as there are different preferences for bread, corn, and rice versus potatoes. As welfare rises, both these effects become less important and the curves for different cities in figure 5-5 converge. Among the poor, cereals account for between

Table 5-6. *Median Household Spending per Person in National Currency per Trimester and U.S. Dollars per Year, by Quartile of Consumption per Person, Ten Latin American Cities*

City and currency	Quartile			
	First	Second	Third	Fourth
Bogotá				
Pesos	521	875	1,333	2,792
Dollars	229	384	586	1,227
Barranquilla				
Pesos	458	771	1,146	2,104
Dollars	201	339	504	924
Cali				
Pesos	396	667	1,208	2,186
Dollars	174	293	531	961
Medellín				
Pesos	333	563	958	2,083
Dollars	146	247	421	915
Santiago				
Escudos	403	772	1,309	2,718
Dollars	220	421	714	1,483
Quito				
Sucres	423	871	1,592	3,359
Dollars	156	320	586	1,236
Guayaquil				
Sucres	435	722	1,393	2,837
Dollars	160	266	512	1,044
Lima				
Soles	1,507	2,699	4,331	8,851
Dollars	220	394	631	1,290
Caracas				
Bolívars	350	740	1,270	2,240
Dollars	320	677	1,162	2,050
Maracaibo				
Bolívars	210	360	540	1,010
Dollars	192	330	494	924

Source: Original ECIEL calculations based on appendix tables C-31 to C-40.

10 and 20 percent of total expenditure, but the share falls very quickly as income increases, to around 5 percent at $1,000 per person per year and to only 2 percent at $2,000 per person. In most cities, the share spent on animal protein foods (meat and poultry, seafood, eggs, and dairy products) is quite stable across the quartiles of consumption per person, so the relation is not presented graphically. The share sometimes rises slightly

Figure 5-4. *Food Budget Share by Median Consumption per Person in Each Quartile*

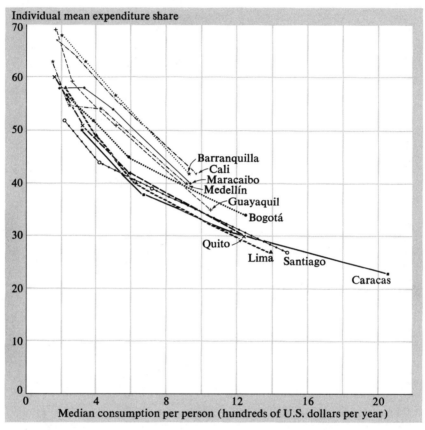

between the first and second quartiles, and usually declines substantially between the third and fourth quartiles.

One other category for which a pronounced relation can be observed between budget share and welfare level is household furnishings and operation. The shares in this category, which includes durables, are undoubtedly biased downward in Caracas because of the short period of reference of the survey, while in Lima they are extremely high because of accelerated inflation in the year preceding the survey. Several cities display a sharp increase in the budget share devoted to this category, over a range of about $300 to $700 of total spending per person. The share grows more slowly thereafter, but does not appear to level off even at much higher levels of consumption per person. This relation is somewhat less apparent when budget shares are related to total income, but the two patterns are generally consistent.

This discussion of the budget structure could be extended to other spending categories, probably with quite similar results. Taking household size into account along with income or total expenditure may show a tighter pattern across cities; this happens for food, but it need not for other categories because differences in prices or in preferences can be substantial. Such differences are more clearly discernible if the effects of variation in household size are first removed. When households are classified by consumption per person, the most notable change between classes is the rapid decline in the budget share spent on food. This share is always at

Figure 5-5. *Budget Share Devoted to Cereals, by Median Consumption per Person in Each Quartile*

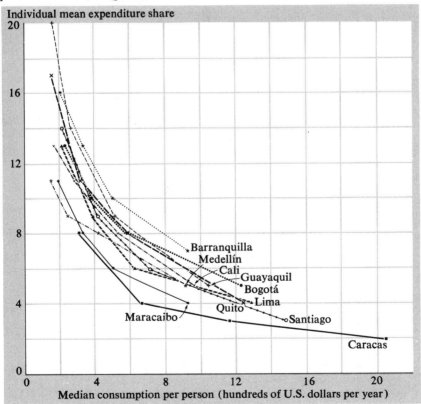

least 50 percent larger in the poorest quartile than it is in the richest, and sometimes it is more than twice as large.[27] Almost equally dramatic is the change in the composition of the diet, with sharply declining shares for cereals and tubers and increasing shares for animal protein foods, fats, and fruits. The other major categories of spending do not, except for household furnishings and operation, vary so greatly across levels of consumption per person.

None of the expenditure values or shares presented really indicate the extent to which economies of scale are present in the household. That is, none of them show the relation between spending and household size or composition that would—if all other expenditures were unchanged—permit a family to maintain a constant level of welfare as it increased in size. Rather, the budget structures show the net result of such economies, the specific needs generated for particular categories by particular members of the household, and the total resources available to the household. Nonetheless, it is evident that some of the differences in spending behavior among expenditure categories reflect differences in the degree to which needs increase less than proportionally as household size increases. They also reflect differences in the extent to which such needs arise from different types of household members, especially differences between adults and children.

To take account of household composition, it has been useful to consider number of members, number of children, age of the oldest child, and age of the household head. The first of these, combined with income or total consumption, is the most important. Many more variables could be considered under this heading—number of adults, the dependency ratio, or the range of children's ages—because household composition is a complicated matter not easily described by any one variable. The evidence of this chapter and of chapter 4 is that household composition and income together account for nearly all of a household's needs and actual behavior; other variables are of much less importance and tend to affect only a few expenditure categories.

In the next chapter all the variables analyzed separately here are considered simultaneously by the use of regression methods to estimate expenditure functions or Engel curves.

27. Since total expenditure includes imputed rent, the share that food takes of money income or expenditure is still higher. For urban households, this effect is not offset by imputed expenditure on home-grown food.

CHAPTER SIX

Expenditure Functions

THE EXPENDITURE STRUCTURES examined in chapters 4 and 5 show how different variables affect the distribution of the household budget but do not distinguish the effects of two or more variables that may be at work simultaneously. For example, households at different ages typically have different incomes and include different numbers of members. Expenditure structures can therefore describe the results of household budgetary decisions but do not explain what factors determined the result. This requires a multivariate model of expenditures. If such a model relates specific expenditure C_r to total expenditure C or total income Y, it is called an Engel curve. These functions can incorporate other variables, such as prices and household characteristics, that are presumed systematically to affect C_r.

Engel curves or expenditure functions may but need not be derived from assumptions about the utility functions that households are assumed to be maximizing. The theory of consumer behavior makes income and prices the chief exogenous variables affecting spending patterns; all other factors, including the sociodemographic characteristics of the household, are absorbed into the utility function. The assumption of a specific form for the utility function leads to a specific shape of the Engel curves and a specific way to incorporate sociodemographic variables. This is done in several of the specialized analyses of the ECIEL data, but not in the standard results.

Engel curves can be estimated in a great many functional forms, no one

191

of which is ideal for all goods and at all levels of income or expenditure.[1] Except perhaps for representing inferior goods, the most generally desirable form is that of a statistical distribution function or sigmoid curve, with an eventual saturation of expenditure either absolutely or in relation to total spending. The forms more often used, including the double logarithmic, linear, quadratic, semilogarithmic, and log-inverse functions, are convenient approximations for particular categories or income ranges.

Four kinds of Engel curves have been estimated from the ECIEL data: double-log, semilog, linear, and quadratic. The linear and double-log functions have been based, in different applications, both on income and on total spending. The semilog function is restricted to income and the quadratic form to expenditure. All these estimates are alike in that they take no account of variations in prices among households. The ECIEL data do not include records of prices actually paid by different households, so it is assumed that all the households faced the same set of prices.[2] No doubt, this assumption is not entirely justified, but some account can be taken of two of the factors, stratum and trimester, most likely to cause differences in the prices associated with different observations. Engel curves can be estimated separately by stratum; and interval (trimester) can be included as one of the exogenous variables. The latter approach reduces the distortion due to inflationary or seasonal price differences, while the first reduces the distortion associated with price differences among neighborhoods and income levels.[3]

1. For an exhaustive review of the theoretical and empirical literature on Engel curve estimation, see Alan Brown and Angus Deaton, "Surveys in Applied Economics: Models of Consumer Behavior," *Economic Journal,* vol. 82 (December 1972), pp. 1145–1236, especially pp. 1171–78.

2. However, in some countries, the survey data include either price paid or unit value (obtained from estimates of expenditure and quantity) for some items, usually a small number of foodstuffs. These data were not retained in the conversion to the common ECIEL format and therefore have not been cleaned or analyzed. See ECIEL, "Resumen del XIV Seminario del Programa de Estudios Conjuntos sobre Integración Latinoamericana (ECIEL)" (Buenos Aires, June 29–July 3, 1970; processed), pp. 19–25.

3. Trimester is included in the standard ECIEL analysis. Separate estimates by stratum were made by Howard Howe and Philip Musgrove, "An Analysis of ECIEL Household Budget Data for Bogotá, Caracas, Guayaquil, and Lima," in Constantino Lluch, Alan A. Powell, and Ross A. Williams, eds., *Patterns in Household Demand and Saving* (New York: Oxford University Press for the World Bank, 1977), pp. 155–98, and Romualdo Roldán, "Funciones Consumo por Tramos de Ingreso," Centro de Estudios de Planificación Nacional (CEPLAN) Documento no. 38 (Santiago: Universidad Católica de Chile, 1974; processed).

Since all the different Engel curves include C or Y, all the expenditure or income effects could be considered together. Comparisons are difficult, however, because of differences in the explanatory variables and in the interpretation of the parameters. Similar or more severe problems arise when one compares the estimates of the effect of family size, the one other variable included in nearly all the analyses. Moreover, the cities or countries studied are not the same for each set of estimates. For these reasons, the double-log estimates are given most attention here, while estimates derived from other functional forms are used for purposes of evaluation or explanation. Appendix B comments on how well the different functional forms explain expenditures, and describes how each form is estimated and its parameters interpreted; R^2 statistics for the double-log formulation are also given there.

Income and Spending

The double logarithmic form of the Engel curve was chosen for the standard ECIEL analysis. The estimating equation is

$$\log C_r = \beta_{or} + \sum_{u=1}^{m_r} \sum_{j=1}^{k_u-1} \beta_{ujr} X_{uj} + \beta_r \log C,$$

where the X_{uj} are a series of sociodemographic variables arranged in m_r groups; group u has k_u classes or individual dummy variables, of which k_u-1 appear in the equation. This form has a number of advantages that recommended it for the initial analyses of the data.[4] It can be estimated by OLS regression for each category separately. It is able to represent well both extremely high and extremely low values of C_r and C. The estimated value of C_r is always nonnegative, and approaches zero when C approaches zero (although it may exceed C in some range). The use of logarithms removes the effect of different national currencies to the constant term β_{or}, making international comparison easy. (The linear form also has this property.) Finally, the parameters β_{ujr} and β_r are easy to interpret: the former indicate proportional changes in C_r between dif-

4. See Brown and Deaton, "Models of Consumer Behavior," and S. J. Prais and H. S. Houthakker, *The Analysis of Family Budgets,* 2d ed. (Cambridge University Press, 1971). The decision to use this form was not based on experiments with the ECIEL data but on the experience of other surveys. Some experiments were undertaken by Roldán, "Funciones Consumo por Tramos de Ingreso," p. 20.

ferent classes of households, while the latter is an elasticity (constant by construction). This form has been found to fit particularly well for categories with relatively high expenditure elasticities. The chief drawback is that the double logarithmic model is not derived from a utility function and does not meet any of the constraints of consumer theory. Even the budget constraint is violated, except when all the elasticities are unitary.

Dependent and Independent Variables

Specific expenditures C_r are related to total expenditure C rather than to income Y or disposable income Y_d, since C is probably reported somewhat more accurately and is more stable over time (has a smaller transitory variance). The model is consistent with the assumption that households first decide, on the basis of income and other factors, how much to spend altogether, and then allocate that spending over categories. Clearly, when C_r is large relative to C, C_r is to a large extent regressed on itself; this has the effect of biasing the estimate of β_r toward 1.0. Even when C_r is small relative to C, the elasticity is biased if in fact the household bases its decisions of how much to spend in each category on its income rather than on total expenditure. This simultaneous equation bias may be in either direction, but it appears to be upward for inelastic categories and downward for highly elastic categories; either way, the effect is to bias the estimates β_r toward unity. However, this bias is assumed to be small for most if not all categories, compared to other sources of error; and if households determine C_r as a function of C, which is itself a function of Y, there is no bias.[5] The same considerations apply to the use of observed consumption in the linear and quadratic Engel curves.

The same expenditure categories were used as in the analysis of expenditure structure in chapters 4 and 5, with the addition of four categories: total transport and communication, taxes, social security payments, and private insurance. A maximum of forty-seven functions are estimated; eight are for aggregates whose components are also analyzed,

5. See Robert Summers, "A Note on Least Squares Bias in Household Expenditure Analysis," *Econometrica*, vol. 27 (January 1959), pp. 121–26. Evidence that the bias is small and that it pushes the elasticities toward 1.0 is given in S. J. Prais, "A Comment," in the same issue, pp. 127–29. Note that the alternative approach—basing C_r on observed income Y—has a different kind of bias, which may well be greater and whose effect is to *increase* the dispersion of the elasticities. This question is discussed later in this chapter.

and the remainder are for categories of spending that are not further disaggregated. The use of logarithms means that C_r is restricted to positive values; only households that actually spent something in category r are included in the regression. No attempt is made to explain why only some households had such expenditures. Households were not grouped for estimation; rather, each consuming unit represents one observation.

Expenditure Elasticities

The elasticities β_r and their standard errors estimated for the forty-seven expenditure categories in the five countries are shown in table 6-1. Only in the cases of vehicle purchases and ceremonial expenditures in Colombia is the coefficient indistinguishable from zero. (No estimates could be made for vehicles in Chile, Ecuador, or Venezuela; only in Peru is there a definite relation between car buying and total spending.) There are no negative elasticities, and thus no inferior goods at this level of aggregation, although some individual goods may be inferior.

Food elasticities are always less than one; that is, food and each of its components are necessities. (Total food expenditure has the lowest or next to lowest elasticity of any of the thirteen principal categories, in all five countries.) Housing is also a necessity, but has a somewhat higher elasticity; at least, this is true for spending on the household's principal dwelling.[6] Other dwellings and maintenance and improvements are, not surprisingly, likely to be luxuries and therefore highly income-elastic. Transportation and other consumption items such as tobacco and personal hygiene are also necessities, although private transportation is generally more of a luxury than public transport.

Medical care, insurance, and transfers show elasticities of around one. Obligatory social security payments have a lower elasticity than private insurance, and the latter can be considered a luxury. Elasticities of around one or greater also characterize clothing, education, and recreational and cultural spending. Within the category of clothing, children's clothes have the lowest elasticity and women's the highest; clothing is equally necessary

6. This does not contradict the evidence of chapter 5 that housing expenditure is income-elastic, because that analysis did not consider household size together with income. When the effect of size is taken into account, the share of the budget devoted to housing is seen to decline slightly as total expenditure or income rises. This distinction is important for many comparisons between the results of chapter 5 and those presented here.

Table 6-1. *Elasticities of Expenditure on Various Spending Categories with Respect to Total Household Expenditure, Five Latin American Countries*

Spending category	Colombia	Chile	Ecuador	Peru	Venezuela
Food	0.662	0.624	0.670	0.474	0.610
	(0.006)	(0.009)	(0.008)	(0.014)	(0.012)
Dairy products and eggs	0.870	0.687	0.902	0.487	0.580
	(0.015)	(0.017)	(0.018)	(0.023)	(0.018)
Cereals	0.447	0.260	0.300	0.167	0.300
	(0.010)	(0.012)	(0.012)	(0.018)	(0.018)
Meat and poultry	0.740	0.755	0.834	0.443	0.744
	(0.014)	(0.016)	(0.019)	(0.023)	(0.020)
Seafood	0.475	0.500	0.424	0.459	0.424
	(0.037)	(0.022)	(0.023)	(0.034)	(0.035)
Vegetables	0.437	0.334	0.427	0.193	0.439
	(0.011)	(0.016)	(0.014)	(0.021)	(0.023)
Fruits	0.821	0.786	0.850	0.831	0.581
	(0.016)	(0.021)	(0.021)	(0.034)	(0.023)
Fats and oils	0.395	0.401	0.433	0.242	0.466
	(0.013)	(0.016)	(0.014)	(0.026)	(0.025)
Sugar and sweets	0.344	0.369	0.554	0.374	0.515
	(0.013)	(0.017)	(0.017)	(0.026)	(0.024)
Hot beverages	0.296	0.447	0.477	0.553	0.382
	(0.013)	(0.018)	(0.017)	(0.038)	(0.026)
Alcoholic beverages	0.546	0.568	0.688	0.456	0.681
	(0.042)	(0.032)	(0.065)	(0.138)	(0.064)
Other beverages	0.518	0.495	0.700	0.430	0.585
	(0.029)	(0.026)	(0.031)	(0.082)	(0.036)
Other foods	0.683	0.584	0.936	0.589	0.594
	(0.021)	(0.027)	(0.031)	(0.045)	(0.040)
Meals away from home	0.859	0.668	0.587	0.721	0.879
	(0.025)	(0.041)	(0.055)	(0.067)	(0.049)
Housing	0.924	0.693	0.961	0.922	0.761
	(0.015)	(0.014)	(0.024)	(0.032)	(0.017)
Family	0.850	0.651	0.851	0.747	0.742
	(0.015)	(0.014)	(0.023)	(0.033)	(0.016)
Other	0.947	n.a.	1.247	1.434	n.a.
	(0.188)		(0.161)	(0.255)	
Maintenance	0.988	0.842	n.a.	0.972	n.a.
	(0.142)	(0.114)		(0.115)	
Furnishings and operation	1.596	1.628	1.358	1.445	1.512
	(0.024)	(0.035)	(0.035)	(0.046)	(0.034)
Furniture, durable goods	1.475	1.717	1.380	1.496	1.308
	(0.076)	(0.098)	(0.092)	(0.111)	(0.090)
Nondurable goods	0.754	0.598	0.573	0.550	0.727
	(0.020)	(0.031)	(0.022)	(0.031)	(0.025)
Services	1.410	1.341	1.086	1.050	1.300
	(0.040)	(0.052)	(0.061)	(0.061)	(0.052)
Clothing	1.244	1.058	1.114	1.049	1.185
	(0.023)	(0.023)	(0.039)	(0.045)	(0.053)
Men's ready-made	0.924	0.910	0.788	0.865	0.804
	(0.031)	(0.025)	(0.034)	(0.045)	(0.067)

Table 6-1 (*continued*)

Spending category	Colombia	Chile	Ecuador	Peru	Venezuela
Women's ready-made	1.192	0.913	0.820	0.950	0.837
	(0.027)	(0.024)	(0.031)	(0.046)	(0.057)
Children's ready-made	0.913	0.582	0.648	0.763	0.696
	(0.029)	(0.056)	(0.076)	(0.088)	(0.056)
Other	0.862	0.779	0.856	1.113	0.985
	(0.082)	(0.038)	(0.047)	(0.078)	(0.082)
Medical care	1.171	0.844	0.904	0.808	1.341
	(0.040)	(0.052)	(0.050)	(0.055)	(0.063)
Education	1.133	1.210	0.902	0.743	1.411
	(0.039)	(0.077)	(0.059)	(0.068)	(0.079)
Recreation, reading, culture	1.187	1.083	0.931	0.984	1.231
	(0.034)	(0.034)	(0.041)	(0.042)	(0.055)
Recreation	1.051	0.947	0.883	1.122	1.004
	(0.031)	(0.037)	(0.039)	(0.042)	(0.047)
Reading material and culture	0.779	0.698	0.536	0.576	0.931
	(0.031)	(0.030)	(0.036)	(0.036)	(0.056)
Transportation, communication	0.688	0.785	0.934	0.814	0.809
	(0.032)	(0.023)	(0.055)	(0.053)	(0.038)
Vehicle purchase	0.178	n.a.	n.a.	0.610	n.a.
	(0.420)			(0.292)	
Private transportation	0.735	0.692	0.551	0.658	0.933
	(0.091)	(0.069)	(0.080)	(0.057)	(0.063)
Public transportation	0.619	0.629	n.a.	0.712	0.530
	(0.030)	(0.028)		(0.064)	(0.044)
Telephone and other communication	0.753	1.280	0.952	1.065	0.488
	(0.047)	(0.053)	(0.052)	(0.072)	(0.060)
Other consumption	0.931	0.831	0.932	0.777	0.666
	(0.016)	(0.022)	(0.021)	(0.024)	(0.022)
Tobacco	0.482	0.495	0.629	0.848	0.518
	(0.034)	(0.024)	(0.045)	(0.056)	(0.045)
Personal care	0.955	0.765	0.936	0.716	0.691
	(0.015)	(0.025)	(0.019)	(0.022)	(0.022)
Ceremonies	0.599	0.665	−0.276	0.507	n.a.
	(0.309)	(0.139)	(0.396)	(0.176)	
Taxes	1.815	0.933	1.033	1.161	1.439
	(0.075)	(0.022)	(0.116)	(0.053)	(0.165)
Insurance	1.026	1.019	0.851	0.770	0.909
	(0.038)	(0.022)	(0.041)	(0.029)	(0.053)
Social security	0.830	1.022	0.830	0.756	0.689
	(0.038)	(0.021)	(0.039)	(0.028)	(0.056)
Other	1.116	n.a.	1.205	0.756	1.253
	(0.204)		(0.383)	(0.033)	(0.090)
Gifts and transfers	1.117	0.890	0.789	1.120	1.318
	(0.060)	(0.104)	(0.067)	(0.096)	(0.088)
Other nonconsumption	1.339	0.966	0.605	0.696	0.717
	(0.108)	(0.132)	(0.095)	(0.151)	(0.114)

Source: Original ECIEL calculations based on the survey data. Standard errors are in parentheses.
n.a. Not available; regression not run for lack of degrees of freedom (nonzero observations).

for all members of the household, but children are more likely to wear used clothes and women to increase the size or quality of their wardrobes. The highest elasticities are for household furnishings and maintenance, particularly furniture, appliances, and other durables. These and services are clearly luxuries, whereas nondurable goods (cleaning supplies, for instance) are necessities.

Because the absolute values of the elasticities may differ considerably among countries, international comparisons are more easily made by means of rankings. For this comparison, the elasticities of twelve of the thirteen principal expenditure categories were ranked in each country, and Spearman's rank correlation coefficient calculated for each pair of countries. (Other nonconsumption spending was excluded, because it is a small and heterogeneous category and because its elasticity varies in rank from four to thirteen.) The results are as follows:

	Colombia	Chile	Ecuador	Peru
Chile	0.776			
Ecuador	0.531	0.293		
Peru	0.685	0.385	0.671	
Venezuela	0.846	0.755	0.315	0.573

These correlations are consistent with a ranking of the five countries in terms of similarity of elasticities, in this order: Chile, Venezuela, Colombia, Peru, Ecuador. That is, the ranking of elasticities in Venezuela is close to that in Chile and in Colombia, differs more from the ranking in Peru, and is very different from the ranking in Ecuador. The same sequence is obtained when the comparison is based on each of the other four countries, except that Chile shows a slightly greater similarity to Colombia than to Venezuela.[7] What makes this ordering interesting is that it corresponds to the ranking of countries by typical, or modal, real household income per person. The pattern of elasticities is therefore a function of real income levels; and countries show more similar patterns as their real income distributions are more alike.

A more detailed examination can be made of relative elasticities within the food and beverage category, the most important one for most house-

7. Because the correlation coefficient involves the squares of differences between rankings, it is insensitive to the *direction* of difference. The ranking Colombia-Venezuela-Chile-Peru-Ecuador obtained by considering the first column of the table is therefore consistent with the ordering Chile-Venezuela-Colombia-Peru-Ecuador: Chile is closer to Colombia than Peru is, but it lies on the opposite side.

holds. In general, milk and eggs, meat, fruits, other foods (including prepared foods), and meals away from home are relative luxuries. Seafood, vegetables, fats and oils, sweets, and beverages are relative necessities. The lowest elasticities occur for cereals. Exceptions to this pattern occur mostly in Peru and Venezuela. Peru is the only country in which spending on seafood increases relative to purchases of meat and poultry as total spending rises.[8] Elasticities for fruits and for milk and eggs are relatively low in Venezuela, perhaps because of relatively high incomes.

The Peruvian results are also notable for a very low elasticity for total food, 0.474, against a range for the other four countries of 0.610 to 0.670. There are two possible explanations for this. First, food expenditures are relatively stable, while total spending in Peru shows a very large transitory variance; second, the Peruvian sample overrepresents high-income households to a greater degree than any other sample, and the elasticity of food is expected to be low for such families. Both factors may have affected other elasticities to a lesser degree. Other international differences in elasticities may be due to differences in incomes or in prices (including the effect of public provision, particularly of education and medical care).

Constancy of Elasticities

The convenience of the double-log model, which permits the elasticity to be represented by a single parameter, β_r, is also one of its principal disadvantages, because no elasticity is likely to be constant over the range of observed expenditure. Almost any good is a luxury at sufficiently low incomes, and gradually becomes a necessity or a declining share of the budget at higher incomes. An elasticity should be expected to decline as income rises, perhaps after an initial rise at the level where households first start to buy the good. However, the value of β_r is an average elasticity over the sample; and since the regressions are unweighted, in every country except Venezuela the estimate is biased toward the value appropriate to the high-income stratum, which is overrepresented in the sample. The amount of bias varies among countries; it is more severe in Peru and Colombia than in Chile and Ecuador.

It is therefore useful to have some idea of how much the elasticity varies

8. This may reflect the success of a government campaign to stimulate the consumption of seafood, for which Peru has abundant resources, rather than of meat, a large share of which must be imported.

among different income levels. Any Engel curve except the double-log model makes the elasticity vary continuously; the most useful comparison is obtained if the double-log model is estimated separately for different strata, allowing the elasticity to be constant within each stratum. This was done by Roldán with the data for Santiago.[9] The lower stratum includes all households with incomes below twice the minimum wage (translated into income), which constitute about one-third of the population. All other households are classed as high-income, and the data are grouped in each stratum (fifty-six and seventy groups, respectively) for estimation. Roldán uses income rather than total spending, and the categories C_i do not exactly match those used by ECIEL, but the comparison of elasticities is nonetheless useful.[10] The results are presented in table 6-2. Although the standard errors of estimate are often large, there are significant differences in the elasticity in almost half the cases. Even when the differences are not statistically significant, as for most categories of food, the point estimates may differ by as much as 0.15 (meat and seafood).

Because these results are for one country only and because comparison is difficult, no strong conclusions can be drawn. Probably, the ECIEL elasticity estimates do not represent the extremes of the income distribution, particularly the lowest incomes. The assumption of a constant elasticity is safer for food (and perhaps for housing) than for such categories as household furnishings, maintenance and services, clothing, recreation, and transportation.

Short-Run and Long-Run Relations

The estimates shown in tables 6-1 and 6-2 show how changes in C_r are related to changes in C or Y over an interval of one trimester. Over longer intervals the relation may not be the same, partly because short-run (current) C or Y contains transitory components that may bias the elasticity either upward (if positively correlated with transitory variations in C_r) or

9. Roldán, "Funciones Consumo por Tramos de Ingreso," especially pp. 9–10, 17–20, 26.

10. Roldán's estimating equation is

$$\log C_r = \beta_{or} + \beta_{Nr} \log N + \beta_r \log Y + \varepsilon,$$

where N is household size. He applies an F-test to determine whether the same equation (same set of parameters) is valid for both strata. Here the only concern is whether β_r differs between them.

Table 6-2. *Elasticities of Expenditures, Various Spending Categories,*
Low-Income and High-Income Households, Urban Chile

Spending category	Low income	High income
Eggs[a]	0.734	0.633
	(0.145)	(0.060)
Cereals[a]	0.190	0.213
	(0.080)	(0.029)
Meat[a]	0.909	0.753
	(0.165)	(0.221)
Seafood[a]	0.400	0.604
	(0.308)	(0.210)
Vegetables[a]	0.366	0.294
	(0.095)	(0.038)
Fruits	1.172	0.708
	(0.206)	(0.055)
Fats and oils[a]	0.274	0.235
	(0.134)	(0.217)
Sugar[a]	0.221	0.275
	(0.118)	(0.224)
Nonalcoholic beverages[a]	0.427	0.483
	(0.124)	(0.051)
Alcohol and tobacco	1.015	0.890
	(0.252)	(0.071)
Meals away from home[a]	1.661	1.127
	(0.601)	(0.118)
Household furnishings	2.778	0.623
	(0.835)	(0.310)
Maintenance	0.543	1.728
	(0.248)	(0.233)
Services	0.528	0.728
	(0.231)	(0.041)
Clothing	1.811	0.965
	(0.208)	(0.042)
Medical care[a]	1.283	1.071
	(0.709)	(0.166)
Recreation	1.944	1.195
	(0.358)	(0.077)
Transportation	0.419	1.279
	(0.141)	(0.053)
Personal care[a]	1.434	1.248
	(0.247)	(0.054)

Source: Romualdo Roldán, "Funciones Consumo por Tramos de Ingreso," Centro de Estudios de Planificación Nacional (CEPLAN) Documento no. 38 (Santiago: Universidad Católica de Chile, 1974; processed), p. 26. Numbers in parentheses are standard errors.

a. Difference not significant at the 95 percent confidence level, using the root mean square of the two estimated standard errors (with the numbers of groups as weights).

downward (if correlated negatively or not at all).[11] Some estimates have been made of permanent elasticities β_r^*, relating C_r to an estimate of permanent income Y^*, using the double-log model and (almost) the identical set of sociodemographic variables as in the standard ECIEL analysis. This investigation is limited to Colombia and to six categories of expenditure.[12] The elasticities may be expected to fall, simply because income elasticities will be lower than expenditure elasticities if the income elasticity of total consumption is less than one. To offset this effect, the estimates β_r^* are divided by the estimated permanent consumption elasticity ($\mu^* = 0.881$) for comparison to the values β_r. The results are as follows:

Category	$\beta_r(C)$	$\beta_r^*(Y^*)$	β_r^*/μ^*
Food and beverages	0.662	0.591	0.671
	(0.006)	(0.015)	
Housing	0.924	0.720	0.817
	(0.015)	(0.026)	
Durables	1.475	1.109	1.257
	(0.076)	(0.088)	
Nondurables	0.754	0.681	0.774
	(0.020)	(0.027)	
Clothing	1.244	1.101	1.250
	(0.023)	(0.040)	
Education	1.133	1.060	1.202
	(0.039)	(0.140)	

The adjusted elasticity is higher, by less than 10 percent, for food, nondurables, clothing, and education. (The differences are not significant at the 95 percent confidence level.) The permanent elasticity is significantly lower for housing (by 16 percent) and durables (17 percent). The current or short-run elasticity for durables appears to be biased upward by the relation between (transitory) purchases of those goods and the associated transitory increases in total expenditure. Note that the estimates β_r^*/μ^*

11. See the discussion in appendix B; Milton Friedman, *A Theory of the Consumption Function* (Princeton University Press, 1957), pp. 206–09; and Jean Crockett, "Biases in Estimating Income-Expenditure Regressions from Cross-Section Data," in Irwin Friend and Robert Jones, eds., *Study of Consumer Expenditures, Incomes and Savings: Proceedings of the Conference on Consumption and Saving* (University of Pennsylvania Press, 1960), vol. 2, pp. 213–22.

12. Philip Musgrove, "The Estimation of Permanent Income in a Cross-Section of Household Budget Data" (Brookings Institution, 1973; processed), pp. 17–30. This document describes a preliminary version of the technique developed in Musgrove, "Determination and Distribution of Permanent Household Income in Urban South America" (Ph.D. dissertation, Massachusetts Institute of Technology, 1974); the first estimates of Y^* are not entirely satisfactory.

are slightly less dispersed than the elasticities β_r: the coefficient of variation falls from 0.273 to 0.247. There ceases to be any significant difference between the elasticities for durables and clothing, or between those for housing and nondurables, when the estimates are based on permanent consumption.

Satisfying the Budget Constraint

As mentioned earlier, the double-logarithmic model of expenditures does not satisfy the household budget constraint at all levels of total expenditure. However, the constraint should be satisfied at the point of means of the different budget shares; how closely it is satisfied can be tested by the statistic $\sum_r g_r \beta_r$, where β_r is the elasticity of expenditure on category r, and g_r is the individual mean budget share in that category discussed in chapter 4 (see table 4-3). This sum should equal 1.0, when all categories are included; if some categories are omitted, then the test is whether $\sum_r g_r \beta_r = \sum_r g_r$, taking only the included categories. Within a category r, the same test can be applied to the components u; that is, $\sum_u g_{ur} \beta_{ur} = g_r \beta_r$.

The shares g_r are weighted, whereas the estimated elasticities β_r are not; the test will give poor results to the extent that the true elasticities are not constant over strata and intervals and to the degree that the unweighted estimates are biased. Most elasticities can be expected to stay constant or to decline with rising income, rather than to rise; so for a sample that over-represents the high-income strata, $\sum_r g_r \beta_r$ is more likely to be too small than too large. A minor problem in making the comparison is that the β_r are estimated from total expenditure, while the g_r are shares of expenditure excluding personal taxes and social security. The comparison is therefore restricted to the latter (smaller) concept. The difference is slight for most households.

When this test is made the ratios are always less than one: the regressions of components, when added up, tend to underestimate the category totals. The problem is worse, the greater the disaggregation of the total.[13] The problem does not seem to be due to sample nonproportionality and the use of unweighted regressions. The worst match is obtained for Peru,

13. This result may be due to errors of observation, leading to a bias of the elasticities toward zero such as is always associated with essentially random errors in variables. Small categories of expenditure are more likely to contain such errors than large aggregates, in which the errors in different components may be offsetting.

where the sample is nonproportional; but the best is obtained for Colombia, which is also overrepresentative of high-income households. There is not much pattern to the relative degrees of satisfaction of the constraint for the different categories of expenditure. The percentage ratio exceeds the overall ratio for a country; that is, the components of a category are more likely to sum to unity than are all categories in the total, for housing, transport, and communication (except in Ecuador), and other consumption (except in Chile). This is reasonable, since these categories have elasticities close to one. No pattern emerges for the other categories. Given the variability of elasticities among countries, no marked ordering is to be expected.

Income Elasticities

The simple expenditure-income relation discussed in chapter 3 can be combined with the expenditure elasticities to yield estimated income-elasticities of expenditure on different categories. The income-elasticity of the rth expenditure category is α_r, where $\alpha_r = \mu \beta_r$. The estimates are biased to the extent that expenditure C_r depends directly on income in a way that varies among categories. Any two elasticities α_r and α_s have the same ratio as the corresponding expenditure elasticities, β_r and β_s. (This is not true of elasticities estimated directly from income.) For a given sample, therefore, the conversion of β_r to α_r does not yield any new information; but since the elasticities μ differ among countries, it is of interest to compare the α_r internationally.

This comparison was limited to the aggregate categories for simplicity, and because the assumption of a separable (two-stage) spending decision probably becomes less satisfactory at lower levels of aggregation. Standard errors were not estimated for the α_r, but since μ is always less than one and is estimated with error, the errors on the α_r necessarily exceed those on the corresponding β_r. These are particularly short-run estimates, since they combine the short-run relations of C_r to C and of C to Y. Hence, except perhaps for household furnishings, they are likely to be understated. The imputed rent that enters housing expenditure and total expenditure is also a component of total income, so the positive association is maintained between C_r and Y for that category.

The chief conclusion to be drawn is that, in general, the income elasticities are not any less dispersed among countries, for a given category, than are the expenditure elasticities. Expenditure on transport and communication is a partial exception in that three of the five values of α_r for this category are indistinguishable, although the β_r are quite different. Otherwise, it does not appear that the α_r are more constant across countries than the β_r or that a low (high) estimate of μ does not offset systematically high (low) values of expenditure elasticities.

Household Characteristics and Spending

A large number of variables X_{uj} are used to represent different socio-demographic characteristics. I consider first the variables common to all the regressions: city, interval or trimester, age of household head, tenure of dwelling, and employment of spouse. Other variables, examined later in this chapter, are used in only one or a few regressions: these variables are type of dwelling, construction material, and number of rooms (related to housing expenditure and furnishing and operation); education of the household head (related to educational and cultural expenditures); and possession of a vehicle or a telephone (related to spending on transportation and communication).[14] A further group of variables, describing the size and composition of the household, are analyzed in the latter part of this chapter; however, household size is an explanatory variable in all the different Engel curves estimated here.

Some of these variables can be used directly as quantitative variables in a regression model (number of household members, for example, is a continuous variable, as is number of years of schooling of the head), or as dummies or qualitative variables. By using dummy variables X_{uj}, the regression equation avoids the assumption of a linear relation over all the values of the independent variable; instead, the coefficients β_{ujr} can be examined to see what form the relation takes. This approach has the drawback, however, that the classes of the variables may not be chosen in the best way to reveal the relation. A particular characteristic may be very important, but its effect may be masked by unsatisfactory choice of classes or dummy variables.[15]

14. I do not consider here the difference between primary and secondary households, which was tested only for Colombia. See appendix A for the definition of secondary households.

15. In principle, this problem can be met by experimenting with different specifications of the dummy variables. The importance of a characteristic can also be examined by a marginal F-test to determine whether the entire block of dummies representing that characteristic has a significant effect on the regression. Neither of these procedures was applied to the estimates except in some initial tests with Colombian data.

The discussion that follows is organized by sociodemographic variable; each of the categories of expenditure that it influences is briefly discussed. Attention is concentrated on the variables that have a significant effect on spending.[16] The results for the variables used in all categories are presented in appendix tables C-41 (Colombia) to C-45 (Venezuela).

City of Residence

In Chile and Peru, only the capital city was surveyed, so there are five non-capital cities to be examined here: Barranquilla, Cali, and Medellín in Colombia, Guayaquil in Ecuador, and Maracaibo in Venezuela. Some rather striking patterns emerge. In either four or five of the non-capital cities, expenditure tends to be higher than in the capital city, for any given total expenditure, for food and beverages, household furnishings (especially durables), recreation, and other consumption expenditures. There is an equally marked tendency for spending in the non-capital cities to be lower on housing, clothing, and education and on transportation in general, or at least on public transport. In some instances, Medellín and Guayaquil behave differently from the rest. It may be significant that these are large cities (Guayaquil is even larger than Quito) with substantial industrial sectors and therefore quite different from the smaller cities of Barranquilla, Cali, and Maracaibo. Some notable patterns also emerge in the allocation of food expenditures. In the non-capital cities, spending is almost invariably higher for high-protein foods (milk and eggs, meat, poultry, and seafood). It tends also to be higher for fats and oils, sweets, and soft drinks. There is a tendency, though less pronounced, toward lower expenditure on cereals, vegetables, and hot beverages, particularly in Colombia. Spending is higher on fruit in the smaller tropical cities of Barranquilla, Cali, and Maracaibo, presumably because of lower prices and greater availability.

Climate is probably also the reason for lower clothing expenditures in Barranquilla, Guayaquil, and Maracaibo. In the case of housing, the chief factor is undoubtedly price, rents being generally higher in the capital cities. Educational expenditures are higher in the capitals, perhaps in part because people come to those cities in order to attend school. It is less obvious what accounts for the uniformly higher spending in the other cities on recreation and on miscellaneous consumption.

16. An expenditure category is not listed if the regression was not estimated or did not pass an F-test of overall significance at the 95 percent confidence level.

Because the Engel curves were not estimated separately by city, there may be bias in these estimates; the city coefficients may include what are actually expenditure effects. In the case of Colombia, Engel curves have been estimated, in linear and quadratic forms, separately by city. The estimated parameters—subsistence expenditures and marginal budget shares—can be transformed into expenditure or income elasticities (see appendix B). A comparison across cities of expenditure elasticities derived from the ELES and the QES suggests that, in fact, elasticities differ markedly: the elasticity for food, for example, ranges from 0.74 (Cali) to 0.86 (Medellín) in the linear model, and from 0.74 (Barranquilla) to 0.82 (Medellín) in the quadratic version. Still greater differences are observed in such categories as durables and education, although for some expenditures the differences are slight.[17] However, these elasticities are evaluated at the point of means, and mean total and specific expenditures differ among cities. Even if a single function correctly described all four cities, the elasticity would differ at different points along it.

A more useful comparison is to evaluate the elasticity at the same value of consumption in all four cities. The ELES results (based on current income Y) are used, and the expenditure elasticity is evaluated at the levels of C_r and C that correspond to median income in the Colombian sample—5,090 pesos. The results appear in table 6-3 (standard errors are not available).

Clearly, there are some cases of large intercity differences. Moreover, most apparent differences in spending behavior are compatible with obvious differences in climate or in the prices and availability of goods and services. However, the differences are slight for the categories of food, housing, and clothing, and not very large for transportation. Incomes tend to be higher in capital cities, but the income distributions of different cities in a country overlap considerably (more in Colombia and Ecuador than in Venezuela). The pooled specification was therefore retained, in the expectation that the bias it introduces would be small.

Spending Variation over Time

The variable trimester—which, like city of residence, characterizes the sample rather than individual households—is singularly difficult to inter-

---

17. Howard J. Howe, "Estimation of the Linear and Quadratic Expenditure Systems: A Cross-Section Case for Colombia" (Ph.D. dissertation, University of Pennsylvania, 1974), p. 255.

Table 6-3. *Elasticities of Expenditure, Various Spending Categories, Medium-Income Households, Urban Colombia*[a]

Spending category	Bogotá	Barranquilla	Cali	Medellín
Food	0.821	0.793	0.764	0.862
Housing	1.064	1.178	1.218	1.046
Durables	1.514	1.951	1.532	1.822
Clothing	1.356	1.463	1.339	1.230
Medical care	1.584	0.189	1.427	1.379
Education	1.058	3.773	1.393	0.985
Recreation	1.332	1.610	1.405	2.256
Transportation	0.956	1.054	1.065	1.127

Source: Calculated from Howard Howe, "Estimation of the Linear and Quadratic Expenditure Systems: A Cross-Section Case for Colombia" (Ph.D. dissertation, University of Pennsylvania, 1974), pp. 176, 178, 181, and 183.

a. Elasticities estimated for a household of four adults and three children of different ages.

pret; it was included in the regressions largely to take some account of price changes during the survey year. Differences among trimesters may be due to cyclical or inflationary changes in real expenditure or to seasonal variations in supply or demand. Moreover, a particular interval in the survey represents different times of the year in different countries. Finally, the seasons in Colombia and Venezuela are the opposite of those in Peru and Chile, while in Ecuador there is virtually no seasonal variation. (For these reasons, no comparative analysis is offered here.) In only a few cases are there clear trends throughout the year; for example, the shares of the budget going to food in Peru and to clothing in Chile rise steadily, while those for furnishings in Ecuador and for recreation in Colombia decline. Such long-term changes probably reflect movements in relative prices or real income; most interinterval differences—for example, spending in one quarter being notably high or low—tend to be seasonal.

Age of the Household Head

Chapter 3 considered the effect of age on total spending, for a given income. Here, I examine the effect of age on the distribution of the budget, with the age of the household head used as a proxy for the age of the household. It is clear from the analysis of chapter 4 that households at different ages have quite different expenditure structures, but this is due partly to differences in total spending, since age is one of the major determinants of household income.

As noted in chapter 3, there is an almost uniform tendency for purchases of durables to decrease after the age of thirty-four; therefore, total expenditure on household furnishing and operation also declines. Expenditures on services rise as a share of the budget for elderly households in Colombia, Peru, and Venezuela, but this does not offset the overall trend. Clothing expenditures follow the same pattern as household furnishings, declining steadily after the age of thirty-four (Colombia and Venezuela) or falling significantly only after forty-nine (Chile, Ecuador, and Peru). There is a less pronounced tendency for miscellaneous consumption spending to decline with age.

Budget shares increase with age for two categories. Expenditure on housing (including imputed rent) rises steadily and significantly in every country except Peru.[18] Spending on communication rises for one or more of the older age groups in every country except Ecuador.

The remaining major expenditure categories show either a nonmonotonic variation with age or no pattern at all. Recreation and transportation are examples of the latter. Food expenditures in Chile, Ecuador, Peru, and Venezuela are highest, in total or at least for some categories, in the middle age groups (thirty-five to sixty-four). In Colombia there is a decline in food expenditures from thirty-four on. This, however, is due to the survey's exclusion of supplementary members in Colombia, so that older households are perceived as smaller, with relatively fewer adults. In all countries, spending on education tends to be highest in the thirty-five to forty-nine age group, when medical expenses tend to be lowest; the latter are highest for the very young and the very old members of a household.

Nearly all the observed variation in the allocation of the budget in different age groups can be explained by three factors. The first, which characterizes spending on food, medical care, and education, is the structure of the household and the needs of its members. The age of the head is simply a useful proxy for a more complete description of the household.[19] The second factor is the accumulation of durable or semidurable goods—housing, furnishings, and clothing—which are acquired at earlier ages so that

18. Under inflation, an imputed rent will rise even though mortgage payments do not. This process will have continued longer for older than for younger households, leading to an apparent rise in the share of the budget spent for housing. Also, older households are somewhat more likely to own than to rent their dwellings.

19. Life cycle might be a still better proxy, but this variable could not be generated reliably from the Venezuela data. Some of the classes might also be too small for analysis.

they can be used longer by the household. Finally, the method of measuring housing expenditure results in an apparent appreciation of the value of the asset. Housing cost measured by either paid rent or mortgage payments would probably show a rise relative to total spending, at least up to the age of fifty, followed by a decline.

The effect of age is analyzed quite differently in the ELES estimates by stratum in Bogotá, Guayaquil, Lima, and Caracas: estimates are made separately for young and old families (head under or over forty-five).[20] Marginal budget shares, β_r, are estimated separately for young and for old households within each of the three strata, for five expenditure categories. Other expenditures, which include household maintenance, medical care, education, transportation, and miscellaneous consumption and nonconsumption items, generally show a higher marginal spending propensity on the part of older households, but the category is too broad for comparison with the disaggregated Engel curve estimates obtained with the double-log model. The results for the remaining four categories—food, housing, durables (including vehicles), and clothing—are unsatisfactory for Lima, because in each stratum one negative share was obtained.[21] The results shown in table 6-4 were obtained for Bogotá, Guayaquil, and Caracas. Younger households have almost uniformly higher marginal propensities to spend on clothing and (with one exception) durables. With two partial exceptions, older households have higher propensities to devote the marginal budget to housing, but the tendency is less pronounced. The propensity to spend on food is usually higher for younger households, but there are two clear exceptions—both, interestingly, in the low-income stratum. These results are altogether consistent with those given by the double-log model.

Housing Tenure

Partly because of the way housing expenditure is measured, it is to be expected that families who own their homes (whether fully paid for or not) will have expenditure structures quite different from those of families

20. Howe and Musgrove, "Analysis of ECIEL Household Budget Data."

21. Since the β_r are required to sum to one, estimates for the other categories are biased upward. The negative estimate occurred for durables in the old, low-income stratum and for food in the old, middle-income and young, high-income strata. Negative values of β_r for durables in Bogotá and Caracas in the low-income stratum are smaller and have much less effect on the results.

who rent. The behavior of the relatively small number of households in neither category—typically families occupying abandoned buildings or who have built their own dwellings in slum areas—should be different from that of either group since they have no disbursements for housing at all. (Rents are still imputed to their dwellings.) To examine these differences, dummy variables for rented and other housing were included in the regressions.

Table 6-4. *Marginal Budget Shares, Four Spending Categories, by Household Income Stratum and Age of Head, Three Latin American Cities*

City and spending category	Low income		Middle income		High income	
	Young	*Old*	*Young*	*Old*	*Young*	*Old*
Bogotá						
Food	0.347	0.390	0.271	0.244	0.161	0.148
	(0.012)	(0.021)	(0.011)	(0.017)	(0.009)	(0.019)
Housing	0.268	0.329	0.319	0.287	0.299	0.254
	(0.009)	(0.072)	(0.013)	(0.019)	(0.017)	(0.034)
Durables	0.046	−0.000	0.059	0.032	0.075	0.057
	(0.002)	(0.000)	(0.002)	(0.002)	(0.004)	(0.007)
Clothing	0.116	0.078	0.095	0.083	0.108	0.075
	(0.004)	(0.004)	(0.004)	(0.006)	(0.006)	(0.010)
Guayaquil						
Food	0.359	0.403	0.443	0.357	0.280	0.111
	(0.018)	(0.021)	(0.038)	(0.016)	(0.017)	(0.014)
Housing	0.235	0.310	0.232	0.319	0.396	0.538
	(0.012)	(0.016)	(0.019)	(0.014)	(0.023)	(0.062)
Durables	0.074	0.028	0.049	0.051	0.049	0.030
	(0.004)	(0.001)	(0.004)	(0.002)	(0.023)	(0.004)
Clothing	0.101	0.073	0.058	0.061	0.074	0.054
	(0.005)	(0.004)	(0.005)	(0.003)	(0.004)	(0.006)
Caracas						
Food	0.548	0.080	0.193	0.163	0.099	0.105
	(0.092)	(0.034)	(0.012)	(0.011)	(0.008)	(0.011)
Housing	0.058	0.471	0.277	0.388	0.367	0.428
	(0.011)	(0.180)	(0.018)	(0.026)	(0.028)	(0.043)
Durables	−0.011	0.023	0.047	0.015	0.045	0.017
	(0.002)	(0.009)	(0.003)	(0.001)	(0.003)	(0.002)
Clothing	0.155	0.166	0.097	0.019	0.854	0.031
	(0.028)	(0.065)	(0.006)	(0.011)	(0.006)	(0.003)

Source: Howard Howe and Philip Musgrove, "An Analysis of ECIEL Household Budget Data for Bogotá, Caracas, Guayaquil, and Lima," in Constantino Lluch, Alan A. Powell, and Ross A. Williams, eds., *Patterns in Household Demand and Saving* (New York: Oxford University Press for the World Bank, 1977), pp. 168, 170, 172. Numbers in parentheses are standard errors.

In every country, households who rent report lower housing expenditure relative to total spending than do households who own their dwellings.[22] Except in Venezuela, spending for shelter is lowest among households in the residual category. Not surprisingly, almost all the significant coefficients for other types of spending are positive; among households who rent, the only exception is for food expenditure in Chile. There seems to be no evidence that, when other factors are taken into account, there is any difference in tastes between families who own and families who rent their dwelling. The latter behave as though the price of housing were lower for them and the price elasticity were less than unitary. They simply increase their spending on all other categories. The same is true, though with some exceptions in Peru and Venezuela, for households who neither own nor rent.[23]

Employment of the Spouse

The allocation of the household budget may depend not only on total spending and family characteristics but also on the way the household income is acquired. The employment of the spouse (nearly always the wife) of the household head might be particularly important, since her employment would leave less time for domestic chores and therefore promote the substitution of market goods and services for labor-intensive activities at home.[24] Employment also creates needs for transportation, work-related clothing, and meals away from home.

A dummy variable was included to indicate whether the spouse is employed, but no account is taken of the employment or income of other

---

22. Mean total spending is typically higher for the latter, but the differences are small. Households in the "other" category are usually quite poor.

23. The only negative coefficient in Peru is for household services, chiefly utilities, and the availability of these is related to the type as well as tenure of the dwelling.

24. This kind of relation is the subject of a growing literature concerned with "household production functions." See, for example, Gary S. Becker, "A Theory of the Allocation of Time," *Economic Journal*, vol. 75 (September 1965), pp. 493–517; and Kelvin Lancaster, *Consumer Demand: A New Approach* (Columbia University Press, 1971). Some of the limitations of this approach are explored in Robert A. Pollak and Michael L. Wachter, "The Relevance of the Household Production Function and Its Implications for the Allocation of Time," *Journal of Political Economy*, vol. 83 (April 1975), pp. 255–77.

Table 6-5. *Coefficients of Employment of the Spouse, Various Spending Categories, Five Latin American Countries*

Spending category	Colombia	Chile	Ecuador	Peru	Venezuela
All food	0.039	−0.083	−0.008	−0.021	−0.055
	(0.015)	(0.022)	(0.019)	(0.032)	(0.028)
Meals away from home	0.204	0.014	0.230	0.011	−0.045
	(0.062)	(0.085)	(0.119)	(0.154)	(0.112)
Housing	−0.189	−0.056	−0.057	−0.082	−0.086
	(0.031)	(0.026)	(0.039)	(0.055)	(0.036)
Furnishings and operation	0.136	0.141	0.080	0.114	0.146
	(0.053)	(0.064)	(0.059)	(0.080)	(0.079)
All clothing	0.113	0.023	0.120	0.002	0.194
	(0.059)	(0.051)	(0.084)	(0.094)	(0.112)
Men's ready-made clothing	−0.008	−0.059	0.104	−0.108	0.074
	(0.075)	(0.054)	(0.071)	(0.100)	(0.146)
Women's ready-made clothing	0.060	0.094	0.056	0.135	0.291
	(0.064)	(0.052)	(0.065)	(0.093)	(0.128)
Recreation	0.142	0.012	0.008	0.068	0.015
	(0.064)	(0.060)	(0.071)	(0.076)	(0.104)
All transportation	0.185	0.044	0.030	0.250	0.122
	(0.056)	(0.046)	(0.096)	(0.101)	(0.069)
Public transportation	0.266	0.153	n.a.	0.202	0.099
	(0.061)	(0.054)		(0.116)	(0.087)
Other	0.048	0.116	−0.001	0.012	0.073
	(0.043)	(0.050)	(0.046)	(0.053)	(0.052)

Source: Original ECIEL calculations based on the survey data. Numbers in parentheses are standard errors.
n.a. Not available.

family members.[25] The employment status of the spouse is not often significant, but if some coefficients with larger errors of estimation are also considered, a reasonable pattern emerges. This is shown in table 6-5. Households in which the spouse works spend less of their budget on hous-

25. Except for the three categories of expenditure on insurance (total, social security, and private insurance payments), where variables are introduced indicating whether the number of people employed is none, one, two, or three or more. Coefficients are estimated for the first three classes. Insurance expenditures are highest, as a share of the budget, when three or more are employed in Peru, and when only one person is employed in Chile and Venezuela; they are lowest when no member is working. No coefficient is significant in Colombia.

ing and (usually) less on food. They regularly spend more on meals away from home, household furnishings and operation, clothing, recreation, transportation, and miscellaneous consumption (Venezuela is an occasional exception). Increased spending is particularly marked for public transport and for women's clothing; expenditure on men's clothing may be shifted either up or down slightly.

Education of the Household Head

Presumably, this variable affects all expenditure categories, either because education changes people's tastes or because more educated households determine their budgets more efficiently to satisfy a given set of tastes.[26] However, the first effect can be examined only by estimating some parameters of a utility function separately for different educational groups, which is impossible in the double-log model. The second effect can be analyzed only after removing transitory variations in total spending, because education is the most important determinant of permanent income. The problem is the same as that considered in chapter 3—determining the effect of education on the propensity to consume.

The education of the head was therefore introduced, as dummy variables for primary, secondary, and higher schooling compared to no formal education, to explain only spending on education and quasi education (reading material and cultural items).[27] The results are shown in table 6-6. If the class with no formal education (which is quite small in all countries) is ignored, expenditure rises with education for both categories in all five countries. However, only at the level of university education are the coefficients significant more often than not. This educational level has a much greater marginal effect on cultural expenditures than on educational spending as compared with the marginal effect of secondary schooling.[28]

26. For a discussion of the latter possibility, see Robert T. Michael, "Education and Consumption," in F. Thomas Juster, ed., *Education, Income and Human Behavior* (McGraw-Hill, 1975), pp. 235–52, or by the same author, *The Effect of Education on Efficiency in Consumption* (National Bureau of Economic Research, 1972).

27. Education also affects total recreational spending, but only the cultural component is considered here.

28. That is, $[\beta(\text{higher}) - \beta(\text{secondary})]$ is larger, relative to $[\beta(\text{secondary}) - \beta(\text{primary})]$, for cultural than for educational expenditures in all five countries.

Size and Characteristics of the Dwelling

Three variables were chosen to characterize the dwelling. The number of rooms is a proxy for the amount of housing the family gets for its money, while the type of dwelling and the material of which it is made are extremely crude indexes of quality. These characteristics were related both to expenditure on housing and to the categories of furnishings and operation of the household. The latter expenditures may be expected to depend on the size of the dwelling, although not necessarily on its quality.

Table 6-6. *Coefficients of Expenditure on Education and Culture, by Educational Level of Head of Household, Five Latin American Countries*

Country and spending category	Educational level		
	Primary	Secondary	Higher
Colombia			
Education	0.365	0.624	0.771
	(0.130)	(0.136)	(0.159)
Culture	−0.017	0.200	0.548
	(0.116)	(0.119)	(0.131)
Chile			
Education	−0.325	0.050	0.354
	(0.354)	(0.353)	(0.367)
Culture	−0.144	−0.104	0.122
	(0.117)	(0.117)	(0.125)
Ecuador			
Education	0.442	0.775	0.998
	(0.250)	(0.258)	(0.277)
Culture	0.147	0.416	0.621
	(0.189)	(0.191)	(0.199)
Peru			
Education	−0.180	0.335	0.723
	(0.459)	(0.458)	(0.461)
Culture	−0.307	−0.127	0.011
	(0.224)	(0.224)	(0.226)
Venezuela			
Education	−0.046	0.137	0.313
	(0.137)	(0.168)	(0.219)
Culture	0.023	0.156	0.474
	(0.119)	(0.131)	(0.158)

Source: Original ECIEL calculations based on the survey data. Numbers in parentheses are standard errors.

The effects of size are presented in table 6-7. Comparisons are made to dwellings of eight or more rooms in four countries. (This variable was not included in the Venezuela survey.) It is clear that expenditure on housing itself, and on the services required to operate it, takes an increasing share of the budget as the number of rooms increases. Results for Colombia, Chile, and Peru indicate that spending falls for durables and for maintenance. Except in Ecuador, there is no systematic pattern for nondurables.[29]

For a given size and construction material, expenditure is greatest on houses (detached or semidetached) everywhere except in Chile; apartments, rooms, boarding houses, tenements, and slum dwellings are "cheaper." This effect is, of course, partly a matter of real quality and partly an artifact of the way housing expenditure is measured. Houses are most likely to have imputed rent, although this occurs (less frequently) for apartments as well; the remaining categories are almost always rented. The estimates related to construction material show concrete dwellings to require the highest expenditures, followed usually by brick, wood, and other materials. Neither the type of dwelling nor its construction has any systematic or significant effect on expenditure for household equipment and operation.

Possession of a Vehicle or a Telephone

One would expect the ownership of a vehicle to raise the share of the budget devoted to transport and communication in total and to shift consumption from public to private transport. Both effects are observed.[30]

---

29. The number of rooms was introduced as a continuous variable, rather than as a block of dummies, in some preliminary regressions for Colombia. The dependent variable is still the logarithm of expenditure, so the coefficient is an estimate of the proportional change in spending resulting from an increase of one room in the size of the dwelling. Coefficients and standard errors are as follows:

Total housing	0.0056	(0.0010)
Principal dwelling	0.0063	(0.0010)
Maintenance	0.0067	(0.0059)
Furnishings and operation	0.0029	(0.0010)
Durables	0.0042	(0.0032)
Nondurables	0.0001	(0.0008)
Services	0.0131	(0.0017)

Except for maintenance, the results are compatible with those presented in table 6-7.

30. The public transport coefficient is not quite significant for Colombia; the regression could not be estimated for Ecuador.

Table 6-7. *Coefficients of Expenditure on House-Related Spending, by Size of Dwelling, Four Latin American Countries*

Country and spending category	Number of rooms in dwelling[a]				
	1–2	3–4	5	6	7
Colombia					
Dwelling	−0.482	−0.307	−0.126	−0.003	0.029
	(0.048)	(0.032)	(0.031)	(0.032)	(0.033)
Maintenance	−0.077	−0.170	0.161	0.033	0.312
	(0.529)	(0.308)	(0.292)	(0.260)	(0.299)
Durables	−0.031	0.394	0.141	0.076	0.017
	(0.244)	(0.164)	(0.150)	(0.152)	(0.159)
Nondurables	−0.042	0.004	0.062	0.028	−0.040
	(0.064)	(0.042)	(0.042)	(0.042)	(0.045)
Services	−0.493	−0.464	−0.193	−0.104	−0.029
	(0.167)	(0.082)	(0.073)	(0.071)	(0.071)
Chile					
Dwelling	−0.529	−0.330	−0.152	−0.030	0.049
	(0.047)	(0.043)	(0.046)	(0.049)	(0.059)
Maintenance	1.054	1.042	0.643	0.599	0.570
	(0.339)	(0.292)	(0.302)	(0.309)	(0.375)
Durables	1.307	0.953	0.426	−0.189	−0.339
	(0.301)	(0.273)	(0.294)	(0.301)	(0.360)
Nondurables	0.042	−0.013	0.022	−0.086	−0.050
	(0.098)	(0.090)	(0.097)	(0.102)	(0.124)
Services	−0.834	−0.681	−0.293	−0.096	−0.097
	(0.153)	(0.131)	(0.135)	(0.139)	(0.163)
Ecuador[b]					
Dwelling	−0.543	−0.366	...	−0.017	0.016
	(0.056)	(0.049)		(0.065)	(0.077)
Durables	0.568	0.308	−0.431	0.373	−0.196
	(0.258)	(0.230)	(0.254)	(0.268)	(0.303)
Nondurables	−0.321	−0.290	−0.265	−0.217	−0.074
	(0.067)	(0.061)	(0.067)	(0.071)	(0.081)
Services	−0.573	−0.426	−0.381	−0.116	−0.011
	(0.151)	(0.127)	(0.127)	(0.130)	(0.139)
Peru					
Dwelling	−0.812	−0.601	−0.294	−0.175	−0.172
	(0.093)	(0.075)	(0.075)	(0.077)	(0.085)
Maintenance	−0.076	0.222	−0.078	−0.282	0.265
	(0.319)	(0.247)	(0.241)	(0.245)	(0.254)
Durables	0.879	0.698	0.764	0.550	0.107
	(0.288)	(0.239)	(0.242)	(0.259)	(0.286)
Nondurables	−0.207	−0.141	0.000	−0.137	−0.089
	(0.084)	(0.070)	(0.070)	(0.073)	(0.081)
Services	−1.255	−0.759	−0.502	−0.348	−0.157
	(0.175)	(0.123)	(0.117)	(0.116)	(0.126)

Source: Original ECIEL calculations based on the survey data. Numbers in parentheses are standard errors.

a. Family's principal residence.

b. Data on maintenance are not available.

Possession of a telephone raises the budget share devoted to communication significantly in Colombia and Venezuela, but not significantly in Ecuador; data on possession of telephones are not available for Chile:

	Colombia	Chile	Ecuador	Peru	Venezuela
Vehicle					
Total					
transportation	1.358	1.049	1.650	0.110	0.811
	(0.057)	(0.044)	(0.087)	(0.087)	(0.048)
Public					
transportation	−0.135	−0.633	n.a.	−0.421	−0.730
	(0.079)	(0.059)		(0.113)	(0.063)
Telephone					
Communication	1.163	n.a.	0.265	1.652	2.311
	(0.083)		(0.673)	(0.574)	(0.082)

Household Size and Composition

The size of the household is perhaps its most fundamental characteristic, the one that has the greatest effect on its needs for different goods and services. Some measure of size, either in total or after classifying people according to age or sex, is therefore included in nearly every Engel curve estimated in each of the five functional forms used.[31]

Proportional Effects of Size on Expenditures

I consider first all the double-log Engel curves which include dummy variables for household size among the regressors. Households are classified in seven size groups: one member, two, three, four or five, six or seven, eight or nine, and ten or more members. One-member households are excluded from the Peruvian sample. The comparison group—that is, the excluded category among the dummy variables—is that of the largest households, except in Chile, where the base class includes one-person households. The coefficients of the dummy variables are shown in appen-

31. If household size and composition determine needs, income determines the possibility of satisfying those needs. All other sociodemographic characteristics, in this view, influence the household's tastes. (For example, age or life cycle is a measure of household composition and therefore affects needs.) In the double-log model, household size is excluded only from the regressions for family dwelling, other housing, private transportation (operation of vehicle), and insurance expenditures.

dix tables C-46 (Colombia) to C-50 (Venezuela). The share of the budget devoted to food rises, in total and for most components, in all five countries as household size increases. This is balanced by almost equally uniform reductions in the shares devoted to housing and to household furnishings. There are opposing trends within these major categories. Expenditure falls for meals away from home, and tends to rise for nondurable household supplies and to fall for services (Peru is a marked exception). Spending on durables is concentrated among small, newly formed households. (See also the discussion in chapter 3.)

Expenditure for public transportation and for personal care also tends to increase with household size, although the coefficients usually cannot be clearly distinguished. It tends to decline for dwelling maintenance and repairs (results are available for only three countries), communication, taxes, transfers including gifts, and other nonconsumption items. These adjustments to changes in household size occupy a rather small share of the budget for most families.

Among foods, increased household size has the greatest effect on cereals and vegetables, including tubers and beans. Spending on these categories rises faster than for total food and beverages, so starches occupy a larger share of the diet. This change is partly at the expense of high-protein foods, the share in the diet tending to fall (or at best not change) for meat, seafood, dairy products, and eggs. Sugar and sweets tend to gain slightly in the diet while fruits, beverages, and other foods become relatively less important. The latter two groups often show declines relative to the total budget and therefore greater declines compared with the increasing budget for food.

For those categories where the budget share does not change monotonically with household size, the dummy variable formulation is very helpful in tracing the shape of the relation. This is the case for spending on durables, other clothing, medical care, and (sometimes) recreation and transportation. For most categories of spending, however, the relation is approximately monotonic, and it is convenient to represent the effect of family size by a single variable in order to simplify the estimation and make it more likely the coefficients will be significant. This was done in a preliminary set of regressions for Colombia, and also (by Roldán) for Chile.[32] In both cases, the logarithm of the number of members (resident

32. The specifications of the Colombian regressions are given in "Resumen del XIII Seminario del Programa de Estudios Conjuntos sobre Integración Económica

members in Colombia) is included; the elasticities are reported in table 6-8.[33] The Chilean estimates are separated by income stratum; those for Colombia are not.

The results are generally compatible with those presented in tables C-46 and C-47; that is, the direction and relative magnitude of the effect are usually the same. The separation by stratum is valuable for suggesting that households at different income levels react differently to size changes. The estimates for the food budget are particularly interesting, since it appears that, while wealthier families expand consumption of cereals and vegetables as rapidly as do poor families, they do not have to reduce their intake of meat and fruit in order to do so. Nor do they increase purchases of fats and oils or sweets at as high a rate.[34]

However, the use of the logarithm is only an approximation to the shape of the relation between expenditure and household size.[35] In the case of total food expenditure, for example, the logarithmic approximation fits quite well for households of two to five members in Colombia and Ecuador, three to five or perhaps seven members in Peru and Chile, and three to nine members in Venezuela. The function fits much less well for extremely large or small households, and also less well for disaggregated categories.

Latinoamericana (ECIEL)" (Lima: December 15–20, 1969; processed), pp. 72–74. The regressions were later respecified in the standard ECIEL format, using blocks of dummies for all variables except total household expenditure. The development of the specification is due largely to Arturo Carlos Meyer; Howard Howe participated in the initial experiments, whose results, for Colombia, are reported in table 6-8. Roldán's results are reported in "Funciones Consumo por Tramos de Ingreso," pp. 26 and 32.

33. Some categories, for which the relation is clearly nonmonotonic, are omitted: durables, clothing, medical care, and recreation.

34. Absolute increases in expenditure on these items are still large, as may be seen from Roldán's estimates of semilogarithmic Engel curves. The coefficient β_{Nr} in that case relates an absolute change in C_r to a proportional change in N, and is the same for the two strata in the cases of cereals, oils, and vegetables. For meat, fruit, and eggs, it is notably higher in the high-income stratum; for sugar and beverages, it is appreciably lower. See Roldán, "Funciones Consumo por Tramos de Ingreso," p. 28.

35. In one model, $d \log C_r$ is $\beta_{Nr} dN/N$, which can be represented, for the change between size N_i and size N_j, as $2\beta_{Nr}(N_i - N_j)/(N_i + N_j)$. In the dummy variable model, $d \log C_r$ is just $\beta_{ri} - \beta_{rj}$. Constancy of the parameter β_{Nr} implied by the logarithmic model then imposes a relation on the β_{ri} as a function of the N_i, and this relation can be tested.

Table 6-8. *Elasticities of Expenditure with Respect to Household Size, Various Spending Categories, Chile and Colombia*

Spending category	Chile		Colombia (all incomes)
	Low income	High income	
Eggs	0.131	0.197	0.058[a]
	(0.065)	(0.051)	(0.024)
Cereals	0.586	0.576	0.335
	(0.035)	(0.024)	(0.160)
Meat and poultry	−0.055	0.091	0.134
	(0.074)	(0.188)	(0.023)
Seafood	0.059	−0.074	0.056
	(0.138)	(0.179)	(0.059)
Vegetables	0.351	0.385	0.255
	(0.042)	(0.032)	(0.018)
Fruits	−0.109	0.101	0.043
	(0.092)	(0.047)	(0.027)
Fats and oils	0.256	−0.022	0.171
	(0.060)	(0.185)	(0.021)
Sugar	0.552	0.093	0.376
	(0.052)	(0.191)	(0.021)
All beverages	0.203	0.082	...
	(0.055)	(0.143)	
Hot beverages	...	...	0.285
			(0.022)
Alcoholic beverages	...	...	−0.070
			(0.074)
Other beverages	...	...	0.072
			(0.048)
Other foods	...	...	−0.075
			(0.036)
Meals away from home	−0.675	−0.149	−0.029
	(0.269)	(0.101)	(0.041)
Alcohol and tobacco	0.220	0.330	0.022[b]
	(0.112)	(0.060)	(0.058)
Maintenance	−0.178	−0.849	−0.006
	(0.111)	(0.199)	(0.181)
Services	0.068	0.068	−0.465
	(0.103)	(0.035)	(0.048)
Transportation	−0.152	0.148	−0.029[c]
	(0.063)	(0.045)	(0.038)
Personal care	0.085	0.006	−0.007
	(0.110)	(0.046)	(0.023)

Source: Data for Chile from Roldán, "Funciones Consumo por Tramos de Ingreso," p. 26; data for Colombia from original ECIEL calculations based on the survey data. Numbers in parentheses are standard errors.
a. Includes dairy products.
b. Tobacco only. Elasticity based on number of adult members.
c. Includes communication.

Table 6-9. Elasticities of Expenditure on Clothing, by Age and Sex of Household Members, Five Latin American Countries

Country and spending category	Number of men				Number of women				Number of children					
	0	1	2	3	0	1	2	3	0	1	2	3	4–5	6–7
Colombia	−0.129 (0.117)	−0.042 (0.104)	−0.048 (0.108)	−0.039 (0.118)	−0.145 (0.208)	0.171 (0.082)	0.096 (0.084)	0.244 (0.092)	0.101 (0.136)	0.222 (0.138)	0.154 (0.137)	0.273 (0.138)	0.181 (0.136)	0.111 (0.145)
Men's	−0.849 (0.220)	−0.441 (0.132)	−0.371 (0.136)	−0.127 (0.148)										
Women's					−0.347 (0.295)	−0.035 (0.094)	0.076 (0.097)	0.208 (0.105)						
Children's									−0.582 (0.170)	−0.600 (0.148)	−0.455 (0.145)	−0.241 (0.147)	−0.140 (0.145)	−0.068 (0.155)
Chile	−0.330 (0.113)	−0.166 (0.100)	−0.030 (0.103)	−0.028 (0.112)	−0.042 (0.130)	−0.031 (0.079)	0.002 (0.080)	0.078 (0.090)	0.055 (0.231)	−0.144 (0.233)	−0.069 (0.233)	−0.193 (0.236)	−0.146 (0.234)	n.a.
Men's	−0.980 (0.165)	−0.499 (0.100)	−0.260 (0.104)	−0.076 (0.114)										
Women's					−0.198 (0.356)	−0.436 (0.081)	−0.281 (0.083)	−0.198 (0.093)						
Children's									−0.714 (0.334)	−0.620 (0.333)	−0.567 (0.334)	−0.598 (0.335)	−0.623 (0.335)	−0.628 (0.351)
Ecuador	−0.532 (0.166)	−0.315 (0.136)	−0.177 (0.141)	−0.177 (0.156)	0.267 (0.224)	−0.167 (0.116)	−0.152 (0.112)	−0.098 (0.120)	−0.625 (0.510)	−0.237 (0.447)	−0.306 (0.449)	−0.366 (0.453)	−0.823 (0.456)	−0.480 (0.486)
Men's	−0.944 (0.177)	−0.407 (0.109)	−0.170 (0.114)	−0.128 (0.127)										
Women's					−0.463 (0.313)	−0.410 (0.089)	−0.203 (0.086)	−0.066 (0.092)						
Children's									0.047 (0.355)	0.051 (0.356)	0.017 (0.356)	0.072 (0.358)	0.052 (0.355)	−0.064 (0.367)
Peru	−0.157 (0.223)	−0.283 (0.117)	−0.188 (0.121)	−0.180 (0.130)	−0.671 (0.423)	−0.098 (0.112)	−0.155 (0.100)	−0.047 (0.102)	−0.134 (0.445)	0.068 (0.404)	0.035 (0.399)	0.105 (0.407)	−0.115 (0.396)	−0.044 (0.419)
Men's	−0.365 (0.329)	−0.485 (0.122)	−0.407 (0.125)	−0.166 (0.135)										
Women's					−0.709 (0.486)	−0.510 (0.111)	−0.424 (0.098)	−0.211 (0.101)						
Children's									−0.014 (0.446)	−0.062 (0.446)	−0.152 (0.445)	−0.107 (0.446)	−0.123 (0.446)	−0.360 (0.466)
Venezuela	0.048 (0.179)	−0.199 (0.138)	−0.069 (0.142)	−0.143 (0.159)	−0.245 (0.334)	0.134 (0.117)	0.141 (0.117)	0.196 (0.128)	1.911 (1.163)	1.648 (1.145)	1.501 (1.143)	1.593 (1.141)	1.386 (1.141)	1.113 (1.155)
Men's	−0.551 (0.289)	−0.189 (0.151)	−0.039 (0.156)	−0.117 (0.176)										
Women's					−0.172 (0.528)	−0.294 (0.120)	−0.118 (0.122)	−0.055 (0.134)						
Children's									−0.536 (0.234)	−0.430 (0.226)	−0.262 (0.223)	−0.335 (0.226)	−0.262 (0.223)	n.a.

Source: Original ECIEL calculations based on the survey data. Numbers in parentheses are standard errors.
n.a. Not available.

Numbers of Adults and Children

Although people of different ages have different needs (whether physical or conventional), they consume the same goods and services in many age categories and vary only in the amount consumed. In those cases, total household size is a reasonable explanatory variable for expenditure.[36] Some goods, however, are bought for the exclusive use of certain members of the household.[37] It is more reasonable, then, to relate spending on such items not to the total number of members but to the number of a particular type. In the double-log analysis, the basic distinction is between adults (over fourteen years old) and children. In the case of clothing, adults are further distinguished by sex, while in the case of educational and quasi-educational spending, three age groups are distinguished in the age interval from six to twenty-five.

Estimates of the effects of households' age and sex composition on clothing expenditures are given in table 6-9. (Comparisons are made with households of four or more men, four or more women, and eight or more children.) Other, nonspecific clothing expenditure is related to total household size; the results are shown in appendix tables C-46 to C-50. Invariably, more tends to be spent on men's clothing when there are more men in the household, and more on women's clothing when there are more women.[38] Expenditure on clothing for children increases with their number in Colombia and, though less systematically, in Venezuela, but no effect can be clearly detected in the other countries. This is undoubtedly

36. A better variable, in theory, is the number of adult-equivalent members, taking account of the smaller needs of children. The conversion to adult equivalence is extremely difficult, however, since observed expenditure behavior does not necessarily reflect physical or other needs accurately. See Brown and Deaton, "Models of Consumer Behavior," pp. 1178–86, for an introduction to this complex question. The only estimates of adult-equivalent consumption based on ECIEL data are those of Howe, "Linear and Quadratic Expenditure Systems," pp. 256–93, where values are derived for the four Colombian cities and compared with estimates from other studies.

37. At a sufficiently low level of aggregation, this is true of virtually all purchases except food and housing (and housing services), and even some foods may be consumed only by certain members. As spending categories are aggregated, this identification with particular individuals disappears for most types of expenditure.

38. At least, this is true if the coefficients for zero members, which are never distinguishable from zero in the case of women because there are almost no households without at least one adult female, are ignored.

because children can wear the clothes of older siblings, at least if they are of the same sex. For this reason, it matters if there are any children at all in the household, but once there are at least two the number has no further discernible effect. Total clothing expenditure does not seem to depend at all on the number of children (only one coefficient, in Colombia, is distinct from zero), but it does tend to rise with the number of men or of women or both. The inclusion of so many variables in the equation makes it difficult to isolate the effects. Thus total spending on clothing is not particularly sensitive to household composition, though it may depend on household size—particularly on the number of adults. Allocation of total clothing expenditure then depends on the presence of children and on the relative numbers of men and women.

Expenditure on tobacco is presumed to depend only on the number of adults in the household; this variable was included in the Engel curve and also in the regression for total other consumption, of which tobacco is a component. The coefficients appear in table 6-10 (comparisons are with families of eight or more adults). Spending in both categories tends to increase with the number of adults, but for tobacco the trend is clear only for Chile. The number of children was also used in the regression for total other consumption, but virtually all the coefficients are indistinguishable from zero. Only in Ecuador is there a clear trend to increased spending; in Chile and Peru expenditure appears to decline as there are more children.[39]

Educational Expenditure and Age Group Sizes

People of school age are divided into three classes: six to eleven, twelve to seventeen, and eighteen to twenty-five. These correspond closely to primary, secondary, and higher levels of schooling (educational spending on older adults is not considered). The numbers of household members in each group were introduced into the Engel curves for spending on education and quasi education (reading material and cultural activities). Results are shown in table 6-11. Comparison is made with families having four or more members in each of the two younger groups and three or more in the oldest group.

---

39. The other two components of other consumption—personal care and ceremonies—are related to total household size (see appendix tables C-46, C-47, and C-49).

Cultural spending is usually unrelated to household composition, or else declines as there are more children under eighteen. There is a clear increase only for additional young adults (who may be supplementary members of the household) in Chile. While having more children may encourage parents to spend more on their cultural upbringing, this effect is usually offset by spending on necessities and, perhaps, by the parents' having less time for cultural activities.

Table 6-10. *Coefficients of Expenditure on Tobacco and Other Consumption, by Number of Adults in Household, Five Latin American Countries*

Country and spending category	Number of adults				
	1	*2*	*3*	*4–5*	*6–7*
Colombia					
Other consumption	−0.376	−0.128	−0.094	−0.085	−0.081
	(0.153)	(0.143)	(0.144)	(0.144)	(0.148)
Tobacco only	−0.371	−0.224	−0.222	−0.265	−0.165
	(0.075)	(0.246)	(0.249)	(0.277)	(0.257)
Chile					
Other consumption	−1.232	−1.016	−0.780	−0.584	−0.283
	(0.172)	(0.160)	(0.161)	(0.160)	(0.170)
Tobacco only	−0.705	−0.664	−0.603	−0.446	−0.481
	(0.182)	(0.153)	(0.154)	(0.151)	(0.161)
Ecuador					
Other consumption	−0.436	−0.307	−0.310	−0.260	−0.200
	(0.117)	(0.097)	(0.096)	(0.094)	(0.101)
Tobacco only	0.148	−0.155	−0.288	−0.196	−0.143
	(0.253)	(0.193)	(0.191)	(0.184)	(0.195)
Peru[a]					
Other consumption	−0.791	−0.381	−0.359	−0.174	−0.059
	(0.350)	(0.090)	(0.082)	(0.075)	(0.078)
Tobacco only	−1.075	−0.167	−0.202	−0.270	−0.194
	(1.174)	(0.200)	(0.176)	(0.156)	(0.160)
Venezuela					
Other consumption	−0.554	−0.369	−0.300	−0.173	−0.106
	(0.122)	(0.094)	(0.095)	(0.093)	(0.098)
Tobacco only	−0.369	−0.102	−0.055	−0.109	−0.050
	(0.245)	(0.166)	(0.166)	(0.164)	(0.173)

Source: Original ECIEL calculations based on the survey data. Numbers in parentheses are standard errors.

a. One-adult households also contain one child, since there are no one-member households in the sample.

Table 6-11. *Coefficients of Expenditure on Education and Culture, by Age of Household Members, Five Latin American Countries*

Spending category and country	Number of members										
	Aged 6–11				Aged 12–17				Aged 18–25		
	0	1	2	3	0	1	2	3	0	1	2
Education											
Colombia	−0.017	−0.065	0.048	0.040	−0.645	−0.323	−0.145	−0.050	−0.328	−0.229	−0.202
	(0.100)	(0.097)	(0.096)	(0.102)	(0.112)	(0.111)	(0.113)	(0.121)	(0.119)	(0.123)	(0.136)
Chile	0.431	0.288	0.610	0.245	−0.417	−0.188	−0.181	0.065	0.400	0.300	0.200
	(0.318)	(0.312)	(0.318)	(0.337)	(0.361)	(0.363)	(0.368)	(0.389)	(0.195)	(0.200)	(0.223)
Ecuador	0.080	−0.050	−0.033	−0.045	−0.551	−0.193	−0.139	−0.077	−0.080	−0.184	−0.036
	(0.183)	(0.182)	(0.183)	(0.197)	(0.193)	(0.191)	(0.196)	(0.205)	(0.127)	(0.128)	(0.141)
Peru	0.088	0.148	0.297	0.189	−0.709	−0.433	−0.228	−0.274	−0.296	−0.024	−0.071
	(0.226)	(0.226)	(0.230)	(0.258)	(0.197)	(0.198)	(0.201)	(0.219)	(0.138)	(0.134)	(0.145)
Venezuela	0.386	0.484	0.345	0.162	−0.570	−0.367	−0.184	−0.401	−0.140	−0.061	−0.086
	(0.243)	(0.241)	(0.247)	(0.271)	(0.264)	(0.267)	(0.274)	(0.289)	(0.160)	(0.168)	(0.191)
Culture											
Colombia	0.325	0.204	0.181	0.137	0.056	−0.024	−0.028	−0.245	0.040	−0.093	−0.002
	(0.088)	(0.090)	(0.091)	(0.097)	(0.102)	(0.104)	(0.106)	(0.115)	(0.098)	(0.100)	(0.110)
Chile	0.374	0.350	0.309	0.345	−0.182	−0.224	−0.215	−0.232	−0.300	−0.213	−0.201
	(0.135)	(0.136)	(0.139)	(0.148)	(0.161)	(0.163)	(0.165)	(0.175)	(0.082)	(0.085)	(0.091)
Ecuador	0.133	0.030	0.047	0.146	0.160	0.055	0.067	0.182	0.024	−0.037	−0.034
	(0.141)	(0.143)	(0.144)	(0.157)	(0.139)	(0.140)	(0.143)	(0.152)	(0.086)	(0.087)	(0.094)
Peru	0.111	0.074	0.154	0.126	0.160	0.244	0.262	0.118	0.011	0.053	−0.046
	(0.137)	(0.139)	(0.141)	(0.154)	(0.124)	(0.126)	(0.129)	(0.142)	(0.073)	(0.072)	(0.078)
Venezuela	0.201	0.126	0.171	0.046	0.247	0.319	0.282	0.014	0.114	−0.022	0.020
	(0.211)	(0.215)	(0.219)	(0.244)	(0.229)	(0.233)	(0.239)	(0.254)	(0.115)	(0.119)	(0.131)

Source: Original ECIEL calculations based on the survey data.

The results for education are more complicated and more interesting. Only in the middle (secondary school) age group does total educational spending in all five countries increase as there are more household members. (Although only a few coefficients are clearly nonzero, the trend is evident everywhere.) The number of children of primary school age has generally no discernible effect, and the trend is likely to be downward or nonmonotonic. Much the same is true in the university-age group: there are consistent trends, but in opposite directions, only in Colombia and Chile. Moreover, the relation is usually steeper for children of secondary school age than for older or younger members. This is not what would be expected if the cost of maintaining a child in school were the same at all levels. Then all the relations should be positive, but, because of high drop-out rates, the strongest association should be observed for the youngest children. However, the results are consistent with the fact that both primary and higher schooling are to a large degree provided by public institutions at very low direct costs to students and their parents. In contrast, secondary schooling is provided chiefly by relatively expensive private schools.[40] Younger or older children do not represent greatly increased needs for spending on education, but their other needs may reduce what can be spent on the schooling of the children of secondary school age.

Committed Expenditures

In the double-log model, a change in the size or composition of the household changes its spending on category r by a constant proportion; that is,

$$\Delta C_r = C_r \Delta \beta_{ujr},$$

where $\Delta \beta_{ujr}$ is the difference in coefficients in two size classes and C_r goes to zero as total spending C goes to zero, whatever the size of the family. In the linear expenditure system and the extended system (LES and ELES), a change in household size or composition affects C_r by a constant

40. For a discussion of relative costs and the effect of this structure on school dropout rates and on the distribution of income, see Martin Carnoy, "Schooling, Income, the Distribution of Income, and Unemployment: A Critical Appraisal," paper presented at the meeting of research institutes participating in the research program on Employment, Under-Employment and Unemployment of Graduates, Paris, OECD Development Centre, December 10–12, 1973.

amount, and the change is proportional to the change in the family's committed or necessary expenditure (γ_r^*):

$$\Delta C_r = (1 - \beta_r)\Delta_\gamma^* \text{ (LES)} \quad \text{or} \quad (1 - \mu\beta_r)\Delta\gamma_r^* \text{ (ELES)}.$$

The quadratic model retains the assumption that household size and composition determine only the committed expenditure, but the change in spending becomes

$$\Delta C_r = (1 - \beta_{1r} - 2\beta_{2r}Z)\Delta\gamma_r^*,$$

where $Z = C - \Sigma_r\gamma_r^*$ is supernumerary expenditure. The expression for ΔC_r combines the constant term of the linear model with a term that is proportional not to C_r but to the square root of $C_r - \gamma_r^*$, since C_r is a function of Z and Z^2.

For categories that can be characterized as necessities, γ_r^* should increase with household size or with the number of those household members who consume that good or service. For luxuries, the opposite effect might be expected: if γ_r^* is negative, and is not interpreted as a subsistence level, larger households may postpone luxury purchases to a higher total spending level than will small households. Over the full range of income, both effects might be observed, as what is a luxury at low income levels comes to be regarded as a necessity at higher levels.

With the ELES, values of γ_r^* were estimated separately for small (four or fewer members) and large (five or more members) households for Bogotá, Guayaquil, Lima, and Caracas. These estimates, for five expenditure categories, appear in table 6-12.[41] The expectation that γ_r^* (large) exceeds γ_r^* (small) is satisfied, usually at a high level of statistical significance, in the first three cities. The opposite patterns hold in Caracas,

41. Values in national currency per trimester are converted to U.S. dollars per year by the overall parity rates presented in chapter 2, adjusted for international differences in relative prices. The food price index excludes all beverages, the clothing index includes footwear, and the housing index is limited to paid or imputed rents, excluding repairs and maintenance. The conversion rates, in dollars per year per unit of national currency per trimester, are:

	Colombia	Ecuador	Peru	Venezuela
Food	0.3914	0.3567	0.1481	0.9153
Housing	0.5784	0.4159	0.2754	0.9153
Clothing	0.3603	0.3462	0.1210	0.9153
Durables	0.3176	0.3253	0.0924	0.9153
Other	0.4393	0.3679	0.1458	0.9153

The aggregate parity is used for other consumption. No account is taken of differential inflation between May 1968 and the survey dates.

Table 6-12. *Committed Expenditures, Various Spending Categories, in National Currency per Trimester and U.S. Dollars per Year, by Household Size, Four Latin American Cities*

Household size and currency	Spending category				
	Food	Housing	Durables	Clothing	Other
Bogotá					
Small					
Pesos	206	166	14	46	116
	(40)	(36)	(5)	(12)	(30)
Dollars	81	96	4	16	51
Large					
Pesos	534	416	41	126	340
	(98)	(89)	(12)	(28)	(73)
Dollars	209	241	13	45	150
Guayaquil					
Small					
Sucres	944	527	31	141	563
	(166)	(90)	(23)	(24)	(73)
Dollars	337	219	10	49	207
Large					
Sucres	2,477	916	113	238	667
	(192)	(104)	(27)	(27)	(85)
Dollars	883	381	37	82	245
Lima					
Small					
Soles	695	592	196	205	668
	(67)	(60)	(38)	(27)	(69)
Dollars	103	162	18	25	97
Large					
Soles	1,108	768	321	307	813
	(82)	(75)	(47)	(34)	(86)
Dollars	164	211	30	37	119
Caracas					
Small					
Bolívars	1,520	1,793	121	390	1,719
	(75)	(126)	(26)	(34)	(52)
Dollars	1,392	1,641	110	357	1,574
Large					
Bolívars	1,372	1,190	86	285	1,183
	(55)	(93)	(19)	(25)	(111)
Dollars	1,256	1,089	79	261	1,083

Source: Howe and Musgrove, "Analysis of ECIEL Household Budget Data," pp. 169, 171, 173, 175. Numbers in parentheses are standard errors.

even for obvious necessities such as food. This may be because in Caracas small families, on average, have higher incomes, or at least higher per capita incomes, than large families and therefore behave as though they have greater needs. Also, the estimates take no account of the composition of the household. (When the estimates are converted to dollars, it is evident that the real values differ greatly among countries, more than can be explained by differences in family size. Food needs for small families in Caracas, for example, appear to be nearly fourteen times as high as for small households in Lima.)

When the ELES is estimated separately by stratum and by age class in the four cities, both of those effects are reduced, if not eliminated. There are then 120 comparisons of γ_r^* (large) and γ_r^* (small) to be made, and of these, 86 show the higher committed expenditure for larger households. The difference is highly significant thirty-five times.[42] The cases in which the reverse is observed are concentrated in Caracas (twelve times out of thirty), in the high-income strata (also twelve times), and among younger households (nineteen times). They are distributed almost equally among housing, durables, clothing, and other expenditures, but occur only three times for food, the one category that can be regarded as almost entirely a necessity.

It is not possible to say more about what the relative values of subsistence expenditure γ_r^* ought to be, both because of household size variation within each size class and because there may be economies of scale in consumption that make γ_r^* increase less than linearly with the number of members. Estimates of the LES for Colombia attempted to take account of both these problems, but individual parameter estimates are often implausible.[43] For households of about three or four members, some interesting scale effects can be detected. There seem to be increasing returns (scale economies) for food, education, durables, and transportation; decreasing returns for housing, medical care, recreation, and miscellaneous expenditures; and constant returns for clothing. It is not clear whether these effects continue for larger households.[44]

42. Howe and Musgrove, "Analysis of ECIEL Household Budget Data," pp. 168–75.

43. Howe, "Linear and Quadratic Expenditure Systems," pp. 256–302. When aggregated to the level of a household's total expenditure, the results are generally more reasonable.

44. For the reasons described earlier, the apparent scale effect in education may reflect not any economies of size, but simply decisions by the household about how

Some of the problems that arise in estimating committed expenditures as a function of household composition are less severe in the quadratic than in the linear model. This happens because the curvilinear form allows a better fit at low incomes and because income and family size are related. There are still substantial differences between γ_r^* for the head of the household and the same parameter for other adults, as well as sizable differences among cities; but the results are more plausible (some of the results are given in table 6-13).[45] The distinction between the head and other adult members gives results that are implausible for food but reasonable for the other categories. (Since the head is usually male, the other adults are slightly more likely to be female; this may account for the usually higher γ_r^* for clothing.) Some of the intercity differences may be due to the price and climatic differences discussed earlier in this chapter; for example, housing needs are uniformly higher in Bogotá and Medellín than in Barranquilla and Cali. The estimates for education fit the cost structure examined in the double-log model: γ_r^* is highest for children of secondary-school age and is zero or nearly zero for the household head.

It is tempting to regard the committed expenditures presented in tables 6-12 and 6-13 as estimates of subsistence levels or of basic human needs; the utility function underlying the linear expenditure system, in fact, treats γ_r^* as a level that a household must consume in order to have any utility at all. It is clear from the results, however, that the estimates can be interpreted this way only for a few categories and then only with great caution. There is no fundamental necessity to consume durable goods or "other consumption," so the parameters at best represent "needs" as defined socially rather than biologically. The fact that the γ_r^* tend to rise with income level is further evidence for this view: "necessities" incorporate much habit formation and are defined relative to what a social stratum considers desirable. It is also evident that while the real values of committed expenditures for all categories and both size classes are fairly similar in Bogotá and Lima—cities with comparable levels and distribu-

---

long to keep children in school. When there are more children, they are likely, at a given level of total expenditure, to leave school earlier, and this will lower educational expenditure per child. These scale effects refer only to committed spending, not to total spending.

45. Howe, "Linear and Quadratic Expenditure Systems," pp. 231–34. The γ_r^* are identified by the assumption that, on average, food represents half of total expenditure. On this assumption, estimates of γ_r^* for food match estimates of a minimum cost diet reasonably well.

Table 6-13. *Committed Expenditures per Trimester, Various Spending Categories, by Type of Household Member, Colombia*
Pesos

City and spending category	Child	Adolescent	Adult	Head
Bogotá				
Food	338	435	729	545
	(11)	(11)	(14)	(34)
Housing	122	249	416	487
	(13)	(13)	(16)	(39)
Durables	12	15	14	76
	(5)	(5)	(6)	(16)
Clothing	50	76	119	130
	(7)	(7)	(8)	(20)
Education	12	101	86	23
	(6)	(6)	(8)	(18)
Barranquilla				
Food	362	495	850	668
	(13)	(3)	(17)	(50)
Housing	55	163	254	463
	(12)	(12)	(15)	(45)
Durables	20	18	32	39
	(5)	(5)	(7)	(21)
Clothing	50	90	119	61
	(7)	(7)	(9)	(27)
Education	20	86	77	−4
	(6)	(6)	(8)	(23)
Cali				
Food	347	484	823	729
	(13)	(16)	(21)	(62)
Housing	96	195	329	374
	(12)	(14)	(19)	(56)
Durables	13	21	21	96
	(6)	(7)	(10)	(29)
Clothing	55	91	112	106
	(7)	(8)	(10)	(30)
Education	18	71	67	37
	(5)	(6)	(7)	(22)
Medellín				
Food	329	478	789	624
	(10)	(12)	(16)	(45)
Housing	118	228	394	498
	(10)	(12)	(15)	(44)
Durables	12	14	22	36
	(3)	(4)	(5)	(13)
Clothing	31	55	77	131
	(4)	(5)	(6)	(17)
Education	20	90	65	10
	(5)	(5)	(7)	(21)

Source: Howe, "Linear and Quadratic Expenditure Systems," pp. 231–34. Numbers in parentheses are standard errors.

tions of household income—they are systematically much lower in Guaya-quil, a poorer city with greater income inequality. The real values are not, however, systematically higher in Caracas.[46] For this reason I stress the effect of household size and composition on total spending in a category, rather than the subsistence level. The chief advantage of the regression analysis in this chapter—whether of complete systems of demand or of individual double-log equations—is not the identification of particular parameters, but the ability to take account simultaneously of household composition and income.

46. For further discussion of this point, see Howe and Musgrove, "Analysis of ECIEL Household Budget Data," pp. 177–79. See also the discussion of how the parameters γ_r^* should be interpreted by Lluch, Powell, and Williams, *Patterns in Household Demand*, pp. 7–16.

CHAPTER SEVEN

Conclusions and Implications

IN REVIEWING the results of this study, this chapter addresses two fundamental questions. What generalizations can be made about urban consumer behavior in Latin America? And what do these findings imply for some of the major social and political issues of development in the region? Neither of these questions can be fully answered here. However, by emphasizing a small number of the most interesting findings and relating them to these basic questions, the bulk of the results may be drawn together so as to indicate their scientific and practical value.

The ECIEL study was designed from the outset to permit and encourage international comparisons, and it would clearly be of great interest to compare this study's findings with the results of similar research in other countries, particularly in other parts of the world where cultural conditions and real income levels are very different. However, since no other studies are exactly comparable in methodology, such a comparison would be hard to make and, moreover, would form a major study in itself. Hence, rather than comparing ten cities with urban areas in other developing countries, the analysis presented here has concentrated on understanding the microeconomic detail of development. Only through such investigations can as full a picture of development be obtained as the one that is beginning to emerge for macroeconomic processes.[1] Such

---

1. See, for example, Hollis B. Chenery and Moises Syrquin, *Patterns of Development, 1950–1970* (London: Oxford University Press for the World Bank, 1975), and the previous macroeconomic studies cited there. Such studies suggest that for understanding the structure and performance of an economy, real income per head and country size (population) are most important, and give no explicit recognition

comparisons also enlarge one's understanding of consumer behavior in general, without necessarily being limited to poor countries.

The ECIEL study was also undertaken in the hope that its results would be of use in the formulation of public policy, in particular of an appropriate strategy for continued or improved development in Latin America. The investigation was not, of course, undertaken specifically to evaluate any existing or proposed government policies. However, its results may well form a useful contribution to such an evaluation. In some cases, information on consumer budgets and household characteristics may by itself suffice to evaluate a policy or at least to discern its deficiencies and to form some idea of its effects.

The remainder of this chapter summarizes a number of patterns evident in the study's results; reviews some of the implications of these findings, concentrating on the distribution of income, the effects of demographic factors, and the process of regional integration; and finally, considers some ways in which this research could usefully be extended, both by further analysis of these data and by the collection of better or complementary information.

Review of Findings

The results selected for review here are grouped approximately according to the chapters in which they were presented, except that chapters 4 through 6 are treated together. A number of conclusions and speculations referring to the macroeconomic sources of differences and similarities among countries and cities are also considered.

The Distribution of Income

In every city, the distribution of total family income looks like a combination of two distributions, which intersect somewhere near median income, with concentration being greater above the median. This sug-

---

of cultural differences except perhaps as these affect development "strategies." This chapter speculates on the possible importance of cultural and regional differences, but only within Latin America; it remains for further research to investigate the validity of the conclusions for Asia, Africa, Europe, or North America.

gests that the overall distribution is generated by two slightly different processes, one of which leads to more inequality than the other. These two hypothetical processes cannot, however, be identified with different factors of production or different kinds of income. It is true that capital income, other than imputed rent, is received almost exclusively by high-income households, and that it is extremely concentrated even among such households. It therefore contributes to inequality at high incomes, but it is received by too few households for its effect to reach down to the median of the distribution. Neither can it be supposed that the slightly greater evenness at low incomes is due to the equalizing effect of transfers. The receipt of transfers, whether public or private, does considerably improve the welfare of the poorest families, but it has almost no overall effect on inequality. Very few families receive any transfers, and those that do are found at all income levels.

The bulk of income inequality is due to inequalities in the distribution of labor income, the principal income received by more than three-quarters of all households, and the only income (apart from imputed rent) of a large majority of households. Within labor incomes, there is no systematic difference in concentration between wages or salaries and independent or self-employment income. Wages and salaries tend to form the larger share of total labor income and also of total income in the middle two quartiles of the distribution, while self-employment income is more common at the extremes of the distribution. The independent labor income of the very poor, of course, is not earned in the same way as that of the rich; among the former it is not likely to be associated with any appreciable capital, while among the latter it is likely to be associated with both physical and human capital. The amount of schooling appears to be the factor that best separates labor incomes into two distributions, with the distribution for the better educated being more unequal.

This finding suggests that, as an economy develops and the educational level of the labor force rises, labor income should become more concentrated. In fact, the opposite appears to happen, and the inequality of income, measured by the Gini coefficient, is inversely related to mean income in these cities. (The range of Gini coefficients is not wide, but the differences are statistically significant.) It therefore seems clear that as education becomes more widespread, the rent—or income differential— it can command declines, although many other factors also affect the relation between income level and inequality of labor incomes. More striking, however, is that as mean income rises, the concentration of incomes within the lower half of the distribution also decreases, and decreases by more than the inequality at higher incomes. That is, the rich in a rich city are somewhat richer than those in a poor city, but the poor in a poor city are very much poorer than those in a rich city. Of course, the absolute difference in incomes is greater between rich families in the two cities than between poor ones. In relative terms, the rich in all these cities are already much alike; development seems to include much catching up by poorer families. This relative gain seems to derive almost entirely from labor income but to be independent of the distinction between wages or salaries and self-employment.

Education is the most powerful source of income differences among families, even if only the schooling of the household head is considered. Occupation appears to generate much income inequality, but the occupational class most clearly distinguishable from other classes—that of professional, technical, and managerial positions—is strongly associated with high levels of schooling. There are no comparably great differences among occupations associated with the same level of education: for example, white-collar jobs pay only slightly more than blue-collar jobs, and both groups show a great heterogeneity of incomes. There are doubtless systematic income differences among skill levels and also among industries or sectors, but these are not clearly identifiable from household budget data.[2]

Age is rather weakly associated with income, and most of the association can be attributed to two factors. First, as the family ages, it is more likely to add working members (adolescent or grown children, or a wife who starts working once her children are older). Second, for people with secondary or higher education, income does rise rather sharply with age, at least up to around the age of fifty; thereafter it may continue to rise or may decline at retirement age. The first effect is more common in low-income families, particularly those with small businesses who can employ the services of children. The second effect is limited to high-income households. For many families, however, neither of these effects occurs, and income is nearly constant all through the working years. This is the

2. For analysis of interindustry and interskill wage differences after controlling for education, see Jorge Salazar-Carrillo, with the assistance of Juan J. Buttari, "The Structure of Wages in LAFTA Countries" (Brookings Institution, 1977; processed).

case for most families with primary schooling or less, who start out with incomes below those of the better educated and then stay at the same level while the latter experience income gains with age. The overall importance of age therefore depends somewhat on the age composition of the population, and still more on the distribution of education.

Large families tend to have higher incomes, but not in proportion to their size. Most families have only one employed member, so all additional members are dependents (except for elderly or disabled members who may receive transfers). In any case, larger families tend to consist more of children, so that in the first place it is more difficult for all the adults to accept employment, and in the second place every employed adult has a large number of dependents. It is not surprising that per capita income declines even more rapidly as the number of children increases.

Very little income variation appears to be due to transitory factors such as illness, short-term unemployment, or unexpected windfalls. There is enough transitory variation—about 10 percent of total relative income variation—to constitute a hardship for very poor families, but there is not enough to account for a significant share of inequality.[3] Further, little inequality can be attributed to differences in family size, which make total family income a poor measure of welfare. It is true that large families tend to look richer and small families to look poorer than they really are, but adjusting for family size simply moves households around in essentially the same distribution. The degree of concentration is hardly affected. Finally, among relatively well-educated households, age accounts for a great deal of income variation. Its effect is much less for less educated families.

It can be concluded, then, that much of income inequality is permanent; that it can be attributed largely to differences in labor earnings, except at very high incomes; and that it is explained by, or at least is strongly associated with, differences in human capital that may account for varying incomes in a given job but that are most important in determining what job a person can hold. The rich may be rich for a variety of reasons, including possession of nonhuman capital and experience. The poor are poor because they have nothing but their labor, and even when that is fully employed it yields low incomes.

3. Transitory factors are of course much more important if the entire economy is experiencing a sharp boom or recession, but even then their contribution to inequality may be slight if all households are affected in the same way.

Assets and Saving

The ECIEL study was not undertaken to learn about household wealth; most of the findings on this subject come from analyzing transactions in particular assets or the receipt of incomes attributable to such assets. There may therefore be a tendency to underestimate ownership of certain forms of wealth, and it is not possible to estimate families' total wealth. Nonetheless, a consistent and plausible picture of asset owning and saving behavior emerges from the analysis.

The great majority of families do not appear to own any financial assets; most do not even have bank accounts, and stocks, bonds, and shares in unincorporated businesses are still more rare. The percentage of families holding such assets rises, naturally, with the income level of the city; it appears also to depend, though here the evidence is more speculative, on the capital market and monetary conditions that determine the safety and rate of return for different forms of wealth. Most families, if they own any assets, own (or are buying) a dwelling; other real property is much less common.[4] Beyond a sufficiently high income level, there seems to be a natural order of asset acquisition: dwellings are acquired first, then cars and bank accounts, then securities and income-producing property. Income and spending rise dramatically with the number of different assets held, so only rich households face a choice among several uses for their savings.[5] These findings are consistent with the very high concentration observed for capital income apart from imputed rent.[6]

The principal determinant of current saving is unquestionably income, whatever form the saving may take. If transitory income is ignored in order to obtain an unbiased saving function, it is clear that saving is not a fixed proportion of permanent or normal income, but rises as income increases. This finding is consistent with the hypothesis that in less developed countries a large fraction of the population is living close to subsistence and therefore cannot save any appreciable part of normal income.

4. With the possible exception of real capital used in a family business; data on this class of asset were not collected in the surveys.
5. Except for housing, the data do not refer to the value of assets; hence the analysis is conducted entirely in terms of whether assets are owned or not.
6. Inclusion of imputed rent can lead to apparently very high shares of capital income at low total incomes if poor households are relatively likely to own their dwellings and richer families are more likely to rent.

As income rises, there is a range in which saving rises rapidly, perhaps eventually becoming a constant fraction of income at levels characteristic of much richer countries.[7] However, the subsistence level cannot easily be estimated, both because it is influenced by many household characteristics and because the concept may confuse the idea of bare physical necessity with that of an apparent threshold defined by short-term behavior. What is clear is that the rate of saving depends on both the level and the distribution of income and that it is probably more sensitive to income differences at some levels than at others.

Life cycle models of consumer behavior imply that the rate of saving should vary substantially over the lifetime, and that overall saving should depend on the level of lifetime or permanent income but should be fairly or completely independent of how that income is distributed through time. The ECIEL data provide little evidence for such long-term relations. There is some variation of the saving rate over the life cycle, but it appears to be due simply to variation in family needs as children are born and grow up. Even if households in Latin America share the long horizons and preferences assumed by such models, they are largely prevented from acting on them by the difficulty of anticipating their real incomes and by their inability to borrow and lend freely to adjust their consumption streams. These factors may also account for the surprisingly high rates of saving by elderly households, where one might expect dissaving.

Family size and composition both appear to influence saving: savings decline as more members (who are usually dependents rather than additional income earners) are added, and this effect is augmented if they are adults (who have greater consumption needs than children). The results do not indicate whether family size and composition shift the household's subsistence level, leaving its saving behavior unchanged at higher incomes, or whether adding more members reduces saving even for income above subsistence. Apparently, when additional family members go to work, the saving rate rises slightly, and this effect holds even when transitory income produced by irregular employment is excluded. The household saving decision is undoubtedly integrated with its labor supply deci-

7. The microeconomic evidence for such a saving function, discussed in chapter 3, provides a rationale for the observation of the same functional shape in macroeconomic aggregates, summarized by Chenery and Syrquin, *Patterns of Development*. At least this is the case for that part of national saving provided by the household sector.

sions, but not much is yet known about this process. The one clear piece of evidence is that higher dependency rates mean lower saving, which, for given incomes of the earners in a household, is equivalent to concluding that saving is lower when income per person is lower.

Some of the variables that have a rather slight effect on total saving affect particular components of saving more dramatically. The most striking example is age or life cycle. Just as there is a pattern of asset acquisition with increasing income, there is a sequential pattern over time at any income level. Durables—which are partly a form of wealth as well as a consumption good—are bought predominantly by young, newly established households, whereas dwellings are usually acquired somewhat later, and financial assets, if they are acquired at all, tend to be accumulated late in life (except perhaps in very high-income families). If educational spending is considered an investment, it also shows a strong age pattern, reaching a peak when the household includes children of secondary-school age. Thus, the level of saving may not depend on the age composition of the population as one would expect from life cycle models, but the composition of saving may be very sensitive to demographic factors.[8]

Determinants of Consumption Behavior

Before discussing the structure of consumption expenditures, it may be useful to review the degree to which the structure depends on particular household characteristics. A great many such characteristics were examined in chapters 4, 5, and 6, and it is one of the interesting findings of the study that several of them do not need to be taken much into consideration, or are sufficiently correlated among themselves that, given the level of aggregation adopted in this study, a single effect can be represented by several variables.

The principal determinants of how a family allocates its expenditures are its income and its composition. Household composition includes the

8. Conclusions about demands for particular assets, and the degree to which they are substitutes, are less firm than findings about total saving, simply because much of the ECIEL analysis was confined to Colombia. See Jean Crockett and Irwin Friend, "Consumption and Saving in Economic Development" (Rodney L. White Center for Financial Research, University of Pennsylvania, Working Paper 22-73, n.d.; processed).

number of members, the proportion of adults and children, the ages of the members, and possibly other variables. Which feature is most important depends on which category of expenditure is analyzed. To the extent that the number of members is important, without further distinction family spending can be said to depend largely on income per person. This simplification explains a great deal of spending behavior, but it ignores possible economies of scale as well as the differences among different types of members.

Income, like household composition, can be represented by a number of variables. It can be replaced, as in much of the ECIEL analysis, by total spending, which removes some of the transitory variation and makes it easier to explain spending in particular categories. It can be represented by factors that explain much income variation, particularly education and to a lesser extent occupation. These factors remove still more of the transitory variation, but at the cost of making only crude distinctions among levels of permanent income and spending.

Curiously, such variables as the employment status of the head of the household or of the spouse, although they appear to be strongly related to income, have little effect on the structure of spending except for a few minor categories. In part, these variables capture only short-term effects; in part, they are unimportant because the level of income matters much more than the form in which it is earned.[9] The surveys provide no evidence on the influence of wealth on the structure of consumption—apart from possible effects on the division of income between saving and consumption—but homeownership has little effect on most categories of spending.

There seem to be no marked differences among cities in the degree to which particular variables are important. Such differences as appear can often be traced to differences in the sample design or the way the survey was carried out, rather than to fundamental features of the economy. Overall, the most powerful determinants of spending behavior are income (or education, which is the best proxy for it), family size, and life cycle stage (which summarizes family composition without regard for the number of members). Other variables such as dwelling tenure, numbers of

9. The analysis does not include any tests of whether different forms of (permanent) income are spent differently: income is assumed to be treated identically for a particular family whether it is earned by labor, derived from capital, transferred, or acquired in some other way.

adults, children, men, or women, are important for explaining only the categories of spending that obviously depend on those features—housing, education, particular types of clothing, and so on.

Three conclusions can be drawn about the degree to which econometric estimates can explain expenditures of particular types. First, it is easier to explain aggregates than small categories, because particular categories substitute for each other within a larger classification, and the exact allocation depends on preferences that are not so well represented by the variables used. Second, spending on necessities—food, housing, and clothing—is more easily explained than purchases of luxuries, again because the latter respond more to particular preferences and opportunities. Thus, it is difficult to use these results to explain or project demand for some goods and services whose expansion is of great interest in economic development, such as appliances for the home and other manufactures. However, the data go far toward explaining how the typical family allocates some 70 to 80 percent of its total spending, and explains still more of the spending behavior of very poor families whom, it is hoped, development will benefit. The third conclusion is that it is harder to explain spending on durable goods than on other items because purchases are infrequent and depend on the past history of purchases and use as much as, or more than, they depend on family characteristics.

The Structure of Expenditure

Because the distribution of income is quite asymmetric and because income is one of the chief determinants of how spending is allocated, this study has concentrated on the structure of expenditure of a typical household located near the middle of the income distribution. When classes of the population are analyzed, discussion centers on a typical rather than an average income for a household in each class. Since most families have incomes well below the mean, the population is appreciably poorer than appears from averages such as those used in national accounts statistics.[10]

10. For example, food and beverages absorb a share of every 100 units of currency spent, ranging from 31 in Venezuela to 38 in Ecuador. For a family with typical characteristics and median income, however, the share ranges from 40 to 50—an increase of 9 or more percentage points. When food, housing, and clothing are combined, the national accounts shares range from 63 to 77 percent, but the typical-family shares range from 71 to 82 percent.

Most of the specific numerical results of the ECIEL study are consistent with the usual patterns found in budget studies. As income rises, necessities, particularly food, absorb less of the budget, and spending rises sharply on durable goods, education, recreation, and travel. Housing occupies a relatively constant share of the budget, opportunities for economies of scale being offset by improvements in quality. Certain categories of spending, particularly on durables and on clothing, are concentrated in the young adult years. Increased family size provokes a shift toward food, since incomes per person decline and there is little room for scale economies.

Two findings associated with this shift are of particular interest. The first is that as the family increases in size, and particularly as children are born, the total budget share devoted to food, housing, and clothing stays nearly constant. The requirement for increased food consumption is met partly by reductions in housing and particularly in spending per person on housing. The second is that the quality of the food budget changes with income per person. As income declines, or as the family is larger, spending on luxury foods—meat, poultry, eggs, dairy products, seafood, and fruit—declines, and the diet consists more of cereal products and of tubers (mostly potatoes). Thus the welfare of a family at any income level cannot be judged from its total spending on large aggregates such as food, but depends on the composition of the diet and other details of the budget. Differences within the food budget (or within the nonfood budget) may be more important among groups or among cities than differences in the overall allocation between food and nonfood.

A few categories of spending take extremely stable shares of the budget: dairy products, meat, fruits, other foods, nondurable goods, clothing, and a heterogeneous category of other consumption items. Budget shares are more variable for such categories as alcoholic beverages, meals away from home, durable goods, and education, and extremely variable for spending on services, private transportation, communication, and gifts and transfers. Relative variability is partly a matter of whether an elasticity is close to 1.0 (implying a share that does not change as income rises) and partly a matter of whether spending is concentrated in a particular age, size, life cycle, or other group in the population.

Age and life cycle appear to affect the shares of the budget devoted to long-lived goods or services (durables, vehicles, and education), to services in general, communication, transfers, medical care, and recreation. They also affect the consumption of alcoholic beverages and of meals away from home but have little impact on purely food categories or on housing.

Household size, somewhat surprisingly, tends to affect nonfood categories more than food categories. The number of children in the family, however, is more notable for its effect on food spending. This reflects the fact that children create needs for food more than they add to needs in most other categories; also, adding children to the family is sure to reduce income per person, whereas an additional adult may add to total income and leave income per person unchanged. A striking example of the importance of the effect of income per person is that expenditures on milk seem to depend more on total family size than on the number of children, although at equal income levels children account for a greater demand for milk than adults.

The analysis of budgetary structure for individual families or groups of households has been complemented by analysis of the structure of the market for each category of spending. That is, the share of total expenditure on any category coming from families in each quartile of the income distribution is estimated and the concentration of the market is measured by the richest quartile's share. There is relatively little concentration for most food categories, nondurable goods, and public transportation, all important categories for low-income households. Concentration among upper-income levels is found for household furnishings, services, education, private transport, and a few other categories. A rough summary of these findings and a comparison across cities of the distribution of income suggest the following conclusion: the degree of market concentration for necessities depends heavily on the concentration of income but not much on the level of income, while for luxuries the concentration depends more on income level and less on inequality in its distribution.[11]

11. This conclusion is based on analysis across income quartiles. Since family size is positively associated with income, the richest quartile (25 percent of households) includes more than 25 percent of the number of people. Therefore, even if all incomes were equal, the top quartile should account for more than one-fourth of the market. If the quartiles were defined on the basis of income per person, the richest quartile would include less than one-fourth of the population, and market concentration would probably decline for necessities and would certainly increase for luxuries.

Aggregate Differences among Cities

The study was made comparable across several cities and countries for two reasons in particular. First, although a small set of household characteristics may explain much of economic behavior in each city, the explanation may not be quite the same for each city. To understand why the same factors could have different effects, the aggregate features of the cities studied must be considered. Second, such features may also explain some of the spending behavior not entirely explained by information about families themselves, even if the household variables have the same effects everywhere. There are specific questions that a comparison across countries may answer. Can differences in behavior among cities or countries be attributed wholly or primarily to differences in the distribution of certain household characteristics? If not, are there any aggregate features of the cities that help explain differences in behavior? Is there any room left for pure differences in preferences, differences that must be called cultural rather than economic?[12]

Such questions cannot, of course, be completely answered since they are not questions about the variables studied here but about the possible importance of factors that have not been studied. However, if expenditure on meat can be completely explained by income and family characteristics, there is no need for an explanation that depends on differences in tastes for meat.[13] If, however, only 50 percent of the variation is explained—or if 100 percent is explained in each of two countries but the two explanations turn out to be quite different—then it is legitimate, perhaps necessary, to speculate on the omitted factors that contribute to a fuller explanation.

Also, these questions may be of interest not only for their own sake, but also for a more practical reason. The better consumer behavior can be understood according to a common pattern and in response to eco-

12. Variables such as education, life cycle, and family size are considered "economic," since they are incorporated in economic theories and have clear effects on economic behavior.

13. Of course, tastes are defined in some relatively long-run sense. Consumers are to some extent creatures of habit, and they may take time to adjust fully to changes in income, prices, or other factors. In the short run, therefore, their apparent "tastes" will be functions of the prices they have recently faced; only in a longer interval will their more fundamental preferences determine their response to price changes.

nomic factors that are relatively easy to study, the more safely can these findings be projected to other cities in these same countries, to other, similar countries, and to the future. If, however, a great deal of behavior can only be explained by cultural factors that differ sharply from place to place or by essentially arbitrary individual preferences, then such generalization becomes dangerous.

Of all the variables studied here, the same ones tend always to be important, and to have the same kind of influence, in all or nearly all cities studied. Much of the difference between cities can be attributed to differences in the distributions of a few fundamental variables. For example, when the labor force is better educated, all incomes are higher, the concentration of income is less, and the relative income gain is always greater for poor families than for rich ones. All this, of course, is due to the interaction of human capital and labor supply with demands for labor in production—they are general equilibrium outcomes. Nonetheless, these interactions in labor markets seem to follow enough of a pattern among cities or countries that their outcome can be understood or even predicted just from information about the supply side. Thus patterns in spending behavior can be predicted by looking only at consumers' demands; the influence of the supply side is indicated by prices and need not be considered otherwise.

The failure of the data to explain some kinds of spending well—as on durable goods, particularly on vehicles—is probably not due to any difference in tastes. It can be explained by small sample sizes, inflationary effects, and the absence of data on current possession and past acquisition of particular goods. For goods and services bought regularly by nearly all families and consumed in fairly short intervals—food, housing, services, household nondurable goods—a large share of the variation among families within a country can be explained.[14] Differences in the degree to which behavior can be explained in each of the countries seem to be largely due to differences in transitory income variation and in sample design among the countries.

Because a given category of spending can be equally well explained with the same set of variables in different countries does not, of course, mean that the econometric parameters or other statistics are everywhere

14. The R^2 statistics range from 0.57 to 0.85 for food, from 0.74 to 0.81 for housing, from 0.38 to 0.57 for clothing (and also for "other consumption"), and from 0.47 to 0.61 for services. See appendix B.

the same. For example, the expenditure elasticity for a particular category varies across countries quite substantially. If the elasticity were considered a feature of the underlying utility function, that would be evidence of fundamental differences in utility or in preferences. However, most of the elasticities are estimated from a model that is inconsistent with utility theory: the estimates are constants, whereas the true elasticities vary with income.[15] When the rankings (rather than the absolute values) of these elasticities are compared across countries, the following interesting result is obtained: as real median income increases, the elasticities shift systematically. That is, the pattern of elasticities is consistent with the ranking of countries in terms of real income, and therefore is (weak) evidence for a common behavior pattern that does not depend on taste differences.

When spending behavior is estimated consistent with utility theory (in the extended linear system), the utility functions appear quite different across cities. However, the model is extremely rigid, and if its parameters are interpreted as describing short-run behavior rather than fundamental needs or wants, once again a consistent pattern emerges. Demand functions vary across cities in accordance with real income levels and also with the degree of income equality.

Drawing together these findings and reaching somewhat beyond the evidence of the study, I conclude that there is a common urban Andean consumer behavior pattern: consumers in these ten cities and five countries are fundamentally alike in their responses to real income and to the set of variables described as family composition. Short-run differences in aggregate behavior are not at all inconsistent with fundamental similarity in behavior at the individual household level.[16]

This is not to say that cultural and individual preferences are of no importance or that economics can explain everything while other factors and the insights of other disciplines can be disregarded. However, when only economic behavior is examined, specifically how incomes are earned and spent, it is unnecessary to invoke cultural differences between populations to explain that behavior.

15. This is the case for the double-logarithmic Engel curves discussed in chapter 6. Other Engel curves derived from linear systems include parameters that do appear in the utility function.

16. The similarity of consumer preferences among cities is examined further in Philip Musgrove, "Price and Income Effects on Budget Allocation: Comparisons Among and Within Latin American Cities" (Brookings Institution, January 1978; processed).

This conclusion must be modified in at least three ways. First, and most obviously, preferences are more similar among countries and also among families for large aggregates of consumption. Colombians appear to drink more coffee than can be explained by its very low price there. The same is true in Chile of wine, and perhaps in Peru of seafood. These preferences are submerged, however, in total food consumption, and much of what seems to be preference, such as the high consumption of potatoes relative to bread in Colombia, may be as well explained by price differences.

Preferences are also expressed in differences in quality—particular cuts of meat, designs of housing, styles of clothing, and so on. Such preferences matter to consumers, but their importance should not be exaggerated. Local markets are attuned to such tastes; here the concern is more with a greater level of abstraction, where these slightly different goods and services can be considered (almost) perfect substitutes.

Second, preferences seem to be more nearly identical for necessities than for luxuries: as income rises, families enjoy more discretionary spending and can express their individual tastes. This is a plausible finding, but it seems to contradict the widespread notion of a "demonstration effect" that would give people in different cultures the same aspirations for modern luxuries, so that preferences should converge rather than diverge as incomes rise. Of course, tastes may converge across populations at the same time that they become more diverse within each population; also the finding of greater diversity for luxuries may simply reflect the greater difficulty of explaining expenditure on these categories. A more sophisticated model of behavior might show great similarities among cities. It may also be true that luxuries are more affected by certain macroeconomic differences among cities or countries, which need to be considered.

Third, the ECIEL study has identified a few aggregate features of the cities analyzed that influence consumption behavior. One such feature is geographic location: cities located in the mountains, away from the seacoast, differ systematically from coastal or near-coastal cities. Much of this difference is associated with relative prices, but there is also an independent effect. Differences in temperature or in climatic variation cause different needs for such items as housing and clothing, and possibly also more indirect differences in needs for food, medical care, and so on. Another feature is the composition of employment in the city, in particular whether a city is largely industrial or includes a large civil service. These occupational differences are probably not associated with tastes, but they affect the distribution and especially the composition of income.

Finally, there is considerable indirect evidence that the rate and variability of changes in price influence consumer behavior, and in this respect there are striking differences between the high inflation rates of Santiago and Lima and the much lower rates in the cities of Colombia, Ecuador, and Venezuela. Two important effects of rapid and, in particular, of variable inflation are, first, that it leads to greater transitory variation in income and spending, making it harder to identify stable relations; and second, that, in the absence of capital market adjustments to maintain real rates of return, it leads to higher consumption relative to saving and to a shift in saving from unprotected financial assets to more protected real assets. The latter effect appears in the very high purchases of durables in Santiago and Lima.

All sorts of government actions affect consumers, so the macroeconomic situation of a country should always be expected to influence spending behavior. Most such actions, however, will be felt through the distribution of incomes or through relative prices. It is important then to see whether other effects are also at work either on consumers' expectations or on their fundamental preferences.

Uses and Implications

The findings of the ECIEL surveys may be useful for evaluating the impact on consumers of economic change or public policy. They may also be valuable for projects such as the construction of national and international price indexes, projections of demand, estimates of tax incidence, and estimates of quantitative consumption necessary for judgments about nutrition, schooling, and (possibly) health. Three broad issues are discussed as examples, all of great political importance and all susceptible to public intervention. These issues are the distribution of income, population growth, and the economic integration of the Andean countries.

The Distribution of Income

The results of the study for income distribution are relevant to public policy in two ways. First, they give some idea of how the income distribution is generated and therefore of how it might be changed. Second, they permit projection of the consequences of redistribution for the structure of consumption. On the first point, the evidence appears to imply the following. In order to reduce the inequality of income appreciably, as opposed to simply redistributing some of the income of a very rich minority, it is necessary to make labor incomes more nearly equal. This is unlikely to be accomplished primarily by creating more jobs exactly like those currently existing, although employment expansion is important both as a way of providing for new labor force entrants and as a way of reducing capital requirements for economic growth.[17] Many families have only one employed member and no other potentially employable members, at least not for full-time work. The only way to raise the living standards of such families is to raise the labor incomes of principal earners; that is, to make labor more productive by adding to human capital, investing more in physical capital, or making better use of existing productive capacity. But efforts of this sort should not be concentrated solely on wage earners. There are many poor salaried people in the urban economy, but the labor income of the very poor tends to come largely from independent work. Equalizing wages and salaries would reduce income inequality around the center of the distribution but affect few of the poorest families, whose poverty is due more to lack of skills, difficulty in access to credit, and product market flaws than to wage policies.

Any substantial equalization of labor incomes would, in the absence of other changes, reduce the overall propensity to save. The impact on economic growth would be considerably less than might appear, however, because saving rates may be fairly constant over some income ranges and because long-run differences in saving rates are smaller than the short-run differences created by transitory factors. Moreover, the reduction in saving resulting from a redistribution of income might be entirely offset by rationalization of capital markets, particularly by a reduction in inflationary and other disincentives to saving by middle-income families.

In fact, a redistribution of income should, after a transitory period of

17. The controversy over how far capital and labor are substitutable in industry, or how much extra employment might be generated by changing the composition of the industrial sector rather than the techniques of production, is not considered here. For a survey of recent studies of these questions, see D. Morawetz, "Employment Implications of Industrialization in Developing Countries: A Survey," *Economic Journal*, vol. 84 (September 1974), pp. 491–542, and the review article by Werner Baer, "Technology, Employment and Development: Empirical Findings," *World Development*, vol. 4 (February 1976), pp. 121–30.

adjustment, have less effect on the balance between saving and consumption than on the composition of consumption. In particular, demand could be expected to increase sharply for high-quality foods if redistribution were directed toward the poor, and for better quality housing and durable goods if redistribution served to expand middle incomes. Shifts such as these would affect import demands, prices, and employment opportunities, and these effects should also be analyzed in evaluating any actual or proposed redistribution of income.

Population Growth

It is clear from this study that income and family composition are the principal household characteristics determining economic behavior and welfare. Family composition and size are in part the result of personal decisions about what kind of consuming unit to form—whether, for example, to group several nuclear families to exploit scale economies, whether to keep young adults attached to nuclear families, and so on. The age distribution within families, however, and the dependency burden carried by each income recipient depend much more on fertility and thus on the rate of population growth. Most households studied here are nuclear families without either individual supplementary members or secondary family units attached to them.[18] Within such households, the number of children, or of children per adult member, is a crucial determinant of the structure of consumption since it determines income per person. Large families tend to be poor—in income per person though not always in total income—and this is especially the case for families with many children.

The data have not been used to study the determinants of fertility, so they do not provide a direct answer to the question whether parents with higher individual incomes tend to have fewer children. If that is the case, economic development can be expected to slow population growth, at least so long as low-income households share in the gains. It is clear that in all ten cities, the lowest levels of total spending are found among families with six or more children, and these levels are sometimes much lower than those of households with five or fewer children. It therefore appears that as a rule it is only very poor parents who have such large numbers of children, and increases in their incomes might have a considerable effect

18. Secondary units typically constitute no more than 5 percent of the total population.

on fertility. A more complete analysis would also take account of the parents' ages, since income and spending tend to rise with age while beyond some age the number of children under fourteen declines. However, families in which there are already six or more children cannot be extremely young, and they are likely to be formed by relatively uneducated adults whose incomes will not rise appreciably as they get older. The omission of age from the analysis therefore probably does not greatly bias the association between income and fertility. Redistribution of income toward the very poor should also reduce population growth, although changes among middle and high incomes might have no effect.

One implication of this pattern is that a reduction in the birthrate would be equivalent in some respects to an increase in incomes. This is true to some extent for all families, but it is only in families with many children per adult that a reduction in fertility would make the difference between being poor or being relatively well off. This is not an argument for reduced fertility by all households, but only for a limitation on the households with more children (usually six or more) than the labor of the adult members can adequately support.

Of course, increased income and reduced family size do not have the same effects on spending. Diets would shift toward high-protein foods in both cases, but food would take a smaller share of the budget if fertility were lower. Demands for housing, durables, services, and recreation would probably increase; demand for schooling might go either up or down, depending on the level of schooling and the balance between the income effect and the child-specific effect.

A second implication is that with or without a slowing of population growth and with or without a redistribution of income the welfare of poor families might be significantly improved by child-related policies such as family allowances or food subsidies. The poor are not uniformly found in large families, nor are all large families poor, but the association is strong enough to constitute an argument for slower population growth and to suggest that demographic and incomes policies should be considered together.

Andean Integration

The five countries studied here have been attempting to integrate their economies not only by the usual device of a common tariff, but by harmonizing their policies on foreign investment and by an ambitious program of joint industrial development. To the extent that integration is successful, it will bring about faster income growth in the Andean countries, with implications for the level and composition of expenditure. An integration scheme raises two other kinds of questions, which would not arise in the development of any of the member economies by itself. First, much of the difference in relative prices among countries has been due to different tariffs or other barriers to trade. As tariffs are made uniform toward the outside world and reduced within the group, price structures should move closer together.[19] This in turn will modify the growth and composition of demand.

Second, achievement of the goals of integration, particularly the creation of an efficient industrial sector, may complement some national objectives and come into conflict with others. In particular, income redistribution in any one country would increase regional demands for some goods but reduce it for others. Similarly, national price policies might further or retard the reduction of intercountry price differences. The interaction of regional and national objectives and actions merits thorough study made possible by the uniformity of data and analysis for the member countries.

This study did not directly investigate either the prospects for regional integration or the probable consequences. The findings nonetheless carry some implications for integration that deserve to be mentioned. The first is that consumption patterns, and the income distributions that give rise to them, are extremely similar in all the cities studied. There is some evidence that they would be still more similar if relative prices were everywhere the same, but in any case there seem to be no profound differences in tastes that would make it difficult for one country's products to be accepted in another country. To the extent that this is true, integration is facilitated both because economies of scale can be more readily exploited and because products need not be greatly differentiated to satisfy different tastes.

A second finding of some importance is that the market for modern

19. Price differences apparently did narrow throughout Latin America between 1960–62 and 1968, although most of this change was probably not the result of integration. See Jorge Salazar-Carrillo, "Price, Purchasing Power and Real Product Comparisons in Latin America," *Review of Income and Wealth,* vol. 19 (March 1973), pp. 117–32.

sector goods—including particularly most of the goods of interest for industrial complementarity agreements—seems to be limited more by the level of income than by the degree of income concentration. Integration may thus offer a greater expansion of the markets for these products than can be obtained by redistributing income within national economies. Such redistribution is likely to have more effect on the markets for traditional goods. To some extent, therefore, international integration and domestic incomes policies are complementary: demand can be increased, or costs reduced, for a great variety of goods and services if both kinds of policies are undertaken jointly.

Extensions of Research

It is traditional but may still be useful to close a study such as this one by discussing the direction of further research. There are four ways in particular in which an extension of this research would lead to a better understanding of household consumer behavior in Latin America.

First, much more can and should be done to analyze the existing data. As indicated earlier, the results presented here were designed to offer a wide range of information and implications, not to settle any particular question definitively. Specific hypotheses can now be stated and tested, and particular policies evaluated, relating to income distribution, population growth, economic integration, or any of many other issues. This study already incorporates many such extensions to the original plan of the ECIEL consumption study, and research has continued on several questions.

Second, at many points it would be useful to combine family budget information with other sorts of data such as information on prices paid by consumers, work experience, multiple employment, and individual incomes (which is missing or incomplete in the ECIEL data); on stocks and past purchases of durable goods and vehicles; on educational history and the educational attainment of individuals; and on health experience and medical needs. These issues all pose questions that are not fully answered by information on current flows of income and spending.

Third, the chief deficiency of these findings for drawing inferences about entire economies is obviously their limitation to just a few large cities. Income concentration and composition may be quite different in rural areas and small towns; even at the same real income level there will be differences in spending as a result of different needs, different relative prices, and greater opportunities for domestic production instead of market purchases. Survey work is considerably more difficult conceptually and more costly in rural areas, but such research is necessary to give a complete picture of the household sector. The present findings can probably be extrapolated to small cities and thus to much of the urban population, but they almost certainly would not represent the rural economy well.

Finally, research like this needs to be repeated at intervals for the simple reason that while consumer behavior is rather stable it nonetheless changes over time as the economy develops. The practice of repeating major surveys at intervals of ten years or less, with research on a smaller scale at shorter intervals, is now widely accepted in developed countries and is coming to be accepted in Latin America as well. To make the best use of such information, it is necessary not only to collect data repeatedly, but also to strengthen the capacity to analyze it and to integrate more fully knowledge about how this fundamental sector of the economy functions. It is the hope of all those concerned in the ECIEL study that it has helped advance these objectives, to the eventual benefit of the people we have tried to examine and understand.

Obtaining and Preparing
the Information

THREE STAGES of the study are discussed here in some detail: data collection, data cleaning, and adjustments to make the sample represent the population.

Data Collection: The Sample

This topic includes the design, structure, and size of the sample; the design of the national questionnaires and their harmonization; the definition of the consuming unit or unit of observation; the choice of periods of reference and the conversion of data to other periods; and the timing and organization of the interviews. This stage actually included some data cleaning, carried out while it was still possible to return to the household for more information or to decide whether to replace it with another unit.

Sample Design

All the samples are multistage: that is, they were not drawn immediately from a country's total population but were selected in stages. In Peru and Venezuela, an initial selection of blocks or groups of households was followed by a selection of dwelling units from among these groups. In Colombia, Chile, and Ecuador, a first-stage selection of neighborhoods or districts was followed by a choice of groups of households, and then by a selection of individual households in Chile and of dwelling units elsewhere. The distinction between households and dwelling units matters only when two or more households share a dwelling.

The Venezuelan sample was selected proportionally, with every household in a given city having the same probability of appearing in the sample. Because the variation in expenditures is greater for high than for low incomes, it was more efficient, and resulted in more accurate estimates, to select a nonproportional sample consisting of a large number of relatively high-income households and a relatively small number with low incomes. This procedure, which permitted comparable accuracy of estimation at all income levels, was adopted in Colombia, Chile, Ecuador, and Peru.

Because there was no prior knowledge of the income distribution in each city, the populations were classified into strata as the basis for nonproportional selection. This classification held for blocks, neighborhoods, or other divisions of the city; every household living in a given division was then assigned to the same stratum. The criterion for assignment was an evaluation of the character of the dwellings in a division based on objective measures such as size, availability of water and electricity, garage, and so on, and subjective assessments of its maintenance and of the income level to which it corresponded. The stratification could be the initial step of the survey: this was the procedure in Chile, where a sample of 15,600 dwellings were classified. In the other countries, the stratification was based on existing information such as censuses of housing or population. Information of this sort may be somewhat obsolete or not exactly suited to the purposes of a budget survey, but it is readily available and can be adjusted where necessary.

The Venezuelan samples, though proportional, were also stratified (three strata in Caracas and four in Maracaibo), with a low-income stratum clearly distinguished. In Colombia, Chile, Ecuador, and Peru, the samples were divided into three strata; in Peru the low-income stratum was further divided between the central city and the surrounding marginal settlements.

In all countries, the sampling fractions (the way the sample was distributed among strata) were chosen to make the estimates as accurate as possible.[1] The sampling fraction for neighborhoods ranged from 1.0 for

---

1. The efficient size for the sample in stratum s is $n_s = np_s\sigma_s/\Sigma_s p_s\sigma_s$, where σ_s is the standard deviation of income or consumption, p_s is the share of total population in the stratum, and n is the total sample size. See Maurice Kendall and Alan Stuart, *The Advanced Theory of Statistics*, 2d ed. (Hafner, 1968), vol. 3, pp. 179–81.

the high stratum in Guayaquil to 0.167 for that stratum in Cali. At the household selection stage, the sampling fraction is typically between 0.2 and 0.4.[2]

The standard formulas for estimating sampling error and errors in parameter estimation assume a random, proportional sample. For more complex samples the errors are likely to be underestimated or overestimated by these formulas, and it is difficult to derive analytical expressions for them. The standard formulas were therefore used.

Sample Structure

Except in Caracas (where the study is based on a one-time survey taken in 1966, before the ECIEL project began), four surveys were taken throughout one year in order to observe seasonal differences while covering a relatively long total interval. However, this posed a problem: if the same families were interviewed repeatedly, they might cease to participate, leaving a small and perhaps unrepresentative sample. On the other hand, if different households were chosen for each survey, sample variations might be misinterpreted as seasonal differences and long-period information could not be obtained for any one family.

The sample structure is thus a compromise, which includes a panel of repeatedly interviewed households; three semipanel groups; and four independent groups. In all, there are eight subsamples, each one selected in the same way from the different strata (except in Chile, where the nonpanel groups include relatively few high-stratum observations):

Interval	*Subsample*							
(trimester)	n_1	n_2	n_3	n_4	n_5	n_6	n_7	n_8
1	n_{11}	n_{21}	n_{31}	n_{41}	n_{51}			
2	n_{12}	n_{22}				n_{62}		
3	n_{13}		n_{33}				n_{73}	
4	n_{14}			n_{44}				n_{84}

While p_s is known, σ_s must be estimated from a presurvey or from exogenous information. See, for example, Rafael Prieto D., *Estructura del Gasto y Distribución del Ingreso Familiar en Cuatro Ciudades Colombianas, 1967–1968* (Bogotá: Universidad de los Andes, 1971), pt. 2, pp. 10–15, which shows how σ_s was estimated from the range of consumption in Colombia.

2. Information on the sampling fraction at each stage is incomplete except for Colombia. See Philip Musgrove and Howard Howe, "ECIEL, Estudio de Consumo e Ingreso Familiar (Antecedentes y Metodología): Version Revisada" (Brookings Institution, 1973; processed), pp. 12–18.

This design concentrates the interviews in the first interval, but includes in each subsequent interval some new households and some that were interviewed previously.

The full design was used in Colombia, Ecuador, and Maracaibo (the Caracas sample consists in effect of the cell n_{51} only). The Chilean sample omitted the semipanels n_2, n_3, and n_4. The Peruvian sample had no repeated interviews, consisting of the independent cells n_{51} through n_{84} only. In Ecuador the subsample classification was used but was not reported in the data, so the effective structure is the same as that for Peru; it is not known which families were reinterviewed.

Sample Size

In principle, the size of a sample should increase with the size and heterogeneity of the population being studied and with the degree of detail and accuracy desired in the estimates of population characteristics. The number of efforts to interview depends also on the expected non-response rate, both initially and as a consequence of attrition in the reinterviewed groups. Finally, the size is constrained by the total resources available for sampling and analysis.

In general, neither the sampling errors nor the nonresponse rates were known in advance, although presurveys were used to project the latter in Colombia, Chile, and Venezuela. Sample sizes were determined by resources, by the structure adopted, and by the size of the city. Table A-1 shows the final samples, by stratum and by interval, for each city. These differ from the number of contacts or interviews for two reasons: the discarding of a few observations in subsequent cleaning and the incorporation of partial or secondary consuming units into primary households in the case of Ecuador.[3]

Several of the cells defined by stratum and trimester are quite small, but these two variables are never analyzed together. The smallest complete sample in a stratum exceeds one hundred observations, as does the smallest quarterly sample over all strata. In a few cases, expenditure patterns are described for groups consisting of as few as forty sample households (see table 4-1), but most analyses are based on larger samples.

3. Secondary units were also consolidated with primary households for some subsequent analyses: see Arturo Carlos Meyer, "Diferencias Internacionales en los Patrones de Consumo," *Ensayos ECIEL*, vol. 1 (November 1974), pp. 173–213.

Table A-1. *Sample Size by City, Trimester, and Income Stratum,*
Ten Latin American Cities

City and income stratum	Trimester				Total
	1	2	3	4	
Bogotá, total	259	174	184	181	798
High	48	20	24	27	119
Middle	93	63	70	68	294
Low	118	91	90	86	385
Barranquilla, total	259	153	165	150	727
High	56	34	41	33	164
Middle	70	43	44	43	200
Low	133	76	80	74	363
Cali, total	200	136	150	150	636
High	43	27	36	29	135
Middle	58	41	44	50	193
Low	99	68	70	71	308
Medellín, total	285	164	177	162	788
High	61	34	36	35	166
Middle	91	54	57	45	247
Low	133	76	84	82	375
Santiago, total	915	834	842	786	3,377
High	241	206	212	191	850
Middle	311	283	290	267	1,151
Low	363	345	340	328	1,376
Quito, total	359	196	194	174	923
High	114	60	62	47	283
Middle	145	82	78	79	384
Low	100	54	54	48	256
Guayaquil, total	398	163	226	259	1,046
High	47	17	27	38	129
Middle	216	88	113	139	556
Low	135	58	86	82	361
Lima, total	326	137	360	534	1,357
High	61	24	90	208	383
Middle	131	52	154	184	521
Low, urban	76	25	78	87	266
Low, slums	58	36	38	55	187
Caracas, total	929	...	...	...	...
High	675	...	...	...	...
Middle	71	...	...	...	...
Low	183	...	...	...	...
Maracaibo, total	475	222	235	241	1,173
High	43	15	22	23	103
Middle (high)	87	42	43	41	213
Middle (low)	30	11	11	12	64
Low	315	154	159	165	793

Source: Original ECIEL calculations based on the survey data.

Data Collection: Interviewing

Questionnaire Design

Two principal kinds of information were collected: financial income and expenditure (flows); and characteristics of the household, its members, and their dwelling (primarily stocks, or long-term information). Income and expenditure were classified by source or type, and the total income of each household member and the expenditures of individual supplementary members were recorded separately. The expenditures of these supplementary members, who contribute to only some parts of the household budget, were then merged with household expenditures. Each member was asked about his or her own income and separate expenditures; most of the expenditure information, as well as that concerning dwelling and family characteristics, was obtained from the household head or spouse.

Some expenditure items, such as mortgage-principal payments and purchases of durables, represent changes in wealth rather than in current consumption. Other asset changes were included to approximate the household's saving, but in general the stock (current value) of assets was not studied. (The chief exception is the value of owned dwellings.)[4] Variables were defined to permit distinctions to be made between consumption and nonconsumption expenditures, between durables and nondurables and services, between total and disposable income, and between regular and (ex ante) transitory income.

It was left to each institute to decide whether to rely on a diary or on memory for data about regular, frequent purchases such as food and tobacco. Pilot tests suggested that the diary method is slightly superior, but it requires more effort on the part of the household and perhaps conditions its expenditures. The diary method was used in Chile, Peru, and Maracaibo, while the entire questionnaire was filled in from memory in Colombia and Ecuador. The Caracas survey used a third procedure: daily visits by the interviewer during the month of reference.

---

4. See "Un Estudio del Ahorro Familiar," ECIEL, "Resumen del Decimonoveno Seminario del Programa de Estudios Conjuntos sobre Integración Económica Latinoamericana (ECIEL)" (Quito: January 15–19, 1973; processed); and chapter 3.

National Questionnaires and Harmonization

Each institute developed its own questionnaire in accordance with its interests, while following a common scheme. For some purposes of national analysis, information may be used directly from the questionnaires, but for the ECIEL study, all the information was converted to a common code designed for the greatest possible international comparability.[5]

The sociodemographic variables and the dwelling characteristics were transferred directly from questionnaire to code, with few problems of aggregation or interpretation. For each household member sex, age, civil status, relation to the household head, schooling, labor force status, and occupation were recorded, and for income recipients, employment sector and total income as well. Migration experience was recorded for the head and the spouse. The dwelling was described by type, number of rooms, construction material, condition, services, and kind of tenure.

Financial variables were harmonized chiefly by aggregation. This eliminated much of the detail of the questionnaires while maintaining a reasonable level of disaggregation for analysis. In some cases, comparability was achieved among most countries at a detailed level; in others, two or more ways of aggregating or classifying the information were followed.

In all, 557 expenditure variables were defined: 509 items, 34 subtotals, 13 categories, and a grand total. A further 54 items refer to income. Finally, 32 variables refer to asset changes and saving. International comparability is best for expenditures, good for most income categories, and relatively poor for wealth and saving variables.[6]

Definition of the Consuming Unit

The questionnaires also differed in the definition of the consuming unit. The principal differences concerned the distinction between primary and

5. A description of all the variables is given in ECIEL, "Estudio de Consumo e Ingreso, Código versión 9 (CODV9)," included as appendix 2 of ECIEL, "Urban Household Income and Consumption Patterns in Latin America: A Comparative Analysis of Colombia, Paraguay, Peru and Venezuela" (Brookings Institution, 1974; processed). A separate document describes the codes for the sociodemographic (nonfinancial) variables.

6. A detailed description of international comparability appears in Musgrove and Howe, "ECIEL, Estudio de Consumo e Ingreso Familiar."

secondary households; the treatment of supplementary members; the inclusion of domestic servants; and the criterion for determining the head of the household. These features are summarized in table A-2. ("Family" and "household" are used synonymously with "consuming unit" in what follows. The unit is defined by a shared budget, not by ties of blood or marriage.)

Provided that all the possible members are included separately or in one or another unit in the questionnaires, the units can be harmonized across countries by aggregation to the largest household concept used in any country. Though this was done to some extent, some differences remain: for example, the information on supplementary members in Colombia was judged to be of very poor quality and was not incorporated, so that Colombian households appear to be slightly smaller than those of

Table A-2. *International Comparability of the Consuming Unit, Five Latin American Countries*

Features of questionnaires	Colombia	Chile	Ecuador	Peru	Venezuela
Definition of unit					
Secondary units	x		x		
Supplementary members	x*		x	x	
(*not incorporated into unit)					
Guests included in primary unit		x			x
Servants included in primary unit		x		x	x
Criterion for head					
Economic (chief income earner) or social (defined by the household)	E	S	E	S	E
Comparability of per capita measures[a]					
Colombia	E	P	E	F	P
Chile		E	P	P	E
Ecuador			E	F	P
Peru				E	P
Venezuela					E

Source: ECIEL, "Resumen del XIV Seminario del Programa de Estudios Conjuntos sobre Integración Económica Latinoamericana (ECIEL)" (Lima; December 15–20, 1969; processed), pp. 32–40, and "Resumen del Decimonoveno Seminario del Programa de Estudios Conjuntos sobre Integración Económica Latinoamericana (ECIEL)" (Buenos Aires, June 29–July 3, 1970; processed), pp. 28–32.

a. E, excellent; F, fair; P, poor.

other countries and to contain relatively fewer adults. Household composition also varies by the inclusion or exclusion of servants and guests.[7]

In general, the criteria for designating the head coincide, but to the extent that they differ, there is some difficulty in classifying households according to the characteristics of the head. The problem arises only for households with several income earners, which are infrequent in Colombia but form about half the population in the other countries.

Periods of Reference

In principle, the period of reference of the financial data should be uniform for all categories of income and expenditure, since only in this way can all the information be made to refer to a well-defined interval; any variation requires that values be imputed multiplicatively if the information is to be made uniform. But it is not possible to apply this principle because the "natural" reporting periods differ greatly among categories. If the period is too short, the data are unrepresentative; if respondents are asked about too long a period, the data become quite inaccurate.

For many variables, there is a natural period of reference corresponding to the frequency of financial receipt or payment: this is the case generally for wage and salary income, transfer income, rent or mortgage payments, and utilities. The use of this natural period, typically one month, minimizes response errors and may be reasonably accurate for imputation over longer periods. For infrequent items such as purchases of durable goods and receipt of transitory income, the multiplicative assumption is likely to be quite inaccurate. The natural choice is the longest reference period, and the response error is ignored. At the opposite extreme, response error rises very quickly for such frequent items as food purchases, so it is natural to choose the shortest period. There is some evidence on the relation of response error to period of reference from expenditure surveys, but not enough to derive analytical expressions for the errors and minimize their effect directly. Generally, the error is negative (amounts are underreported) and increases in absolute size with the length of the recall period, at least beyond the natural period. For

7. In all the analyses reported here, only the largest concept of household size was used; this includes members who were temporarily absent or who contributed only partially to the household budget.

such items as semidurable goods and irregular income from capital or other sources, the two sources of error may be of comparable magnitude.

For all these reasons, the ECIEL researchers agreed to use different periods of reference for different categories, with (usually) a uniform period within each category. The exception is Caracas, where all the data (except on vehicle purchases) have a monthly reference period. The natural period of receipt or payment was used whenever it could be defined. All observations refer to a period of one week, one month, three months, or one year. Table A-3 summarizes the periods used in each country. In Quito, there is a difference between the first and subsequent intervals for many categories with a monthly or quarterly reference period.

Table A-3. *Periods of Reference, Various Spending Categories, Five Latin American Countries*

Spending category	Colombia	Chile	Ecuador[a]	Peru	Venezuela[b]
Housing	M	T	A/T	T/A	M
Food	W	W	W	W	W
Alcoholic beverages	M	W	T/M	W	W
Tobacco	M	W	A/M	M	W
Repairs	T	T	A/T	T	W
Household services	M	T	T/M	T	M
Cleaning	M	W	T/M	M	W
Furnishing	T	T	A/T	T	T
Clothing	T	T	A/T	T	T
Personal care	M	W	T/M	M	W
Medical care	T	T	A/M	T	W
Recreation	T	W	T/M	T	W
Education	M/T	T	A/T	T	W
Vehicle	T	T	A/T	A	T
Transport	M	T	T	M	W
Insurance	T	T	T	A	W
Taxes	T	T	T	A	T
Income by person	M/T	T	A/T	M/T	M
Income by type	T	T	A/T	M/T	M

Source: ECIEL, "Resumen del XIV Seminario ECIEL" (Buenos Aires, June 29–July 3, 1970; processed), pp. 68–69; and correspondence with the collaborating institutes. W, weekly; M, monthly; T, quarterly; A, annual. Colombia and Peru had moving interview dates; dates in other countries were fixed.
a. The first of two periods refers to Quito in the first interval.
b. The periods refer to Maracaibo; periods in Caracas were monthly except for vehicle purchases, which was annual.

To adjust the data to a quarterly basis, weekly estimates were multiplied by thirteen, and monthly values by three; annual values were divided by four. No conversion was made from a weekly to a monthly basis. Note, however, that the respondent may actually use a different period of reference in arriving at the reported value. For example, he may estimate his weekly expenditure on tobacco and multiply it by four to get the monthly estimate sought by the interviewer. In this case, quarterly expenditures would be underestimated by one-thirteenth, since the weekly figure would be multiplied first by four and then by three. It cannot be determined how often this occurred or how it affects the data generally.

Only quarterly estimates were aggregated to form estimates of total income and total expenditure. (Aggregation and reconciliation of monthly or weekly observations would have required the unjustifiable assumption that flows recorded for the whole quarter were distributed uniformly throughout it.) In some cases, the reconciliation of these totals required information on changes in debts and assets, which also have a quarterly period of reference.

In a sense, there is no particular problem in aggregating data with initially different reference periods, since any procedure that maximizes the accuracy of the estimated quarterly value for each variable separately also maximizes the accuracy with which their sum is estimated. There might be a serious problem if the period of reference had to be uniform for all variables, since small percentage errors in some variables would significantly affect the totals while large errors in other variables would have no such effect. Where the period was chosen separately for each variable or group of related variables, it was unnecessary to choose between the accuracy of the components and that of totals.

There is still a difficulty, however, in aggregating variables with both of the following properties: errors in reporting increase rapidly in absolute value as the period increases; and imputed values differ significantly from true values because of seasonal or inflationary factors.

The first property may require a very short period, with the result that the long period value is considerably over- or underestimated, even if one week's expenditure is estimated quite accurately. In the ECIEL samples, this problem probably exists only for food expenditures, which constitute a large share of total expenditure for low-income families. For this reason, an error as large as 30 percent of estimated total expenditures was allowed in reconciling income and outflow. The problem becomes general and severe if there is rapid inflation during the quarter; then all items with short periods of reference tend to be overestimated relative to all long-period items unless some correction is made for price change.

Distribution of Interviews through Time

Where problems of this sort are sufficient to bias the estimates for individual households, it may still be possible to estimate accurately the quarterly income and expenditure of the population, by properly distributing the interviews throughout the survey period. Suppose, for example, that every sample household can accurately report a week's food expenditures, and that the total food expenditure of the population increases by 12 percent between the first and last weeks of the quarter (1 percent per week, linearly). If all the families are interviewed in the last week, total food expenditure for the quarter will be overstated by between 5 and 6 percent of the true value, whereas if one-thirteenth of the families are interviewed each week, the total will be correctly estimated. Of course, if this problem affects all variables, then the proportions of expenditure in different categories will not be biased as much as the money amounts, when all interviews occur in the same week.

The period of reference also varies among countries according to whether it ends on the day of the interview (a moving period) or refers to a fixed previous period. When all the interviews for an interval are completed in a short time, there is little difference between these methods; when the interviews are spread throughout the year, the use of a moving period almost removes the distinction between intervals for categories with a quarterly or longer reference period. For example, a household at the end of the first interval and one at the start of the second can have twelve weeks in common, whereas the data for two observations in the same interval may overlap by only one week.

The surveys in the different countries were meant to be contemporaneous, but each institute chose its own calendar. (The dates of the interviews were indicated in chapter 1.) The four intervals fell within twelve months in Chile, Peru, and Maracaibo; in Ecuador, the interviews spread out over eighteen months in unequal intervals; and in Colombia, the interviews scheduled for May 1967 were taken one year later, maintaining the seasonal distribution. In Chile and Ecuador, there was a slight overlap of intervals. The period of interviewing was one week per interval in Maracaibo, one month in Colombia, and the entire interval in Chile, Ecuador, and Peru. Seasonal effects can be much more sharply distinguished in the first two cases than in the last three.

In all the analyses of the ECIEL data, no account has been taken of the fact that some households were interviewed repeatedly. If a household was interviewed four times, a complete annual record exists; annual estimates can be made for households interviewed three or fewer times by replacing the missing data with observations from other households or by multiplying the available record by the appropriate constant, exactly as is done in constructing quarterly estimates from observations over shorter periods. Experiments with a small number of households that were interviewed four times (twenty-six families in Medellín) suggest that fairly accurate annual records can be constructed, but the best way to do this depends partly on the variable whose value is to be estimated and partly on whether it is desired to estimate individual household values or only the mean value in the sample.[8]

Interview Organization and Control

Interviewers were divided into small groups whose supervisors were responsible for the quality of the questionnaire data. The supervisors sometimes accompanied the interviewers on a first visit to a household, visited a subsample of households to make sure they had been interviewed and to check the accuracy of the replies, and went themselves to interview families who initially chose not to participate. As part of the field work, the questionnaires were checked for logical consistency and for a rough balance of income and expenditure. Extreme values were examined at this stage in Venezuela and Colombia, and in the latter country checks were made of the consistency over time of data from panel households. In general, these procedures were designed to prevent the later rejection of observations, since the samples were relatively small. In this stage, as in later stages, the cost of data cleaning was less than that of replacement, so a balance was struck between accuracy and the total cost of collecting and cleaning the information.

8. These experiments are reported in Philip Musgrove, "Household Income and Expenditure Data," reproduced in annex A of ECIEL, "Urban Household Income and Consumption Patterns."

Data Cleaning

In preparing the data for economic analysis, it was necessary to remove all errors that would not pass through subsequent stages of cleaning and examination. This initial, mechanical purification of the sample was therefore quite thorough. Later stages may be described as logical, arithmetic, and economic, or statistical, cleaning. Each stage saw an increase in the amount of information used to select a particular value for examination and a decrease in the likelihood that the value was erroneous. In the final stages of data cleaning, therefore, efforts were made to select only those values most likely to contain errors.[9]

Stages of Cleaning

The data passed through seven steps before being considered acceptably clean.

1. Checking the sequence of the punched cards to which the data were transcribed from questionnaires or coding sheets to make sure observations were complete and properly ordered. (Card images were maintained in later magnetic tape and disk files to ensure compatibility between different forms of data storage.)

2. Correction of nonnumerical and blank entries introduced in transcription. (Blanks—which were distinguished from zeros—often indicated slips of the decimal place in transcribing information.)

3. Conversion to the common ECIEL code. This involved adjustment to a common period of reference as well as aggregation and redefinition of variables. Given the diversity of questionnaires and coding formats, this stage was complex and different for each country. Nonresponses were indicated by a code to permit the exclusion of those observations from

9. Some criterion is required to keep the investigator from being overwhelmed by a mass of values that could be selected as possibly erroneous by rigorous tests but that in fact have only a low probability of containing errors. See Howard Howe and Roberto Villaveces, "Data Preparation for Latin American Comparisons of Consumption," in Nancy D. Ruggles, ed., *The Role of the Computer in Economic and Social Research in Latin America* (National Bureau of Economic Research, 1974), pp. 269–89, for a discussion of these criteria.

subsequent analyses if desired. In order not to leave subtotals and categories unfilled, nonresponse items were treated as zeros (left out of sums).

4. Correction of invalid codes (numbers for which no meaning was defined).

5. Checking logical consistency. This involved about fifty relations among financial and nonfinancial variables. For example, parents must be at least thirteen years older than their children; age and education must be consistent; a house may not show both mortgage payments and rent; and payments for utilities must (usually) correspond to the services installed in the house.

6. Checking arithmetic consistency. This required that reported totals be no less than the sum of their components (totals greater than sums were allowed because of possible nonresponses for some components).

7. Detection and correction of extreme values. A preliminary inspection was made of the univariate distribution; then (except in Ecuador) a regression test was also used to identify values that were extreme in relation to a set of explanatory variables—that is, values whose residuals from the regression line were large.

If there is no prior univariate inspection, the multivariate test may find only the obviously (and absolutely) extreme values. If, however, the regression test is applied after censoring the univariate distribution, it is much better able to find relatively large errors and even to pick out more severe errors from a background of less severe ones. Tests in which errors were deliberately introduced into a body of data show that the multivariate test is more likely to find erroneous values, and less likely to detect extreme but correct values, than a univariate procedure.[10]

After each stage of data cleaning, the participating institutes were consulted about the invalid or possibly erroneous values detected. Mistakes in transcribing the data were caught and corrected from the questionnaires. Some apparent inconsistencies could be explained by specific conditions or customs of the city or country under study. Decisions on replacing or eliminating values were made jointly by the institutes and the study's coordinators. All values that could not be either accepted or corrected were replaced by nonresponse codes.

10. See Philip Musgrove, "Detecting Errors in Economic Survey Data: Multivariate vs. Univariate Procedures," *Annals of Economic and Social Measurement*, vol. 3 (April 1974), pp. 333–45 (Brookings Technical Series Reprint T-007).

Sample Analysis and Adjustment

Data cleaning consists of efforts to detect and correct errors in individual values of variables (although other variables, and even other observations, may be used in the tests). Data that have passed this stage are clean—that is, as free as possible of invalid, inconsistent, or inaccurate information—but they do not necessarily represent the population from which the sample was drawn.

Weighting the Sample

If a nonproportional sample is to yield unbiased information, the observations must be weighted. The weight of each sample household is simply the number of households in the population it represents. In a one-time, proportional sample, all the weights are equal. In the ECIEL samples, the weights differ among observations because the sample sizes are different in different intervals, as well as because of nonproportionality among strata. The rule for assigning weights is that the weighted sample size should equal the population (of households) for each stratum separately and thus for the sample as a whole. (The population frequencies are obtained from the same sources of information used to stratify the population. The subsamples into which the sample is divided do not affect the calculation of the weights, since they do not refer to population characteristics.)

If N_s is the population number of households in stratum s, and n_{si} of them are sampled in interval i, and there are four intervals altogether, there are two possible criteria for the weights w_{si}. One is to have the weighted sample frequency sum to the population over the entire year:

$$\sum_{i=1}^{4} = w_{si}n_{si} = N_s,$$

subject to $w_{si}n_{si} = w_{sj}n_{sj}$ for two different quarters i and j. Then,

$$w_{si}n_{si} = N_s/4,$$

or

(1) $$w_{si} = N_s/4n_{si}.$$

The other criterion is to have each quarter separately sum to the population:

(2) $$w_{si} = N_s/n_{si},$$

so that each weight is four times as large. For all statistics in which the weights appear in both the numerator and the denominator—relative frequencies, moments, indexes of concentration, regression coefficients—it does not matter if all the weights are multiplied by a constant, but it does matter when computing totals. Thus the sum of the values x_h over all households h using the weights in equation 1 is an estimate of the total *quarterly* flow of x in the population, since x has a quarterly period of reference after conversion of the data. The same sum with the weights in equation 2 is an estimate of the total *annual* flow, while the quarterly estimates are obtained by summing within each interval separately.

The weights were assigned according to equation 1 in Colombia, Peru, and Maracaibo, and according to equation 2 in Chile, Ecuador, and Caracas. The discrepancy between the two Venezuelan cities is explained by the fact that only one wave of interviews was taken in Caracas but four in Maracaibo; since the two cities are combined for some analyses, the weighted sum over all observations in each one must equal the population.

The weights are calculated in one step, reflecting the sample actually obtained. This collapses two estimates that are sometimes made separately: a weight based on the anticipated sample and an adjustment factor (calculated as $1/(1 - R)$) that takes account of the nonresponse rate R. The weights take no account of any characteristic except interval and stratum. Adjustments to make the sample represent the population with respect to other features are made only if required as a result of tests of sample composition.

Because the weight of an observation is inversely proportional to sample size in any interval, a household that is interviewed two or more times will have different weights in different intervals. This is not desirable for constructing annual (or six- or nine-month) records for individual families, but within the entire sample the low weight of a household in one quarter is balanced by the presence of a greater number of households. If a portion of the sample (other than the portions defined by interval and stratum) is analyzed separately, the weights must be adjusted. This would be required, for example, for separate studies of panel and nonpanel families.

The weights vary considerably among cities (because of differences in overall sampling fractions) and among quarters and strata. The ratio of the largest to the smallest weight is 1.1 in Caracas and 3.3 in Maracaibo; both samples were meant to be proportional, but proportionality was less well achieved in Maracaibo, where there are also differences in sample size among quarters. The ratio ranges from 4.9 to 8.3 in the four Colombian cities and in Santiago and Guayaquil; it reaches 19.7 in Quito and 135 in Lima, where the sample most heavily overrepresents high-income families. If all the weights are adjusted to the same basis—dividing those for Chile, Ecuador, and Caracas by four—then a high-stratum observation typically has a weight of about 100, though this is lower in Ecuador, Peru, and Chile and higher in Bogotá and Cali. Low-stratum observations are assigned weights of about 200 in Ecuador and Chile, and 500 or more in Peru and Colombia, with occasional values over 1,000. The weights in the middle stratum are intermediate.

Sample Biases

The weighting procedure ensures that the sample represents the population with respect to the strata, but it may still be biased in either of two other respects. First, the sample may differ from the population in the distribution of some important classifying characteristic such as household size or the occupation of the head. Such a difference can arise either because the sample, as initially chosen, is unrepresentative (includes too few households of some kinds and too many of others) or because attrition makes an initially representative sample lose that character. Global attrition or simple reduction in sample size is entirely compensated for by the weights, but differential attrition, the loss of more households of one kind than of another, is not.

The second type of bias is that the sample, though representative in each of several characteristics, may give inaccurate values of incomes or expenditures for the population. This problem may also arise because of the initial character of the sample or it may be induced by the experience of repeated interviews. If households modify their responses or their actual behavior because being interviewed is a tedious process or because they are made aware of their budget pattern and decide to change it, this conditioning will bias the data of the second and subsequent intervals.

The first type of bias produces a difference between distributions of the affected characteristic. The appropriate test is the χ^2 test of frequency differences. The second kind of bias, if it affects enough households, will make mean values differ. The appropriate tests here are the t-test for pairs of means and the F-test for groups of means; both are provided by an analysis of variance of the variable whose mean may be biased.[11]

If exogenous information is available, it can be used in either of these tests of the sample.[12] In most cases, however, there is no reliable exogenous information; it is precisely to get such information that the survey was undertaken. Such data as exist may be unsuitable because of conceptual differences (national censuses do not necessarily use the same unit of observation as the surveys) or because of obsolescence (in times of inflation especially, older estimates of income and expenditure means cannot be used as standards). For this reason, the samples were tested internally by exploiting the subsample and interval structure to detect biases.

The logic of this procedure is as follows. In the absence of differential attrition and conditioning, all the subsamples interviewed in a given interval should give the same picture of the population. If either bias is present, subsamples should differ according to the number of previous interviews, and subsamples being interviewed for the first time cannot be affected. To ensure that there are no differences resulting from the initial sample selection, each new subsample (n_{62}, n_{73}, n_{84}) can be compared with the subsamples interviewed in the first interval, once the latter are found to be consistent. Also, in the absence of bias, a repeatedly interviewed subsample should not change from one interval to another except in ways that can be explained by inflation or by seasonal variation (real income growth is not likely to be large in one year). The latter factors must be evaluated by exogenous information.

The χ^2 test was applied to the following variables in each country: household size, labor force status of head (employed or not employed),

11. The hypotheses and test statistics used in both procedures are described in detail in ECIEL, "Urban Household Income and Consumption Patterns," annex D.
12. This was done in Venezuela, where the final sample was compared with a much larger presample from which only a few variables were obtained.

age of head (twelve to thirty-four, thirty-five to forty-nine, fifty to sixty-four, sixty-five and over), and household income. Dwelling tenure was also tested in Colombia.[13]

When a distribution was found to be biased, it was corrected by assigning adjustment factors or auxiliary weights. If, for example, too many households of a particular class were found in the sample, they received a factor less than one. The adjustment was applied to particular subsample and interval cells, keeping the average factor equal to one for each cell.

The tests are repeated after adjustment to check that the adjustment has not distorted any other distribution, and the process continues until all the distributions are acceptable. The final weight of an observation is then its stratum-interval weight multiplied by its interval-subsample-class adjustment factor. Several adjustment factors may be applied multiplicatively to the same observation if it belongs to a group that requires adjustment for two or more characteristics. This procedure has been used to detect and correct biases in the following variables and subsample and interval cells:

Barranquilla: tenure n_{22}; income n_{84};

Cali: labor force status n_{12}, n_{13}, n_{14}; tenure n_{62}; household size n_{73};

Medellín: household size n_{12}, n_{13}, n_{14};

Chile: household size n_{51}; age of head n_{84}.

No biases were detected in Bogotá, Ecuador, or Peru. In Ecuador and Peru, the subsamples were not distinguished within each interval, and only interinterval differences could be detected.

The F-statistics test whether there are overall or systematic differences in mean values. Differences between pairs of cells may be submerged in this analysis, but a binary comparison can be made between cells using the t-statistic. The hypotheses tested are that means are equal within intervals and within subsamples or (in the case of interaction) equal for cells with the same interview experience. Because of sample replacement within panel groups, the latter hypothesis is only partially tested. Where

13. The results of these tests are described in the following ECIEL documents: Doc. C.63, December 3, 1971, "Análisis de la Muestra Peruana"; Doc. C.65, May 8, 1972, "Análisis de la Muestra Colombiana"; Doc. C.80, June 19, 1973, "Análisis de la Muestra para Maracaibo"; and Doc. C.83, December 21, 1973, "Análisis de la Muestra del Ecuador" (Brookings Institution; processed). Similar analyses were conducted for Chile but have not been presented in a working document.

there is no independent subsample or interval distinction, as in Ecuador and Peru, the analysis of variance becomes a test of interval or subsample differences.

The analysis was conducted for the following fifteen financial variables: total income; total expenditure; food and beverages; housing; furnishings and operation; clothing; medical care; education; recreation and culture; transport and communication; other consumption; taxes; insurance; gifts; and other nonconsumption items.

Since the tests on total income failed, additional tests of capital income and salary income were made in Peru, and of these variables plus transitory income in Maracaibo. Test failures for some expenditure categories in Ecuador led to further tests of some components: tobacco, personal care, ready-made clothing, furniture, and so forth. Any errors in the data detected by the tests were corrected and the analysis was repeated. A considerable number of test failures remain uncorrected, particularly those indicating variations among subsamples. Some seasonal or inflationary effects were also found, especially in Chile.

Four conclusions emerge from the test results. First, conditioning—which, it was feared, might seriously impair the sample and against which precautions were taken in the sample design—is insignificant. Second, differences among subsamples are nearly always significant. Third, differences among intervals, often caused by seasonal or inflationary factors, are usually important, though these occur slightly less frequently than subsample differences. Because expenditures rather than budget shares were tested, a small change in income or total expenditure from one interval to another can cause differences for all or nearly all categories of expenditure. Finally, there are considerable differences among countries, and these are strongly associated with differences in sample structure. The more complex the sample, the more likely it is that evidence of intersubsample or interinterval differences will be found. Adjusting the statistics for different degrees of freedom does not erase these differences.

When bias is found among mean values by the analysis of variance, no obvious adjustment can be made. Examination of the data may, however, indicate the source of the bias and permit its correction. For example, difficulties in converting the data to a common period of reference in Quito were detected and corrected in this way. It is difficult to detect conditioning because households lost from the panel and semipanel groups were often replaced (as in Colombia and Maracaibo), so that not all the observations in a cell will, in fact, be of households with comparable interview experience. If the observations are reclassified by actual rather than planned number of interviews, the panel groups are too small for analysis.[14]

14. For example, although in the Colombian sample 1,129 observations were classified as belonging to the panel (n_1), only 460 of these were of households whose interview experience fitted the correct pattern. In the fourth quarter, the panel included 228 households, but only 66 of these were actually interviewed four times. The number ranges from 8 in Cali to 26 in Medellín.

Econometric Specification and Interpretation

THE ECONOMETRIC MODELS used in chapters 2, 3, and 6 to describe relations among variables are described here in some detail. The results derived from several different Engel curve specifications presented in chapter 6 are also assessed to see whether a particular model best explains either all kinds or certain categories of spending. Finally, I consider the accuracy of estimation for the most widely used econometric specification, the double-logarithmic Engel curves relating particular expenditures to total expenditure.

Estimation of Normal and Permanent Income

A number of the consumption functions and Engel curves estimated from the ECIEL data use neither consumption C nor income Y as the principal explanatory variable. Instead, they use an unobservable income concept designed to represent the "normal" or "permanent" situation of the family. The reason for this is that transitory variations in observed income or consumption bias the estimates of the parameters β_r in the way described by the classical errors-in-variables model.[1]

1. For a brief description of the problem and derivation of the bias, see J. Johnston, *Econometric Methods*, 2d ed. (McGraw-Hill, 1972), pp. 281–91. An interpretation of the bias in the permanent income model appears in Milton Friedman, *A Theory of the Consumption Function* (Princeton University Press, 1957), pp. 31–37.

Suppose the true relation to be estimated is

$$(1) \qquad C_r = \tilde{\beta}_{or} + \sum_u \sum_j \tilde{\beta}_{ujr} X_{uj} + \tilde{\beta}_r \tilde{Y} + \epsilon_r,$$

where $\tilde{Y}$ is a stable or long-term income concept. However, $\tilde{Y}$ cannot be observed, so the regression actually estimated is

$$(2) \qquad C_r = \beta_{or} + \sum_u \sum_j \beta_{ujr} X_{uj} + \beta_r Y + \epsilon_r,$$

where $Y = \tilde{Y} + v$, and v is an "error" or transitory element. The estimator β_r is then related to the parameter $\tilde{\beta}_r$ by

$$(3) \qquad \beta_r = \frac{\tilde{\beta}_r}{1 + \sigma_v^2/\sigma_Y^2},$$

where σ_v^2 and σ_Y^2 are, respectively, the variances of v and $\tilde{Y}$. To remove this bias, an estimate of $\tilde{Y}$ must be found, or else a technique other than OLS regression must be used, incorporating further restrictions on the model. Both approaches have been used to analyze the ECIEL data.[2]

Normal Income

The simpler approach is that of instrumental variables. The variable $\tilde{Y}$ is defined as normal income Y_N, which is assumed to be a function of observable variables, X, with a well-behaved error ϵ:[3]

$$(4) \qquad Y_N = X\beta + \epsilon \quad \text{or} \quad \log Y_N = X\beta + \epsilon.$$

Expression 4 is estimated by OLS regression, after which $\hat{Y}_N$ can be used in estimating equation 1.

2. However, β_r is not necessarily a bad estimate; it is the correct one for short-term relations between C_r and Y when the effect of transitory variation may be included. It is incorrect—and $\tilde{\beta}_r$ is preferable—only when it is desired to suppress this effect and estimate a long-term relation.

3. The linear specification is used by Jean Crockett and Irwin Friend, "Consumption and Saving in Economic Development" (Rodney L. White Center for Financial Research, University of Pennsylvania, Working Paper 22-73, n.d.; processed), and the logarithmic form by Howard J. Howe, "Estimation of the Linear and Quadratic Expenditure Systems: A Cross-Section Case for Colombia" (Ph.D. dissertation, University of Pennsylvania, 1974). Howe uses dummy classifying variables for X; Crockett and Friend use mean incomes of households in various classes. Howe includes age among the exogenous variables, where Crockett and Friend exclude it in order to estimate a lifetime income concept.

Permanent Income

In this approach, $\tilde{Y}$ is defined as permanent income Y^*, again related to observable variables X:

(5) $$\log Y^* = X\beta + \epsilon.$$

However, the assumptions of the permanent income hypothesis are also used; specifically, that

(6) $$\log C^* = W\kappa + \mu^* \log Y^*,$$

where C^* is permanent consumption (expenditure); μ^* is a permanent elasticity (equal to one in Friedman's formulation); and W denotes observable variables. On the assumption that observed income and consumption consist of permanent and transitory components, related multiplicatively, the model becomes

(7) $$\log C = W\kappa + \mu^* X\beta + \mu^* \epsilon + \log C^{**}$$
$$\log Y = X\beta + \epsilon + \log Y^{**},$$

where C^{**} and Y^{**} are the transitory components. The parameters μ^*, β, and κ are estimated by a sequence of OLS and 2SLS (two-stage) regression, beginning with OLS regression of $\log C$ and $\log Y$ against W and X. The 2SLS estimation exploits the assumption that $\log C^{**}$ and $\log Y^{**}$ are uncorrelated, so the covariance of the errors in expression 7 can be interpreted.[4] Estimation of expression 7 yields the consumption function 6 directly. The estimate $\hat{Y}^*$ can then be used to estimate Engel curves, as in equation 1.

The Direction of Bias

It is evident from equation 3 that β_r is generally an underestimate of the long-term elasticities or marginal spending propensities. An exception to this pattern occurs when the transitory component, v, of Y (or of C) is positively correlated with transitory variation v_r in expenditure C_r: then

4. The complete estimating procedure is described in Philip Musgrove, "Determination and Distribution of Permanent Household Income in Urban South America" (Ph.D. dissertation, Massachusetts Institute of Technology, 1974), pp. 21–33.

$\tilde{\beta}_r$ tends to be overestimated. An example is the relation between spending on durable goods and total expenditure. The permanent share of spending on durables is low for most households, but they make occasional large purchases. These raise not only C_r but also C, leading to a high estimate of the parameter $\tilde{\beta}_r$.[5]

Specification and Interpretation of Engel Curves

Engel curves have been estimated from the ECIEL data in five different functional forms. I consider here the estimation and interpretation of only the parameters associated with income or total expenditure or with sociodemographic characteristics of the household.

The Double Logarithmic Model

The regression equation in this model is

$$(8) \qquad \log C_r = \beta_{or} + \sum_{u=1}^{m_r} \sum_{j=1}^{k_u-1} \beta_{ujr} X_{uj} + \beta_r \log C + \epsilon_r.$$

The variables X_{uj} are dummy (qualitative) variables representing sociodemographic characteristics of the household. They are organized into m_r groups, where the number of classes in the group m_u is k_u. To prevent singularity of the exogenous variable matrix, one class must be omitted from each group. The omitted classes are absorbed into the constant term β_{or}. Variable X_{uj} is 1 when the household belongs to the jth class of variable or group u, and zero otherwise.

Differentiating equation 1 with respect to C yields

$$(9) \qquad \frac{d \log C_r}{d \log C} = \frac{CdC_r}{C_r dC} = \beta_r,$$

so that β_r is the rth expenditure elasticity. Differentiating with respect to a qualitative variable X_{uj} yields

$$(10) \qquad d \log C_r = \frac{dC_r}{C_r} = \beta_{ujr} dX_{uj}.$$

5. This problem arises because C_r represents expenditure on durables, not consumption of durables in the sense of depreciation. If C_r could be measured as consumption, the only difficulty would arise with errors in C, and equation 3 would hold.

Since X_{uj} is either zero or one, it can change by only one. Setting $dX_{uj} = 1$ gives the interpretation of β_{ujr} as the percentage change in C_r associated with a change from $X_{uj} = 0$ to $X_{uj} = 1$. This corresponds to the difference between the household being in the "base" class of the variable u (the class omitted from the regression) and being in the class j. The percentage change in C_r between the jth and the ith classes is given by $\beta_{ujr} - \beta_{uir}$.

A relation of the form 8 is a curve that passes through the origin and for given values of the X_{uj} shows the relation between C_r and C. If $\beta_r < 1$, the curve bends away from the vertical axis; if $\beta_r > 1$, it bends toward that axis; and if $\beta_r = 1$, the curve becomes a straight line through the origin. The slope of a line from the origin to a point on the curve is the average share of total expenditure C devoted to category r. The slope of the curve at that point is the marginal expenditure share dC_r/dC.

When one of the variables $X_{uj} = 1$, the curve is shifted up or down by a constant percentage, as indicated by β_{ujr}. The family of lines described by the regression has as many members as there are combinations of values of the X_{uj}.

This specification does not respect the household budget constraint

$$(11) \qquad\qquad \sum_r C_r = C.$$

That is, the estimated values $\hat{C}_r$ do not satisfy it, since upon exponentiating equation 8,

$$(12) \qquad \sum_r \hat{C}_r = \sum_r \exp\left(\beta_{or} + \sum_u \sum_j \beta_{ujr} X_{uj}\right) C^{\beta_r},$$

which does not equal C unless all the elasticities $\beta_r = 1$ and $\sum_r \exp\left(\beta_{or} + \sum_u \sum_j \beta_{ujr} X_{uj}\right) = 1$. However, a regression with a constant term (β_{or}) passes through the point defined by the mean values of all the variables, so that

$$(13) \qquad \overline{\log C_r} = \beta_{or} + \sum_u \sum_j \beta_{ujr} \bar{X}_{uj} + \beta_r \overline{\log C},$$

where $\bar{X}_{uj}$ is the probability that $X_{uj} = 1$. This does not mean the regression passes through the point $(\bar{C}_r, \bar{C}, \bar{X}_{uj} \ldots)$ and therefore satisfies expression 11; it is the means of the logarithms of C_r and C that satisfy equation 13. How well the regression explains the budget at the mean value of total expenditure can be tested by multiplying equation 9 by the average budget share $C_r/C = g_r$:

$$(14) \qquad \frac{C_r}{C} \cdot \frac{C}{C_r} \frac{dC_r}{dC} = \frac{dC_r}{dC} = \frac{C_r}{C} \beta_r = g_r \beta_r.$$

The derivatives or marginal budget shares dC_r/dC should satisfy the relation derived from equation 4, that

$$(15) \qquad \sum_r \frac{dC_r}{dC} = \sum_r g_r \beta_r = 1.$$

Therefore, the extent to which equation 15 is satisfied is a measure of how well the double-log model explains expenditure variation *at mean total expenditure*.

Because all the variables in equation 8 are observable and because no restriction of the model links any expenditure C_r to any other expenditure C_s, the equations are estimated individually by ordinary least squares (OLS) regression. Provided the error ϵ_r has a zero mean and constant variance, all the parameter estimates are unbiased, consistent, and efficient. The same approach is used (in chapter 3) to estimate two relations between C and total income Y. The first is

$$(16) \qquad \log C = \mu_o + \mu \log Y + \epsilon,$$

where μ is the income elasticity of total expenditure when all other household characteristics are allowed to vary. If instead these are fixed, the relation is

$$(17) \qquad \log C = \mu_o + \sum_{u=1}^{m} \sum_{j=1}^{k_u-1} \beta_{uj} X_{uj} + \mu \log Y + \epsilon.$$

Substitution of expression 16 into 8 leads to a relation of C_r to Y:

$$(18) \qquad \log C_r = \beta_{or} + \sum_u \sum_j \beta_{ujr} X_{uj} + \beta_r \mu_o + \beta_r \mu \log Y + \epsilon_r,$$

where $\beta_r \mu = \alpha_r$ can be considered an estimate of the income elasticity of expenditure in category r. This estimate is based on the assumption that the household first decides how much to spend in total, on the basis of its income, and then decides how to allocate that expenditure. This is a reasonable assumption for long-run values of income and spending but is much less acceptable for short intervals.

The Semilogarithmic Model

The regression equation is

(19) $$C_r = \beta_{or} + \sum_u \sum_j \beta_{ujr} X_{uj} + \beta_r \log C + \epsilon_r.$$

In the only application of this form to the ECIEL data, the X_{uj} are replaced by the logarithm of household size, and no dummy variables are used.[6] Differentiating 19 with respect to C yields

(20) $$\frac{dC_r}{dC} = \frac{\beta_r}{C}.$$

Multiplying by C/C_r gives the expenditure elasticity

(21) $$\frac{d \log C_r}{d \log C} = \frac{C}{C_r}\frac{dC_r}{dC} = \frac{\beta_r}{C_r},$$

which declines as C_r increases, and therefore as C increases, for $\beta_r > 0$. (The constraint 15 is satisfied only at the point where $\sum_r \beta_r = C$.) Similarly, an elasticity with respect to family size N can be calculated from

(22) $$C_r = \beta_{or} + \beta_{Nr} \log N + \beta_r \log C + \epsilon_r$$

as

(23) $$\frac{d \log C_r}{d \log N} = \frac{\beta_{Nr}}{C_r}.$$

The Linear Expenditure System (LES)

The Engel curve in this system has the form

(24) $$C_r = p_r\gamma_r + \beta_r(C - \sum_r p_r\gamma_r) + \epsilon_r.$$

The parameter β_r is the marginal budget share of category r, since

(25) $$\frac{dC_r}{dC} = \beta_r.$$

6. Romualdo Roldán, "Funciones Consumo por Tramos de Ingreso," Centro de Estudios de Planificación Nacional (CEPLAN) Documento no. 38 (Santiago: Universidad Católica de Chile, 1974; processed), p. 14. This permits calculation of an "elasticity" of expenditure C_r with respect to household size.

The parameters γ_r are "committed" or minimum or "subsistence" quantities of goods consumed; multiplied by prices p_r, they become committed expenditures. This formulation corresponds to the utility function

$$(26) \qquad\qquad U = \sum_r \beta_r \log (q_r - \gamma_r),$$

where q_r is the quantity consumed. Then $q_r > \gamma_r$ is required, so $C_r = p_r q_r > p_r \gamma_r = \gamma_r^*$. If prices are not observed, only the quantity γ_r^* can be estimated. Beyond the level $\sum_r \gamma_r^*$, marginal total expenditure is allocated as shown by the shares β_r; the quantity $C - \sum \gamma_r^* = Z$ is referred to as supernumerary expenditure.

Since the Engel curves are derived from a utility function, they must satisfy the budget constraint 11; that is,

$$(27) \qquad \sum_r C_r = \left(\sum_r \beta_r\right) C + \left(1 - \sum_r \beta_r\right) \sum_r \gamma_r^* = C,$$

from which $\sum_r \beta_r = 1$ is required. The equations are linked together by this requirement (or equivalently, by the fact that expenditure on each good depends on the prices of all other goods). The β_r can still be estimated by OLS regression, however.

Sociodemographic variables X_{uj} can be incorporated into equation 24 in the form

$$(28) \qquad C_r = \sum_u \sum_j \gamma_{ujr}^* X_{uj} + \beta_r (C - \sum_u \sum_j \sum_r \gamma_{ujr}^* X_{uj}) + \epsilon_r.$$

As in the double-log model (equation 8), the variables X_{uj} affect the level of expenditure C_r only by shifting the intercept of the function; they do not affect its slope β_r.

The elasticity of C_r with respect to C is found from equation 24 as

$$(29) \qquad\qquad \frac{C}{C_r} \cdot \frac{dC_r}{dC} = \frac{\beta_r C}{C_r}.$$

This declines as C increases, provided that $\gamma_r^* - \beta_r \sum_r \gamma_r^* < 0$, which is the normal case when $\beta_r > 0$.

The Extended Linear Expenditure System (ELES)

The LES is extended by supposing that saving can be treated as an additional category for which the committed level γ^* is zero. The Engel curve in equation 28 is modified by the inclusion of a constant marginal propensity to consume $\mu < 1$, so that C_r can be related to income Y thus:

$$(30) \quad C_r = \sum_u \sum_j \gamma^*_{ujr} X_{uj} + \mu \beta_r \left(Y - \sum_u \sum_j \sum_r \gamma^*_{ujr} X_{uj} \right) + \epsilon_r.$$

The income-elasticity of C_r, analogous to equation 29, is $\beta_r Y/C_r$; the expenditure-elasticity remains $\beta_r C/C_r$. The ELES Engel curves satisfy the budget restriction in equation 11, yielding the total consumption or expenditure function

$$(31) \quad C = \sum_r \gamma^*_r + \mu \left(Y - \sum_r \gamma^*_r \right) = \mu Y + (1 - \mu) \sum_r \gamma^*_r.$$

The Quadratic Expenditure System (QES)

The Engel curve differs from the linear form by its inclusion of the square of supernumerary expenditure:

$$(32) \quad C_r = \sum_u \sum_j \gamma^*_{ujr} X_{uj} + \beta_{1r} \left(C - \sum_u \sum_j \sum_r \gamma^*_{ujr} X_{uj} \right)$$

$$\beta_{2r} \left(C - \sum_u \sum_j \sum_r \gamma^*_{ujr} X_{uj} \right)^2 + \epsilon_r.$$

In addition to the requirement that $\sum_r \beta_{1r} = 1$ (retained from the LES) the system must meet the condition that $\sum_r \beta_{2r} = 0$ in order to satisfy the budget constraint. The marginal budget share is

$$(33) \quad \frac{dC_r}{dC} = \beta_{1r} + 2\beta_{2r} \left(C - \sum_u \sum_j \sum_r \gamma^*_{ujr} X_{uj} \right),$$

which is no longer constant unless $\beta_{2r} = 0$. Multiplying equation 33 by C/C_r yields the expenditure elasticity

$$(34) \quad \frac{d \log C_r}{d \log C} = \frac{(\beta_{1r} + 2\beta_{2r} Z)C}{\sum_u \sum_j \gamma^*_{ujr} X_{uj} + \beta_{1r} Z + \beta_{2r} Z^2},$$

where Z is supernumerary expenditure. Expression 34 can be rewritten as

$$(35) \quad \frac{(\beta_{1r} + 2\beta_{2r} Z)C}{C + (\beta_{1r} - 1)Z + \beta_{2r} Z^2}.$$

The Choice of Engel Curve

Chapter 6 presented all but a few of the estimates obtained using double-log Engel curves with the ECIEL data, and discussed results from other models when these illuminate the standard results or help evaluate specific effects on household expenditures. Here, I consider interpretations of the two principal variables affecting spending, income (or total expenditure), and household size, and their implications for the choice of the proper Engel curve.

The Shape of the Expenditure Function

The selection of a functional form involves two choices: whether to relate specific expenditures to income or to total expenditure, and how to introduce sociodemographic variables. The results of chapter 6 do not clearly indicate the best solutions, but they do suggest certain approaches.

Note first that the linear form of the Engel curve is unduly restrictive: virtually all the expenditure relations in the data are curvilinear. This is most striking when a quadratic term is added to the LES specification for Colombia. For all four cities, the expenditure function is nonlinear for food, recreation, durables, transportation, and miscellaneous expenditures, while it is approximately linear for housing, clothing, medical care, and education.[7] These last four categories have elasticities fairly close to 1.0 in the double-log model. The superiority of the quadratic over the linear form is likewise evident in the more reasonable values of the committed expenditures by type of member (table 6-13).

Nonlinearity over the entire income range also appears when the ELES is estimated separately by stratum. The marginal budget shares (table 6-4) often differ significantly among strata, although not always in a consistent way across cities and age groups.[8] These results suggest that the

7. See Howe, "Linear and Quadratic Expenditure Systems," pp. 219–27 and 230–36.

8. Howard Howe and Philip Musgrove, "An Analysis of ECIEL Household Budget Data for Bogotá, Caracas, Guayaquil and Lima," in Constantino Lluch, Alan A. Powell, and Ross A. Williams, eds., *Patterns in Household Demand and Saving* (New York: Oxford University Press for the World Bank, 1977), tables 7.4–7.7.

great advantages of the linear form—compatibility with a utility function and ease of estimation—are obtained at a rather high price. The linear form may be best for some individual expenditure categories (housing and clothing, for example), but if the budget constraint is to hold, the same form must be used for all categories. These comparisons reinforce Howe's tentative conclusion that the quadratic form, despite the difficulty of estimation, deserves to be investigated and used more frequently. Where individual equations rather than the entire system are of interest, the double-log form continues to be fairly satisfactory. The semilogarithmic function is sometimes preferable for food expenditures, because it approaches saturation much more quickly. The results available for Chile suggest that the semilog form is, for this reason, as good as or better than the double-log, for food categories that are not relative luxuries (seafood, fats and oils, vegetables, and sugar). The double-log is preferable for luxury categories relative to total food spending (meat, eggs, fruits, and beverages).[9] For nonfood categories, the double-log specification is always preferable.

The Effect of Household Size

Virtually all the results derived from the ECIEL surveys support the expectation that the size and composition of the household are important determinants of spending. However, the analysis of this relation depends to a large extent on the way the household is classified (that is, by size alone, by ages of various members, and so on); it also involves a choice of which parameters of the expenditure function are to depend on household composition. Two approaches to the latter issue have been followed, allowing either constant proportional shifts or changes in the level of committed expenditure. In both cases, the parameter relating C_r to C or Y does not depend on household composition. To take account of the effects of household composition, several classifications were used, based on age (and for clothing, on sex as well). A comparison of the results permits some tentative conclusions about how the number and types of members of a family influence its spending decisions.

9. Roldán, "Funciones Consumo por Tramos de Ingreso," pp. 45–48. The comparison is based on the variance of the residuals from the regression. Interestingly, there is no difference in the relative merits of the two forms between the low- and high-income strata.

First, the various members of a household obviously make different demands on its resources. Many categories of expenditures can be fairly well explained by the number of members alone, but even in those cases precision is gained by classifying members.[10] For other categories (for example, clothing, education, and tobacco), total size provides very little explanation and it is necessary to classify members in order to obtain meaningful results.

Second, the classification appropriate for one kind of expenditure may be neither helpful nor necessary for others. Age is the most important distinguishing feature; but for some expenditures all children or all adults can be considered alike, while for others it is necessary to distinguish by school age groups, by sex, or perhaps by other characteristics.[11] The choice of classification has to depend on some a priori knowledge or hypotheses about behavior. Particularly when expenditures rather than quantities bought must be explained, the classification must take account of differences in prices faced by different members. Secondary schooling is usually more expensive than primary schooling; women's clothing may cost more than men's; members who eat away from home regularly will pay more for their food, and so on.

Third, the effects of household size are not always monotonic: additional household members introduce both income (per person) effects and substitution effects. Even when the effects are monotonic, they may be difficult to represent by a single variable. A careful choice of dummy variables is therefore likely to give better results. This is mainly a question of representing the behavior of very large or very small households. For median sizes, the relation may be more regular and can perhaps be approximated by a constant linear or proportional effect. It is also in this range that economies of scale are likely to be least important.

10. The best example is food. The double-log functions based on total household size give generally reasonable results, but it is clear from the linear and quadratic estimates that the food needs of adults, adolescents, and children are quite different from each other, and these differences should be incorporated in the Engel curves.

11. In principle, one could introduce a sufficiently fine classification—say, by sex and by three or four age classes—into all the regressions and let the parameter estimates indicate which factors are most important for each category of spending. However, the presence of interactions among classes of members may only mean that few or none of the coefficients will be significant. This problem arises, for example, in the case of clothing expenditures (table 6-9), even though there are still quite enough degrees of freedom.

Finally, it is not very satisfactory to suppose that household size and composition affect only the level of committed expenditure, and that the relation between specific and total expenditure is thereafter the same for all households. For example, the quadratic form gives more plausible results than the linear function, partly because the marginal propensity depends on supernumerary expenditure. If the ELES is estimated separately by strata, the propensities among strata are associated with differences in the estimates of committed expenditure. This suggests that the double-log model is somewhat superior, although the restriction to a constant proportional effect may be unduly severe. This argument refers to goods and services that can be bought in any amount—that are divisible. For some categories of spending there may be indivisibilities represented by committed expenditure, and it may be reasonable to suppose that the marginal spending propensity is independent of the size and composition of the household. Education may be an example, at least when tuition is a large share of total spending in the category; private transportation may be another.

The Accuracy of Estimation (Double-Log Specification)

The accuracy of the expenditure estimates cannot be compared across different functional forms unless the errors (residuals) from the regressions are transformed so as to be comparable. And even if this is done, the choice of specification depends on more than the error variance or the proportion of total variance explained. For a given specification, the accuracy can be compared across expenditure categories and countries. Table B-1 shows the R^2 statistics for all the double-log expenditure functions (regressions with unusually low F-statistics are also indicated).

Most of the R^2 statistics are satisfactorily large, considering the short-run nature of the data and the absence of information on prices and on personal tastes. Very low statistics (under 0.2) occur only for expenditures on minor food items, vehicle purchases, public transportation, tobacco, and the category of other nonconsumption items.

Second, the R^2 and F-statistics are generally, though not invariably, larger for the categories than for their components. This suggests that the components are substitutes for one another and that the distribution of expenditure among them is explained by characteristics not included in the regressions.

Table B-1. *Accuracy of Estimation of Double-Log Expenditure Functions*[a]

Spending category	Colombia	Chile	Ecuador	Peru	Venezuela
Food and beverages	0.854	0.614	0.826	0.569	0.652
Dairy products and eggs	0.588	0.383	0.619	0.381	0.420
Cereals	0.588	0.302	0.572	0.301	0.344
Meat and poultry	0.575	0.447	0.577	0.341	0.452
Seafood	0.277	0.241	0.342	0.230	0.158
Vegetables and tubers	0.457	0.202	0.476	0.207	0.334
Fruits	0.536	0.366	0.537	0.391	0.293
Fats and oils	0.358	0.218	0.468	0.179	0.215
Sugar and sweets	0.383	0.189	0.469	0.244	0.270
Hot beverages	0.344	0.215	0.372	0.247	0.160
Alcoholic beverages	0.206	0.221	0.379	0.168[b]	0.224
Other beverages	0.322	0.207	0.384	0.345	0.156
Other foods	0.348	0.171	0.423	0.168	0.167
Meals away from home	0.404	0.168	0.218	0.166	0.181
Housing	0.810	0.769	0.822	0.739	0.782
Principal	0.796	0.754	0.813	0.699	0.777
Other	0.904	n.a.	0.669	0.706	n.a.
Maintenance	0.378	0.247	n.a.	0.342	n.a.
Furnishings and operation	0.707	0.544	0.645	0.611	0.536
Furniture and durable goods	0.332	0.249	0.324	0.321	0.244
Nondurable goods	0.484	0.208	0.565	0.419	0.371
Services	0.611	0.478	0.529	0.572	0.467
Clothing	0.574	0.451	0.468	0.392	0.379
Men's ready-made	0.423	0.406	0.355	0.330	0.265
Women's ready-made	0.496	0.386	0.442	0.415	0.314
Children's ready-made	0.457	0.301	0.302	0.354	0.333
Other	0.268	0.201	0.316	0.294	0.290
Medical care	0.395	0.179	0.272	0.274	0.400
Education	0.568	0.411	0.511	0.479	0.457
Recreation and culture	0.515	0.403	0.431	0.488	0.325
Recreation	0.408	0.276	0.391	0.463	0.296
Reading and culture	0.461	0.330	0.352	0.361	0.302
Transportation, communication	0.582	0.570	0.655	0.467	0.558
Vehicle purchase	0.018[b]	n.a.	n.a.	0.205[b]	n.a.
Private transportation	0.202	0.171	0.266	0.222	0.260
Public transportation	0.224	0.192	n.a.	0.220	0.143
Telephone and other communication	0.540	0.397	0.380	0.422	0.753
Other	0.563	0.401	0.602	0.558	0.389
Tobacco	0.161	0.211	0.259	0.325	0.124
Personal care	0.616	0.282	0.614	0.529	0.382
Ceremonies	0.498	0.229	0.647	0.319	n.a.
Taxes	0.664	0.493	0.442	0.464	0.300
Insurance	0.513	0.555	0.452	0.461	0.340
Social security	0.436	0.559	0.464	0.485	0.285
Other	0.450	n.a.	0.528	0.386	0.573
Gifts and transfers	0.360	0.219	0.276	0.385	0.392
Other nonconsumption	0.439	0.225	0.226	0.164	0.278

Source: Original ECIEL calculations based on the survey data.
n.a. Not available.
a. R^2 statistics.
b. Not significant at the 95 percent confidence level of the F test.

Third, the more durable the goods in any category are, the more difficult it is to explain expenditures. For example, the regression for vehicle purchases is never significant; the independent variables do not explain a significant share of the variation among households in such expenditures. Within the category of furnishings and maintenance, R^2 is lowest for durables (except in Ecuador) and highest for services (except in Chile). Spending in this category probably depends on the households' existing stock of durables, its wealth in other forms, and its expectations about inflation and rates of return on assets; and none of these variables are measured in the data.

The estimates tend to be most accurate in Colombia and Ecuador, particularly for the major categories of food, housing, and clothing. The estimates might be expected to be less precise in Chile because of inflation (whose effect is not entirely absorbed by the dummy variables for the quarters), in Peru because of the relatively large transitory variation in spending, and in Venezuela because the Caracas survey covers only one month. However, the observed international differences are seldom large and are usually reasonable, given the differences among the samples.

Finally, rank correlation coefficients were computed for the R^2 statistics corresponding to twelve principal expenditure categories (omitting other nonconsumption spending). The highest statistics always occur for housing and food, and household furnishing. The least well explained categories are (except in Venezuela) medical care, and gifts and transfers. The coefficients are as follows:

	Colombia	Chile	Ecuador	Peru
Chile	0.797			
Ecuador	0.832	0.797		
Peru	0.727	0.580	0.783	
Venezuela	0.517	0.490	0.713	0.497

The rankings are very similar for Colombia, Chile, and Ecuador, the countries in which the sample design was most nearly identical. Venezuela is exceptional, largely because of the one-interval sample survey in Caracas. Ecuador seems to be the modal or typical country; its ranking does not differ greatly from that of any other country.

Statistical Tables

THE TABLES in this appendix enlarge on the discussion in chapters 5 and 6. All of them are original ECIEL calculations based on the survey data; the figures in tables C-1 to C-40 have been rounded and may not add to totals. Standard errors are given in parentheses in tables C-41 to C-50.

Table C-1. *Individual Budget Structure by Income Quartile, Bogotá*[a]

Spending category	Income quartile			
	First	*Second*	*Third*	*Fourth*
Food and beverages	58.95	52.00	47.01	36.11
Dairy products and eggs	6.43	6.26	6.42	5.84
Cereals	12.22	10.36	8.74	5.34
Meat and poultry	10.53	10.19	9.06	7.67
Seafood	0.06	0.10	0.13	0.31
Vegetables and tubers	11.29	9.09	7.44	4.46
Fruits	2.18	2.36	2.46	2.33
Fats and oils	3.33	2.52	2.08	1.22
Sugar and sweets	2.63	2.08	1.63	1.04
Hot beverages	3.72	2.86	2.29	1.28
Alcoholic beverages	0.25	0.52	0.36	0.62
Other beverages	0.23	0.12	0.21	0.27
Other foods	0.57	0.41	0.41	0.42
Meals away from home	5.51	5.13	5.78	5.31
Housing	21.58	25.65	27.49	26.06
Principal dwelling	21.27	25.22	26.85	24.71
Other	0.06	0.02	0.05	0.09
Maintenance	0.24	0.41	0.59	1.27
Furnishings and operation	3.25	3.03	4.13	8.03
Durables	0.73	0.85	1.28	4.03
Nondurables	2.13	1.54	1.58	1.44
Services	0.40	0.64	1.27	2.57
Clothing	5.36	6.11	7.65	9.10
Men's	1.62	1.61	2.37	3.04
Women's	1.87	2.20	2.85	3.93
Children's	1.81	2.21	2.29	1.85
Other	0.06	0.08	0.14	0.28
Medical care	1.48	1.20	1.49	2.99
Education	2.36	5.45	4.70	6.14
Recreation and culture	0.94	1.32	1.66	2.91
Recreation	0.54	0.85	1.11	2.12
Reading and culture	0.40	0.47	0.55	0.79
Vehicle operation	0.00	0.01	0.09	1.47
Public transportation	3.41	2.45	2.50	2.02
Communication	0.17	0.18	0.26	0.69
Other consumption	2.31	2.04	2.16	2.12
Tobacco	0.28	0.36	0.24	0.22
Personal care	1.74	1.68	1.85	1.84
Ceremonies	0.29	0.00	0.07	0.05
Insurance	0.00	0.11	0.10	0.26
Gifts and transfers	0.20	0.38	0.56	1.78
Other nonconsumption	0.00	0.08	0.19	0.23

a. Colombian (four-city) quartiles.

Table C-2. *Individual Budget Structure by Income Quartile,*
Barranquilla[a]

	Income quartile			
Spending category	First	Second	Third	Fourth
Food and beverages	65.43	61.48	57.23	41.35
Dairy products and eggs	7.24	7.15	7.02	5.68
Cereals	14.56	12.22	10.79	6.78
Meat and poultry	15.08	14.24	15.75	11.40
Seafood	1.51	1.38	0.97	0.75
Vegetables and tubers	7.79	6.70	5.53	4.14
Fruits	3.51	3.35	3.08	2.35
Fats and oils	3.27	2.75	2.69	1.72
Sugar and sweets	3.09	2.33	1.94	1.19
Hot beverages	1.75	1.34	1.10	0.77
Alcoholic beverages	0.82	1.75	1.27	0.92
Other beverages	0.58	0.85	0.65	0.56
Other foods	1.17	1.14	0.82	0.72
Meals away from home	5.08	6.28	5.62	4.38
Housing	15.30	14.12	17.20	22.50
Principal dwelling	14.74	13.42	16.17	21.11
Other	0.00	0.00	0.00	0.12
Maintenance	0.56	0.71	1.03	1.27
Furnishings and operation	3.05	3.77	5.67	7.33
Durables	0.72	1.25	2.88	2.14
Nondurables	2.30	2.13	1.99	1.61
Services	0.03	0.40	0.80	3.57
Clothing	3.92	6.27	6.38	7.72
Men's	0.97	2.17	2.22	2.41
Women's	1.86	2.22	2.15	3.32
Children's	0.91	1.65	1.72	1.62
Other	0.18	0.23	0.29	0.37
Medical care	1.87	2.66	1.91	3.30
Education	2.23	3.29	3.31	5.55
Recreation and culture	1.30	1.57	1.86	2.46
Recreation	0.86	0.92	1.10	1.61
Reading and culture	0.44	0.65	0.76	0.84
Vehicle operation	0.00	0.20	0.08	2.92
Public transportation	2.77	2.06	2.03	1.46
Communication	0.06	0.18	0.18	0.83
Other consumption	3.76	3.71	3.37	2.76
Tobacco	0.97	0.83	0.68	0.48
Personal care	2.46	2.63	2.46	2.09
Ceremonies	0.33	0.25	0.23	0.19
Insurance	0.00	0.01	0.00	0.19
Gifts and transfers	0.23	0.63	0.53	1.50
Other nonconsumption	0.07	0.05	0.25	0.11

a. Colombian (four-city) quartiles.

Table C-3. *Individual Budget Structure by Income Quartile, Cali*[a]

Spending category	Income quartile			
	First	*Second*	*Third*	*Fourth*
Food and beverages	67.56	59.50	52.62	40.64
Dairy products and eggs	5.87	7.45	7.98	7.13
Cereals	12.07	9.42	7.88	5.55
Meat and poultry	17.51	15.45	14.00	10.61
Seafood	0.17	0.19	0.35	0.26
Vegetables and tubers	11.24	8.47	6.62	4.55
Fruits	4.13	3.42	2.99	2.57
Fats and oils	4.29	3.21	2.64	1.53
Sugar and sweets	4.10	2.96	2.25	1.57
Hot beverages	3.38	2.44	2.02	1.37
Alcoholic beverages	0.17	0.45	0.41	0.73
Other beverages	0.09	0.13	0.30	0.39
Other foods	0.69	0.67	0.50	0.41
Meals away from home	3.86	5.24	4.67	3.95
Housing	14.04	17.63	19.40	23.28
Principal dwelling	13.93	17.50	18.36	22.16
Other	0.00	0.00	0.00	0.13
Maintenance	0.11	0.14	1.04	0.98
Furnishings and operation	3.00	3.59	5.05	8.83
Durables	0.64	1.32	1.73	3.57
Nondurables	2.25	1.78	1.63	1.40
Services	0.11	0.49	1.69	3.86
Clothing	4.78	5.97	8.17	8.01
Men's	1.46	2.08	3.05	2.86
Women's	1.82	2.46	3.12	3.36
Children's	1.32	1.34	1.85	1.37
Other	0.18	0.09	0.14	0.42
Medical care	0.83	1.28	1.55	2.02
Education	1.34	2.36	3.16	3.90
Recreation and culture	1.12	2.17	2.33	2.49
Recreation	0.69	1.38	1.51	1.61
Reading and culture	0.43	0.79	0.82	0.88
Vehicle operation	0.00	0.00	0.02	1.66
Public transportation	2.44	2.10	1.77	1.33
Communication	0.04	0.11	0.41	1.02
Other consumption	2.99	2.92	2.60	2.69
Tobacco	0.61	0.70	0.50	0.48
Personal care	2.35	2.15	2.09	1.98
Ceremonies	0.04	0.08	0.00	0.23
Insurance	0.00	0.02	0.17	0.28
Gifts and transfers	0.39	0.73	0.74	1.96
Other nonconsumption	0.04	0.09	0.13	0.28

a. Colombian (four-city) quartiles.

Table C-4. *Individual Budget Structure by Income Quartile, Medellín*[a]

Spending category	Income quartile			
	First	Second	Third	Fourth
Food and beverages	61.46	55.59	50.90	38.87
Dairy products and eggs	7.86	8.23	7.64	6.83
Cereals	10.54	8.88	8.11	4.97
Meat and poultry	14.20	13.47	13.17	10.75
Seafood	0.00	0.04	0.10	0.19
Vegetables and tubers	9.76	8.23	7.05	4.52
Fruits	1.59	1.65	2.05	1.82
Fats and oils	2.79	2.60	2.03	1.40
Sugar and sweets	5.74	4.30	3.15	1.85
Hot beverages	3.88	3.33	2.23	1.31
Alcoholic beverages	0.16	0.22	0.35	0.54
Other beverages	0.06	0.11	0.14	0.31
Other foods	0.46	0.35	0.46	0.48
Meals away from home	4.41	4.19	4.42	3.88
Housing	20.47	23.18	22.25	26.23
Principal dwelling	20.28	23.00	21.81	24.47
Other	0.17	0.01	0.15	0.78
Maintenance	0.02	0.17	0.30	0.98
Furnishings and operation	2.16	2.37	3.93	6.55
Durables	0.35	0.54	1.33	2.40
Nondurables	1.63	1.45	1.18	1.13
Services	0.18	0.38	1.42	3.02
Clothing	3.26	4.08	4.48	6.16
Men's	0.74	1.09	1.19	1.62
Women's	1.31	1.56	1.82	3.01
Children's	1.00	1.07	0.95	1.19
Other	0.22	0.38	0.52	0.34
Medical care	0.71	1.28	2.48	3.09
Education	1.92	2.95	4.02	4.85
Recreation and culture	0.98	1.21	1.62	2.45
Recreation	0.80	0.78	1.03	1.69
Reading and culture	0.18	0.44	0.59	0.76
Vehicle operation	0.36	0.15	0.32	1.23
Public transportation	2.19	1.88	1.50	1.26
Communication	0.03	0.09	0.12	0.19
Other consumption	2.30	2.36	2.44	2.43
Tobacco	1.00	0.92	0.74	0.50
Personal care	1.30	1.44	1.50	1.53
Ceremonies	0.00	0.00	0.20	0.40
Insurance	0.00	0.00	0.03	0.49
Gifts and transfers	0.27	0.41	1.37	1.86
Other nonconsumption	0.06	0.17	0.20	0.50

a. Colombian (four-city) quartiles.

Table C-5. *Individual Budget Structure by Income Quartile, Santiago*

Spending category	Income quartile			
	First	Second	Third	Fourth
Food and beverages	51.28	43.44	38.91	29.61
Dairy products and eggs	4.66	4.59	4.30	3.46
Cereals	12.19	9.16	7.73	4.30
Meat and poultry	8.54	8.60	8.16	7.17
Seafood	1.24	0.98	0.97	0.80
Vegetables and tubers	8.74	7.00	5.64	3.48
Fruits	2.31	2.36	2.32	2.12
Fats and oils	2.81	2.15	1.84	1.19
Sugar and sweets	3.17	2.37	2.02	1.27
Hot beverages	1.88	1.50	1.32	0.93
Alcoholic beverages	0.95	1.00	0.80	0.82
Other beverages	0.68	0.77	0.63	0.59
Other foods	1.13	0.84	0.75	0.66
Meals away from home	2.98	2.12	2.45	2.83
Housing	23.92	24.61	27.03	29.30
Principal dwelling	23.46	23.82	26.23	28.49
Other	n.a.	n.a.	n.a.	n.a.
Maintenance	0.47	0.78	0.80	0.81
Furnishings and operation	4.47	7.50	6.38	9.48
Durables	2.26	5.52	3.97	4.01
Nondurables	1.70	1.45	1.34	1.18
Services	0.52	0.53	1.07	4.30
Clothing	8.94	11.24	13.27	13.24
Men's	4.23	5.30	6.55	6.64
Women's	3.17	4.20	5.03	5.10
Children's	0.37	0.30	0.25	0.25
Other	1.17	1.44	1.45	1.25
Medical care	1.25	1.33	1.16	1.48
Education	0.28	0.52	0.71	1.41
Recreation and culture	2.02	2.80	3.18	4.26
Recreation	1.02	1.58	1.92	2.70
Reading and culture	0.99	1.22	1.26	1.56
Vehicle operation	0.06	0.08	0.32	2.33
Public transportation	3.61	2.99	3.23	2.43
Communication	0.09	0.23	0.39	1.02
Other consumption	3.70	4.53	4.80	4.55
Tobacco	1.59	1.82	2.01	1.57
Personal care	1.93	2.40	2.51	2.55
Ceremonies	0.18	0.31	0.29	0.42
Insurance	n.a.	n.a.	n.a.	n.a.
Gifts and transfers	0.14	0.24	0.28	0.53
Other nonconsumption	0.17	0.39	0.27	0.33

n.a. Not available.

Table C-6. *Individual Budget Structure by Income Quartile, Quito*[a]

	Income quartile			
Spending category	First	Second	Third	Fourth
Food and beverages	58.97	49.65	41.70	29.72
Dairy products and eggs	5.91	6.13	6.31	5.41
Cereals	14.82	11.26	8.85	5.29
Meat and poultry	6.00	8.20	7.41	5.49
Seafood	0.60	0.59	0.64	0.54
Vegetables and tubers	8.22	7.01	5.36	3.10
Fruits	2.33	2.26	2.57	1.87
Fats and oils	3.38	2.78	2.20	1.38
Sugar and sweets	3.66	2.79	2.33	1.65
Hot beverages	1.79	1.63	1.23	0.76
Alcoholic beverages	0.49	0.28	0.36	0.51
Other beverages	0.32	0.49	0.57	0.53
Other foods	0.55	0.53	0.56	0.59
Meals away from home	10.74	4.94	2.97	2.40
Housing	19.22	20.87	26.44	38.22
Principal dwelling	19.02	20.63	24.10	33.59
Other	0.12	0.06	1.40	3.95
Maintenance	0.07	0.18	0.94	0.69
Furnishings and operation	4.34	6.42	4.54	7.32
Durables	1.85	4.05	1.88	3.84
Nondurables	2.24	1.70	1.48	1.18
Services	0.25	0.67	1.18	2.29
Clothing	8.77	11.64	11.39	9.60
Men's	3.66	5.20	4.69	3.92
Women's	3.89	4.99	5.49	4.88
Children's	0.35	0.26	0.17	0.11
Other	0.87	1.19	1.03	0.69
Medical care	2.94	3.15	3.22	2.49
Education	0.61	1.52	1.62	2.06
Recreation and culture	0.99	1.16	2.26	1.98
Recreation	0.68	0.68	1.62	1.41
Reading and culture	0.31	0.49	0.64	0.57
Vehicle operation	0.00	0.00	0.18	0.82
Public transportation	0.02	0.07	0.02	0.08
Communication	0.07	0.28	0.70	0.80
Other consumption	2.38	3.24	3.78	2.75
Tobacco	0.51	0.79	0.88	0.58
Personal care	1.75	2.31	2.24	1.82
Ceremonies	0.12	0.14	0.66	0.35
Insurance	0.00	0.01	0.08	0.10
Gifts and transfers	1.06	0.95	3.35	2.60
Other nonconsumption	0.45	0.71	0.52	0.69

a. Ecuadorean (two-city) quartiles.

Table C-7. *Individual Budget Structure by Income Quartile, Guayaquil*[a]

	Income quartile			
Spending category	*First*	*Second*	*Third*	*Fourth*
Food and beverages	68.05	61.07	50.22	35.44
Dairy products and eggs	5.64	7.52	7.08	5.45
Cereals	17.62	14.26	10.48	5.67
Meat and poultry	11.33	12.85	10.97	8.18
Seafood	3.31	2.52	1.71	1.15
Vegetables and tubers	8.76	7.47	5.51	3.47
Fruits	2.75	2.52	2.00	2.05
Fats and oils	4.62	3.74	2.55	1.61
Sugar and sweets	3.61	3.10	2.56	2.06
Hot beverages	2.45	1.65	1.17	0.80
Alcoholic beverages	0.14	0.61	0.39	0.81
Other beverages	0.64	1.11	1.21	0.92
Other foods	0.60	0.51	0.56	0.62
Meals away from home	6.48	2.97	3.92	2.65
Housing	17.34	18.32	20.60	30.65
Principal dwelling	17.34	18.08	19.60	28.02
Other	0.00	0.00	0.44	1.55
Maintenance	0.00	0.23	0.57	1.08
Furnishings and operation	3.13	4.24	6.47	8.12
Durables	0.36	1.82	3.72	3.91
Nondurables	2.29	1.72	1.36	1.05
Services	0.49	0.69	1.39	3.16
Clothing	4.00	5.01	7.83	8.84
Men's	1.44	2.34	3.81	3.75
Women's	1.78	1.94	3.08	4.10
Children's	0.22	0.15	0.19	0.20
Other	0.56	0.58	0.74	0.79
Medical care	1.30	2.25	1.93	2.42
Education	0.66	1.55	2.34	2.42
Recreation and culture	0.92	1.76	1.97	2.15
Recreation	0.42	0.92	1.13	1.48
Reading and culture	0.50	0.84	0.85	0.67
Vehicle operation	0.00	0.05	0.36	0.80
Public transportation	0.00	0.00	0.01	0.00
Communication	0.05	0.07	0.16	0.52
Other consumption	3.47	3.29	3.23	3.14
Tobacco	0.63	0.62	0.67	0.76
Personal care	2.83	2.66	2.48	2.20
Ceremonies	0.00	0.00	0.08	0.18
Insurance	0.07	0.03	0.18	0.28
Gifts and transfers	0.77	1.98	4.25	4.61
Other nonconsumption	0.22	0.21	0.13	0.19

a. Ecuadorean (two-city) quartiles.

Table C-8. *Individual Budget Structure by Income Quartile, Lima*

Spending category	Income quartile			
	First	Second	Third	Fourth
Food and beverages	53.87	46.66	41.32	31.12
Dairy products and eggs	7.37	6.57	5.43	4.58
Cereals	10.62	8.77	6.89	4.58
Meat and poultry	12.97	12.16	10.69	8.15
Seafood	1.77	1.51	1.45	1.03
Vegetables and tubers	8.15	6.98	4.99	3.40
Fruits	2.41	2.30	2.32	2.33
Fats and oils	1.90	1.60	1.19	0.86
Sugar and sweets	1.88	1.35	1.16	0.95
Hot beverages	0.80	0.78	0.59	0.48
Alcoholic beverages	0.20	0.46	0.68	0.14
Other beverages	0.10	0.13	0.12	0.14
Other foods	1.56	1.14	0.98	1.03
Meals away from home	4.06	2.91	4.84	3.38
Housing	16.14	17.34	20.79	25.98
Principal dwelling	15.10	15.55	19.02	22.81
Other	0.07	0.36	0.16	1.34
Maintenance	0.97	1.44	1.61	1.83
Furnishings and operation	7.50	9.91	8.97	11.64
Durables	4.66	6.80	5.30	6.79
Nondurables	2.23	1.94	1.89	1.47
Services	0.61	1.17	1.78	3.38
Clothing	7.10	7.10	9.20	8.14
Men's	2.77	3.26	4.38	3.58
Women's	3.03	2.81	3.59	3.56
Children's	0.47	0.31	0.26	0.22
Other	0.84	0.72	0.97	0.77
Medical care	2.61	1.94	2.04	1.87
Education	1.11	1.68	1.57	2.45
Recreation and culture	2.08	2.68	2.70	3.02
Recreation	0.88	1.14	1.68	1.92
Reading and culture	1.20	1.54	1.02	1.10
Vehicle operation	0.29	2.62	1.36	3.50
Public transportation	3.16	3.84	3.30	2.20
Communication	0.10	0.15	0.36	0.49
Other consumption	4.10	3.91	4.99	4.59
Tobacco	0.63	0.56	0.73	0.78
Personal care	3.34	3.30	3.57	3.24
Ceremonies	0.13	0.05	0.69	0.56
Insurance	1.22	1.32	1.60	2.20
Gifts and transfers	0.17	0.29	0.56	0.77
Other nonconsumption	0.53	0.31	0.87	0.50

Table C-9. *Individual Budget Structure by Income Quartile, Caracas*[a]

	Income quartile			
Spending category	First	Second	Third	Fourth
Food and beverages	46.67	38.29	32.66	24.41
Dairy products and eggs	7.40	5.99	5.17	3.95
Cereals	6.30	4.56	3.43	2.23
Meat and poultry	9.23	8.07	7.81	5.67
Seafood	1.25	1.02	0.94	0.56
Vegetables and tubers	5.76	4.52	3.29	2.14
Fruits	2.65	2.45	1.96	1.67
Fats and oils	2.33	1.88	1.23	0.88
Sugar and sweets	1.63	1.39	1.06	0.81
Hot beverages	1.91	1.20	0.89	0.63
Alcoholic beverages	1.14	1.36	1.05	1.00
Other beverages	1.37	1.17	0.88	0.67
Other foods	1.27	1.26	0.93	0.81
Meals away from home	4.43	3.43	3.94	2.83
Housing	24.01	26.05	29.21	31.60
Principal dwelling	24.01	26.05	29.20	31.50
Other	n.a.	n.a.	n.a.	n.a.
Maintenance	0.00	0.00	0.02	0.09
Furnishings and operation	4.19	5.02	5.92	7.37
Durables	0.66	1.37	1.41	1.46
Nondurables	2.07	1.88	1.63	1.39
Services	1.46	1.78	2.88	4.45
Clothing	5.94	6.98	6.14	6.39
Men's	1.42	1.54	1.70	1.58
Women's	2.13	2.76	2.14	2.46
Children's	1.79	1.75	1.26	1.29
Other	0.60	0.93	1.05	1.07
Medical care	2.27	3.93	3.62	4.80
Education	1.50	2.94	3.77	4.89
Recreation and culture	2.68	2.86	3.16	4.13
Recreation	2.27	2.43	2.53	3.39
Reading and culture	0.41	0.43	0.63	0.73
Vehicle operation	1.41	3.45	5.02	4.71
Public transportation	4.58	3.41	2.93	1.89
Communication	0.25	0.56	0.97	1.08
Other consumption	4.91	4.29	3.51	3.11
Tobacco	2.12	1.59	1.15	1.14
Personal care	2.78	2.70	2.36	1.97
Ceremonies	0.00	0.00	0.00	0.00
Insurance	0.09	0.11	0.26	0.42
Gifts and transfers	0.47	0.78	0.92	1.59
Other nonconsumption	0.08	0.15	0.13	0.21

n.a. Not available.
a. Venezuelan (two-city) quartiles.

Table C-10. *Individual Budget Structure by Income Quartile, Maracaibo*[a]

Spending category	Income quartile			
	First	Second	Third	Fourth
Food and beverages	57.67	58.15	52.84	41.70
Dairy products and eggs	11.70	11.89	10.46	8.42
Cereals	9.93	8.42	6.91	4.74
Meat and poultry	9.64	11.97	12.04	9.92
Seafood	1.32	1.24	0.95	0.66
Vegetables and tubers	4.12	4.42	3.50	2.78
Fruits	4.52	4.04	3.97	2.87
Fats and oils	2.27	2.79	2.14	1.77
Sugar and sweets	2.42	1.90	1.69	1.28
Hot beverages	2.35	2.09	1.78	1.33
Alcoholic beverages	1.02	1.21	1.24	1.11
Other beverages	1.26	1.10	1.23	0.95
Other foods	1.70	1.46	1.30	1.04
Meals away from home	5.10	5.57	5.32	4.55
Housing	19.68	17.13	18.13	21.62
Principal dwelling	19.68	17.13	18.13	21.55
Other	n.a.	n.a.	n.a.	n.a.
Maintenance	0.00	0.00	0.00	0.07
Furnishings and operation	4.84	5.44	7.05	9.92
Durables	2.51	3.03	4.37	5.47
Nondurables	2.09	2.07	1.91	1.68
Services	0.24	0.34	0.77	2.77
Clothing	2.80	3.07	4.03	4.65
Men's	0.79	1.23	1.51	1.85
Women's	0.93	0.66	1.24	1.61
Children's	0.81	0.92	1.02	0.87
Other	0.28	0.27	0.26	0.31
Medical care	1.02	0.80	1.29	1.66
Education	0.85	0.92	1.59	2.73
Recreation and culture	1.98	2.93	3.15	3.67
Recreation	1.77	2.61	2.68	2.87
Reading and culture	0.21	0.32	0.47	0.80
Vehicle operation	0.36	0.40	1.37	3.74
Public transportation	4.81	4.78	3.70	2.46
Communication	0.02	0.01	0.19	0.41
Other consumption	5.36	5.51	5.39	4.00
Tobacco	1.34	1.57	1.92	1.06
Personal care	4.02	3.93	3.47	2.94
Ceremonies	0.00	0.01	0.00	0.00
Insurance	0.10	0.12	0.09	0.24
Gifts and transfers	0.05	0.16	0.50	0.53
Other nonconsumption	0.09	0.12	0.12	0.14

n.a. Not available.
a. Venezuelan (two-city) quartiles.

Table C-11. *Shares of Total Expenditure in Each Category Generated in Each Income Quartile, Bogotá*

Spending category	Income quartile			
	First	Second	Third	Fourth
Food and beverages	13.20	18.67	25.50	42.52
Dairy products and eggs	10.50	16.46	26.42	46.42
Cereals	15.86	21.70	27.74	34.70
Meat and poultry	12.34	18.60	24.09	44.91
Seafood	2.24	8.64	16.89	71.31
Vegetables and tubers	18.08	21.53	27.59	32.82
Fruits	9.01	15.74	24.92	50.20
Fats and oils	18.37	22.48	26.91	32.32
Sugar and sweets	16.74	22.35	24.68	36.10
Hot beverages	17.00	24.57	27.29	31.24
Alcoholic beverages	4.28	9.57	17.33	69.14
Other beverages	7.02	9.67	25.47	55.85
Other foods	11.33	13.76	20.93	54.80
Meals away from home	9.53	14.63	23.22	52.45
Housing	7.86	15.97	24.01	52.01
Principal dwelling	8.06	16.52	24.04	51.26
Other	4.08	1.35	10.24	87.53
Maintenance	3.52	4.43	25.08	66.75
Furnishings and operation	4.58	7.09	19.18	68.88
Durables	2.81	4.51	19.66	72.79
Nondurables	11.68	15.22	22.98	49.92
Services	2.35	5.33	15.90	76.52
Clothing	5.86	11.98	22.09	59.85
Men's	4.82	12.31	21.95	60.59
Women's	4.89	9.44	19.48	65.84
Children's	9.43	17.55	27.50	45.55
Other	4.14	2.28	19.07	74.13
Medical care	4.42	9.72	14.69	70.85
Education	5.51	13.86	17.83	62.67
Recreation and culture	4.05	7.13	14.60	73.73
Recreation	3.59	6.15	13.52	76.26
Reading and culture	5.38	9.95	17.70	66.50
Vehicle operation	0.00	1.33	0.17	98.64
Public transportation	12.71	15.03	27.69	44.51
Communication	1.73	5.98	11.86	80.74
Other consumption	10.07	13.15	23.16	53.26
Tobacco	12.30	15.37	18.36	53.51
Personal care	9.23	13.40	23.92	53.21
Ceremonies	20.16	0.00	25.30	53.51
Insurance	0.00	4.01	7.31	89.69
Gifts and transfers	1.26	4.80	12.69	80.65
Other nonconsumption	0.43	7.76	30.05	61.18

Table C-12. *Shares of Total Expenditure in Each Category Generated in Each Income Quartile, Barranquilla*

Spending category	Income quartile			
	First	*Second*	*Third*	*Fourth*
Food and beverages	14.51	19.72	26.17	39.27
Dairy products and eggs	12.78	18.03	25.75	43.12
Cereals	16.96	21.67	26.55	34.53
Meat and poultry	13.47	17.42	27.43	41.26
Seafood	14.93	25.58	23.29	36.36
Vegetables and tubers	16.30	21.15	24.34	37.88
Fruits	13.43	19.11	26.95	40.30
Fats and oils	15.68	19.74	27.13	37.02
Sugar and sweets	18.69	22.92	24.60	33.75
Hot beverages	18.00	22.05	25.73	34.13
Alcoholic beverages	8.78	23.52	26.89	40.07
Other beverages	10.71	22.53	25.99	41.30
Other foods	15.18	19.01	24.98	40.28
Meals away from home	12.51	19.16	25.10	42.99
Housing	9.23	11.71	19.17	59.63
Principal dwelling	9.55	12.04	19.92	58.18
Other	2.25	0.00	0.00	100.13
Maintenance	5.37	7.81	10.17	76.44
Furnishings and operation	6.00	9.82	19.16	64.61
Durables	3.94	7.05	26.09	62.13
Nondurables	15.05	19.46	23.74	41.32
Services	0.11	4.24	7.42	88.22
Clothing	7.00	14.50	20.74	57.45
Men's	5.92	15.57	22.38	55.62
Women's	7.71	13.28	18.08	60.57
Children's	7.43	15.77	24.18	52.06
Other	5.47	11.34	15.99	67.42
Medical care	7.98	14.26	15.93	61.80
Education	6.41	10.19	17.93	65.27
Recreation and culture	7.70	12.60	19.91	59.57
Recreation	7.84	12.11	18.07	61.73
Reading and culture	7.45	13.51	23.59	55.62
Vehicle operation	0.00	1.11	1.57	97.52
Public transportation	16.58	18.94	23.34	40.76
Communication	1.52	6.10	8.61	84.97
Other consumption	14.30	18.65	25.23	41.56
Tobacco	19.07	19.46	25.99	34.82
Personal care	12.40	19.10	23.76	44.42
Ceremonies	19.48	12.21	36.15	32.83
Insurance	0.00	1.13	0.00	100.32
Gifts and transfers	1.23	12.12	8.95	77.59
Other nonconsumption	8.61	6.54	28.96	56.11

Table C-13. *Shares of Total Expenditure in Each Category Generated in Each Income Quartile, Cali*

Spending category	Income quartile			
	First	Second	Third	Fourth
Food and beverages	12.80	18.69	25.48	42.17
Dairy products and eggs	8.09	14.28	25.13	51.34
Cereals	15.27	21.17	25.24	37.68
Meat and poultry	12.93	17.65	26.53	41.95
Seafood	4.98	12.06	28.49	52.20
Vegetables and tubers	16.53	22.44	25.31	35.14
Fruits	13.42	17.28	24.65	44.01
Fats and oils	17.04	22.65	27.13	32.52
Sugar and sweets	16.89	22.67	24.73	35.46
Hot beverages	16.65	21.26	26.06	35.36
Alcoholic beverages	1.81	13.54	19.23	65.36
Other beverages	0.93	7.04	22.16	67.67
Other foods	12.90	17.58	25.38	43.97
Meals away from home	7.24	17.25	24.51	49.83
Housing	6.01	11.93	21.59	59.40
Principal dwelling	6.12	12.36	22.20	58.22
Other	0.00	0.00	0.00	100.00
Maintenance	4.30	4.02	10.64	80.11
Furnishings and operation	4.85	5.88	16.69	71.67
Durables	4.96	2.61	17.41	74.19
Nondurables	11.93	18.60	22.72	46.44
Services	0.21	2.02	12.08	84.95
Clothing	4.96	10.84	22.46	60.53
Men's	3.93	10.17	22.94	61.82
Women's	4.29	10.82	21.93	61.71
Children's	7.62	13.17	25.43	52.60
Other	7.87	5.44	10.00	75.03
Medical care	4.58	9.69	16.90	67.87
Education	2.30	10.32	21.53	64.46
Recreation and culture	4.40	9.38	22.70	62.23
Recreation	4.47	8.35	22.71	63.25
Reading and culture	4.36	11.43	22.71	60.21
Vehicle operation	0.00	0.00	0.48	99.52
Public transportation	12.89	19.83	24.63	42.01
Communication	0.00	1.82	13.58	82.93
Other consumption	9.88	15.45	22.57	51.25
Tobacco	8.72	18.57	24.37	47.62
Personal care	10.55	15.75	22.59	50.33
Ceremonies	4.36	0.00	15.83	77.34
Insurance	0.00	0.00	6.82	91.63
Gifts and transfers	3.41	8.46	11.24	76.46
Other nonconsumption	1.61	3.13	10.66	86.17

Table C-14. *Shares of Total Expenditure in Each Category Generated in Each Income Quartile, Medellín*

Spending category	Income quartile			
	First	Second	Third	Fourth
Food and beverages	11.73	18.65	26.28	42.89
Dairy products and eggs	9.46	17.83	23.48	48.77
Cereals	13.73	20.21	28.79	36.84
Meat and poultry	10.59	17.13	26.70	45.09
Seafood	0.00	5.56	11.96	83.34
Vegetables and tubers	14.24	20.29	27.84	37.30
Fruits	8.00	14.89	23.66	52.92
Fats and oils	13.26	20.91	27.36	37.90
Sugar and sweets	16.78	22.95	28.90	30.97
Hot beverages	16.43	23.81	28.27	31.13
Alcoholic beverages	3.87	10.66	14.62	69.88
Other beverages	2.63	7.54	16.42	73.01
Other foods	9.06	12.45	21.20	57.99
Meals away from home	9.20	17.09	24.24	48.87
Housing	7.70	14.14	19.65	58.05
Principal dwelling	8.20	15.05	20.83	55.43
Other	1.62	0.00	3.42	94.69
Maintenance	0.24	4.02	4.32	91.83
Furnishings and operation	3.81	6.37	15.10	74.29
Durables	2.13	3.12	14.13	80.04
Nondurables	11.84	17.68	23.74	45.85
Services	0.84	3.02	11.11	84.72
Clothing	5.39	10.05	18.30	65.88
Men's	4.45	9.44	22.06	63.62
Women's	4.76	8.74	16.21	70.01
Children's	7.85	12.75	19.21	60.17
Other	4.97	12.00	15.61	66.88
Medical care	3.27	5.18	24.58	66.32
Education	4.62	9.90	19.29	65.77
Recreation and culture	4.24	9.15	16.33	69.69
Recreation	4.78	8.30	15.04	71.74
Reading and culture	3.08	11.28	19.59	66.14
Vehicle operation	3.41	2.77	11.59	81.87
Public transportation	13.35	16.78	24.70	44.41
Communication	2.89	14.48	18.53	67.78
Other consumption	8.69	13.22	21.95	55.97
Tobacco	14.47	18.53	28.12	38.10
Personal care	8.36	14.27	21.76	55.34
Ceremonies	0.00	0.00	11.70	86.99
Insurance	0.00	0.00	2.70	95.30
Gifts and transfers	1.08	4.72	18.83	74.52
Other nonconsumption	1.84	1.75	13.48	80.52

Table C-15. *Shares of Total Expenditure in Each Category Generated in Each Income Quartile, Santiago*

	Income quartile			
Spending category	*First*	*Second*	*Third*	*Fourth*
Food and beverages	15.60	21.12	25.92	37.29
Dairy products and eggs	13.22	20.30	26.07	40.20
Cereals	19.54	24.65	27.13	28.70
Meat and poultry	13.11	19.45	25.65	41.70
Seafood	14.00	18.25	25.37	42.88
Vegetables and tubers	18.82	24.09	26.98	29.99
Fruits	11.75	19.13	24.90	43.97
Fats and oils	18.20	22.22	27.84	31.70
Sugar and sweets	18.74	23.29	26.06	31.75
Hot beverages	16.30	21.91	28.49	33.58
Alcoholic beverages	12.66	17.40	25.37	44.07
Other beverages	12.85	20.45	25.66	39.93
Other foods	16.28	20.27	23.62	39.60
Meals away from home	12.59	15.43	21.31	50.30
Housing	9.65	14.15	22.95	53.06
Principal dwelling	9.80	14.06	22.89	53.05
Other	0.00	0.00	0.00	0.00
Maintenance	5.46	16.58	24.46	53.35
Furnishings and operation	7.53	18.08	21.53	52.67
Durables	8.60	25.39	25.36	40.63
Nondurables	14.37	18.32	26.36	40.67
Services	2.53	3.84	12.06	81.09
Clothing	9.17	16.43	24.49	49.80
Men's	8.51	15.92	24.48	50.98
Women's	8.83	16.14	24.26	50.63
Children's	16.90	20.18	21.57	41.95
Other	12.05	19.05	25.82	42.63
Medical care	10.73	24.93	17.84	46.33
Education	3.60	8.75	15.97	71.92
Recreation and culture	7.02	15.38	21.21	56.06
Recreation	6.27	15.95	21.07	56.50
Reading and culture	8.31	14.41	21.44	55.67
Vehicle operation	1.11	0.82	7.61	90.21
Public transportation	14.76	20.12	27.07	37.99
Communication	3.16	7.14	13.08	75.71
Other consumption	10.01	18.90	25.17	45.78
Tobacco	11.01	18.92	26.80	43.39
Personal care	9.92	19.20	24.69	46.07
Ceremonies	7.11	17.19	22.47	52.95
Insurance	n.a.	n.a.	n.a.	n.a.
Gifts and transfers	5.04	8.78	16.80	68.61
Other nonconsumption	6.43	13.09	34.87	44.80

n.a. Not available.

Table C-16. *Shares of Total Expenditure in Each Category Generated in Each Income Quartile, Quito*

Spending category	Income quartile			
	First	*Second*	*Third*	*Fourth*
Food and beverages	10.97	17.79	26.48	44.88
Dairy products and eggs	7.06	14.37	26.00	52.75
Cereals	13.91	20.83	27.46	37.79
Meat and poultry	6.64	16.15	27.97	49.36
Seafood	7.97	13.31	26.05	53.68
Vegetables and tubers	12.95	21.41	28.39	37.12
Fruits	7.21	14.83	27.83	50.01
Fats and oils	12.23	20.06	27.60	40.11
Sugar and sweets	11.95	18.05	26.08	43.74
Hot beverages	11.76	20.77	27.48	40.36
Alcoholic beverages	6.88	9.31	16.46	68.30
Other beverages	3.53	12.10	24.45	59.28
Other foods	6.21	11.91	22.67	59.28
Meals away from home	21.66	17.79	21.02	39.71
Housing	3.45	7.32	17.63	72.17
Principal dwelling	3.94	8.36	18.58	69.66
Other	0.31	0.20	7.97	92.61
Maintenance	0.58	3.54	33.04	62.98
Furnishings and operation	3.99	15.02	14.38	67.32
Durables	3.37	19.74	11.40	66.40
Nondurables	9.42	14.71	21.64	54.30
Services	0.94	5.24	14.89	79.59
Clothing	5.86	14.48	26.43	53.35
Men's	6.06	15.36	25.95	52.69
Women's	5.22	12.98	26.19	55.79
Children's	11.32	22.97	22.27	41.84
Other	7.42	17.18	30.94	43.88
Medical care	5.58	21.35	23.12	50.33
Education	2.46	8.90	22.39	66.77
Recreation and culture	3.48	7.28	26.22	63.56
Recreation	3.32	5.76	26.41	64.79
Reading and culture	3.82	10.90	25.69	59.28
Vehicle operation	0.00	0.00	5.97	95.42
Public transportation	n.a.	n.a.	n.a.	n.a.
Communication	0.70	4.47	26.22	69.79
Other consumption	4.56	13.35	29.11	53.20
Tobacco	5.26	14.52	29.44	51.24
Personal care	5.14	14.42	25.86	54.50
Ceremonies	0.64	6.14	43.39	48.64
Insurance	0.00	1.15	18.22	80.83
Gifts and transfers	2.93	4.71	30.68	61.69
Other nonconsumption	3.01	15.00	13.75	68.86

n.a. Not available.

Table C-17. *Shares of Total Expenditures in Each Category Generated in Each Income Quartile, Guayaquil*

Spending category	Income quartile			
	First	Second	Third	Fourth
Food and beverages	12.03	19.13	25.69	43.08
Dairy products and eggs	7.71	17.84	26.88	47.54
Cereals	16.79	22.61	27.82	32.74
Meat and poultry	9.58	18.23	26.22	45.91
Seafood	15.35	20.49	24.72	39.45
Vegetables and tubers	14.58	21.76	26.47	37.04
Fruits	9.78	15.39	21.38	53.22
Fats and oils	15.47	22.24	25.97	36.26
Sugar and sweets	11.24	17.42	23.30	47.71
Hot beverages	16.08	20.62	23.87	38.97
Alcoholic beverages	2.40	11.62	11.07	75.60
Other beverages	5.74	15.75	27.69	50.75
Other foods	7.06	10.47	20.69	61.53
Meals away from home	13.67	16.05	24.11	46.09
Housing	4.45	8.96	16.37	70.12
Principal dwelling	4.89	9.69	16.86	68.46
Other	0.00	0.00	7.10	92.64
Maintenance	0.00	5.17	21.23	73.90
Furnishings and operation	3.60	8.47	21.25	66.59
Durables	2.27	8.28	25.31	64.18
Nondurables	13.61	17.95	23.93	44.43
Services	1.17	4.52	13.56	80.72
Clothing	4.39	10.19	24.29	61.11
Men's	4.16	10.55	27.99	57.18
Women's	4.11	9.49	20.89	65.27
Children's	9.27	10.56	27.64	53.73
Other	5.51	11.57	22.72	60.72
Medical care	8.10	11.91	20.44	59.25
Education	2.51	10.13	22.89	64.50
Recreation and culture	3.79	12.44	21.71	61.78
Recreation	2.73	9.85	19.22	68.07
Reading and culture	5.85	17.46	26.52	49.59
Vehicle operation	0.24	0.85	13.37	85.41
Public transportation	n.a.	n.a.	n.a.	n.a.
Communication	1.10	2.97	10.91	84.91
Other consumption	7.69	13.45	22.10	56.63
Tobacco	6.77	11.82	20.84	61.00
Personal care	8.70	15.22	23.30	52.89
Ceremonies	0.00	0.00	13.09	89.22
Insurance	0.91	1.44	4.43	93.54
Gifts and transfers	2.14	7.37	24.05	66.31
Other nonconsumption	6.22	20.46	15.28	60.44

n.a. Not available.

Table C-18. *Shares of Total Expenditure in Each Category Generated in Each Income Quartile, Lima*

Spending category	Income quartile			
	First	Second	Third	Fourth
Food and beverages	18.09	21.26	25.81	34.95
Dairy products and eggs	17.00	21.86	24.75	36.42
Cereals	21.02	24.00	25.72	29.31
Meat and poultry	17.02	22.14	25.75	35.13
Seafood	16.69	20.45	26.43	36.84
Vegetables and tubers	22.49	25.10	24.34	27.99
Fruits	14.91	17.25	22.95	44.89
Fats and oils	21.68	23.71	25.12	28.98
Sugar and sweets	20.71	20.16	23.14	35.73
Hot beverages	16.93	23.22	24.60	34.85
Alcoholic beverages	7.98	27.14	41.64	22.64
Other beverages	9.70	18.29	28.33	47.78
Other foods	19.08	19.25	21.49	39.74
Meals away from home	14.48	12.63	31.76	41.87
Housing	8.59	12.07	22.07	57.56
Principal dwelling	9.78	12.76	24.28	53.51
Other	0.45	3.81	2.60	92.97
Maintenance	6.21	14.37	22.06	57.67
Furnishings and operation	9.61	17.72	21.88	50.87
Durables	10.00	20.81	22.41	46.82
Nondurables	16.25	18.66	25.28	40.45
Services	4.67	8.32	18.46	68.87
Clothing	12.13	14.47	25.30	48.36
Men's	11.83	14.53	27.77	46.22
Women's	12.13	15.05	23.34	49.87
Children's	20.08	17.21	22.80	39.56
Other	10.96	11.68	23.84	53.77
Medical care	15.31	16.26	24.47	44.12
Education	7.22	15.09	17.58	60.25
Recreation and culture	8.97	15.30	22.30	53.47
Recreation	6.72	10.71	24.42	58.87
Reading and culture	12.57	22.63	18.94	45.22
Vehicle operation	2.00	20.90	14.03	62.63
Public transportation	13.02	21.67	23.01	42.20
Communication	4.92	11.69	19.79	63.30
Other consumption	11.69	14.76	26.90	47.11
Tobacco	11.06	14.19	22.23	53.42
Personal care	13.01	16.91	25.02	45.43
Ceremonies	4.31	1.48	46.71	49.92
Insurance	8.48	13.03	22.96	56.16
Gifts and transfers	6.74	9.24	16.49	68.29
Other nonconsumption	11.92	12.84	38.12	38.57

Table C-19. *Shares of Total Expenditure in Each Category Generated in Each Income Quartile, Caracas*

Spending category	Income quartile			
	First	*Second*	*Third*	*Fourth*
Food and beverages	16.87	20.65	25.29	37.26
Dairy products and eggs	16.90	20.43	25.46	37.30
Cereals	21.07	23.40	24.59	31.12
Meat and poultry	15.63	20.34	26.99	37.04
Seafood	17.70	20.86	28.51	33.06
Vegetables and tubers	20.40	23.72	24.85	31.28
Fruits	15.63	21.22	24.24	39.16
Fats and oils	20.81	24.68	23.35	30.94
Sugar and sweets	16.86	21.63	24.49	37.04
Hot beverages	22.72	21.05	22.40	33.41
Alcoholic beverages	13.79	20.46	21.26	44.26
Other beverages	18.10	22.74	25.19	34.08
Other foods	13.84	20.80	23.96	41.01
Meals away from home	14.63	17.36	29.40	38.63
Housing	9.28	15.25	23.80	51.84
Principal dwelling	9.29	15.26	23.81	51.85
Other	0.00	0.00	0.00	0.00
Maintenance	0.00	0.00	14.54	78.20
Furnishings and operation	7.21	13.61	22.78	56.67
Durables	4.84	19.48	23.02	52.95
Nondurables	14.31	18.53	24.87	42.53
Services	5.36	8.51	21.91	64.60
Clothing	10.83	17.88	24.85	46.63
Men's	10.17	17.18	26.40	46.26
Women's	10.71	18.62	24.14	46.57
Children's	15.29	20.33	23.04	41.65
Other	6.29	13.96	26.20	53.72
Medical care	5.68	14.24	23.84	56.59
Education	4.85	13.19	23.73	58.56
Recreation and culture	8.37	12.58	21.78	57.51
Recreation	8.89	13.13	21.99	56.21
Reading and culture	6.12	10.19	20.87	62.45
Vehicle operation	4.59	14.79	28.75	52.04
Public transportation	20.34	21.51	28.52	29.70
Communication	3.71	12.37	28.91	55.05
Other consumption	15.55	19.73	24.97	39.81
Tobacco	19.14	21.17	22.54	37.73
Personal care	13.65	18.96	26.27	40.92
Ceremonies	0.00	0.00	0.00	0.00
Insurance	2.32	4.41	19.00	72.65
Gifts and transfers	4.94	9.66	21.54	64.08
Other nonconsumption	3.79	17.26	22.81	54.62

Table C-20. *Shares of Total Expenditure in Each Category Generated in Each Income Quartile, Maracaibo*

	Income quartile			
Spending category	First	Second	Third	Fourth
Food and beverages	16.93	22.44	27.33	33.30
Dairy products and eggs	16.95	22.24	26.98	33.88
Cereals	20.60	24.53	26.40	28.57
Meat and poultry	13.80	21.18	28.30	36.69
Seafood	21.62	25.74	26.41	26.29
Vegetables and tubers	18.16	24.92	25.65	31.32
Fruits	17.65	22.21	28.27	31.93
Fats and oils	16.33	25.07	25.66	32.98
Sugar and sweets	20.76	21.45	25.54	32.14
Hot beverages	20.05	23.06	25.65	31.18
Alcoholic beverages	12.69	23.05	27.85	36.52
Other beverages	14.96	20.09	29.82	34.97
Other foods	20.00	22.00	25.82	32.14
Meals away from home	14.94	21.81	29.43	33.66
Housing	12.20	15.88	22.74	49.19
Principal dwelling	12.23	15.92	22.79	49.06
Other	0.00	0.00	0.00	0.00
Maintenance	0.00	0.00	0.00	100.00
Furnishings and operation	8.83	12.30	21.82	57.04
Durables	9.07	12.45	23.92	54.57
Nondurables	15.43	20.13	26.20	38.35
Services	2.04	4.62	12.07	81.58
Clothing	10.75	15.12	24.11	50.14
Men's	8.45	16.03	23.32	52.37
Women's	10.91	10.55	23.10	55.77
Children's	13.57	18.64	27.67	40.66
Other	14.22	19.41	21.68	43.80
Medical care	9.63	10.07	21.77	58.51
Education	6.17	8.63	20.29	65.14
Recreation and culture	9.13	15.84	23.62	51.53
Recreation	10.00	17.00	24.57	48.45
Reading and culture	5.22	10.62	19.36	65.38
Vehicle operation	3.91	3.77	17.23	74.97
Public transportation	20.73	27.27	27.24	24.90
Communication	1.06	2.09	18.77	77.54
Other consumption	15.84	21.34	27.84	34.82
Tobacco	14.91	20.52	34.47	29.91
Personal care	16.27	21.68	25.20	36.95
Ceremonies	0.00	0.00	0.00	0.00
Insurance	7.62	10.04	12.20	70.61
Gifts and transfers	2.57	11.30	26.43	59.35
Other nonconsumption	16.01	13.56	22.37	51.14

Table C-21. *Individual Budget Structure by Family Size Class, Bogotá*

	Number of members			
Spending category	*1–2*	*3–5*	*6–8*	*9 or more*
Food and beverages	43.75	46.18	48.38	46.98
Dairy products and eggs	4.57	6.20	6.70	5.72
Cereals	7.71	7.99	9.00	10.01
Meat and poultry	10.80	8.90	9.31	8.87
Seafood	0.23	0.19	0.17	0.08
Vegetables and tubers	6.42	7.50	7.58	8.32
Fruits	1.99	2.32	2.53	2.13
Fats and oils	2.19	2.15	2.16	2.11
Sugar and sweets	1.58	1.62	1.76	1.99
Hot beverages	2.73	2.15	2.44	2.61
Alcoholic beverages	0.41	0.47	0.53	0.28
Other beverages	0.23	0.25	0.20	0.13
Other foods	0.46	0.43	0.46	0.41
Meals away from home	4.42	6.01	5.54	4.32
Housing	35.59	25.74	23.89	25.52
Principal dwelling	35.48	25.03	22.99	24.81
Other	0.06	0.04	0.09	0.00
Maintenance	0.05	0.67	0.81	0.71
Furnishings and operation	3.85	5.70	4.57	4.22
Durables	1.54	2.45	1.75	1.22
Nondurables	1.49	1.68	1.55	1.74
Services	0.81	1.57	1.27	1.26
Clothing	4.43	8.05	7.23	6.93
Men's	1.43	2.81	2.14	1.62
Women's	2.63	3.26	2.56	2.66
Children's	0.36	1.79	2.34	2.56
Other	0.01	0.18	0.18	0.09
Medical care	1.35	2.50	1.59	1.30
Education	1.64	3.02	6.17	7.19
Recreation and culture	1.33	2.04	1.84	1.51
Recreation	0.81	1.14	1.25	1.05
Reading and culture	0.52	0.63	0.58	0.45
Vehicle operation	1.33	0.53	0.27	0.49
Public transportation	3.02	2.47	2.42	2.62
Communication	0.31	0.47	0.30	0.23
Other consumption	1.62	2.15	2.28	2.05
Tobacco	0.39	0.26	0.30	0.18
Personal care	1.23	1.87	1.80	1.79
Ceremonies	0.00	0.02	0.18	0.09
Insurance	0.10	0.09	0.15	0.19
Gifts and transfers	1.65	0.91	0.70	0.60
Other nonconsumption	0.03	0.17	0.12	0.16

Table C-22. *Individual Budget Structure by Family Size Class, Barran-quilla*

Spending category	Number of members			
	1–2	*3–5*	*6–8*	*9 or more*
Food and beverages	55.58	57.08	56.34	60.28
Dairy products and eggs	5.63	6.72	7.08	6.85
Cereals	9.77	10.35	11.11	13.90
Meat and poultry	11.70	14.24	14.52	14.16
Seafood	1.67	1.14	1.08	1.38
Vegetables and tubers	7.70	6.25	5.90	6.42
Fruits	3.58	3.30	2.90	3.15
Fats and oils	3.02	2.56	2.62	2.84
Sugar and sweets	2.65	2.34	1.93	2.46
Hot beverages	1.21	1.31	1.18	1.42
Alcoholic beverages	1.21	1.38	1.14	1.04
Other beverages	0.74	0.67	0.62	0.72
Other foods	0.90	1.05	0.97	0.96
Meals away from home	5.77	5.78	5.27	4.96
Housing	18.64	17.08	17.29	15.60
Principal dwelling	17.89	16.00	16.53	14.78
Other	0.01	0.06	0.00	0.03
Maintenance	0.73	1.02	0.76	0.78
Furnishings and operation	4.52	4.66	5.14	4.16
Durables	2.71	1.61	1.71	1.33
Nondurables	1.73	2.25	1.86	2.09
Services	0.08	0.80	1.57	0.73
Clothing	5.88	6.24	5.74	5.76
Men's	2.24	2.13	1.70	1.76
Women's	2.78	2.47	2.26	2.16
Children's	0.66	1.24	1.61	1.63
Other	0.20	0.40	0.17	0.21
Medical care	5.99	2.73	1.76	2.29
Education	0.12	2.34	4.41	4.20
Recreation and culture	1.42	1.83	1.77	1.61
Recreation	0.88	1.10	1.12	1.05
Reading and culture	0.54	0.73	0.65	0.56
Vehicle operation	1.06	0.36	1.02	0.56
Public transportation	1.92	2.54	1.89	1.97
Communication	0.18	0.27	0.35	0.22
Other consumption	4.02	3.75	3.39	3.01
Tobacco	0.80	0.81	0.74	0.74
Personal care	3.16	2.60	2.31	2.24
Ceremonies	0.07	0.34	0.34	0.03
Insurance	0.00	0.03	0.05	0.07
Gifts and transfers	0.66	0.89	0.75	0.25
Other nonconsumption	0.01	0.19	0.12	0.01

Table C-23. *Individual Budget Structure by Family Size Class, Cali*

	Number of members			
Spending category	*1–2*	*3–5*	*6–8*	*9 or more*
Food and beverages	59.16	56.88	55.60	60.23
Dairy products and eggs	7.47	7.05	6.87	6.55
Cereals	7.82	9.08	8.94	11.16
Meat and poultry	16.15	15.73	13.67	15.19
Seafood	0.26	0.28	0.22	0.12
Vegetables and tubers	7.47	7.97	8.28	9.29
Fruits	2.73	3.32	3.44	3.86
Fats and oils	2.73	3.03	3.07	3.70
Sugar and sweets	2.70	2.70	3.05	3.32
Hot beverages	2.46	2.34	2.53	2.55
Alcoholic beverages	0.33	0.45	0.33	0.55
Other beverages	0.23	0.20	0.22	0.17
Other foods	0.56	0.61	0.57	0.62
Meals away from home	8.27	4.13	4.42	3.15
Housing	17.89	19.15	17.48	15.69
Principal dwelling	17.61	18.75	16.85	15.14
Other	0.00	0.06	0.00	0.03
Maintenance	0.28	0.34	0.63	0.52
Furnishings and operation	3.79	4.80	4.96	4.67
Durables	1.36	1.70	1.65	1.59
Nondurables	1.69	1.79	1.84	2.01
Services	0.73	1.30	1.47	1.07
Clothing	6.08	6.43	7.15	4.29
Men's	2.21	2.37	2.38	1.25
Women's	3.28	2.61	2.68	1.65
Children's	0.11	1.22	1.93	1.22
Other	0.49	0.22	0.15	0.17
Medical care	1.65	1.35	1.26	1.37
Education	0.00	1.71	3.06	4.30
Recreation and culture	1.85	2.01	1.97	1.43
Recreation	1.10	1.30	1.25	0.91
Reading and culture	0.74	0.70	0.72	0.52
Vehicle operation	0.00	0.26	0.48	0.44
Public transportation	2.29	1.92	1.94	2.19
Communication	0.49	0.32	0.34	0.26
Other consumption	3.37	2.80	2.86	2.60
Tobacco	1.26	0.50	0.57	0.52
Personal care	2.11	2.19	2.23	1.97
Ceremonies	0.00	0.10	0.06	0.11
Insurance	0.00	0.07	0.10	0.22
Gifts and transfers	2.11	0.89	0.74	0.64
Other nonconsumption	0.15	0.12	0.15	0.03

Table C-24. *Individual Budget Structure by Family Size Class, Medellín*

Spending category	Number of members			
	1–2	*3–5*	*6–8*	*9 or more*
Food and beverages	51.45	53.31	51.39	54.04
Dairy products and eggs	8.88	8.47	7.56	6.60
Cereals	7.76	8.20	8.05	9.13
Meat and poultry	11.81	13.02	13.04	13.42
Seafood	0.10	0.10	0.06	0.03
Vegetables and tubers	7.07	7.33	7.28	8.59
Fruits	1.60	1.71	1.84	1.76
Fats and oils	2.59	2.35	2.11	2.31
Sugar and sweets	3.18	3.69	3.80	4.66
Hot beverages	3.11	2.74	2.61	3.13
Alcoholic beverages	0.16	0.25	0.43	0.25
Other beverages	0.18	0.16	0.18	0.08
Other foods	0.29	0.49	0.45	0.38
Meals away from home	4.72	4.79	3.99	3.70
Housing	24.42	23.34	23.65	20.85
Principal dwelling	24.24	22.98	23.04	19.97
Other	0.04	0.13	0.37	0.32
Maintenance	0.13	0.23	0.24	0.57
Furnishings and operation	3.02	3.43	3.94	3.30
Durables	1.10	1.06	1.06	1.01
Nondurables	1.34	1.34	1.42	1.38
Services	0.58	1.03	1.46	0.91
Clothing	4.74	4.68	4.13	4.11
Men's	1.52	1.49	0.77	0.92
Women's	2.88	1.97	1.94	1.34
Children's	0.20	0.88	1.11	1.38
Other	0.14	0.33	0.31	0.47
Medical care	0.97	2.02	1.81	1.53
Education	1.90	1.81	3.40	5.34
Recreation and culture	2.10	1.62	1.56	1.11
Recreation	1.64	1.07	1.08	0.78
Reading and culture	0.46	0.56	0.48	0.33
Vehicle operation	1.37	0.61	0.29	0.31
Public transportation	2.35	1.73	1.64	1.78
Communication	0.05	0.09	0.10	0.13
Other consumption	2.34	2.41	2.33	2.38
Tobacco	1.02	0.76	0.91	0.74
Personal care	1.28	1.40	1.42	1.52
Ceremonies	0.04	0.25	0.01	0.12
Insurance	0.19	0.07	0.17	0.07
Gifts and transfers	0.63	1.17	0.91	0.54
Other nonconsumption	0.01	0.14	0.25	0.31

Table C-25. *Individual Budget Structure by Family Size Class, Santiago*

Spending category	Number of members			
	1–2	*3–5*	*6–8*	*9 or more*
Food and beverages	37.16	39.59	44.17	45.95
Dairy products and eggs	3.71	4.36	4.53	3.80
Cereals	6.47	7.50	10.09	12.48
Meat and poultry	7.23	8.24	8.64	7.52
Seafood	0.74	1.02	1.17	0.88
Vegetables and tubers	4.85	6.19	6.74	7.75
Fruits	2.05	2.36	2.32	2.09
Fats and oils	1.87	1.97	2.08	2.21
Sugar and sweets	1.95	2.00	2.53	3.11
Hot beverages	1.44	1.32	1.52	1.52
Alcoholic beverages	0.92	0.85	1.03	0.67
Other beverages	0.59	0.70	0.66	0.62
Other foods	0.70	0.90	0.83	0.89
Meals away from home	4.63	2.18	2.04	2.42
Housing	33.39	26.44	22.97	18.94
Principal dwelling	32.63	25.68	22.30	18.48
Other	n.a.	n.a.	n.a.	n.a.
Maintenance	0.76	0.76	0.67	0.46
Furnishings and operation	7.21	7.29	6.55	5.45
Durables	3.61	4.08	4.00	3.46
Nondurables	1.11	1.41	1.62	1.50
Services	2.49	1.80	0.93	0.49
Clothing	9.05	12.23	1.89	13.52
Men's	3.76	5.99	6.03	7.00
Women's	4.01	4.56	4.30	4.28
Children's	0.06	0.36	0.25	0.51
Other	1.22	1.32	1.31	1.72
Medical care	1.43	1.37	1.18	0.99
Education	0.24	0.78	0.97	0.71
Recreation and culture	3.02	2.95	3.02	4.12
Recreation	1.95	1.68	1.72	2.62
Reading and culture	1.06	1.26	1.31	1.50
Vehicle operation	0.79	0.80	0.53	0.26
Public transportation	2.78	2.92	3.24	4.11
Communication	0.59	0.48	0.28	0.24
Other consumption	3.35	4.47	4.65	5.55
Tobacco	1.08	1.76	1.92	2.74
Personal care	2.03	2.42	2.36	2.54
Ceremonies	0.24	0.29	0.37	0.26
Insurance	n.a.	n.a.	n.a.	n.a.
Gifts and transfers	0.62	0.29	0.16	0.04
Other nonconsumption	0.29	0.33	0.28	0.06

n.a. Not available.

Table C-26. *Individual Budget Structure by Family Size Class, Quito*

Spending category	Number of members			
	1–2	*3–5*	*6–8*	*9 or more*
Food and beverages	47.39	46.26	44.79	44.88
Dairy products and eggs	5.51	6.47	5.86	5.04
Cereals	6.14	9.87	11.26	12.78
Meat and poultry	4.79	7.59	6.78	5.78
Seafood	0.51	0.64	0.60	0.52
Vegetables and tubers	3.58	6.08	6.45	7.01
Fruits	1.81	2.32	2.38	2.17
Fats and oils	1.83	2.55	2.67	2.42
Sugar and sweets	1.71	2.73	2.89	2.76
Hot beverages	1.30	1.06	1.44	1.26
Alcoholic beverages	0.65	0.46	0.40	0.16
Other beverages	0.65	0.57	0.39	0.23
Other foods	0.45	0.66	0.54	0.44
Meals away from home	17.70	4.72	2.71	4.25
Housing	25.77	25.97	26.21	25.44
Principal dwelling	25.12	24.21	24.22	22.97
Other	0.57	1.20	1.49	2.13
Maintenance	0.08	0.57	0.50	0.34
Furnishings and operation	4.27	5.48	6.41	4.87
Durables	1.85	2.67	3.57	2.21
Nondurables	1.47	1.65	1.73	1.85
Services	0.95	1.16	1.11	0.80
Clothing	10.90	9.67	10.28	10.84
Men's	5.10	3.54	4.50	5.05
Women's	4.73	4.86	4.75	4.46
Children's	0.00	0.32	0.19	0.29
Other	1.07	0.94	0.84	1.04
Medical care	2.41	2.99	2.81	3.62
Education	0.30	1.20	1.63	2.34
Recreation and culture	2.42	1.50	1.49	1.19
Recreation	1.81	0.98	1.04	0.79
Reading and culture	0.61	0.52	0.45	0.40
Vehicle operation	0.10	0.25	0.26	0.35
Public transportation	n.a.	n.a.	n.a.	n.a.
Communication	0.43	0.54	0.38	0.36
Other consumption	3.16	3.46	2.74	2.18
Tobacco	0.78	0.70	0.64	0.59
Personal care	2.14	2.21	1.92	1.57
Ceremonies	0.23	0.55	0.18	0.03
Insurance	0.08	0.05	0.04	0.01
Gifts and transfers	1.69	1.74	1.83	3.07
Other nonconsumption	0.55	0.45	0.82	0.34

n.a. Not available.

Table C-27. *Individual Budget Structure by Family Size Class, Guayaquil*

Spending category	Number of members			
	1–2	*3–5*	*6–8*	*9 or more*
Food and beverages	52.95	52.22	53.30	55.37
Dairy products and eggs	5.49	6.43	6.87	6.27
Cereals	6.66	10.66	12.59	15.44
Meat and poultry	7.99	11.28	10.99	11.25
Seafood	1.53	2.06	2.17	2.50
Vegetables and tubers	4.78	6.26	6.46	6.43
Fruits	1.59	2.37	2.45	2.28
Fats and oils	2.28	3.26	3.10	3.09
Sugar and sweets	2.45	2.74	3.01	2.67
Hot beverages	1.56	1.56	1.39	1.45
Alcoholic beverages	0.48	0.42	0.62	0.41
Other beverages	1.06	1.08	0.97	0.79
Other foods	0.42	0.61	0.58	0.54
Meals away from home	16.46	3.31	2.01	2.25
Housing	26.70	22.94	20.10	20.45
Principal dwelling	26.17	21.74	19.08	19.71
Other	0.49	0.74	0.34	0.39
Maintenance	0.05	0.45	0.68	0.35
Furnishings and operation	4.09	6.16	5.97	4.29
Durables	0.62	3.01	2.95	1.73
Nondurables	1.60	1.57	1.57	1.59
Services	1.86	1.58	1.44	0.97
Clothing	6.60	5.83	7.21	6.35
Men's	2.66	2.59	3.37	2.64
Women's	3.17	2.37	2.96	2.88
Children's	0.07	0.29	0.15	0.12
Other	0.71	0.58	0.73	0.71
Medical care	1.70	2.32	1.92	1.67
Education	0.18	1.41	2.47	2.00
Recreation and culture	1.75	1.78	1.70	1.72
Recreation	0.84	1.04	1.04	0.97
Reading and culture	0.91	0.74	0.66	0.75
Vehicle operation	0.13	0.37	0.38	0.13
Public transportation	n.a.	n.a.	n.a.	n.a.
Communication	0.21	0.22	0.20	0.16
Other consumption	3.70	3.43	3.06	3.17
Tobacco	1.08	0.56	0.67	0.70
Personal care	2.62	2.75	2.34	2.45
Ceremonies	0.00	0.13	0.05	0.02
Insurance	0.02	0.13	0.19	0.12
Gifts and transfers	1.70	2.77	3.08	4.00
Other nonconsumption	0.25	0.15	0.26	0.07

n.a. Not available.

Table C-28. *Individual Budget Structure by Family Size Class, Lima*

Spending category	Number of members			
	1–2	*3–5*	*6–8*	*9 or more*
Food and beverages	35.14	42.28	44.09	44.91
Dairy products and eggs	5.23	6.06	6.09	5.81
Cereals	4.59	7.09	7.95	8.97
Meat and poultry	10.15	11.07	11.05	10.90
Seafood	1.06	1.32	1.56	1.47
Vegetables and tubers	3.68	5.64	6.00	6.47
Fruits	1.76	2.51	2.30	2.20
Fats and oils	1.23	1.35	1.43	1.41
Sugar and sweets	0.84	1.18	1.41	1.58
Hot beverages	0.77	0.71	0.65	0.58
Alcoholic beverages	0.56	0.28	0.39	0.44
Other beverages	0.10	0.10	0.14	0.13
Other foods	1.18	1.07	1.32	1.10
Meals away from home	3.99	3.81	3.78	3.84
Housing	33.67	21.17	18.91	18.55
Principal dwelling	30.75	19.81	16.90	15.87
Other	1.37	0.26	0.39	0.96
Maintenance	1.55	1.11	1.61	1.73
Furnishings and operation	8.22	9.41	9.92	8.78
Durables	6.23	5.61	6.41	5.07
Nondurables	1.25	1.98	1.82	1.95
Services	0.75	1.82	1.69	1.76
Clothing	6.08	8.10	7.78	7.91
Men's	2.64	3.55	3.52	3.40
Women's	2.53	3.01	3.32	3.65
Children's	0.38	0.46	0.27	0.16
Other	0.53	1.09	0.68	0.69
Medical care	2.68	2.27	2.09	1.86
Education	0.33	1.48	1.85	1.93
Recreation and culture	2.76	2.79	2.48	2.54
Recreation	1.18	1.60	1.26	1.36
Reading and culture	1.58	1.19	1.22	1.17
Vehicle operation	3.06	1.26	2.40	1.90
Public transportation	2.00	3.26	2.76	3.43
Communication	0.39	0.31	0.26	0.23
Other consumption	3.58	4.32	4.32	4.82
Tobacco	0.53	0.65	0.69	0.73
Personal care	2.75	3.51	3.19	3.54
Ceremonies	0.31	0.16	0.44	0.56
Insurance	0.70	1.52	1.63	1.72
Gifts and transfers	0.14	0.42	0.49	0.43
Other nonconsumption	0.51	0.53	0.61	0.47

Table C-29. *Individual Budget Structure by Family Size Class, Caracas*

	Number of members			
Spending category	*1–2*	*3–5*	*6–8*	*9 or more*
Food and beverages	35.37	33.55	36.05	42.84
Dairy products and eggs	5.15	5.29	5.91	6.76
Cereals	3.32	3.46	4.54	6.64
Meat and poultry	7.77	7.62	7.58	8.35
Seafood	1.05	0.86	0.91	1.27
Vegetables and tubers	3.78	3.75	3.88	5.00
Fruits	2.41	2.14	2.11	2.37
Fats and oils	1.32	1.48	1.63	2.14
Sugar and sweets	0.98	1.10	1.30	1.79
Hot beverages	1.14	1.06	1.20	1.52
Alcoholic beverages	1.53	1.15	1.04	0.98
Other beverages	0.94	0.98	1.02	1.29
Other foods	0.56	1.09	1.15	1.16
Meals away from home	5.11	3.45	3.61	3.46
Housing	32.01	29.09	25.69	23.52
Principal dwelling	32.01	29.09	25.62	23.50
Other	n.a.	n.a.	n.a.	n.a.
Maintenance	0.00	0.00	0.08	0.02
Furnishings and operation	5.74	5.64	5.79	4.99
Durables	1.86	1.26	1.15	0.66
Nondurables	1.85	1.67	1.78	1.87
Services	2.02	2.70	2.83	2.43
Clothing	6.45	6.05	6.78	6.41
Men's	1.99	1.33	1.73	1.67
Women's	2.60	2.44	2.33	1.96
Children's	0.65	1.47	1.71	1.99
Other	1.22	0.81	1.01	0.79
Medical care	2.73	3.95	3.73	2.97
Education	1.04	2.74	4.76	3.40
Recreation and culture	2.63	3.33	3.42	2.60
Recreation	2.13	2.76	2.85	2.14
Reading and culture	0.50	0.57	0.57	0.46
Vehicle operation	3.43	4.39	3.29	1.59
Public transportation	3.54	3.01	2.97	4.38
Communication	0.67	0.83	0.65	0.49
Other consumption	4.23	3.79	3.81	4.83
Tobacco	1.68	1.43	1.43	1.88
Personal care	2.54	2.36	2.38	2.96
Ceremonies	0.00	0.00	0.00	0.00
Insurance	0.15	0.21	0.20	0.40
Gifts and transfers	1.46	0.92	0.93	0.57
Other nonconsumption	0.04	0.15	0.18	0.10

n.a. Not available.

Table C-30. *Individual Budget Structure by Family Size Class,*
Maracaibo

	Number of members			
Spending category	1–2	3–5	6–8	9 or more
Food and beverages	48.56	50.02	53.38	56.93
Dairy products and eggs	9.62	10.04	11.12	11.07
Cereals	7.35	6.53	7.45	9.17
Meat and poultry	9.73	11.23	10.73	11.10
Seafood	0.96	0.95	1.01	1.27
Vegetables and tubers	3.77	3.65	3.47	4.12
Fruits	3.43	3.50	3.78	4.74
Fats and oils	2.04	2.17	2.23	2.50
Sugar and sweets	1.62	1.93	1.70	1.84
Hot beverages	1.71	1.78	1.92	2.05
Alcoholic beverages	1.33	0.99	1.23	1.23
Other beverages	1.20	1.16	1.08	1.12
Other foods	0.81	1.37	1.52	1.34
Meals away from home	4.88	4.57	5.70	5.25
Housing	24.86	21.14	17.42	15.81
Principal dwelling	24.86	21.09	17.41	15.81
Other	n.a.	n.a.	n.a.	n.a.
Maintenance	0.00	0.04	0.01	0.00
Furnishings and operation	5.97	7.82	6.65	6.07
Durables	3.16	4.42	3.70	3.50
Nondurables	1.76	2.01	1.92	1.88
Services	1.05	1.39	0.94	0.69
Clothing	3.43	3.44	3.88	3.78
Men's	1.64	1.26	1.38	1.37
Women's	1.28	1.19	1.10	0.92
Children's	0.17	0.78	1.09	1.14
Other	0.34	0.20	0.31	0.35
Medical care	1.50	1.47	1.02	0.83
Education	0.71	1.63	1.57	1.73
Recreation and culture	2.15	3.14	3.23	2.47
Recreation	1.66	2.61	2.76	2.19
Reading and culture	0.49	0.53	0.47	0.28
Vehicle operation	1.72	1.73	1.38	1.26
Public transportation	4.36	3.56	4.04	4.14
Communication	0.24	0.23	0.10	0.11
Other consumption	4.87	4.65	5.22	5.56
Tobacco	1.61	1.32	1.49	1.65
Personal care	3.26	3.33	3.73	3.91
Ceremonies	0.01	0.00	0.01	0.00
Insurance	0.06	0.17	0.14	0.11
Gifts and transfers	0.58	0.32	0.30	0.23
Other nonconsumption	0.16	0.11	0.13	0.08

n.a. Not available.

Table C-31. *Individual Mean Expenditure Shares of Households Classified by Quartiles of Expenditure per Person, Bogotá*

	Quartile			
Spending category	First	Second	Third	Fourth
Food and beverages	57.14	52.05	44.90	34.37
Dairy products and eggs	6.50	6.64	6.54	5.21
Cereals	12.63	9.76	7.89	4.66
Meat and poultry	10.20	10.44	8.81	7.27
Seafood	0.03	0.11	0.18	0.34
Vegetables and tubers	10.89	8.66	6.82	4.16
Fruits	2.06	2.52	2.64	2.19
Fats and oils	3.04	2.57	1.87	1.13
Sugar and sweets	2.63	1.92	1.43	0.97
Hot beverages	3.76	2.61	1.97	1.19
Alcoholic beverages	0.30	0.38	0.44	0.71
Other beverages	0.14	0.20	0.26	0.24
Other foods	0.52	0.45	0.35	0.45
Meals away from home	4.43	5.81	5.70	5.85
Housing	22.73	24.49	27.97	27.11
Rent (paid, imputed)	22.47	24.19	26.72	25.94
Maintenance, repairs	0.26	0.19	1.24	1.05
Household goods and services	2.65	3.66	4.60	8.68
Durables	0.41	0.95	1.71	4.56
Nondurables	1.87	1.79	1.45	1.42
Services	0.37	0.91	1.44	2.70
Clothing	4.93	6.86	8.16	9.36
Men's	1.24	2.01	2.76	3.06
Women's	1.56	2.49	2.98	4.38
Children's	2.09	2.29	2.21	1.63
Other	0.05	0.08	0.21	0.28
Medical care	1.26	0.99	1.92	3.32
Education	4.57	4.76	5.04	5.13
Recreation and culture	1.06	1.33	1.74	3.17
Recreation	0.62	0.88	1.19	2.32
Reading and culture	0.43	0.46	0.55	0.84
Vehicle operation	0.00	0.00	0.35	1.32
Public transportation	3.07	2.76	2.14	2.09
Communication	0.08	0.23	0.32	0.78
Other consumption	2.21	2.27	1.94	2.20
Tobacco	0.23	0.38	0.19	0.27
Personal care	1.76	1.83	1.70	1.89
Ceremonies	0.22	0.06	0.05	0.04
Gifts and transfers	0.25	0.29	0.67	1.87
Other nonconsumption	0.05	0.15	0.09	0.27
Unspecified and rounding	0.00	0.16	0.16	0.33
Addenda:				
Upper limit of expenditure per person	708	1,125	1,945	24,750
Mean value of total expenditure	3,760	5,530	8,350	17,940

Table C-32. *Individual Mean Expenditure Shares of Households Classified by Quartiles of Expenditure per Person, Barranquilla*

Spending category	Quartile			
	First	Second	Third	Fourth
Food and beverages	67.68	62.93	57.03	42.48
Dairy products and eggs	7.47	7.29	7.05	5.56
Cereals	15.95	13.31	9.98	6.61
Meat and poultry	15.66	15.10	14.85	11.28
Seafood	1.55	1.23	1.22	0.81
Vegetables and tubers	7.57	7.02	5.73	4.59
Fruits	3.50	3.34	3.07	2.61
Fats and oils	3.39	2.94	2.46	1.90
Sugar and sweets	3.12	2.42	2.02	1.35
Hot beverages	1.78	1.48	1.10	0.79
Alcoholic beverages	0.94	1.44	1.46	0.97
Other beverages	0.61	0.76	0.73	0.56
Other foods	1.11	1.16	0.98	0.72
Meals away from home	5.02	5.43	6.39	4.72
Housing	14.77	15.14	16.04	21.42
Rent (paid, imputed)	14.33	14.44	14.90	20.31
Maintenance, repairs	0.44	0.70	1.14	1.00
Household goods and services	2.78	3.31	5.53	7.25
Durables	0.45	1.08	2.06	2.93
Nondurables	2.25	2.05	2.28	1.59
Services	0.08	0.18	1.18	2.73
Clothing	3.83	5.39	6.94	7.52
Men's	0.91	1.72	2.54	2.36
Women's	1.62	2.03	2.44	3.23
Children's	1.14	1.51	1.64	1.50
Other	0.16	0.12	0.31	0.43
Medical care	1.38	1.75	2.49	3.99
Education	2.60	3.57	2.71	4.97
Recreation and culture	1.09	1.50	1.94	2.43
Recreation	0.72	0.95	1.17	1.52
Reading and culture	0.37	0.56	0.77	0.91
Vehicle operation	0.01	0.00	0.24	2.48
Public transportation	2.63	2.16	2.17	1.56
Communication	0.03	0.12	0.24	0.74
Other consumption	3.16	3.75	3.75	3.16
Tobacco	0.94	0.84	0.78	0.50
Personal care	2.16	2.69	2.63	2.24
Ceremonies	0.06	0.22	0.33	0.42
Gifts and transfers	0.03	0.32	0.79	1.56
Other nonconsumption	0.01	0.06	0.11	0.27
Unspecified and rounding	0.00	0.00	0.02	0.17
Addenda:				
Upper limit of expenditure per person	630	946	1,523	15,770
Mean value of total expenditure	3,940	5,080	6,930	13,890

Table C-33. *Individual Mean Expenditure Shares of Households Classified by Quartiles of Expenditure per Person, Cali*

	Quartile			
Spending category	*First*	*Second*	*Third*	*Fourth*
Food and beverages	67.37	63.90	54.75	42.02
Dairy products and eggs	5.55	7.37	7.89	6.93
Cereals	12.60	10.71	8.19	5.43
Meat and poultry	16.97	17.10	14.41	10.98
Seafood	0.10	0.21	0.24	0.37
Vegetables and tubers	11.61	9.36	7.49	4.57
Fruits	4.48	3.34	3.16	2.65
Fats and oils	4.72	3.26	2.78	1.73
Sugar and sweets	4.43	3.40	2.36	1.51
Hot beverages	3.41	2.94	2.13	1.35
Alcoholic beverages	0.28	0.12	0.56	0.66
Other beverages	0.06	0.10	0.30	0.35
Other foods	0.78	0.63	0.51	0.44
Meals away from home	2.38	5.36	4.71	5.04
Housing	14.42	15.59	19.06	22.59
Rent (paid, imputed)	14.28	15.38	18.49	21.48
Maintenance, repairs	0.14	0.20	0.57	1.00
Household goods and services	2.83	2.87	4.39	8.96
Durables	0.54	0.47	1.21	4.32
Nondurables	2.22	1.93	1.84	1.35
Services	0.08	0.47	1.35	3.29
Clothing	4.22	6.11	7.03	8.24
Men's	1.12	2.24	2.50	2.99
Women's	1.58	2.09	2.75	3.78
Children's	1.42	1.73	1.59	1.01
Other	0.10	0.05	0.20	0.45
Medical care	0.55	0.96	1.67	2.15
Education	1.88	2.24	3.04	2.78
Recreation and culture	1.02	1.52	2.38	2.68
Recreation	0.56	0.96	1.53	1.81
Reading and culture	0.46	0.56	0.86	0.88
Vehicle operation	0.00	0.04	0.12	1.25
Public transportation	2.73	1.80	1.95	1.50
Communication	0.00	0.06	0.31	0.96
Other consumption	2.79	2.88	3.05	2.61
Tobacco	0.63	0.45	0.74	0.51
Personal care	2.16	2.38	2.24	1.91
Ceremonies	0.00	0.05	0.08	0.19
Gifts and transfers	0.50	0.22	0.57	2.21
Other nonconsumption	0.01	0.11	0.08	0.29
Unspecified and rounding	1.68	1.70	1.60	1.76
Addenda:				
Upper limit of expenditure per person	550	932	1,621	14,690
Mean value of total expenditure	2,850	4,390	6,390	13,820

Table C-34. *Individual Mean Expenditure Shares of Households Classified by Quartiles of Expenditure per Person, Medellín*

	Quartile			
Spending category	*First*	*Second*	*Third*	*Fourth*
Food and beverages	62.52	55.06	53.70	40.02
Dairy products and eggs	6.70	8.22	8.63	7.23
Cereals	11.12	8.70	8.45	5.30
Meat and poultry	14.68	13.75	13.56	10.25
Seafood	0.00	0.03	0.03	0.23
Vegetables and tubers	10.82	7.96	7.16	4.68
Fruits	1.60	1.74	1.90	1.79
Fats and oils	2.91	2.42	2.32	1.48
Sugar and sweets	6.39	4.26	3.41	1.80
Hot beverages	4.02	3.22	2.61	1.49
Alcoholic beverages	0.23	0.20	0.29	0.47
Other beverages	0.01	0.05	0.12	0.38
Other foods	0.44	0.41	0.41	0.47
Meals away from home	3.61	4.11	4.79	4.45
Housing	19.91	21.67	21.98	27.67
Rent (paid, imputed)	19.59	21.38	21.64	26.34
Maintenance, repairs	0.12	0.26	0.29	0.62
Household goods and services	2.22	2.51	3.48	5.88
Durables	0.49	0.62	0.94	2.14
Nondurables	1.63	1.52	1.27	1.09
Services	0.10	0.37	1.26	2.65
Clothing	2.70	4.30	4.45	5.98
Men's	0.49	1.11	1.16	1.70
Women's	0.86	1.64	2.03	2.84
Children's	1.00	1.29	0.82	1.07
Other	0.35	0.26	0.43	0.37
Medical care	0.70	1.54	1.59	3.19
Education	2.67	3.51	3.31	3.63
Recreation and culture	0.71	1.15	1.84	2.27
Recreation	0.59	0.77	1.24	1.51
Reading and culture	0.12	0.38	0.59	0.76
Vehicle operation	0.53	0.07	0.02	1.29
Public transportation	1.97	2.07	1.68	1.31
Communication	0.05	0.11	0.10	0.14
Other consumption	2.25	2.54	2.34	2.37
Tobacco	0.98	0.94	0.69	0.65
Personal care	1.26	1.60	1.48	1.38
Ceremonies	0.00	0.00	0.17	0.34
Gifts and transfers	0.14	0.54	1.14	1.71
Other nonconsumption	0.05	0.25	0.32	0.24
Unspecified and rounding	3.58	4.68	4.05	4.30
Addenda:				
Upper limit of expenditure per person	460	767	1,439	21,410
Mean value of total expenditure	2,980	4,310	5,460	13,200

Table C-35. *Individual Mean Expenditure Shares of Households Classified by Quartiles of Expenditure per Person, Santiago*

	Quartile			
Spending category	*First*	*Second*	*Third*	*Fourth*
Food and beverages	52.18	44.46	38.98	27.33
Dairy products and eggs	4.47	4.98	4.44	3.08
Cereals	14.11	9.46	6.41	3.39
Meat and poultry	8.19	8.59	8.92	6.69
Seafood	1.33	1.02	0.88	0.76
Vegetables and tubers	9.30	6.80	5.51	3.19
Fruits	2.20	2.51	2.36	2.02
Fats and oils	2.85	2.27	1.77	1.08
Sugar and sweets	3.52	2.41	1.74	1.14
Hot beverages	1.93	1.55	1.22	0.91
Alcoholic beverages	0.96	0.97	0.78	0.87
Other beverages	0.60	0.70	0.77	0.58
Other foods	1.11	0.86	0.75	0.64
Meals away from home	1.61	2.33	3.43	2.98
Housing	23.12	26.30	26.54	29.28
Rent (paid, imputed)	22.72	25.57	25.79	28.31
Maintenance, repairs	0.41	0.73	0.75	0.97
Household goods and services	2.85	4.48	7.55	12.85
Durables	1.01	2.61	5.11	6.96
Nondurables	1.72	1.45	1.31	1.17
Services	0.12	0.43	1.13	4.72
Clothing	9.73	11.46	13.00	12.51
Men's	4.77	5.54	6.50	5.88
Women's	3.37	4.29	4.78	5.10
Children's	0.41	0.40	0.17	0.18
Other	1.18	1.23	1.55	1.35
Medical care	0.89	1.22	1.26	1.86
Education	0.34	0.61	0.77	1.20
Recreation and culture	2.30	2.67	3.13	4.15
Recreation	1.13	1.44	1.88	2.78
Reading and culture	1.17	1.23	1.26	1.37
Vehicle operation	0.02	0.14	0.36	2.23
Public transportation	3.97	3.30	2.91	2.09
Communication	0.09	0.23	0.32	1.08
Other consumption	4.18	4.69	4.60	4.13
Tobacco	2.16	1.93	1.64	1.28
Personal care	1.93	2.50	2.63	2.35
Ceremonies	0.10	0.26	0.33	0.51
Gifts and transfers	0.09	0.11	0.20	0.80
Other nonconsumption	0.16	0.25	0.31	0.44
Unspecified and rounding	0.08	0.08	0.07	0.05
Addenda:				
Upper limit of expenditure per person	576	990	1,760	36,944
Mean value of total expenditure	2,354	3,630	4,990	10,162

Table C-36. *Individual Mean Expenditure Shares of Households Classified by Quartiles of Expenditure per Person, Quito*

	Quartile			
Spending category	First	Second	Third	Fourth
Food and beverages	59.72	50.64	41.67	30.45
Dairy products and eggs	5.82	6.08	6.58	5.22
Cereals	17.34	11.42	7.92	4.41
Meat and poultry	6.74	7.89	6.63	5.45
Seafood	0.54	0.71	0.59	0.54
Vegetables and tubers	9.72	6.87	4.55	2.90
Fruits	2.56	2.46	2.05	1.95
Fats and oils	3.81	2.78	2.01	1.29
Sugar and sweets	4.31	2.75	2.11	1.45
Hot beverages	1.84	1.62	1.27	0.74
Alcoholic beverages	0.32	0.30	0.51	0.55
Other beverages	0.15	0.49	0.61	0.62
Other foods	0.56	0.54	0.47	0.67
Meals away from home	5.92	6.10	5.88	4.47
Housing	19.19	20.96	28.24	35.62
Rent (paid, imputed)	19.04	20.07	25.79	31.86
Maintenance, repairs	0.15	0.34	0.76	0.55
Household goods and services	4.23	4.97	5.15	7.97
Durables	1.65	2.74	2.52	4.43
Nondurables	2.39	1.80	1.38	1.15
Services	0.19	0.44	1.25	2.39
Clothing	8.87	11.38	11.08	9.51
Men's	3.75	4.77	4.88	3.79
Women's	3.99	5.00	5.07	4.93
Children's	0.44	0.26	0.11	0.11
Other	0.69	1.34	1.02	0.68
Medical care	2.35	3.47	3.03	2.91
Education	0.95	1.28	1.62	1.75
Recreation and culture	0.53	1.39	2.09	2.28
Recreation	0.27	0.84	1.62	1.60
Reading and culture	0.27	0.55	0.47	0.68
Vehicle operation	0.00	0.00	0.17	0.82
Public transportation	0.05	0.05	0.05	0.05
Communication	0.07	0.25	0.55	0.91
Other consumption	2.26	3.06	3.11	3.52
Tobacco	0.49	0.84	0.72	0.65
Personal care	1.74	2.08	2.20	1.99
Ceremonies	0.02	0.13	0.19	0.88
Gifts and transfers	1.14	1.69	2.12	2.87
Other nonconsumption	0.60	0.48	0.63	0.63
Unspecified and rounding	0.04	0.38	0.49	0.71
Addenda:				
Upper limit of expenditure per person	671	1,197	2,398	57,038
Mean value of total expenditure	2,934	4,996	8,380	19,978

Table C-37. *Individual Mean Expenditure Shares of Households Classified by Quartiles of Expenditure per Person, Guayaquil*

	Quartile			
Spending category	*First*	*Second*	*Third*	*Fourth*
Food and beverages	68.53	59.05	50.66	34.81
Dairy products and eggs	6.09	7.28	7.31	5.23
Cereals	20.00	13.92	8.86	4.53
Meat and poultry	12.34	12.28	10.89	7.90
Seafood	3.52	2.31	1.59	1.09
Vegetables and tubers	9.12	7.35	5.23	3.20
Fruits	2.81	2.46	2.10	1.88
Fats and oils	4.83	3.43	2.59	1.47
Sugar and sweets	3.79	2.91	2.54	1.99
Hot beverages	2.36	1.58	1.26	0.73
Alcoholic beverages	0.22	0.45	0.59	0.74
Other beverages	0.65	1.05	1.30	0.94
Other foods	0.66	0.44	0.61	0.57
Meals away from home	2.13	3.33	5.69	4.45
Housing	16.00	18.16	21.07	31.95
Rent (paid, imputed)	15.86	17.83	20.28	29.26
Maintenance, repairs	0.14	0.33	0.63	0.83
Household goods and				
services	3.61	3.38	6.33	8.96
Durables	1.28	1.24	2.79	4.86
Nondurables	2.25	1.73	1.40	0.93
Services	0.08	0.41	2.14	3.18
Clothing	4.01	6.99	7.60	7.43
Men's	1.62	3.17	3.56	3.23
Women's	1.74	2.88	3.05	3.35
Children's	0.22	0.17	0.21	0.15
Other	0.43	0.76	0.79	0.70
Medical care	1.36	2.19	1.84	2.60
Education	1.07	1.76	2.10	2.23
Recreation and culture	1.10	1.66	2.04	2.15
Recreation	0.61	0.84	1.11	1.48
Reading and culture	0.49	0.82	0.93	0.67
Vehicle operation	0.00	0.22	0.29	0.73
Public transportation	0.00	0.00	0.01	0.00
Communication	0.01	0.04	0.22	0.55
Other consumption	3.26	3.19	3.46	3.17
Tobacco	0.47	0.77	0.76	0.70
Personal care	2.79	2.43	2.69	2.23
Ceremonies	0.00	0.00	0.01	0.25
Gifts and transfers	0.90	2.64	3.83	4.57
Other nonconsumption	0.12	0.30	0.10	0.24
Unspecified and rounding	0.03	0.42	0.45	0.61
Addenda:				
Upper limit of expenditure				
per person	620	1,099	2,074	27,834
Mean value of total				
expenditure	3,051	5,215	7,761	19,260

Table C-38. *Individual Mean Expenditure Shares of Households Classified by Quartiles of Expenditure per Person, Lima*

	Quartile			
Spending category	First	Second	Third	Fourth
Food and beverages	57.63	49.39	39.64	27.26
Dairy products and eggs	7.79	6.43	5.86	3.97
Cereals	12.52	8.92	6.17	3.53
Meat and poultry	13.45	13.20	10.54	6.90
Seafood	1.93	1.60	1.40	0.87
Vegetables and tubers	9.21	6.81	5.02	2.67
Fruits	2.03	2.32	2.76	2.24
Fats and oils	1.97	1.76	1.21	0.65
Sugar and sweets	1.98	1.57	1.10	0.75
Hot beverages	0.86	0.83	0.56	0.42
Alcoholic beverages	0.29	0.32	0.50	0.34
Other beverages	0.12	0.19	0.10	0.08
Other foods	1.67	1.39	0.94	0.75
Meals away from home	3.82	4.06	3.47	3.95
Housing	14.73	18.36	20.77	26.11
Rent (paid, imputed)	14.15	16.85	18.86	22.44
Maintenance, repairs	0.54	1.44	1.62	2.17
Household goods and services	5.54	6.38	11.34	14.48
Durables	2.64	3.54	7.37	9.75
Nondurables	2.46	1.96	1.82	1.32
Services	0.44	0.88	2.15	3.41
Clothing	5.84	8.37	8.39	8.85
Men's	2.37	3.85	3.72	3.98
Women's	2.76	3.43	3.21	3.57
Children's	0.23	0.31	0.38	0.35
Other	0.49	0.77	1.07	0.96
Medical care	1.98	1.66	2.20	2.64
Education	1.13	1.34	1.84	2.45
Recreation and culture	2.01	2.47	2.65	3.29
Recreation	0.84	1.04	1.52	2.17
Reading and culture	1.16	1.43	1.13	1.12
Vehicle operation	0.39	1.69	2.53	2.99
Public transportation	3.99	3.16	2.75	2.35
Communication	0.10	0.14	0.37	0.48
Other consumption	4.36	4.21	4.79	4.23
Tobacco	0.59	0.74	0.64	0.74
Personal care	3.53	3.42	3.56	2.94
Ceremonies	0.24	0.05	0.59	0.54
Gifts and transfers	0.34	0.29	0.36	0.78
Other nonconsumption	0.20	0.73	0.59	0.68
Unspecified and rounding	1.76	1.81	1.78	3.41
Addenda:				
Upper limit of expenditure per person	2,147	3,434	5,987	146,705
Mean value of total expenditure	11,800	17,850	25,990	60,740

Table C-39. *Individual Mean Expenditure Shares of Households
Classified by Quartiles of Expenditure per Person, Caracas*

	Quartile			
Spending category	*First*	*Second*	*Third*	*Fourth*
Food and beverages	50.44	37.92	31.03	22.80
Dairy products and eggs	7.82	6.49	4.90	3.32
Cereals	7.61	4.22	2.86	1.86
Meat and poultry	9.54	8.88	7.41	4.98
Seafood	1.44	0.95	0.81	0.56
Vegetables and tubers	6.26	4.21	3.20	2.07
Fruits	2.73	2.29	2.03	1.68
Fats and oils	2.65	1.73	1.17	0.79
Sugar and sweets	1.89	1.29	0.97	0.75
Hot beverages	1.99	1.26	0.87	0.53
Alcoholic beverages	1.06	1.11	1.22	1.16
Other beverages	1.50	1.09	0.90	0.60
Other foods	1.51	1.08	1.03	0.64
Meals away from home	4.47	3.30	3.58	3.31
Housing	23.72	29.41	29.76	27.95
Rent (paid, imputed)	23.71	29.41	29.67	27.93
Maintenance, repairs	0.01	0.00	0.09	0.01
Household goods and services	3.99	4.44	5.73	8.33
Durables	0.29	0.93	1.06	2.60
Nondurables	2.12	1.79	1.62	1.44
Services	1.57	1.72	3.04	4.23
Clothing	5.37	6.12	6.53	7.40
Men's	1.35	1.71	1.17	2.00
Women's	1.72	2.01	2.75	2.99
Children's	1.78	1.55	1.50	1.26
Other	0.52	0.86	1.10	1.17
Medical care	1.45	2.93	3.90	6.32
Education	1.43	3.81	3.77	4.06
Recreation and culture	2.29	2.75	3.70	4.08
Recreation	1.89	2.22	3.09	3.41
Reading and culture	0.40	0.53	0.61	0.67
Vehicle operation	0.80	2.17	5.00	6.59
Public transportation	4.38	4.02	2.68	1.74
Communication	0.18	0.69	0.95	1.05
Other consumption	4.85	4.14	3.77	3.07
Tobacco	1.98	1.58	1.41	1.04
Personal care	2.87	2.56	2.36	2.03
Ceremonies	0.00	0.00	0.00	0.00
Gifts and transfers	0.34	0.63	0.93	1.85
Other nonconsumption	0.07	0.14	0.18	0.18
Unspecified and rounding	0.69	0.83	2.07	4.58
Addenda:				
Upper limit of expenditure per person	558	1,029	1,667	10,886
Mean value of total expenditure	2,476	4,069	6,050	11,951

Table C-40. *Individual Mean Expenditure Shares of Households Classified by Quartiles of Expenditure per Person, Maracaibo*

	Quartile			
Spending category	First	Second	Third	Fourth
Food and beverages	58.16	57.88	53.83	39.59
Dairy products and eggs	12.39	11.06	10.88	7.97
Cereals	10.82	8.34	6.36	4.19
Meat and poultry	9.91	11.67	12.52	9.48
Seafood	1.18	1.30	1.06	0.59
Vegetables and tubers	4.09	4.11	3.80	2.76
Fruits	4.69	4.24	3.69	2.68
Fats and oils	2.46	2.46	2.45	1.59
Sugar and sweets	2.25	1.97	1.72	1.28
Hot beverages	2.32	2.05	1.86	1.26
Alcoholic beverages	0.66	1.31	1.27	1.35
Other beverages	1.08	1.42	1.25	0.77
Other foods	1.61	1.50	1.25	1.11
Meals away from home	4.69	6.35	5.31	4.15
Housing	19.30	17.54	18.30	21.52
Rent (paid, imputed)	19.30	17.54	18.30	21.44
Maintenance, repairs	0.00	0.00	0.00	0.08
Household goods and services	4.44	5.46	6.73	10.91
Durables	2.26	3.06	4.07	6.14
Nondurables	2.05	2.01	1.91	1.75
Services	0.12	0.39	0.75	3.01
Clothing	2.49	3.42	4.24	4.49
Men's	0.81	1.10	1.64	1.88
Women's	0.57	0.90	1.43	1.55
Children's	0.83	1.09	0.90	0.79
Other	0.28	0.33	0.26	0.24
Medical care	0.68	0.85	1.02	2.24
Education	0.75	1.03	1.47	2.94
Recreation and culture	1.99	2.88	2.98	3.99
Recreation	1.82	2.52	2.52	3.14
Reading and culture	0.17	0.36	0.46	0.85
Vehicle operation	0.44	0.75	1.26	3.63
Public transportation	4.79	4.34	4.22	2.28
Communication	0.05	0.01	0.16	0.43
Other consumption	6.34	5.40	4.76	3.68
Tobacco	1.61	1.68	1.50	1.07
Personal care	4.72	3.72	3.26	2.60
Ceremonies	0.01	0.00	0.00	0.00
Gifts and transfers	0.13	0.14	0.28	0.72
Other nonconsumption	0.06	0.09	0.17	0.15
Unspecified and rounding	0.38	0.21	0.58	3.43
Addenda:				
Upper limit of expenditure per person	291	442	734	5,415
Mean value of total expenditure	1,709	2,380	3,008	5,320

Table C-41. Coefficients of Sociodemographic Variables Included in All Expenditure Functions, Colombia

Spending category	City			Trimester			Age of head			Tenure		Spouse employed
	Barranquilla	Cali	Medellin	1	2	3	35–49	50–64	Over 64	Rented	Other	
Food and beverages	0.163	0.117	0.011	0.065	0.078	0.075	−0.004	−0.019	−0.047	0.040	0.179	0.039
	(0.012)	(0.012)	(0.012)	(0.012)	(0.013)	(0.013)	(0.011)	(0.013)	(0.020)	(0.009)	(0.021)	(0.015)
Dairy products and eggs	0.127	0.141	0.241	−0.129	0.013	0.001	−0.059	−0.119	−0.035	0.093	0.176	0.050
	(0.030)	(0.031)	(0.030)	(0.029)	(0.032)	(0.032)	(0.027)	(0.032)	(0.050)	(0.023)	(0.054)	(0.037)
Cereals	0.206	−0.044	−0.191	−0.026	0.002	0.041	0.059	0.055	−0.017	−0.014	0.094	−0.006
	(0.020)	(0.021)	(0.020)	(0.020)	(0.022)	(0.021)	(0.018)	(0.021)	(0.034)	(0.015)	(0.036)	(0.025)
Meat and poultry	0.475	0.439	0.309	0.043	0.180	0.119	0.041	0.059	0.150	0.063	0.213	−0.010
	(0.028)	(0.029)	(0.028)	(0.028)	(0.030)	(0.030)	(0.025)	(0.030)	(0.047)	(0.022)	(0.051)	(0.035)
Seafood	0.378	0.228	0.229	0.124	0.086	0.220	0.052	0.065	0.086	0.026	0.108	0.008
	(0.071)	(0.083)	(0.092)	(0.060)	(0.076)	(0.072)	(0.062)	(0.072)	(0.114)	(0.052)	(0.128)	(0.079)
Vegetables	−0.190	−0.041	−0.118	−0.015	−0.013	0.045	0.009	0.014	−0.010	−0.009	0.098	0.007
	(0.023)	(0.024)	(0.023)	(0.023)	(0.025)	(0.024)	(0.020)	(0.024)	(0.039)	(0.018)	(0.042)	(0.029)
Fruits	0.152	0.245	−0.236	0.068	0.051	0.081	0.008	−0.044	0.010	0.048	0.114	0.052
	(0.033)	(0.035)	(0.034)	(0.033)	(0.037)	(0.036)	(0.030)	(0.036)	(0.057)	(0.026)	(0.061)	(0.042)
Fats and oils	0.172	0.173	−0.082	0.051	−0.027	−0.019	0.044	0.048	0.025	−0.023	0.043	−0.006
	(0.026)	(0.028)	(0.026)	(0.026)	(0.029)	(0.028)	(0.024)	(0.028)	(0.045)	(0.020)	(0.048)	(0.033)
Sugar and sweets	0.143	0.375	0.513	−0.012	−0.002	0.059	0.010	−0.011	0.030	0.010	0.080	0.019
	(0.027)	(0.028)	(0.026)	(0.026)	(0.029)	(0.028)	(0.024)	(0.028)	(0.045)	(0.021)	(0.048)	(0.034)
Hot beverages	−0.599	−0.100	−0.059	−0.049	−0.104	−0.010	0.055	0.152	0.081	−0.013	−0.003	−0.034
	(0.028)	(0.029)	(0.027)	(0.027)	(0.030)	(0.029)	(0.025)	(0.029)	(0.047)	(0.021)	(0.050)	(0.035)
Alcoholic beverages	0.100	0.101	−0.138	−0.091	0.043	0.069	−0.029	−0.093	−0.455	0.091	0.251	−0.060
	(0.080)	(0.096)	(0.091)	(0.078)	(0.091)	(0.088)	(0.071)	(0.092)	(0.165)	(0.063)	(0.164)	(0.094)
Other beverages	0.360	0.354	0.338	0.140	0.124	0.104	0.144	0.192	0.240	0.166	0.240	−0.068
	(0.052)	(0.063)	(0.063)	(0.056)	(0.066)	(0.062)	(0.049)	(0.058)	(0.092)	(0.042)	(0.093)	(0.065)
Other foods	0.581	0.084	−0.009	0.128	−0.029	0.108	−0.055	−0.088	0.221	0.040	0.156	0.029
	(0.043)	(0.046)	(0.045)	(0.043)	(0.048)	(0.047)	(0.039)	(0.047)	(0.075)	(0.034)	(0.081)	(0.055)
Meals away from home	−0.083	−0.146	−0.191	0.357	0.216	0.236	−0.076	−0.130	−0.394	0.053	0.368	0.204
	(0.049)	(0.053)	(0.051)	(0.051)	(0.057)	(0.057)	(0.044)	(0.055)	(0.093)	(0.039)	(0.091)	(0.062)
Housing	−0.299	−0.302	−0.090	−0.049	0.043	0.034	0.023	0.092	0.236	−0.111	−1.758	−0.189
	(0.026)	(0.027)	(0.029)	(0.024)	(0.027)	(0.026)	(0.022)	(0.026)	(0.042)	(0.020)	(0.051)	(0.031)
Principal dwelling	−0.313	−0.297	−0.112	−0.066	0.042	0.027	−0.00002	0.111	0.295	−0.058	−1.828	−0.213
	(0.027)	(0.027)	(0.029)	(0.025)	(0.027)	(0.027)	(0.022)	(0.027)	(0.042)	(0.020)	(0.052)	(0.031)

Table C-41 (continued)

Spending category	City			Trimester			Age of head			Tenure		Spouse employed
	Barranquilla	Cali	Medellin	1	2	3	35–49	50–64	Over 64	Rented	Other	
Other	-1.025	-0.105	0.116	-0.208	-0.417	-0.231	-0.042	0.231	0.199	-0.006	-1.684	-0.138
	(0.420)	(0.560)	(0.448)	(0.536)	(0.591)	(0.540)	(0.436)	(0.474)	(0.568)	(0.389)	(0.648)	(0.535)
Maintenance	-0.162	-0.308	-0.230	0.116	-0.162	0.662	-0.155	-0.316	-0.507	-0.896	-0.072	0.254
	(0.238)	(0.248)	(0.260)	(0.231)	(0.273)	(0.293)	(0.229)	(0.269)	(0.354)	(0.216)	(0.502)	(0.273)
Furnishings and opera-tion	0.158	0.125	-0.035	0.101	0.105	0.099	-0.150	-0.258	-0.251	0.190	0.417	0.136
	(0.043)	(0.044)	(0.047)	(0.041)	(0.046)	(0.045)	(0.038)	(0.045)	(0.071)	(0.033)	(0.076)	(0.053)
Durables	-0.065	0.067	0.327	-0.267	-0.218	-0.277	-0.278	-0.483	-0.888	0.090	0.290	0.118
	(0.122)	(0.133)	(0.149)	(0.123)	(0.144)	(0.142)	(0.107)	(0.136)	(0.233)	(0.095)	(0.254)	(0.148)
Nondurables	0.176	-0.001	-0.193	0.062	0.029	0.066	-0.044	-0.083	-0.173	0.050	0.291	0.048
	(0.035)	(0.036)	(0.038)	(0.034)	(0.037)	(0.037)	(0.030)	(0.037)	(0.058)	(0.027)	(0.062)	(0.043)
Services	0.403	0.288	0.271	-0.116	0.053	0.043	-0.045	0.053	0.210	0.210	0.525	0.186
	(0.065)	(0.062)	(0.071)	(0.062)	(0.069)	(0.069)	(0.056)	(0.067)	(0.100)	(0.047)	(0.140)	(0.074)
Clothing	-0.117	0.012	-0.174	-0.530	-0.668	-0.659	-0.171	-0.323	-0.569	0.055	0.383	0.113
	(0.047)	(0.050)	(0.047)	(0.046)	(0.052)	(0.051)	(0.042)	(0.053)	(0.087)	(0.037)	(0.087)	(0.059)
Men's	-0.031	0.066	-0.204	-0.489	-0.520	-0.454	-0.186	-0.193	-0.028	0.069	0.232	-0.008
	(0.062)	(0.064)	(0.066)	(0.059)	(0.068)	(0.068)	(0.055)	(0.070)	(0.121)	(0.049)	(0.115)	(0.075)
Women's	-0.022	0.169	-0.079	-0.394	-0.503	-0.430	-0.177	-0.112	-0.362	0.100	0.289	0.060
	(0.055)	(0.058)	(0.055)	(0.053)	(0.060)	(0.059)	(0.049)	(0.061)	(0.097)	(0.043)	(0.102)	(0.067)
Children's	-0.267	-0.189	-0.186	-0.381	-0.658	-0.621	0.102	0.053	-0.008	0.096	0.307	0.040
	(0.055)	(0.060)	(0.058)	(0.054)	(0.064)	(0.063)	(0.049)	(0.061)	(0.159)	(0.044)	(0.105)	(0.067)
Other	-0.107	0.047	0.213	0.303	-0.060	-0.179	-0.055	-0.105	-0.175	0.099	0.067	0.168
	(0.179)	(0.192)	(0.180)	(0.160)	(0.185)	(0.173)	(0.155)	(0.178)	(0.298)	(0.128)	(0.354)	(0.197)
Medical care	0.055	0.087	0.120	-0.002	0.050	0.102	-0.224	-0.097	0.002	0.091	0.494	-0.050
	(0.078)	(0.093)	(0.081)	(0.081)	(0.090)	(0.091)	(0.072)	(0.088)	(0.130)	(0.063)	(0.147)	(0.102)
Education	-0.189	-0.335	-0.188	-0.028	-0.414	-0.385	0.236	0.247	0.328	0.065	0.356	-0.024
	(0.059)	(0.067)	(0.062)	(0.060)	(0.069)	(0.067)	(0.062)	(0.074)	(0.137)	(0.048)	(0.128)	(0.077)
Recreation and culture	0.183	0.234	0.139	0.175	0.128	0.017	-0.138	-0.125	-0.411	0.163	0.267	0.142
	(0.051)	(0.054)	(0.053)	(0.051)	(0.057)	(0.056)	(0.046)	(0.057)	(0.092)	(0.040)	(0.098)	(0.064)
Recreation	-0.168	-0.027	-0.090	0.071	0.093	-0.032	-0.182	-0.217	-0.324	0.107	0.223	0.007
	(0.061)	(0.064)	(0.063)	(0.060)	(0.067)	(0.067)	(0.054)	(0.066)	(0.112)	(0.047)	(0.117)	(0.073)
Reading and culture	0.423	0.410	0.345	0.192	0.054	0.074	0.064	0.155	-0.044	0.160	0.268	0.095
	(0.046)	(0.049)	(0.049)	(0.048)	(0.053)	(0.052)	(0.046)	(0.054)	(0.088)	(0.037)	(0.095)	(0.059)

336

Transportation and communication	-0.102 (0.045)	-0.011 (0.048)	-0.393 (0.047)	-0.017 (0.045)	0.100 (0.050)	0.038 (0.049)	0.011 (0.041)	-0.013 (0.049)	-0.100 (0.078)	0.069 (0.035)	0.235 (0.084)	0.185 (0.056)
Private transportation	0.102 (0.134)	0.086 (0.162)	-0.285 (0.140)	-0.164 (0.133)	0.104 (0.152)	0.076 (0.147)	-0.070 (0.135)	0.061 (0.150)	0.071 (0.206)	0.175 (0.108)	0.555 (0.379)	0.029 (0.172)
Public transportation	-0.123 (0.049)	-0.063 (0.053)	-0.255 (0.050)	-0.042 (0.050)	0.063 (0.054)	0.027 (0.054)	-0.020 (0.045)	-0.072 (0.054)	-0.174 (0.088)	0.034 (0.039)	0.180 (0.090)	0.266 (0.061)
Communication	0.024 (0.069)	0.236 (0.074)	-0.364 (0.096)	-0.039 (0.075)	0.099 (0.085)	0.103 (0.083)	-0.007 (0.071)	0.178 (0.080)	0.241 (0.121)	0.286 (0.057)	0.320 (0.152)	0.183 (0.093)
Other consumption	0.398 (0.034)	0.219 (0.036)	0.070 (0.034)	0.055 (0.034)	0.045 (0.037)	0.007 (0.037)	-0.056 (0.031)	-0.122 (0.038)	-0.227 (0.060)	0.091 (0.027)	0.124 (0.062)	0.048 (0.043)
Tobacco	-0.022 (0.077)	0.155 (0.085)	0.158 (0.078)	0.005 (0.069)	-0.134 (0.080)	-0.034 (0.077)	-0.083 (0.063)	0.011 (0.078)	-0.002 (0.111)	0.141 (0.054)	0.188 (0.131)	-0.060 (0.089)
Personal care	0.253 (0.031)	0.139 (0.033)	-0.163 (0.031)	0.006 (0.031)	-0.010 (0.034)	0.033 (0.034)	-0.069 (0.028)	-0.144 (0.034)	-0.287 (0.053)	0.095 (0.024)	0.187 (0.057)	0.038 (0.040)
Ceremonies	0.917 (0.748)	1.057 (0.890)	-1.177 (0.720)	0.343 (0.684)	0.437 (0.672)	-1.047 (0.806)	0.074 (0.617)	0.063 (0.677)	-0.299 (0.883)	-0.226 (0.589)	-2.284 (1.626)	0.004 (0.863)
Taxes	0.408 (0.217)	0.520 (0.183)	0.354 (0.143)	-0.045 (0.162)	0.001 (0.209)	0.219 (0.211)	0.184 (0.163)	0.509 (0.175)	0.811 (0.239)	-0.204 (0.138)	1.111 (0.561)	0.022 (0.226)
Insurance	0.141 (0.139)	0.068 (0.067)	0.195 (0.063)	0.245 (0.072)	0.170 (0.081)	0.217 (0.082)	-0.084 (0.059)	-0.096 (0.080)	-0.334 (0.171)	0.171 (0.055)	0.205 (0.138)	-0.010 (0.104)
Social security	0.099 (0.166)	0.033 (0.060)	0.116 (0.063)	0.164 (0.072)	0.092 (0.073)	0.120 (0.072)	-0.081 (0.052)	-0.161 (0.073)	-0.225 (0.164)	0.191 (0.049)	0.236 (0.122)	0.035 (0.093)
Private insurance	-0.644 (0.439)	0.175 (0.461)	-0.089 (0.369)	-0.450 (0.797)	-0.684 (0.815)	-0.771 (0.808)	0.013 (0.355)	0.152 (0.406)	-0.584 (0.666)	-0.097 (0.309)	-0.056 (1.455)	0.100 (0.683)
Gifts and transfers	-0.185 (0.119)	0.172 (0.125)	-0.007 (0.116)	-0.474 (0.101)	-0.303 (0.129)	-0.443 (0.124)	-0.022 (0.103)	0.022 (0.124)	0.087 (0.175)	0.025 (0.088)	0.454 (0.236)	0.184 (0.140)
Other nonconsumption	-0.113 (0.206)	-0.046 (0.189)	0.245 (0.178)	-0.392 (0.202)	-0.100 (0.240)	-0.076 (0.237)	0.047 (0.155)	0.159 (0.228)	-0.008 (0.424)	0.231 (0.146)	0.456 (0.456)	-0.623 (0.204)

Table C-42. Coefficients of Sociodemographic Variables Included in All Expenditure Functions, Chile

Spending category	Trimester			Age of head			Tenure		Spouse employed
	1	2	3	35–49	50–64	Over 64	Rented	Other	
Food and beverages	-0.089	-0.025	-0.003	0.067	0.041	0.018	-0.064	0.002	-0.083
	(0.021)	(0.021)	(0.021)	(0.020)	(0.021)	(0.028)	(0.016)	(0.033)	(0.022)
Dairy products and eggs	-0.093	-0.066	-0.020	0.053	-0.011	0.072	0.026	0.075	-0.066
	(0.036)	(0.037)	(0.037)	(0.035)	(0.038)	(0.050)	(0.028)	(0.059)	(0.039)
Cereals	-0.249	-0.140	-0.030	0.145	0.064	0.075	-0.010	-0.025	-0.118
	(0.027)	(0.027)	(0.027)	(0.025)	(0.028)	(0.037)	(0.021)	(0.043)	(0.029)
Meat and poultry	-0.069	-0.131	-0.060	0.129	0.135	0.216	0.058	-0.032	-0.080
	(0.035)	(0.035)	(0.035)	(0.033)	(0.036)	(0.048)	(0.027)	(0.056)	(0.037)
Seafood	-0.334	-0.280	-0.144	0.083	0.078	0.057	0.039	-0.151	-0.037
	(0.047)	(0.048)	(0.045)	(0.045)	(0.049)	(0.066)	(0.037)	(0.076)	(0.051)
Vegetables and tubers	-0.032	0.249	0.014	0.087	0.019	0.014	0.025	-0.004	-0.089
	(0.035)	(0.036)	(0.036)	(0.034)	(0.037)	(0.049)	(0.027)	(0.056)	(0.038)
Fruits	0.044	0.130	0.062	0.096	0.015	0.089	0.046	-0.045	-0.063
	(0.044)	(0.044)	(0.044)	(0.042)	(0.045)	(0.061)	(0.034)	(0.071)	(0.047)
Fats and oils	-0.091	-0.062	0.067	0.088	0.084	0.036	0.026	-0.109	-0.084
	(0.035)	(0.036)	(0.035)	(0.033)	(0.036)	(0.049)	(0.027)	(0.056)	(0.038)
Sugar and sweets	0.052	-0.110	0.043	0.079	0.070	0.069	-0.018	-0.135	-0.099
	(0.038)	(0.038)	(0.038)	(0.036)	(0.039)	(0.052)	(0.029)	(0.061)	(0.041)
Hot beverages	-0.215	-0.226	-0.025	0.064	0.062	0.030	0.067	-0.012	-0.085
	(0.040)	(0.040)	(0.040)	(0.038)	(0.041)	(0.055)	(0.031)	(0.064)	(0.044)
Alcoholic beverages	-0.042	-0.012	-0.001	0.001	0.010	0.027	-0.007	-0.314	-0.024
	(0.074)	(0.076)	(0.076)	(0.069)	(0.075)	(0.099)	(0.056)	(0.133)	(0.079)
Other beverages	0.167	0.314	0.118	0.014	0.041	0.003	0.014	-0.086	0.043
	(0.056)	(0.057)	(0.060)	(0.051)	(0.056)	(0.077)	(0.042)	(0.091)	(0.057)
Other foods	-0.352	-0.231	-0.149	-0.036	-0.053	0.018	0.099	0.067	0.002
	(0.059)	(0.059)	(0.058)	(0.056)	(0.061)	(0.083)	(0.046)	(0.092)	(0.064)
Meals away from home	-0.218	-0.038	0.026	-0.202	-0.084	-0.161	0.130	-0.072	0.014
	(0.081)	(0.085)	(0.088)	(0.078)	(0.082)	(0.117)	(0.062)	(0.153)	(0.085)
Housing	-0.138	-0.087	-0.023	0.002	0.034	0.149	-0.230	-0.114	-0.056
	(0.024)	(0.024)	(0.024)	(0.023)	(0.025)	(0.033)	(0.019)	(0.039)	(0.026)
Principal dwelling	-0.176	-0.097	-0.024	-0.020	0.047	0.199	-0.204	-0.108	-0.037
	(0.024)	(0.025)	(0.025)	(0.023)	(0.025)	(0.033)	(0.020)	(0.040)	(0.026)
Maintenance	0.237	0.195	-0.054	-0.209	0.056	0.059	-0.793	-0.647	0.004
	(0.195)	(0.224)	(0.232)	(0.173)	(0.191)	(0.272)	(0.147)	(0.383)	(0.184)

Furnishings and operation	0.344 (0.059)	0.042 (0.061)	−0.088 (0.061)	−0.163 (0.058)	−0.305 (0.063)	−0.245 (0.084)	0.051 (0.048)	0.134 (0.102)	0.141 (0.064)
Durables	0.341 (0.144)	0.310 (0.164)	0.065 (0.163)	−0.443 (0.143)	−0.592 (0.162)	−0.783 (0.237)	−0.113 (0.124)	0.140 (0.260)	0.005 (0.160)
Nondurables	−0.026 (0.051)	−0.051 (0.053)	−0.010 (0.053)	0.058 (0.050)	−0.066 (0.055)	−0.112 (0.073)	−0.048 (0.041)	−0.073 (0.087)	0.017 (0.056)
Services	0.115 (0.080)	0.113 (0.087)	0.040 (0.087)	−0.123 (0.083)	−0.190 (0.089)	−0.037 (0.117)	0.041 (0.066)	−0.019 (0.192)	0.327 (0.084)
Clothing	−0.246 (0.048)	−0.130 (0.049)	−0.067 (0.049)	0.011 (0.046)	−0.108 (0.054)	−0.158 (0.072)	0.078 (0.038)	0.193 (0.080)	0.023 (0.051)
Men's	−0.340 (0.052)	−0.125 (0.054)	−0.033 (0.053)	−0.064 (0.049)	−0.136 (0.056)	−0.022 (0.078)	0.049 (0.040)	0.028 (0.088)	−0.059 (0.054)
Women's	−0.345 (0.050)	−0.235 (0.052)	−0.129 (0.051)	0.028 (0.048)	−0.007 (0.054)	−0.038 (0.073)	0.047 (0.039)	0.091 (0.085)	0.094 (0.052)
Children's	−0.258 (0.126)	−0.221 (0.134)	−0.112 (0.131)	0.031 (0.103)	−0.172 (0.160)	0.199 (0.313)	0.160 (0.100)	−0.023 (0.190)	0.588 (0.137)
Other	0.101 (0.075)	−0.037 (0.083)	−0.201 (0.082)	0.056 (0.075)	−0.107 (0.083)	−0.042 (0.117)	0.112 (0.061)	0.081 (0.136)	0.017 (0.083)
Medical care	0.346 (0.106)	0.203 (0.116)	0.220 (0.120)	0.093 (0.107)	0.249 (0.113)	0.409 (0.143)	0.209 (0.083)	0.350 (0.197)	0.067 (0.114)
Education	0.031 (0.134)	0.180 (0.158)	0.575 (0.135)	0.016 (0.139)	0.058 (0.155)	−0.436 (0.237)	0.070 (0.104)	0.268 (0.224)	−0.231 (0.136)
Recreation and culture	0.175 (0.055)	0.249 (0.057)	0.092 (0.057)	−0.028 (0.054)	0.150 (0.058)	−0.089 (0.080)	0.212 (0.043)	0.019 (0.096)	0.012 (0.060)
Recreation	0.097 (0.071)	0.222 (0.073)	0.091 (0.075)	−0.083 (0.069)	0.064 (0.073)	−0.112 (0.109)	0.202 (0.055)	0.133 (0.136)	−0.138 (0.072)
Reading and culture	0.097 (0.049)	−0.092 (0.051)	−0.008 (0.050)	0.050 (0.051)	0.179 (0.053)	0.076 (0.071)	0.079 (0.039)	0.153 (0.086)	−0.004 (0.053)
Transportation and communication	0.113 (0.043)	0.148 (0.044)	0.166 (0.044)	0.043 (0.041)	0.256 (0.044)	0.172 (0.059)	0.021 (0.033)	−0.145 (0.071)	0.044 (0.046)
Private transportation	0.316 (0.109)	0.470 (0.111)	0.417 (0.110)	0.028 (0.111)	0.038 (0.117)	−0.086 (0.164)	−0.016 (0.089)	−0.360 (0.280)	0.043 (0.105)
Public transportation	0.068 (0.050)	0.071 (0.052)	0.117 (0.053)	0.010 (0.049)	0.174 (0.052)	0.001 (0.070)	0.060 (0.040)	−0.043 (0.081)	0.153 (0.054)
Communication	−0.532 (0.097)	−0.218 (0.101)	−0.190 (0.101)	0.176 (0.101)	0.521 (0.102)	0.520 (0.127)	−0.053 (0.075)	−0.027 (0.229)	−0.301 (0.105)

Table C-42 (continued)

Spending category	Trimester			Age of head			Tenure		Spouse employed
	1	2	3	35-49	50-64	Over 64	Rented	Other	
Other consumption	0.291	0.335	0.231	-0.139	-0.105	-0.361	0.120	-0.006	0.116
	(0.046)	(0.047)	(0.047)	(0.045)	(0.053)	(0.068)	(0.036)	(0.079)	(0.050)
Tobacco	0.101	0.252	0.221	-0.066	-0.033	-0.210	0.033	0.001	-0.018
	(0.051)	(0.053)	(0.054)	(0.049)	(0.056)	(0.077)	(0.040)	(0.095)	(0.052)
Personal care	0.237	0.212	0.171	0.038	0.280	0.144	0.151	0.008	0.066
	(0.051)	(0.053)	(0.053)	(0.049)	(0.053)	(0.072)	(0.040)	(0.088)	(0.056)
Ceremonies	-0.644	-0.191	-0.281	-0.065	0.402	0.760	0.563	0.173	-0.034
	(0.308)	(0.325)	(0.359)	(0.292)	(0.284)	(0.483)	(0.220)	(0.618)	(0.267)
Taxes	-0.080	0.082	-0.016	0.033	-0.183	0.069	0.028	-0.109	0.109
	(0.045)	(0.045)	(0.045)	(0.041)	(0.046)	(0.071)	(0.035)	(0.077)	(0.047)
Insurance	-0.350	-0.133	-0.078	-0.052	-0.171	-0.214	0.042	-0.029	0.159
	(0.045)	(0.044)	(0.044)	(0.040)	(0.046)	(0.072)	(0.035)	(0.072)	(0.053)
Social security	-0.340	-0.132	-0.078	0.047	-0.170	-0.213	0.039	-0.030	0.171
	(0.045)	(0.044)	(0.044)	(0.039)	(0.046)	(0.072)	(0.034)	(0.072)	(0.052)
Gifts and transfers	0.206	0.720	0.211	-0.080	-0.132	-0.254	0.072	-0.157	-0.355
	(0.211)	(0.225)	(0.248)	(0.206)	(0.221)	(0.314)	(0.163)	(0.395)	(0.207)
Other nonconsumption	-0.076	-0.271	-0.256	0.193	-0.136	-1.067	0.052	0.453	0.161
	(0.306)	(0.326)	(0.355)	(0.261)	(0.291)	(0.431)	(0.217)	(0.560)	(0.310)

340

Table C-43. Coefficients of Sociodemographic Variables Included in All Expenditure Functions, Ecuador

Spending category	Guayaquil	Trimester			Age of head			Tenure		Spouse employed
		1	2	3	35–49	50–64	Over 64	Rented	Other	
Food and beverages	0.151	0.015	0.046	0.048	-0.032	-0.011	-0.077	0.177	0.290	-0.008
	(0.013)	(0.018)	(0.021)	(0.020)	(0.017)	(0.019)	(0.027)	(0.016)	(0.026)	(0.019)
Dairy products and eggs	-0.005	-0.053	-0.064	-0.030	-0.034	-0.006	-0.037	0.204	0.349	-0.120
	(0.030)	(0.039)	(0.046)	(0.044)	(0.037)	(0.043)	(0.061)	(0.035)	(0.059)	(0.041)
Cereals	0.007	-0.086	-0.060	-0.012	0.058	0.094	0.062	0.019	0.070	-0.067
	(0.019)	(0.025)	(0.030)	(0.029)	(0.024)	(0.028)	(0.039)	(0.026)	(0.037)	(0.026)
Meat and poultry	0.464	-0.039	0.109	0.024	0.011	-0.037	-0.004	0.215	0.305	-0.025
	(0.031)	(0.041)	(0.049)	(0.047)	(0.039)	(0.045)	(0.065)	(0.037)	(0.061)	(0.043)
Seafood	0.474	0.105	-0.005	0.042	0.059	0.052	0.087	-0.022	0.136	-0.005
	(0.040)	(0.048)	(0.058)	(0.054)	(0.046)	(0.053)	(0.077)	(0.043)	(0.074)	(0.055)
Vegetables	-0.021	-0.030	0.054	0.076	0.125	0.120	0.070	0.092	0.284	-0.019
	(0.023)	(0.030)	(0.036)	(0.034)	(0.029)	(0.033)	(0.047)	(0.027)	(0.045)	(0.032)
Fruits	0.002	0.123	0.158	-0.062	0.013	-0.071	-0.092	0.112	0.214	-0.052
	(0.035)	(0.046)	(0.055)	(0.052)	(0.043)	(0.050)	(0.071)	(0.041)	(0.068)	(0.048)
Fats and oils	0.179	0.045	0.059	0.092	0.076	0.075	0.083	0.098	0.171	-0.037
	(0.023)	(0.030)	(0.036)	(0.034)	(0.028)	(0.033)	(0.046)	(0.027)	(0.044)	(0.031)
Sugar and sweets	-0.024	0.142	0.180	0.125	0.002	0.021	-0.057	0.117	0.310	-0.034
	(0.029)	(0.038)	(0.045)	(0.043)	(0.036)	(0.042)	(0.059)	(0.034)	(0.057)	(0.040)
Hot beverages	0.060	-0.009	0.070	-0.034	0.092	0.149	0.042	0.070	0.156	0.014
	(0.029)	(0.037)	(0.045)	(0.042)	(0.036)	(0.041)	(0.058)	(0.034)	(0.056)	(0.039)
Acoholic beverages	0.880	0.273	0.164	-0.097	0.234	0.199	0.276	0.112	0.398	0.099
	(0.116)	(0.157)	(0.173)	(0.176)	(0.145)	(0.165)	(0.262)	(0.131)	(0.237)	(0.156)
Other beverages	0.644	-0.139	-0.021	-0.136	-0.071	-0.114	-0.094	0.146	0.338	0.032
	(0.048)	(0.062)	(0.073)	(0.072)	(0.060)	(0.069)	(0.103)	(0.057)	(0.097)	(0.068)
Other foods	-0.200	0.391	0.251	-0.004	-0.028	-0.085	-0.323	0.184	0.341	-0.017
	(0.051)	(0.067)	(0.077)	(0.073)	(0.063)	(0.072)	(0.103)	(0.060)	(0.100)	(0.070)
Meals away from home	0.091	-0.368	-0.147	0.136	0.153	-0.066	-0.129	0.451	0.514	0.230
	(0.092)	(0.127)	(0.155)	(0.151)	(0.111)	(0.130)	(0.203)	(0.115)	(0.193)	(0.119)
Housing	-0.119	-0.161	-0.089	-0.054	0.039	0.094	0.280	-0.276	-1.846	-0.057
	(0.032)	(0.038)	(0.045)	(0.043)	(0.035)	(0.041)	(0.057)	(0.046)	(0.062)	(0.039)
Principal dwelling	-0.084	-0.174	0.079	-0.046	0.050	0.102	0.280	-0.299	-1.902	-0.035
	(0.032)	(0.037)	(0.044)	(0.042)	(0.035)	(0.040)	(0.057)	(0.046)	(0.061)	(0.039)
Other dwellings	-0.089	0.145	0.168	0.087	0.162	0.002	0.392	0.088	-0.436	0.074
	(0.026)	(0.242)	(0.284)	(0.285)	(0.287)	(0.312)	(0.342)	(0.300)	(0.458)	(0.303)

Table C-43 (continued)

Spending category	Guayaquil	Trimester			Age of head			Tenure		Spouse employed
		1	2	3	35–49	50–64	Over 64	Rented	Other	
Furnishings and operation	−0.069 (0.047)	0.390 (0.056)	0.300 (0.067)	0.231 (0.064)	−0.081 (0.053)	−0.302 (0.061)	−0.406 (0.086)	0.263 (0.053)	0.561 (0.084)	0.080 (0.059)
Durables	0.057 (0.116)	0.032 (0.162)	0.240 (0.190)	0.075 (0.193)	−0.251 (0.129)	−0.238 (0.157)	−0.137 (0.129)	0.141 (0.131)	0.454 (0.218)	0.039 (0.139)
Nondurables	−0.172 (0.030)	0.178 (0.036)	0.098 (0.042)	0.050 (0.040)	−0.028 (0.033)	−0.114 (0.039)	−0.278 (0.054)	0.015 (0.033)	0.161 (0.053)	−0.029 (0.037)
Services	0.437 (0.076)	−0.233 (0.086)	−0.059 (0.103)	−0.033 (0.098)	0.062 (0.083)	−0.058 (0.094)	−0.021 (0.130)	0.339 (0.079)	0.631 (0.137)	0.156 (0.089)
Clothing	−0.821 (0.061)	0.858 (0.081)	0.271 (0.096)	0.100 (0.092)	−0.069 (0.077)	−0.130 (0.093)	−0.596 (0.129)	0.137 (0.074)	0.398 (0.123)	0.120 (0.084)
Men's	−0.120 (0.054)	0.297 (0.074)	0.202 (0.088)	0.072 (0.085)	−0.139 (0.063)	−0.142 (0.082)	−0.260 (0.117)	0.121 (0.065)	0.392 (0.112)	0.104 (0.071)
Women's	−0.397 (0.049)	0.436 (0.066)	0.028 (0.079)	−0.126 (0.076)	−0.086 (0.061)	−0.045 (0.073)	−0.321 (0.106)	0.051 (0.059)	0.191 (0.099)	0.056 (0.065)
Children's	0.239 (0.121)	−0.381 (0.180)	−0.128 (0.222)	−0.095 (0.203)	−0.249 (0.132)	−0.126 (0.182)	−0.243 (0.320)	0.237 (0.151)	0.314 (0.235)	−0.306 (0.150)
Other	−0.654 (0.076)	0.819 (0.101)	0.200 (0.118)	0.031 (0.117)	−0.072 (0.093)	0.048 (0.107)	−0.281 (0.154)	0.285 (0.090)	0.461 (0.154)	0.061 (0.102)
Medical care	0.318 (0.081)	−0.292 (0.107)	−0.053 (0.131)	−0.152 (0.128)	−0.193 (0.099)	−0.209 (0.116)	0.009 (0.167)	0.188 (0.095)	0.449 (0.166)	0.058 (0.106)
Education	0.543 (0.074)	−0.325 (0.091)	0.049 (0.124)	−0.022 (0.106)	0.039 (0.099)	0.131 (0.115)	−0.337 (0.163)	0.068 (0.082)	0.210 (0.145)	0.009 (0.095)
Recreation and culture	0.208 (0.052)	−0.071 (0.066)	−0.037 (0.080)	−0.160 (0.076)	−0.120 (0.065)	0.019 (0.074)	−0.248 (0.102)	0.103 (0.062)	0.320 (0.108)	0.008 (0.071)
Recreation	−0.109 (0.062)	−0.264 (0.078)	0.047 (0.099)	−0.114 (0.092)	−0.095 (0.078)	−0.110 (0.085)	−0.362 (0.141)	0.121 (0.073)	0.414 (0.131)	−0.164 (0.081)
Reading and culture	0.342 (0.046)	0.009 (0.059)	0.045 (0.070)	−0.045 (0.067)	0.071 (0.061)	0.139 (0.068)	0.232 (0.090)	0.045 (0.054)	0.317 (0.099)	−0.002 (0.063)

	C1	C2	C3	C4	C5	C6	C7	C8	C9	C10
Transportation and communication	-0.167 (0.069)	-0.155 (0.089)	-0.080 (0.101)	-0.026 (0.100)	0.136 (0.092)	0.209 (0.099)	-0.010 (0.137)	0.210 (0.079)	0.264 (0.156)	0.030 (0.096)
Private transportation	0.290 (0.110)	-0.074 (0.140)	0.171 (0.164)	0.098 (0.141)	0.110 (0.154)	0.126 (0.172)	-0.168 (0.284)	0.423 (0.139)	0.056 (0.243)	0.147 (0.165)
Communication	-0.105 (0.073)	-0.173 (0.093)	-0.114 (0.107)	0.009 (0.106)	0.173 (0.099)	0.286 (0.104)	0.006 (0.144)	0.148 (0.083)	0.391 (0.169)	-0.095 (0.101)
Other consumption	0.121 (0.033)	0.050 (0.044)	-0.022 (0.051)	0.070 (0.049)	-0.064 (0.042)	-0.078 (0.050)	-0.227 (0.069)	0.141 (0.040)	0.264 (0.066)	-0.001 (0.046)
Tobacco	0.033 (0.070)	0.114 (0.090)	0.218 (0.113)	0.148 (0.108)	0.120 (0.089)	0.127 (0.105)	-0.055 (0.151)	0.137 (0.083)	0.252 (0.146)	-0.076 (0.093)
Personal care	0.238 (0.031)	0.022 (0.041)	0.010 (0.048)	0.138 (0.046)	-0.091 (0.039)	-0.044 (0.045)	-0.216 (0.063)	0.108 (0.037)	0.232 (0.062)	-0.038 (0.043)
Ceremonies	0.897 (0.650)	-0.322 (1.072)	1.035 (1.560)	1.533 (1.879)	⋮	⋮	⋮	⋮	⋮	⋮
Taxes	0.350 (0.185)	-0.629 (0.230)	-0.158 (0.279)	0.379 (0.269)	0.218 (0.238)	-0.084 (0.246)	0.279 (0.327)	0.027 (0.200)	0.400 (0.393)	-0.083 (0.207)
Insurance	0.070 (0.060)	-0.118 (0.078)	-0.014 (0.086)	0.036 (0.081)	-0.005 (0.071)	-0.179 (0.086)	-0.551 (0.183)	0.086 (0.068)	0.298 (0.114)	-0.025 (0.081)
Social security	0.063 (0.057)	-0.115 (0.074)	-0.029 (0.081)	0.049 (0.078)	0.022 (0.067)	-0.186 (0.082)	-0.617 (0.173)	0.080 (0.065)	0.260 (0.108)	-0.006 (0.078)
Private insurance	0.903 (0.552)	0.456 (0.722)	0.722 (0.719)	0.434 (0.637)	-0.857 (0.580)	-0.101 (0.781)	-0.498 (1.502)	0.028 (0.528)	0.715 (0.645)	-0.736 (0.594)
Gifts and transfers	0.349 (0.109)	-0.649 (0.140)	-0.038 (0.168)	-0.132 (0.160)	0.076 (0.141)	0.631 (0.152)	0.564 (0.229)	0.220 (0.126)	0.413 (0.217)	-0.089 (0.145)

343

Table C-44. Coefficients of Sociodemographic Variables Included in All Expenditure Functions, Peru

Spending category	Trimester			Age of head			Tenure		Spouse employed
	1	2	3	35-49	50-64	Over 64	Rented	Other	
Food and beverages	-0.128	-0.117	0.037	0.072	0.084	0.040	0.103	0.104	-0.021
	(0.029)	(0.039)	(0.028)	(0.031)	(0.034)	(0.045)	(0.024)	(0.044)	(0.032)
Dairy products and eggs	-0.168	-0.264	0.112	0.009	-0.015	-0.087	0.107	-0.188	0.117
	(0.048)	(0.065)	(0.046)	(0.051)	(0.057)	(0.074)	(0.040)	(0.073)	(0.053)
Cereals	-0.224	-0.154	0.031	0.108	0.151	0.082	-0.037	0.084	0.024
	(0.038)	(0.052)	(0.037)	(0.041)	(0.045)	(0.059)	(0.032)	(0.058)	(0.042)
Meat and poultry	-0.282	-0.196	-0.033	0.064	0.155	0.123	0.074	-0.065	-0.037
	(0.048)	(0.065)	(0.046)	(0.051)	(0.057)	(0.075)	(0.040)	(0.074)	(0.053)
Seafood	-0.025	-0.125	-0.080	0.116	0.212	0.247	0.180	0.088	0.033
	(0.073)	(0.097)	(0.067)	(0.078)	(0.085)	(0.114)	(0.059)	(0.118)	(0.078)
Vegetables and tubers	-0.319	-0.227	-0.116	0.149	0.191	0.093	0.007	0.173	0.013
	(0.045)	(0.060)	(0.043)	(0.048)	(0.053)	(0.069)	(0.037)	(0.068)	(0.049)
Fruits	-0.027	-0.459	-0.099	0.073	0.108	0.054	0.238	0.054	-0.054
	(0.072)	(0.099)	(0.069)	(0.077)	(0.086)	(0.111)	(0.060)	(0.112)	(0.079)
Fats and oils	-0.164	-0.229	-0.050	0.131	0.138	0.125	0.008	-0.047	-0.017
	(0.055)	(0.077)	(0.050)	(0.057)	(0.063)	(0.083)	(0.045)	(0.081)	(0.059)
Sugar and sweets	0.071	-0.089	0.038	0.046	0.022	0.184	0.042	-0.006	0.011
	(0.056)	(0.075)	(0.053)	(0.059)	(0.066)	(0.087)	(0.047)	(0.082)	(0.060)
Hot beverages	-0.122	-0.170	0.050	0.061	0.097	0.177	0.056	0.018	-0.024
	(0.082)	(0.112)	(0.074)	(0.086)	(0.095)	(0.127)	(0.066)	(0.115)	(0.085)
Alcoholic beverages	-0.533	0.065	-0.422	-0.364	-0.029	-0.090	-0.053	0.642	-0.061
	(0.323)	(0.407)	(0.297)	(0.370)	(0.411)	(0.552)	(0.264)	(0.468)	(0.393)
Other beverages	0.068	0.442	0.378	-0.371	-0.055	0.289	0.016	-0.561	0.129
	(0.162)	(0.304)	(0.221)	(0.200)	(0.216)	(0.329)	(0.153)	(0.251)	(0.209)
Other foods	-0.067	-0.261	-0.034	0.090	-0.041	0.002	0.137	0.288	0.145
	(0.094)	(0.129)	(0.090)	(0.099)	(0.111)	(0.149)	(0.078)	(0.137)	(0.101)
Meals away from home	0.497	0.409	0.213	-0.113	-0.194	-0.267	0.019	0.444	0.011
	(0.139)	(0.190)	(0.137)	(0.149)	(0.168)	(0.223)	(0.118)	(0.219)	(0.154)
Housing	-0.066	0.106	-0.137	0.061	0.038	0.097	-0.226	-0.775	-0.082
	(0.059)	(0.071)	(0.049)	(0.054)	(0.060)	(0.079)	(0.045)	(0.080)	(0.055)
Principal dwelling	-0.138	0.033	-0.134	-0.009	-0.003	0.078	-0.162	-0.812	-0.092
	(0.062)	(0.075)	(0.051)	(0.056)	(0.063)	(0.083)	(0.047)	(0.083)	(0.058)

Other dwellings	−0.143 (0.379)	−0.879 (0.469)	0.793 (0.425)	−0.275 (0.452)	−0.871 (0.479)	−1.221 (0.533)	−0.216 (0.331)	−1.643 (0.830)	0.408 (0.396)
Maintenance	−0.291 (0.204)	0.050 (0.243)	−0.265 (0.165)	0.063 (0.189)	0.153 (0.212)	0.375 (0.280)	−0.444 (0.153)	0.041 (0.294)	−0.016 (0.185)
Furnishings and operation	0.395 (0.085)	0.387 (0.104)	0.119 (0.071)	−0.352 (0.079)	−0.335 (0.088)	−0.194 (0.115)	0.199 (0.063)	0.143 (0.114)	0.114 (0.080)
Durables	0.457 (0.200)	0.316 (0.233)	−0.108 (0.173)	−0.288 (0.177)	−0.364 (0.202)	−0.570 (0.284)	0.021 (0.155)	0.097 (0.258)	0.480 (0.180)
Nondurables	0.234 (0.058)	0.211 (0.071)	−0.007 (0.048)	−0.006 (0.054)	−0.110 (0.060)	−0.142 (0.078)	0.121 (0.043)	−0.003 (0.078)	0.015 (0.054)
Services	−0.455 (0.111)	−0.289 (0.134)	−0.021 (0.087)	−0.103 (0.103)	0.008 (0.113)	0.217 (0.142)	0.191 (0.078)	−0.497 (0.169)	−0.133 (0.100)
Clothing	0.214 (0.086)	−0.011 (0.118)	−0.070 (0.084)	−0.078 (0.092)	−0.276 (0.112)	−0.456 (0.144)	0.261 (0.073)	0.212 (0.133)	0.002 (0.094)
Men's	−0.099 (0.091)	−0.329 (0.131)	0.064 (0.090)	−0.155 (0.097)	−0.191 (0.115)	−0.142 (0.154)	0.168 (0.078)	−0.181 (0.144)	−0.108 (0.100)
Women's	0.401 (0.085)	0.141 (0.116)	−0.077 (0.087)	−0.088 (0.092)	−0.149 (0.105)	−0.201 (0.141)	0.373 (0.073)	0.084 (0.130)	0.135 (0.093)
Children's	−0.207 (0.196)	−0.350 (0.235)	0.086 (0.183)	−0.433 (0.166)	−0.552 (0.249)	−0.343 (0.324)	0.094 (0.158)	−0.156 (0.296)	−0.149 (0.198)
Other	−0.090 (0.160)	−0.526 (0.215)	−0.465 (0.179)	−0.018 (0.178)	−0.057 (0.197)	−0.256 (0.268)	−0.111 (0.141)	0.169 (0.224)	0.321 (0.165)
Medical care	−0.277 (0.121)	−0.231 (0.150)	0.055 (0.111)	−0.264 (0.123)	−0.146 (0.138)	0.168 (0.177)	0.043 (0.098)	−0.063 (0.174)	−0.075 (0.124)
Education	−0.244 (0.112)	−0.112 (0.153)	−0.052 (0.110)	0.260 (0.162)	0.149 (0.162)	−0.069 (0.222)	−0.061 (0.184)	−0.237 (0.184)	−0.075 (0.118)
Recreation and culture	0.025 (0.069)	−0.111 (0.095)	0.081 (0.066)	−0.276 (0.074)	−0.168 (0.083)	−0.069 (0.107)	0.227 (0.058)	0.053 (0.108)	−0.068 (0.067)
Recreation	−0.066 (0.085)	−0.287 (0.119)	−0.001 (0.081)	−0.359 (0.090)	−0.386 (0.100)	−0.208 (0.132)	0.252 (0.071)	0.039 (0.136)	−0.036 (0.094)
Reading and culture	0.149 (0.059)	0.114 (0.081)	0.202 (0.056)	−0.131 (0.066)	0.061 (0.072)	0.212 (0.091)	0.074 (0.049)	−0.160 (0.092)	0.091 (0.064)
Transportation and communication	−0.097 (0.093)	−0.276 (0.126)	0.063 (0.089)	−0.089 (0.100)	−0.018 (0.111)	0.151 (0.143)	−0.117 (0.077)	0.247 (0.145)	0.250 (0.101)
Vehicle purchase	1.053 (0.615)	0.477 (0.705)	−0.170 (0.502)	−0.298 (0.543)	−0.841 (0.651)	−0.199 (0.970)	0.080 (0.478)	1.052 (0.103)	0.108 (0.646)
Private transportation	−0.301 (0.107)	−0.168 (0.155)	0.020 (0.095)	−0.080 (0.116)	−0.027 (0.127)	0.236 (0.177)	−0.058 (0.085)	0.021 (0.206)	0.157 (0.125)

Table C-44 (continued)

Spending category	Trimester			Age of head			Tenure		Spouse employed
	1	2	3	35-49	50-64	Over 64	Rented	Other	
Public transportation	-0.265	-0.633	0.103	0.377	0.187	0.192	-0.094	0.250	0.202
	(0.111)	(0.145)	(0.111)	(0.119)	(0.133)	(0.172)	(0.094)	(0.160)	(0.116)
Communication	-0.513	-0.916	-0.180	0.122	0.442	0.591	0.084	-0.583	0.006
	(0.133)	(0.181)	(0.141)	(0.159)	(0.166)	(0.205)	(0.116)	(0.267)	(0.157)
Other consumption	-0.081	-0.258	0.110	0.018	0.024	-0.132	0.240	0.050	0.012
	(0.049)	(0.067)	(0.047)	(0.053)	(0.064)	(0.080)	(0.041)	(0.076)	(0.053)
Tobacco	-0.199	-0.250	0.150	0.052	0.255	-0.043	0.334	0.090	-0.188
	(0.110)	(0.168)	(0.105)	(0.125)	(0.143)	(0.185)	(0.092)	(0.185)	(0.122)
Personal care	0.010	-0.172	-0.041	0.035	0.162	0.102	0.160	-0.074	0.040
	(0.045)	(0.062)	(0.043)	(0.048)	(0.054)	(0.070)	(0.038)	(0.070)	(0.049)
Ceremonies	-0.657	-1.175	0.348	0.425	0.635	-0.551	0.013	-0.441	0.562
	(0.357)	(0.521)	(0.294)	(0.359)	(0.407)	(0.491)	(0.312)	(0.668)	(0.375)
Taxes	-0.122	0.089	0.204	0.034	-0.077	0.357	0.143	-0.371	-0.228
	(0.121)	(0.156)	(0.108)	(0.124)	(0.137)	(0.178)	(0.095)	(0.201)	(0.126)
Insurance	-0.209	-0.126	-0.209	-0.029	-0.002	-0.081	0.080	0.013	-0.115
	(0.061)	(0.082)	(0.057)	(0.063)	(0.073)	(0.097)	(0.050)	(0.091)	(0.074)
Social security	-0.277	-0.177	-0.207	0.027	0.051	-0.010	0.094	0.056	-0.177
	(0.059)	(0.079)	(0.055)	(0.060)	(0.071)	(0.094)	(0.048)	(0.088)	(0.071)
Private insurance	-0.116	-0.103	-0.214	0.049	-0.065	-0.179	0.007	0.019	-0.083
	(0.070)	(0.094)	(0.066)	(0.072)	(0.084)	(0.111)	(0.058)	(0.105)	(0.085)
Gifts and transfers	0.021	-0.332	-0.103	-0.019	0.176	-0.069	0.071	-0.732	-0.324
	(0.195)	(0.250)	(0.201)	(0.214)	(0.237)	(0.333)	(0.170)	(0.294)	(0.222)
Other nonconsumption	0.322	0.240	0.591	-0.078	-0.264	0.120	0.124	0.369	-0.294
	(0.333)	(0.480)	(0.327)	(0.327)	(0.369)	(0.534)	(0.272)	(0.451)	(0.303)

Table C-45. *Coefficients of Sociodemographic Variables Included in All Expenditure Functions, Venezuela*

Spending category	Guayaquil	Trimester			Age of head			Tenure		Spouse employed
		1	2	3	35–49	50–64	Over 64	Rented	Other	
Food and beverages	0.102 (0.022)	−0.074 (0.027)	0.031 (0.032)	−0.049 (0.031)	0.027 (0.017)	0.031 (0.022)	−0.071 (0.040)	0.016 (0.017)	−0.040 (0.040)	−0.055 (0.028)
Dairy products and eggs	0.332 (0.033)	−0.030 (0.042)	0.043 (0.049)	0.031 (0.049)	0.035 (0.027)	0.145 (0.035)	0.111 (0.061)	0.064 (0.026)	0.016 (0.062)	−0.031 (0.043)
Cereals	0.039 (0.033)	−0.110 (0.041)	0.059 (0.049)	−0.016 (0.048)	0.071 (0.026)	0.153 (0.034)	0.048 (0.060)	−0.030 (0.026)	−0.119 (0.061)	0.022 (0.042)
Meat and poultry	0.241 (0.037)	−0.033 (0.047)	−0.016 (0.055)	−0.036 (0.055)	0.079 (0.030)	0.067 (0.038)	0.009 (0.070)	0.085 (0.029)	−0.011 (0.070)	−0.087 (0.048)
Seafood	0.527 (0.074)	−0.181 (0.096)	−0.007 (0.111)	−0.325 (0.110)	0.114 (0.053)	0.204 (0.067)	0.063 (0.125)	0.115 (0.052)	0.227 (0.144)	−0.0001 (0.084)
Vegetables	−0.418 (0.043)	−0.119 (0.054)	−0.049 (0.063)	−0.144 (0.062)	0.014 (0.034)	0.097 (0.044)	0.063 (0.079)	0.033 (0.034)	0.035 (0.079)	−0.020 (0.055)
Fruits	0.355 (0.043)	0.088 (0.055)	0.129 (0.064)	0.059 (0.064)	0.097 (0.034)	0.165 (0.044)	0.195 (0.081)	0.038 (0.034)	−0.008 (0.079)	0.031 (0.055)
Fats and oils	0.182 (0.047)	−0.024 (0.059)	−0.027 (0.068)	−0.065 (0.068)	0.030 (0.036)	0.037 (0.047)	0.105 (0.086)	0.062 (0.036)	0.050 (0.085)	0.009 (0.059)
Sugar and sweets	0.098 (0.045)	−0.052 (0.058)	0.111 (0.065)	−0.063 (0.064)	−0.006 (0.035)	0.072 (0.045)	0.051 (0.081)	0.004 (0.035)	−0.147 (0.082)	0.102 (0.056)
Hot beverages	0.338 (0.049)	0.032 (0.062)	−0.029 (0.073)	−0.037 (0.072)	0.057 (0.039)	0.174 (0.049)	0.259 (0.090)	0.021 (0.038)	−0.182 (0.092)	−0.111 (0.061)
Alcoholic beverages	1.011 (0.134)	−0.277 (0.192)	−0.113 (0.235)	−0.098 (0.236)	−0.361 (0.094)	−0.242 (0.124)	−0.550 (0.258)	0.034 (0.089)	0.099 (0.265)	0.296 (0.138)
Other beverages	0.235 (0.067)	0.064 (0.091)	−0.009 (0.106)	0.013 (0.106)	−0.100 (0.053)	−0.104 (0.070)	0.030 (0.134)	0.037 (0.052)	0.284 (0.126)	0.108 (0.083)
Other foods	0.232 (0.073)	0.146 (0.093)	0.326 (0.108)	0.151 (0.108)	−0.233 (0.057)	−0.386 (0.074)	−0.429 (0.138)	0.059 (0.056)	−0.073 (0.135)	−0.075 (0.091)
Meals away from home	0.436 (0.089)	−0.173 (0.113)	0.001 (0.133)	−0.036 (0.136)	−0.072 (0.070)	−0.417 (0.093)	−0.549 (0.170)	−0.130 (0.070)	0.083 (0.170)	−0.045 (0.112)
Housing	−0.238 (0.029)	0.098 (0.035)	−0.024 (0.041)	−0.018 (0.041)	0.054 (0.022)	0.108 (0.029)	0.212 (0.052)	−0.052 (0.024)	0.003 (0.052)	−0.086 (0.036)
Principal dwelling	−0.250 (0.029)	0.094 (0.036)	−0.030 (0.042)	−0.019 (0.041)	0.044 (0.022)	0.111 (0.029)	0.239 (0.051)	−0.034 (0.024)	0.005 (0.053)	−0.095 (0.036)

Table C-45 (continued)

Spending category	Guayaquil	Trimester			Age of head			Tenure		Spouse employed
		1	2	3	35–49	50–64	Over 64	Rented	Other	
Furnishings and operation	0.483	−0.008	−0.246	−0.044	−0.178	−0.193	−0.227	0.025	−0.263	0.146
	(0.062)	(0.078)	(0.091)	(0.090)	(0.049)	(0.064)	(0.114)	(0.049)	(0.116)	(0.079)
Durables	1.735	0.389	−0.377	0.194	−0.302	−0.330	−0.076	0.103	0.019	−0.056
	(0.163)	(0.187)	(0.223)	(0.213)	(0.126)	(0.163)	(0.375)	(0.125)	(0.314)	(0.197)
Nondurables	0.003	−0.185	−0.085	−0.125	−0.041	−0.007	−0.111	0.018	−0.109	0.090
	(0.046)	(0.057)	(0.067)	(0.066)	(0.036)	(0.047)	(0.085)	(0.036)	(0.085)	(0.058)
Services	−0.072	0.069	−0.014	−0.100	0.020	0.006	0.398	0.066	−0.457	0.285
	(0.102)	(0.151)	(0.179)	(0.179)	(0.077)	(0.098)	(0.178)	(0.070)	(0.231)	(0.117)
Clothing	−0.712	−0.369	−0.333	0.443	−0.176	−0.336	−0.513	−0.129	0.165	0.194
	(0.096)	(0.125)	(0.143)	(0.140)	(0.073)	(0.101)	(0.188)	(0.073)	(0.185)	(0.112)
Men's	−0.428	−0.179	−0.194	0.341	−0.183	−0.253	−0.184	−0.077	−0.100	0.074
	(0.120)	(0.143)	(0.171)	(0.155)	(0.094)	(0.122)	(0.242)	(0.091)	(0.248)	(0.146)
Women's	−0.572	−0.010	−0.126	0.366	−0.108	−0.204	−0.106	−0.006	0.201	0.291
	(0.110)	(0.145)	(0.165)	(0.157)	(0.083)	(0.108)	(0.222)	(0.080)	(0.197)	(0.128)
Children's	−0.925	−0.524	−0.484	0.223	−0.071	−0.093	−0.296	−0.073	0.096	0.064
	(0.105)	(0.139)	(0.156)	(0.154)	(0.077)	(0.118)	(0.025)	(0.079)	(0.205)	(0.113)
Other	−0.780	−0.008	0.228	0.818	−0.135	0.008	0.222	−0.038	0.265	0.018
	(0.164)	(0.235)	(0.255)	(0.253)	(0.117)	(0.154)	(0.316)	(0.114)	(0.302)	(0.183)
Medical care	−0.662	−0.447	−0.456	−0.457	−0.115	−0.091	0.006	0.078	0.266	0.019
	(0.118)	(0.152)	(0.181)	(0.178)	(0.093)	(0.118)	(0.209)	(0.090)	(0.221)	(0.147)
Education	−0.688	−0.005	0.671	0.351	0.269	0.273	0.685	0.302	0.165	−0.052
	(0.132)	(0.174)	(0.189)	(0.200)	(0.110)	(0.145)	(0.269)	(0.101)	(0.247)	(0.157)
Recreation and culture	0.521	−0.075	0.481	−0.265	−0.056	−0.125	−0.223	0.162	−0.179	0.015
	(0.085)	(0.107)	(0.129)	(0.124)	(0.068)	(0.090)	(0.165)	(0.065)	(0.160)	(0.104)
Recreation	0.230	−0.055	0.077	−0.173	0.008	−0.119	−0.212	0.191	0.045	−0.143
	(0.084)	(0.103)	(0.123)	(0.121)	(0.065)	(0.083)	(0.165)	(0.064)	(0.163)	(0.097)
Reading and culture	0.446	−0.403	−0.435	−0.234	0.035	0.106	0.212	0.130	−0.196	0.015
	(0.093)	(0.124)	(0.152)	(0.144)	(0.078)	(0.098)	(0.177)	(0.068)	(0.180)	(0.111)

Transportation and communication	−0.039 (0.055)	−0.123 (0.069)	−0.013 (0.080)	−0.104 (0.078)	−0.061 (0.043)	−0.054 (0.057)	−0.247 (0.102)	−0.003 (0.043)	0.220 (0.101)	0.122 (0.069)
Private transportation	0.200 (0.118)	−0.071 (0.174)	−0.121 (0.201)	−0.205 (0.209)	0.003 (0.091)	−0.125 (0.117)	−0.371 (0.219)	0.112 (0.082)	−0.034 (0.284)	0.098 (0.129)
Public transportation	−0.210 (0.069)	−0.137 (0.085)	−0.019 (0.098)	−0.092 (0.096)	0.055 (0.054)	0.065 (0.070)	−0.250 (0.123)	−0.013 (0.055)	0.169 (0.124)	0.099 (0.087)
Communication	−0.511 (0.103)	−0.110 (0.149)	−0.182 (0.182)	−0.149 (0.173)	0.052 (0.079)	−0.037 (0.094)	0.477 (0.162)	0.068 (0.069)	−0.031 (0.222)	0.003 (0.113)
Other consumption	0.137 (0.041)	−0.148 (0.051)	−0.059 (0.060)	−0.090 (0.060)	−0.102 (0.033)	−0.108 (0.043)	−0.171 (0.076)	0.045 (0.033)	−0.174 (0.077)	0.073 (0.052)
Tobacco	−0.017 (0.080)	−0.040 (0.101)	−0.046 (0.119)	−0.028 (0.117)	−0.144 (0.063)	−0.121 (0.080)	−0.128 (0.149)	0.011 (0.061)	−0.258 (0.160)	−0.110 (0.098)
Personal care	0.309 (0.041)	−0.108 (0.051)	−0.037 (0.060)	−0.071 (0.059)	−0.053 (0.032)	−0.047 (0.042)	0.014 (0.075)	0.021 (0.032)	−0.102 (0.076)	0.133 (0.052)
Taxes	0.148 (0.339)	0.526 (0.554)	0.753 (0.627)	0.733 (0.713)	−0.103 (0.236)	−0.195 (0.291)	−0.337 (0.531)	−0.107 (0.217)	0.059 (0.560)	0.043 (0.298)
Insurance	0.226 (0.083)	0.029 (0.102)	−0.117 (0.117)	0.004 (0.118)	−0.105 (0.069)	−0.191 (0.087)	−0.251 (0.177)	0.038 (0.069)	−0.156 (0.153)	0.112 (0.107)
Social security	0.506 (0.077)	0.115 (0.091)	−0.092 (0.106)	0.029 (0.105)	−0.051 (0.063)	−0.238 (0.082)	−0.293 (0.182)	0.086 (0.065)	0.235 (0.139)	−0.007 (0.098)
Private insurance	0.037 (0.156)	0.344 (0.282)	0.353 (0.302)	0.140 (0.322)	−0.183 (0.145)	−0.163 (0.163)	0.099 (0.282)	0.210 (0.137)	0.126 (0.351)	−0.037 (0.206)
Gifts and transfers	−0.792 (0.171)	−0.019 (0.243)	0.763 (0.288)	0.375 (0.274)	0.082 (0.133)	0.084 (0.168)	0.163 (0.331)	0.088 (0.125)	0.128 (0.379)	−0.001 (0.207)
Other nonconsumption	0.964 (0.235)	−0.443 (0.335)	−0.350 (0.446)	−0.094 (0.434)	−0.033 (0.198)	0.161 (0.230)	0.378 (0.387)	−0.249 (0.184)	0.065 (0.421)	0.164 (0.272)

Table C-46. Coefficients of Household Size Variables in Expenditure Functions, Colombia

	Number of members					
Spending category	1	2	3	4–5	6–7	8–9
Food and beverages	-0.518 (0.052)	-0.302 (0.023)	-0.232 (0.019)	-0.135 (0.015)	-0.084 (0.015)	-0.034 (0.016)
Dairy products and eggs	-0.399 (0.013)	-0.119 (0.058)	-0.029 (0.047)	0.036 (0.037)	0.078 (0.037)	0.099 (0.040)
Cereals	-0.996 (0.089)	-0.586 (0.039)	-0.454 (0.032)	-0.348 (0.025)	-0.214 (0.025)	-0.117 (0.027)
Meat and poultry	-0.568 (0.126)	-0.273 (0.055)	-0.218 (0.045)	-0.114 (0.035)	-0.091 (0.035)	-0.053 (0.038)
Seafood	-0.731 (0.324)	0.095 (0.155)	-0.034 (0.120)	-0.167 (0.087)	-0.109 (0.086)	-0.102 (0.091)
Vegetables and tubers	-0.783 (0.109)	-0.508 (0.045)	-0.349 (0.037)	-0.224 (0.029)	-0.174 (0.028)	-0.061 (0.031)
Fruits	-0.193 (0.152)	-0.148 (0.067)	-0.072 (0.054)	-0.023 (0.042)	0.003 (0.042)	0.006 (0.042)
Fats and oils	-0.672 (0.130)	-0.298 (0.053)	-0.265 (0.042)	-0.175 (0.033)	-0.126 (0.033)	-0.071 (0.035)
Sugar and sweets	-0.749 (0.122)	-0.712 (0.052)	-0.579 (0.042)	-0.352 (0.033)	-0.245 (0.033)	-0.136 (0.036)
Hot beverages	-0.787 (0.121)	-0.491 (0.054)	-0.427 (0.044)	-0.294 (0.035)	-0.170 (0.034)	-0.129 (0.037)
Alcoholic beverages	n.a.	0.280 (0.194)	-0.030 (0.142)	0.231 (0.103)	0.069 (0.100)	0.149 (0.108)
Other beverages	-0.614 (0.377)	-0.169 (0.118)	-0.104 (0.091)	-0.052 (0.071)	-0.056 (0.069)	-0.086 (0.075)
Other foods	0.354 (0.249)	-0.014 (0.089)	0.014 (0.071)	0.052 (0.054)	-0.010 (0.053)	0.030 (0.057)
Meals away from home	-0.051 (0.222)	0.082 (0.105)	-0.004 (0.082)	0.009 (0.065)	0.065 (0.063)	0.015 (0.069)
Total housing	0.412 (0.108)	0.315 (0.049)	0.311 (0.040)	0.192 (0.031)	0.104 (0.030)	0.095 (0.033)
Maintenance	-0.191 (1.366)	-0.260 (0.515)	0.333 (0.358)	-0.153 (0.264)	-0.131 (0.253)	-0.289 (0.273)

Furnishings and operation	0.374 (0.185)	0.117 (0.083)	0.323 (0.067)	0.249 (0.053)	0.194 (0.052)
					0.197 (0.056)
Durables	−0.074 (0.642)	0.666 (0.275)	0.309 (0.200)	0.272 (0.160)	0.028 (0.154)
					−0.000 (0.165)
Nondurables	−0.198 (0.150)	−0.303 (0.067)	−0.123 (0.055)	−0.061 (0.042)	−0.064 (0.042)
					−0.029 (0.046)
Services	0.274 (0.368)	0.104 (0.148)	0.326 (0.108)	0.275 (0.085)	0.229 (0.083)
					0.181 (0.088)
Other clothing	−1.101 (1.186)	0.061 (0.361)	0.352 (0.281)	0.065 (0.190)	0.079 (0.192)
					0.016 (0.204)
Medical care	−0.042 (0.466)	0.395 (0.170)	0.456 (0.130)	0.212 (0.101)	0.172 (0.010)
					0.156 (0.106)
Recreation, reading material, culture	0.810 (0.284)	0.193 (0.111)	0.262 (0.085)	0.159 (0.066)	0.158 (0.065)
					0.027 (0.070)
Recreation	0.940 (0.363)	0.015 (0.129)	0.132 (0.103)	0.004 (0.078)	0.104 (0.076)
					0.011 (0.082)
Transport and communication	0.090 (0.228)	−0.031 (0.091)	−0.129 (0.074)	−0.063 (0.058)	−0.131 (0.056)
					−0.140 (0.061)
Public transport	0.004 (0.247)	−0.073 (0.098)	−0.081 (0.080)	−0.032 (0.063)	−0.057 (0.062)
					−0.025 (0.067)
Communication	−0.721 (0.320)	−0.034 (0.176)	−0.119 (0.130)	−0.175 (0.102)	−0.192 (0.099)
					−0.226 (0.107)
Personal care	−0.076 (0.147)	−0.124 (0.063)	−0.067 (0.050)	0.009 (0.040)	0.024 (0.039)
					0.049 (0.042)
Ceremonies	−0.844 (1.648)	0.388 (1.097)	−0.011 (1.108)	0.423 (0.640)	0.245 (0.708)
					0.341 (0.748)
Taxes	2.535 (0.608)	1.018 (0.294)	1.254 (0.297)	0.390 (0.209)	0.487 (0.207)
					0.052 (0.215)
Gifts and transfers	1.511 (0.571)	0.736 (0.234)	0.619 (0.196)	0.410 (0.160)	0.234 (0.156)
					0.138 (0.168)
Other nonconsumption	0.773 (1.141)	0.718 (0.593)	0.696 (0.300)	0.307 (0.221)	0.147 (0.228)
					0.053 (0.239)

n.a. Not available.

Table C-47. *Coefficients of Household Size Variables in Expenditure Functions, Chile*[a]

	Number of members				
Spending category	*2*	*3*	*4–5*	*6–7*	*8–9*
Food and beverages	0.031 (0.031)	0.092 (0.030)	0.181 (0.028)	0.276 (0.030)	0.368 (0.038)
Dairy products and eggs	0.056 (0.058)	0.222 (0.055)	0.303 (0.051)	0.356 (0.055)	0.263 (0.068)
Cereals	−0.076 (0.042)	0.010 (0.040)	0.253 (0.037)	0.490 (0.040)	0.694 (0.050)
Meat and poultry	0.268 (0.056)	0.325 (0.054)	0.313 (0.049)	0.333 (0.053)	0.341 (0.066)
Seafood	−0.091 (0.084)	−0.116 (0.079)	0.030 (0.074)	0.036 (0.078)	0.058 (0.093)
Vegetable and tubers	0.086 (0.057)	0.164 (0.055)	0.358 (0.050)	0.456 (0.054)	0.663 (0.067)
Fruits	0.122 (0.070)	0.054 (0.067)	0.222 (0.061)	0.132 (0.066)	1.000 (0.082)
Fats and oils	0.087 (0.057)	0.115 (0.055)	0.119 (0.050)	0.123 (0.053)	0.237 (0.065)
Sugar and sweets	−0.201 (0.060)	−0.121 (0.057)	0.040 (0.053)	0.177 (0.056)	0.276 (0.069)
Hot beverages	−0.068 (0.060)	−0.089 (0.057)	−0.053 (0.053)	−0.015 (0.056)	−0.026 (0.069)
Alcoholic beverages	−0.066 (0.062)	−0.139 (0.060)	−0.131 (0.054)	−0.183 (0.058)	−0.049 (0.072)
Other beverages	0.015 (0.117)	−0.107 (0.113)	−0.062 (0.101)	−0.059 (0.108)	0.072 (0.135)
Other foods	−0.041 (0.093)	0.068 (0.090)	0.031 (0.083)	0.007 (0.089)	0.065 (0.106)
Meals away from home	−0.616 (0.098)	−0.637 (0.093)	−0.770 (0.086)	−0.731 (0.091)	−0.507 (0.111)
Total housing	0.088 (0.126)	−0.032 (0.119)	−0.084 (0.109)	−0.191 (0.117)	−0.322 (0.145)
Maintenance	−0.410 (0.036)	−0.579 (0.035)	−0.437 (0.033)	−0.607 (0.035)	−0.114 (0.044)
	(0.322)	(0.322)	(0.302)	(0.318)	(0.378)

	(1)	(2)	(3)	(4)	(5)
Furnishings and operation	-0.059 (0.093)	-0.198 (0.090)	-0.345 (0.083)	-0.389 (0.089)	-0.506 (0.113)
Durables	0.220 (0.261)	-0.228 (0.247)	-0.158 (0.232)	-0.049 (0.246)	-0.038 (0.302)
Nondurables	0.134 (0.085)	0.049 (0.081)	0.131 (0.075)	0.270 (0.080)	0.193 (0.100)
Services	-0.404 (0.123)	-0.593 (0.120)	-0.740 (0.116)	-1.162 (0.132)	-1.204 (0.178)
Other clothing	-0.062 (0.133)	-0.039 (0.125)	0.084 (0.114)	0.064 (0.121)	0.211 (0.149)
Medical care	0.051 (0.164)	0.137 (0.162)	-0.060 (0.149)	-0.001 (0.163)	-0.131 (0.212)
Recreation, reading material, culture	-0.192 (0.089)	-0.150 (0.085)	-0.188 (0.077)	-0.143 (0.083)	-0.023 (0.105)
Recreation	-0.045 (0.112)	-0.133 (0.107)	-0.147 (0.097)	-0.075 (0.105)	0.046 (0.128)
Transportation and communication	-0.202 (0.067)	-0.181 (0.064)	-0.189 (0.059)	-0.199 (0.064)	-0.084 (0.080)
Public transportation	-0.275 (0.080)	-0.195 (0.077)	-0.155 (0.070)	-0.095 (0.075)	0.057 (0.092)
Communication	-0.101 (0.146)	-0.226 (0.144)	-0.386 (0.134)	-0.677 (0.149)	-1.007 (0.182)
Personal care	-0.122 (0.080)	-0.012 (0.077)	0.083 (0.070)	0.078 (0.076)	0.145 (0.095)
Ceremonies	-0.438 (0.505)	-0.060 (0.484)	-0.299 (0.434)	-0.376 (0.472)	-0.234 (0.502)
Taxes	0.082 (0.078)	-0.089 (0.071)	-0.080 (0.065)	-0.110 (0.069)	-0.276 (0.084)
Gifts and transfers	-0.299 (0.280)	-0.380 (0.291)	-0.576 (0.257)	-0.802 (0.293)	-0.863 (0.421)
Other nonconsumption	-0.326 (0.486)	-0.451 (0.436)	-0.702 (0.409)	-1.142 (0.430)	-0.916 (0.553)

a. Households of only one member are excluded from the Chilean sample.

Table C-48. Coefficients of Household Size Variables in Expenditure Functions, Ecuador

Spending category	Number of members					
	1	2	3	4-5	6-7	8-9
Total food expenditure	-0.462 (0.041)	-0.327 (0.034)	-0.263 (0.030)	-0.178 (0.026)	-0.144 (0.026)	-0.104 (0.028)
Dairy products	-0.119 (0.113)	-0.040 (0.077)	-0.032 (0.066)	0.051 (0.056)	0.049 (0.055)	0.002 (0.061)
Cereals	-1.459 (0.074)	-1.145 (0.049)	-0.804 (0.042)	-0.508 (0.036)	-0.366 (0.035)	-0.208 (0.039)
Meat and poultry	-0.054 (0.133)	-0.098 (0.084)	-0.141 (0.068)	-0.030 (0.058)	-0.090 (0.057)	-0.016 (0.062)
Seafood	-0.440 (0.167)	-0.381 (0.104)	-0.269 (0.084)	-0.253 (0.070)	-0.097 (0.069)	-0.015 (0.074)
Vegetables	-1.035 (0.095)	-0.535 (0.062)	-0.372 (0.050)	-0.236 (0.043)	-0.160 (0.042)	-0.104 (0.046)
Fruits	-0.015 (0.131)	-0.250 (0.091)	-0.023 (0.076)	-0.007 (0.065)	0.037 (0.064)	0.065 (0.070)
Fats and oils	-0.720 (0.094)	-0.401 (0.060)	-0.245 (0.050)	-0.135 (0.042)	-0.078 (0.042)	-0.044 (0.046)
Sugar and sweets	-0.809 (0.110)	-0.641 (0.074)	-0.476 (0.064)	-0.235 (0.054)	-0.136 (0.053)	-0.086 (0.059)
Hot beverages	-0.377 (0.109)	-0.187 (0.074)	-0.218 (0.063)	-0.095 (0.054)	-0.095 (0.053)	-0.118 (0.058)
Alcoholic beverages	1.009 (0.400)	0.707 (0.373)	0.444 (0.282)	0.664 (0.239)	0.315 (0.230)	0.144 (0.253)
Other beverages	0.352 (0.201)	0.039 (0.128)	-0.002 (0.110)	0.031 (0.095)	-0.062 (0.095)	-0.124 (0.104)
Other foods	0.293 (0.222)	0.237 (0.133)	0.192 (0.111)	0.147 (0.093)	0.148 (0.092)	0.056 (0.100)
Meals outside the home	1.299 (0.234)	0.776 (0.222)	0.485 (0.214)	0.013 (0.188)	-0.124 (0.182)	-0.129 (0.206)
Total housing	0.242 (0.087)	0.297 (0.072)	0.255 (0.064)	0.212 (0.055)	0.097 (0.054)	0.082 (0.059)

354

Furnishings and operation	0.481 (0.132)	0.258 (0.109)	0.319 (0.095)	0.243 (0.082)	0.249 (0.080)	0.225 (0.088)
Durable goods	0.669 (0.406)	0.294 (0.283)	0.694 (0.243)	0.593 (0.204)	0.409 (0.196)	0.335 (0.216)
Nondurables	−0.746 (0.087)	−0.378 (0.069)	−0.232 (0.060)	−0.213 (0.051)	−0.143 (0.050)	−0.050 (0.055)
Services	0.866 (0.209)	0.690 (0.180)	0.388 (0.154)	0.450 (0.136)	0.484 (0.134)	0.516 (0.148)
Other clothing	0.147 (0.278)	−0.262 (0.193)	−0.363 (0.164)	−0.368 (0.138)	−0.318 (0.135)	−0.221 (0.147)
Medical care	0.868 (0.298)	0.334 (0.212)	0.483 (0.177)	0.246 (0.149)	0.189 (0.145)	0.311 (0.160)
Recreation, reading material, culture	0.665 (0.176)	0.162 (0.134)	−0.032 (0.116)	0.027 (0.100)	0.032 (0.098)	0.012 (0.107)
Recreation	0.772 (0.213)	0.331 (0.161)	0.200 (0.136)	0.185 (0.115)	0.173 (0.112)	0.099 (0.123)
Transport and communication	0.517 (0.265)	0.719 (0.192)	0.429 (0.155)	0.362 (0.135)	0.269 (0.132)	0.320 (0.148)
Communication	0.618 (0.281)	0.838 (0.200)	0.532 (0.162)	0.412 (0.141)	0.299 (0.138)	0.351 (0.154)
Personal care	0.029 (0.096)	0.076 (0.079)	0.106 (0.069)	0.051 (0.059)	−0.034 (0.058)	−0.011 (0.064)
Taxes	0.792 (0.640)	0.777 (0.380)	0.349 (0.344)	0.294 (0.290)	0.152 (0.292)	0.020 (0.318)
Gifts and transfers	0.536 (0.377)	−0.504 (0.279)	−0.690 (0.233)	−0.320 (0.191)	−0.159 (0.184)	−0.249 (0.204)
Other nonconsumption	1.220 (0.612)	0.302 (0.429)	0.719 (0.376)	0.727 (0.297)	0.561 (0.288)	0.355 (0.316)

Table C-49. *Coefficients of Household Size Variables in Expenditure Functions, Peru*[a]

Spending category	Number of members				
	2	3	4-5	6-7	8-9
Total food expenditure	-0.550 (0.075)	-0.310 (0.051)	-0.220 (0.039)	-0.122 (0.038)	-0.089 (0.040)
Dairy products	-0.564 (0.129)	-0.419 (0.084)	-0.277 (0.065)	-0.111 (0.062)	-0.115 (0.066)
Cereals	-1.041 (0.102)	-0.765 (0.067)	-0.516 (0.051)	-0.319 (0.049)	-0.205 (0.052)
Meat and poultry	-0.524 (0.136)	-0.326 (0.085)	-0.284 (0.065)	-0.093 (0.062)	-0.104 (0.066)
Seafood	-0.295 (0.209)	-0.270 (0.132)	-0.176 (0.093)	-0.170 (0.087)	-0.084 (0.095)
Vegetables	-0.661 (0.124)	-0.421 (0.079)	-0.262 (0.060)	-0.103 (0.057)	-0.017 (0.061)
Fruits	-0.587 (0.206)	0.067 (0.126)	0.016 (0.096)	0.064 (0.092)	0.050 (0.098)
Fats and oils	-0.518 (0.146)	-0.359 (0.099)	-0.344 (0.072)	-0.190 (0.068)	-0.154 (0.073)
Sugar and sweets	-0.520 (0.156)	-0.421 (0.100)	-0.406 (0.075)	-0.199 (0.071)	-0.053 (0.077)
Hot beverages	0.170 (0.217)	-0.017 (0.142)	0.048 (0.104)	0.085 (0.100)	0.081 (0.106)
Alcoholic beverages	0.616 (0.979)	-0.279 (0.641)	0.032 (0.436)	-0.060 (0.415)	0.045 (0.436)
Other beverages	-0.604 (0.523)	-0.300 (0.295)	0.059 (0.264)	0.119 (0.236)	-0.132 (0.242)
Other foods	0.098 (0.274)	-0.184 (0.168)	-0.036 (0.125)	-0.088 (0.120)	-0.024 (0.127)
Meals away from home	1.044 (0.396)	0.315 (0.245)	0.165 (0.190)	0.020 (0.183)	-0.030 (0.191)
Total housing	0.551 (0.131)	0.231 (0.091)	0.207 (0.070)	0.088 (0.067)	0.070 (0.070)
Maintenance	1.819 (0.543)	0.669 (0.309)	0.582 (0.234)	0.719 (0.221)	0.382 (0.225)

Furnishings and operation	-0.409	-0.114	-0.060	0.026	-0.022
	(0.192)	(0.132)	(0.102)	(0.097)	(0.102)
Durable goods	0.691	0.276	0.078	0.156	-0.320
	(0.539)	(0.319)	(0.235)	(0.218)	(0.232)
Nondurables	-0.821	-0.455	-0.226	-0.181	-0.110
	(0.132)	(0.090)	(0.069)	(0.067)	(0.069)
Services	-0.080	-0.044	-0.049	-0.027	-0.024
	(0.274)	(0.167)	(0.125)	(0.118)	(0.119)
Other clothing	0.618	0.896	0.518	0.299	0.034
	(0.527)	(0.290)	(0.225)	(0.208)	(0.219)
Medical care	0.380	0.019	0.072	0.080	0.240
	(0.307)	(0.203)	(0.158)	(0.148)	(0.156)
Recreation, reading material, culture	-0.039	-0.048	-0.064	-0.050	-0.123
	(0.180)	(0.124)	(0.095)	(0.091)	(0.096)
Recreation	-0.149	-0.001	-0.034	-0.074	-0.028
	(0.219)	(0.152)	(0.113)	(0.108)	(0.116)
Transport and communciation	-0.097	0.162	-0.071	-0.075	0.003
	(0.242)	(0.165)	(0.125)	(0.121)	(0.128)
Public transport	-0.569	-0.140	-0.304	-0.216	-0.164
	(0.293)	(0.198)	(0.155)	(0.151)	(0.160)
Communication	-0.151	0.068	0.104	0.091	0.117
	(0.374)	(0.238)	(0.176)	(0.169)	(0.178)
Personal care	-0.462	-0.244	-0.121	-0.059	-0.084
	(0.116)	(0.080)	(0.061)	(0.059)	(0.063)
Ceremonies	0.460	0.255	0.120	0.106	0.731
	(0.833)	(0.620)	(0.415)	(0.407)	(0.433)
Taxes	0.369	0.429	0.198	-0.023	-0.167
	(0.297)	(0.210)	(0.159)	(0.151)	(0.160)
Gifts and transfers	-0.328	-0.253	-0.102	-0.162	-0.341
	(0.555)	(0.334)	(0.278)	(0.247)	(0.262)

a. Households of only one member are excluded from the Peruvian sample.

Table C-50. *Coefficients of Household Size Variables in Expenditure Functions, Venezuela*

Spending category	Number of members					
	1	2	3	4-5	6-7	8-9
Total food expenditure	-0.392 (0.076)	-0.393 (0.036)	-0.310 (0.033)	-0.234 (0.027)	-0.157 (0.028)	-0.073 (0.031)
Dairy products	-0.498 (0.123)	-0.509 (0.056)	-0.336 (0.052)	-0.244 (0.042)	-0.140 (0.043)	-0.023 (0.047)
Cereals	-0.032 (0.115)	-0.890 (0.055)	-0.713 (0.050)	-0.515 (0.042)	-0.348 (0.043)	-0.125 (0.046)
Meat and poultry	-0.345 (0.135)	-0.217 (0.063)	-0.109 (0.057)	-0.065 (0.047)	-0.069 (0.048)	-0.083 (0.053)
Seafood	-0.098 (0.274)	-0.050 (0.113)	-0.140 (0.099)	-0.097 (0.082)	-0.034 (0.085)	-0.008 (0.091)
Vegetables	-0.632 (0.155)	-0.485 (0.072)	-0.370 (0.065)	-0.255 (0.054)	-0.284 (0.055)	-0.132 (0.060)
Fruits	-0.342 (0.168)	-0.444 (0.073)	-0.372 (0.066)	-0.298 (0.054)	-0.262 (0.058)	-0.168 (0.061)
Fats and oils	-0.406 (0.178)	-0.551 (0.077)	-0.385 (0.070)	-0.237 (0.058)	-0.232 (0.059)	-0.180 (0.063)
Sugar and sweets	-0.423 (0.161)	-0.541 (0.074)	-0.376 (0.067)	-0.245 (0.055)	-0.228 (0.057)	-0.100 (0.062)
Hot beverages	-0.570 (0.182)	-0.436 (0.082)	-0.333 (0.073)	-0.264 (0.060)	-0.176 (0.061)	-0.110 (0.066)
Alcoholic beverages	0.541 (0.522)	-0.013 (0.197)	-0.020 (0.185)	-0.101 (0.155)	-0.082 (0.158)	-0.239 (0.178)
Other beverages	-0.078 (0.249)	-0.282 (0.117)	-0.169 (0.103)	-0.097 (0.086)	-0.184 (0.088)	-0.142 (0.096)
Other foods	-0.350 (0.307)	-0.693 (0.123)	-0.177 (0.108)	-0.190 (0.089)	-0.093 (0.091)	-0.115 (0.099)
Meals away from home	0.577 (0.326)	0.137 (0.151)	-0.129 (0.137)	-0.099 (0.112)	-0.071 (0.114)	-0.005 (0.125)
Total housing	0.200 (0.098)	0.142 (0.048)	0.159 (0.044)	0.145 (0.036)	0.058 (0.036)	-0.019 (0.040)

Furnishings and operation	0.388 (0.228)	0.229 (0.104)	0.057 (0.095)	0.179 (0.078)	0.043 (0.080)	0.114 (0.087)
Durable goods	-0.743 (0.598)	0.604 (0.281)	0.210 (0.251)	-0.137 (0.198)	-0.156 (0.203)	-0.185 (0.217)
Nondurables	-0.144 (0.171)	-0.156 (0.077)	-0.144 (0.070)	0.003 (0.057)	-0.013 (0.059)	0.026 (0.064)
Services	0.881 (0.334)	0.229 (0.174)	0.133 (0.158)	0.253 (0.132)	0.240 (0.135)	0.229 (0.150)
Other clothing	0.550 (0.724)	0.371 (0.249)	-0.243 (0.229)	-0.320 (0.178)	-0.118 (0.180)	-0.014 (0.204)
Medical care	0.576 (0.417)	0.534 (0.203)	0.608 (0.181)	0.393 (0.152)	0.184 (0.156)	0.282 (0.170)
Recreation, reading material, culture	-0.257 (0.314)	0.284 (0.149)	0.183 (0.133)	0.160 (0.109)	0.268 (0.111)	0.334 (0.122)
Recreation	0.175 (0.383)	0.191 (0.147)	0.133 (0.129)	0.094 (0.105)	0.220 (0.107)	0.210 (0.116)
Transport and communication	-0.284 (0.199)	0.217 (0.092)	0.070 (0.084)	-0.040 (0.069)	-0.026 (0.070)	-0.054 (0.077)
Public transport	-0.541 (0.274)	-0.097 (0.114)	-0.230 (0.102)	-0.236 (0.084)	-0.120 (0.085)	-0.055 (0.093)
Communication	0.502 (0.354)	0.194 (0.181)	-0.144 (0.153)	-0.025 (0.130)	-0.090 (0.137)	-0.154 (0.157)
Personal care	-0.607 (0.144)	-0.345 (0.068)	-0.352 (0.062)	-0.248 (0.051)	-0.194 (0.052)	-0.114 (0.057)
Taxes	1.513 (0.811)	1.742 (0.636)	0.858 (0.550)	1.123 (0.493)	0.877 (0.494)	0.848 (0.561)
Gifts and transfers	1.262 (0.692)	0.460 (0.299)	-0.041 (0.272)	0.215 (0.232)	0.141 (0.236)	-0.164 (0.258)
Other nonconsumption	-0.004 (0.938)	0.083 (0.411)	0.074 (0.349)	0.338 (0.289)	0.397 (0.296)	-0.192 (0.337)

Index

Adults: household expenditures, 223–24, propensity to consume, 105–08
Age: and consumption, 88, 90, 108–10, 122; effect on budget allocation, 143–44, 244–45; effect on education expenditures, 224; effect on household expenditures, 208–10; effect on income, 62–63, 72–73, 74, 77–78; and income inequality, 237; and purchase of durables and housing, 82; and savings, 109, 240, 241
Ahluwalia, Montek, 38n
Aitchison, J., 32n, 37n
Allende government, 19–20
Andean Pact, 5–6
Ando, Albert, 109n
Arellano V., Aquiles, 24
Argentina, 5, 7n
Assets: demand for, 115–18; household-held, 119–20, 239
Aulestia, Alfonso, 114n
Automobiles: and public transportation, 216–18; share of household budget for, 133, 167, 169, 216–17
Ayal, Eliezer B., 10n

Baer, Werner, 251n
Bank accounts, 119, 120, 239
Becker, Gary S., 212n
Blades, Derek W., 4n
Blinder, Alan S., 121n
Bolivia, 5
Bonuses, 39, 40
Brazil, 5, 9n
Bronfenbrenner, Martin, 34n, 37n
Brown, Alan, 192n, 193n, 223n

Brown, J. A. C., 32n, 37n
Budget, household: categories, 124–25, 133; defined, 123; factors influencing distribution, 135–36, 137–39, 142–44; global mean shares, 165–71; income and allocation of, 139, 140, 144; income concentration and, 125; individual mean shares, 158–65; intercity variations, 132–33, 135–36; marginal shares, 210–11. *See also* Expenditures
Buttari, Juan J., 40n, 237n

Calvo S., Haroldo, 24
Capital income: concentration, 50, 53, 236; and imputed rent, 50, 56; as percent of total income, 40, 49–50
Carney, J. B., 133n
Carnoy, Martin, 227n
Cartagena Agreement. *See* Andean Pact
Cereal products: and children, 175; household expenditures for, 186–87; share of food budget for, 162, 173, 175
Chaigneau C., Sergio, 15n, 21
Champernowne, D. G., 37n
Chenery, Hollis B., 95n, 234n, 240n
Children: and household expenditures, 142–43, 171–72, 174–78, 223–24, 252–53; and propensity to consume, 106, 107
Chile, 2, 5; Allende government in, 19–20; inflation rate, 17
Cities in ECIEL survey, 7–8, 15
Clark, Lincoln H., 133n
Cline, William R., 22, 23, 26n, 37n, 39n, 53n

361